ROUTES OF PASSAGE

ROUTES OF PASSAGE

RETHINKING THE AFRICAN DIASPORA

VOLUME 1 • PART 1

Edited by

Ruth Simms Hamilton

Michigan State University Press • *East Lansing*

Michigan State University Press
East Lansing, Michigan 48823-5245

Printed and bound in the United States of America.

13 12 11 10 09 08 07   1 2 3 4 5 6 7 8 9 10

LIBRARY OF CONGRESS CATALOGING-IN-PUBLICATION DATA
Routes of passage : rethinking the African diaspora / edited by Ruth
Simms Hamilton.
p. cm. — (African diaspora research)
Includes bibliographical references.
ISBN-13: 978-0-87013-632-0
ISBN-10: 0-87013-632-1 (alk. paper)
1. African diaspora. I. Hamilton, Ruth Simms. II. Series.
DT16.5.R68 2003
909.'0496—dc21
2003001308

Cover and book design by Sharp Des!gns, Inc., Lansing, Michigan

Visit Michigan State University Press on the World Wide Web at **www.msupress.msu.edu**

Ruth Simms Hamilton

was a teacher and researcher at Michigan State University for thirty-five years, and she won many awards for her work. Dr. Hamilton taught courses on international inequality and development, comparative race relations, international migration and diasporas, Third World urbanization and change, and sociological theory. She was professor of Sociology and Urban Affairs, director of the African Diaspora Research Project, and a core faculty member of the African Studies Center and Center for Latin American and Caribbean Studies at Michigan State University.

Dr. Hamilton served as a trustee of the Teachers Insurance and Annuity Association, a subsidiary of the TIAA-CREF group of financial services companies, from 1989 to 2003. TIAA-CREF created the TIAA-CREF Ruth Simms Hamilton Research Fellowship in 2004, to honor the memory and outstanding work of Dr. Hamilton.

At the time of her death, in November 2003, Dr. Hamilton was finalizing plans for the African Diaspora Research Project Series at Michigan State University Press. *Routes of Passage: Rethinking the African Diaspora* is the first volume in that series.

Contents

Introduction

THIS INTRODUCTORY VOLUME IS A COMPILATION OF ESSAYS WRITTEN AND contributed by authors of diverse national origins and who represent a range of disciplinary backgrounds and area studies, including anthropology; African, Caribbean, and Latin American studies; history; library science; linguistics and languages; religious studies; and sociology. Most are associated with the African Diaspora Research Project (ADRP) and as such have been pioneers in African diaspora studies and instrumental in defining and rethinking the field.

This book is the first of a two-part volume. Both publications are organized to complement the conceptual framework advanced in the first chapter of this book, which provides an orientation to the global approach and the key issues guiding the studies and research of the ADRP.

ENVISIONING THE AFRICAN DIASPORA AS A FIELD OF STUDY

For three decades, numerous papers, books, monographs, and journals have been written in the effort to reduce the tremendous gaps in our knowledge about various dimensions of the African diaspora. This "fact-finding" phase of the field continues to be exciting and extraordinarily productive. Most of the works, however, exhibit a low degree of theoretical integration, while others, encoded in grand abstractions, are absent empirical data. Another complication encountered by students of diaspora studies is the lack of in-depth comparative-historical analysis that goes beyond the observation that there is variation, socially and culturally, from one community to another. Perhaps the most critical problem is the failure to sustain, within an interdisciplinary context, a higher level of theoretical innovation.

While there is cause for concern, the distinguished scholar Elliott Skinner calls attention to the three-stage progression of new intellectual disciplines.[1] Phase 1, the period of delineation and definition, has all the excitement inherent in the pioneering experience of exploring new frontiers. Phase 2, essentially a micro-level fact-finding stage, is generally a time when the concepts and definitions created during phase 1 are used as the basis for detailed case studies and field research. Finally, there is phase 3, or the mature stage. At this point in the development process there begins to emerge a more systematic assessment of the collected body of data with two major thrusts: challenges to or the reinterpretation of the original conceptual models, and the formulation of new models that build upon the knowledge of phases 1 and 2 but at the same time suggest innovative theoretical approaches or untried avenues of exploration. To move African diaspora studies to a more mature phase of intellectual development requires rethinking and (re)envisioning where we have been, where we are, and how we see the future of this developing field. It implies trying new paths and *routes* to frame heuristic questions; it requires intellectual *passages* to higher levels of social thought, analysis, and intellectual development. Authors in this text raise awareness about expanding parameters of social and geographical space, pursuing unexplored areas of research and analysis, and the need to build paradigms within a world or global frame of reference.

In the opening paper, "Rethinking the African Diaspora: Global Dynamics," Ruth Simms Hamilton provides a conceptualization of the African diaspora as a global social formation. Looking at demographic distributions and settlement patterns in every part of the world, Hamilton is concerned with the social identities of peoples of the African diaspora. Why have they persisted as identifiable communities over centuries? Given the specificity of each of their histories, is it possible that certain shared experiences permit a conceptualization of global collective social identity (re)formations? Using a range of data and concrete examples of specific diaspora experiences and relations, Hamilton contends that all share a history conditioned by and within the larger world ordering system that the diaspora is constitutive of and mediated within, contributing to and impacted by, transforming relations and in turn transformed by them. Importantly, collective identity formations are inscribed by historical social experiences conditioned by the multi-layered socio-cultural, economic, and political processes within a global system of domination and unequal social relations. Four intersecting components frame the discussion for exploring the changing bases of global identity formations: (1) geosocial mobility and displacement—the circulatoriness phenomenon; (2) Africa-diaspora-homeland connections: myths and realities; (3) social inequality and oppression—relations of domination and subordination; and (4) communities of consciousness and agency—cultural production and endurance. Readers will note that the organization of the two-part volume is linked to these four components.

Hubert Gerbeau noted, "The absence of studies does not necessarily mean the absence of a subject requiring study."[2] Edward A. Alpers argues in "The African Diaspora in the Northwestern Indian Ocean: Reconsideration of an Old Problem and New Directions for Research" that if the African diaspora is really a global phenomenon, scholars cannot continue to be taciturn about the African heritage in the Indian Ocean and Asia. There is a great need to focus on the history and development of African diaspora communities in India, Pakistan, Sri Lanka, the Arabian Peninsula, and the Persian Gulf. While broadening the geographical span is imperative, it is also important to go beyond the limitations of conventional study by crossing disciplinary boundaries, employing different language and methodological skills, engaging in joint projects, and complementing work on politics, economics, and social history with research on the "principles of aesthetics." The latter requires interdisciplinary work of historians, social scientists, and students of literature and the arts (especially ethnomusicologists specializing in African and Arab music and dance). Alpers provides the reader with a strong historical orientation to the African presence in Asia and the world of the Indian Ocean, along with fascinating examples, including "arts of the sea" associated with African sailors, some traditions of which remain noticeable at the port of Bal-Haf, on the Gulf of Aden.

"The Diaspora in Yemen" by Tim Carmichael reinforces the Alpers paper by sharing ideas about the richness of investigating the historical relations between Ethiopia and Yemen, which can be traced over two millennia through commercial exchanges. Of particular interest is how new socio-cultural identities emerge as a result of transnational migrations, intermarriage, and deeply embedded views of social hierarchy, including skin color, race, ethnicity/nationality, and occupational status. Carmichael brings attention to *muwalladin*, mixed people of Ethiopian and Yemeni descent, the *'abid*, descendants of former slave communities in the south, and the *akhdam*, believed to be of African ancestry and predating the rise of Islam yet "denied the benefits of respectability" in Yemen.

Joseph E. Harris, a historian and scholar of African studies and pioneer of African diaspora studies, contends that the situation of African people in world politics constitutes a major challenge of the twenty-first century. In "Historicizing the

African Diaspora" he notes the need for research on the implications of Africa-diaspora relations within the global African community, and between the diaspora and particular African states. For the latter, the dispersion of Africans since the 1960s is today a major problem in the external affairs of contemporary African states.

In "African American Studies in Libraries: Collection Development and Management Priorities" New York Public Library, Schomburg Center for Research in Black Culture chief Howard Dodson makes a compelling argument for the implications of a global comparative framework of African diaspora studies for libraries and collection strategies. This global paradigmatic framework requires a comprehensive strategy for identifying and providing access to a massive and as yet relatively inaccessible corpus of manuscripts, archival and organizational records, personal papers, photographs, prints, and ephemera. Collections must be intensified and, in the case of the Americas, they must be hemispheric, requiring comparative and collaborative collections for series published by and about blacks in Latin America and the Caribbean, preserving, and providing access to primary research sources. Moreover, new information technology demands changes in databases, on-line bibliographic services, including CD-ROM technology, telefacsimile, and other new technologies.

Milfred C. Fierce and Jorge Silva Castillo provide useful windows of understanding regarding different conceptual and institutional developments of diaspora studies in the Americas. In "The Diaspora in Indo-Afro-Ibero-America" Silva Castillo takes the position that studies on Africa should not be separated from studies of Afro-Latin Americans and Afro-Americans. Although there is great disdain for and ignorance about Africa in Latin America, the larger culture has three roots: African, European, and Indian. He calls for more comparative work in various Latin American countries; more scientific research related to self-identity and African origins; and the increased involvement of sociologists and political scientists in developing and conducting research. The majority of work on the diaspora is conducted by historians, anthropologists, folklorists, and religionists. In a similar context, in "Two Academic Programs in the African Diaspora: Afro-Brazilian Studies and U.S. Africana Studies" Fierce argues that these two countries are the best laboratories in the world for studying relations between blacks and whites. Although race relations, ideologies, and practices have taken different paths in Brazil and the United States, both are experiencing ongoing challenges to end discrimination. However, there is little development of programs in Afro-Brazilian studies in a country with the largest concentration of people of African descent outside of Nigeria.

Conditioning Situations of Geosocial Mobility

Since the inception of the diaspora age, the movement of African populations, across time and space, has been conditioned by systemic and global political, military, economic, and cultural forces. This displacement and circulatoriness of populations involves not only physical movements but also complex social processes that can only be understood within the historical context of larger collective experiences. Whether movements are forced, voluntary, or something in between, the result is a presence and crystallization of communities of African people in every part of the world. In this text are papers providing situational and historical explanations of the proliferation of African diaspora passages and circulatoriness in the Middle East, Asia, Germany, Australia, and Russia.

"African Diaspora Passages from the Middle East to East Asia," by Michael C. Thornton, complements the earlier paper by Alpers in reference to the Northwestern Indian Ocean. Thornton provides a broad overview of circulatoriness and settlement in the Africa, Asia, and Middle East zone of passage, and covers a time frame extending from ancient periods through the twentieth century. His paper is divided into two parts: the first focusing on the African presence in the Middle East and South Asia, primarily India and Pakistan, and the second on East Asia, mainly China and Japan. He shows the connections between the rise of the Islamic empire in the seventh century and the surge and dispersion of numerous Africans to Asia and the Middle East up to the fourteenth century. Many served in caliphates as soldiers and sailors, while others, especially eunuchs, played significant roles in governance of the state. Around the fifteenth century forward, as in the Atlantic, some Africans were enslaved, some were manumitted, and some were free; some were private and public servants; and some were concubines, traders, pearl divers, plantation laborers, artisans, and so on. Later, the changing global political economy brought occupying European and North American forces to Asia during World Wars I and II, the Korean conflict, and the Vietnam wars. Thornton addresses one result of these globalizing forces: the creation of Afro-Asian social identities. This discussion is reinforced in a second paper by Thornton, "Portrait of the Past: Black Servicemen in Asia, 1899–1952."

John T. Greene, in "Two Courtiers of African Descent in the Kingdom of Judah: Yehudi and Ebedmelech," confirms the presence of Africans in the Judean court during the final two decades before the Exile, sixth century B.C.E., and reminds readers of the presence of black African troops in the region long before displacements of the modern era.

In "Portrait of the Past: African Moslems in Yugoslavia" Michael C. Thornton draws attention to one instance of global passages of Africans to Eastern Europe in an area currently a volatile center of ethnic strife. Little is known of African Moslems in the former Yugoslavia, but further research and knowledge is warranted.

The arrival of peoples of the African diaspora in Australia is not well known.[3] Hence, in "The World Is All of One Piece: The African Diaspora and Transportation to Australia" Cassandra Pybus takes us on an odyssey through many interlinked and connecting routes from North America, the Caribbean, Africa, and the United Kingdom. In the eighteenth century, the result was the passage of a small number of African and diaspora male felons, who became part of the British convict colony at Sydney Cove, later Sydney, Australia.

Two papers provide different yet concurring perspectives on African people in the former Union of the Soviet Socialist Republics (USSR). In "A Little-Known Chapter in African American and Russian Cooperation" Joy Gleason Carew presents a fascinating account of major contributions of African American technical experts to agricultural cotton enterprises and industrial development in the former USSR in the early twentieth century. Among them were graduates of Tuskegee Institute (now Tuskegee University), some of whom were former students of famous scientist George Washington Carver. Later, African American artists and intellectuals joined them. Most of these individuals returned to the United States, but a number settled in the USSR, married, and had children, thus giving rise to generations of African descent Russians with legacies and connections to relatives in the United States and to their native Russian homeland. In "A Perspective on African Diaspora: Cultural Workers and Communities in Russia," Michael C. Thornton provides a brief overview of African people from Czarist Russia through the early twentieth century revolution and rise of Bolshevik power. He explores the international significance of the Russian Revolution and the USSR to Africa and its diaspora as theory and praxis for anti-racist, anti-colonial, and national liberation struggles. Critical questions are raised about the relationship between humane (and nonracialist) socialist ideology and practice in global diaspora experiences.

In "Passages and Portraits of African Descent People in Germany: From Ancient Times to the 1960s" Ruth Simms Hamilton advances a brief assessment of the early history of African people in Germany. Using case studies of Black American intellectual cultural workers such as W. E. B. DuBois, Angela Davis, Ernest Just, and Oliver Wendell Harrington, she examines some of the experiences and conditioning situations related to their respective passages to Germany. Pilgrimage and exilic processes, and the dwelling in distant liminal spaces of "in-betweenness" are some of the concepts used to discuss identity transformations within the context of African diaspora geosocial mobility and transitoriness.

Oppression, Terror, and Actions of Resistance

World War I was a major force in the geosocial mobility and displacement of global African people after the period of enslavement. As a global phenomenon, the time-space of the war and its aftermath encompassed colonialism and profound changes in technologies, economies, and labor demands. These forces and processes provide the context for analyzing the changing social conditions and impact of the Great War on Global Africa and vice versa. For Africa and its diaspora the implications were enormous including the emergence of new communities of social consciousness and agency, the creation of effective strategies of resistance to terror and oppression, and major identity transformations at individual and collective levels. Importantly, it was a time of significant transitions and transitoriness for "everyday people": the poorly paid urban laborers and mine workers, the rural poor, and tillers of the soil; struggling families, men and women, children and the elderly; the illiterate and dispossessed. For them it meant, among other things, forced labor, the terror of displacement and loss of life and land, and leaving their homelands and traversing distant routes across land, water, and terrain never before imagined. The moral costs and "blood price" were very high.

In "African Resistance to German Colonialism and Its Legacies, 1884–1913," Ruth Simms Hamilton and Getahun Benti acquaint readers with the nature of German colonialism from the late-nineteenth-century partitioning of Africa up to 1913, the eve of World War I. Germany's colonial economies of trade encompassed the West African countries of Togo and Cameroon in West Africa; and their economies of the labor reserves comprised Tanganyika (Republic of Tanzania) and South-West Africa (Namibia) in the east and southern parts of the continent. Africans vigorously opposed German land appropriation, which resulted in the first major genocide of the twentieth century. While using terror and brutality to maintain order and "racial purity," Germans also managed to create new social identities: mixed African and German *mischlingskinder* and so-called Rehobothers.

In "Reassessing Diaspora Connections and Consciousness: Global Africa and World War I" Ruth Simms Hamilton demonstrates how the military labor of global Africa was essential to the exploits of both Axis and Allied forces and was indeed central to "making the world safe for democracy." The latter raises an important question: If the victims of imperialism, colonialism, and racism were its defenders, why, at the same time, did they develop new levels of consciousness, experience new visions of freedom, and act in ways to bring their image of a decent society closer to reality? Three case studies are part of the analysis: The South African Native Labor Contingent, the British West Indies Regiment, and the black regiments of the United States Armed Forces. Individually and collectively they illustrate shared experiences as common laborers in the service of their armed oppressors; continued racialization, deprivation, and exclusion from opportunity structures; the use of degrees of freedom to resist as means of empowerment; the intersection of routes of passage across physical and social boundaries; and transformed identities as cultural actors transmitting and sharing knowledge and insights with each other and the folks remaining in their homeplaces. All shared a larger history of interlinked, interdependent, and world-changing social, political, and economic events and forces.

According to Dana S. Hale, use of colonial military forces to advance European conquest began long before World War I. The *Tirailleurs Sénégalais*, the subject of "Brothers in Arms? African Soldiers in Interwar France," are an excellent example. They were constituted in 1857, with continued expansion over time. Hale provides a persuasive and poignant view of their use and abuse by French military officials, and their positioning and representation as "primitive" colonials stationed at the center of French/European civilization and civil society. Following WWI, an increasing scale of violence and resistance was directed by Africans toward their colonial oppressors. Veterans who returned to their homelands contributed significantly to the sense of urgency for change and the reclamation of Africa for the Africans. A glimpse of these spaces and terrains of activism is advanced by Ruth Simms Hamilton in "Increasing Resistance to Colonialism in Africa after the 'Great War.'"

Two papers demonstrate the intersections of gender, race, and nation and some of the physical and structural consequences for African peoples. In "Orchestrating Race, Nation, and Gender: African Peacekeepers in Germany, 1919–1920," Ruth Simms Hamilton argues that the German state and its apparatuses, along with strategic civil organizations, used the presence of African soldiers (largely *Tirailleurs Sénégalais*) to rally nationalist sentiment which was really directed toward France. This campaign illustrates the relationship between racism and nationalism, both of which are articulated through sexism and gender. In "Anti-Black Reigns of Terror in Great Britain and the Americas in 1919: Similarity and Simultaneity," the circulatoriness phenomenon at war's end was linked to large-scale geosocial mobility of African and diaspora peoples in search of jobs and "betterment," as well as their postwar demobilization. In the United States, the Great Migration of black Americans from the rural South to the urban North, West, and South was in full swing. In Britain, black colonial pre-war and wartime workers, and men of the demobilized military, were in a similar position to their U.S. counterparts. Given the nature of the global economy at the time, all found themselves in fierce competition with whites (North American and British) for jobs, housing, neighborhoods of meaning, and places to call "home." While much has been written about the lynching and rioting in the United States, especially the Red Hot Summer of 1919, little is known of the reverberations of terror and resistance to it in Great Britain and the British Caribbean. The "sameness and simultaneity" of terror, violence, and counteractions suggest a patterning of actions globally yet a grounding in historical specificities locally. These examples reinforce the argument that the shared history of Africa and its diaspora is conditioned by and within the larger world ordering system, constitutive of and mediated within it while at the same time transforming relations as it is being transformed by them.

N O T E S

1. Remarks made by Elliott Skinner, Franz Boas Professor of Anthropology Emeritus, Columbia University, at a conference, "Transformation and Resiliency in Africa," 12–13 October 1977, Washington, D.C.
2. Hubert Gerbeau, "The Slave Trade in the Indian Ocean: Problems Facing the Historian and Research to be Undertaken," *African Slave Trade from the Fifteenth to the Nineteenth Century* (Paris: Unesco, 1979), quoted in Edward A. Alpers, "The African Diaspora in the Northwestern Indian Ocean: Reconsideration of an Old Problem and New Directions for Research" in this book.
3. I am grateful to my friend, former student, and colleague Jim McAllister of the School of Psychology and Sociology, Central Queensland University, Australia, for bringing the following works to my attention: Lawrence T. Udo-Ekbo, *The Africans in Australia: Expectations and Shattered Dreams* (Henley Beach, South Australia: Seaview Press, 1999) and Richard Waterhouse, *From Minstrel Show to Vaudeville: The Australian Popular Stage 1788–1914* (New South Wales, Australia: New South Wales University Press, 1999).

Rethinking the African Diaspora: Global Dynamics

Ruth Simms Hamilton, with Kimberly Eison Simmons,
Raymond Familusi, and Michael Hanson

INTRODUCTION

Global Africa, the geographically and socio-culturally diverse peoples of Africa and its diaspora, is linked through complex networks of social relationships and processes. Whether examined at the level of the household, neighborhood, village, city, province, state, or region, the experiences of these dispersed peoples are multi-layered, interactively varied, and complex, and yet constituted of and mediated within a global and unequal social ordering system. Here, our task is to actively engage in disaggregating these complexities in relation to the problems identified for social action and analysis, the development of a more definitive knowledge base, and the promotion of public understanding and informed discussion.

This introductory chapter discusses the framework that has guided the research of the African Diaspora Research Project (ADRP) in the above-mentioned task.[1] It presents a general overview of the relational processes that constitute this framework, enhanced with empirical examples drawn from (trans)localities and regions of the world. These illustrations are not meant to be exhaustive but to provide selected windows into diaspora realities at different points in time and space.[2] Such instances may function as heuristic devices, and thus stimulate and generate thinking about

This chapter was unfinished at the time of Ruth Simms Hamilton's death. Kimberly Eison Simmons, Raymond Familusi, and Michael Hanson edited this piece on Dr. Hamilton's behalf.

specific and broader levels of experiences and inform our approaches to problem solving within, across, and between communities of global Africa.

This framework is embedded within a historical and global context that is based on the view that the African diaspora came into being as the result of evolving global forces. It thus can be equated to a roadmap, albeit one that is constantly redrawn according to practice, changing spheres of knowledge and understanding, and contested terrains of thinking and analyses of this diaspora as a worldwide historical social formation.

Articulated over time and grounded within and spanning across places and spaces, four fields of social relations constitute the core of our analysis of the African diaspora as a global social formation.

Geosocial Mobility and Displacement

This circulatoriness phenomenon, the experience of ongoing and continuous geosocial mobility and displacement throughout the African diaspora, focuses on processes of structural change and the redistribution of populations. Geosocial mobility impacts age and gender distribution and processes of racialization, as well as how ethnicities and nationalities are defined and redefined. It focuses on large-scale socio-historical contexts and collective experiences. Circulatoriness describes and maps the actual movements of people in the African diaspora across time and space and involves a "proliferation of departures" from the fifteenth century to the present, which have been involuntary, semi-voluntary, and voluntary. Circulatoriness also maps the process of identity reformation due to mobility. From new socio-racial categories, to new languages, to competing notions of nationality and citizenship, circulatoriness illustrates how identities change as they are changed.

African Diaspora Connections

Myths and realities of homeland relations focus on the networks, connections, and social construction of homelands and the relationships—both real and mythical—that people in the African diaspora have with Africa as a symbolic place or homeland. In this way, Africa, and what it is imagined to be, becomes the place of origin or a point of departure for people in the African diaspora. Thus, the idea of returning to Africa exists and is realized, mythologized, or even discarded as people contemplate their relationship with Africa in terms of what it represents and means to them. Those who have a strong connection to—and sense of—Africa as homeland often form networks with others who share in this, building alliances based on similar experiences and worldviews and shared circumstances in the African diaspora.

POWER, DOMINATION, INEQUALITY

Structurations of black dispossession focus on social inequality and oppression, relations of domination and subordination (class, gender, nation, race, and religion), and how these inequalities have been created and institutionalized, paying close attention to race as a social construction based on ideas of biological difference.

AGENTS OF RESISTANCE

Diasporic identities and communities of consciousness focus on agency, cultures of endurance, resistance, and actions of people of African descent as subjects and creators of their history. What people do to assert themselves, what they create, and how they remember their past contribute to the formation of communities of consciousness that arise out of very particular experiences based on structural inequalities.

Intersecting and overlapping, dynamic and multilayered, these fields of relations provide the analytical tools by which ADRP researchers have sought to conceptualize important dimensions of the collective experiences and complexities embedded within the African diaspora as a living example.

While an extensive and critical discussion of diaspora is beyond the parameters of this essay, it is important to briefly note that the meaning associated with the concept has changed over time.[3] Ancient Greeks used the concept to designate a nationality, or some part of it, dispersed among nations but maintaining its own culture.[4] The Greeks, however, primarily dispersed as conquerors, as expansionists, both politically and territorially, and the definition that evolved from this context has for much of the modern era been supplanted by a more qualified, or restricted, understanding of diaspora as it applies to peoples displaced from a homeland by violent socio-political forces, such as Africans, Armenians, Jews, and Palestinians.

Late twentieth-century scholarship saw something of a re-emergence of the Greek notion of diaspora that encompasses an increasingly heterogeneous collection of dispersed populations—clusters of Cubans and Mexicans in the United States, Pakistanis in Britain, Corsicans in France, and even corporate executives assigned overseas are described as diasporas. In parallel fashion, the notion of diaspora has become prominent in poststructuralist strains of social theory challenging modernist conceptualizations of national, ethnic, and racial boundaries.[5] Thus, the postmodern semantic domain of diaspora has become quite broad, ranging from nation and multiculturalism to nomadic ideas.[6]

From the viewpoint of the ADRP, the concept of diaspora represents a mode of analysis—an approach to history, a method of inquiry—rooted in the historical experiences of a socially identifiable global aggregate of dispersed and interconnected networks of peoples. The concept of diaspora connotes people whose social relationships have been largely inscribed by their geographical displacement at historically significant moments. All diasporas have defining moments of inception, though smaller movements and dispersions might precede them.[7] These defining moments are the major turning points in history that establish the scope, extensiveness, and severity of the displacement, as well as its future significance. This displacement invariably occurred under duress, instigated by powerful social forces such as state exile, slave bondage, land appropriation/seizure, racial/ethnic cleansing, and genocide. Thus, diasporas tend to share a common historical experience of forced displacement, transitoriness of routes and passages, (re)rootings, and dwelling in multiple locations. For the Armenian diaspora, for example, the defining historical moment was the 1915 slaughter and expulsion perpetuated by the Ottoman Turkish state.

For the African diaspora, the *maafa*,[8] this moment was the massive trafficking and dispersion of human cargo and enslavement that occurred primarily from the sixteenth to the early twentieth centuries. This displacement of people against their will and over vast physical spaces was one of the largest in the history of the modern world. It created the first diaspora of the modern era, and it is one of the most salient linking points in understanding identity formation within the African diaspora. Globally, millions of Africans survived and far too many died when they experienced the *maafa*—this momentous period of collective human trauma, passages of violence, terror, degradation, and bondage. Joseph Harris's mapping of the slave trade provides an impressive visual representation of the global and temporal scale of the *maafa*.

Africans displaced during the *maafa* originated from different ethnic groups and regions of Africa—primarily from south of the Sahara, from Senegambia to Angola. They embodied complex and varied cultural, economic, and political histories. These Africans were already products of centuries of geosocial mobility by way of trading routes and networks that conveyed slaves, free people, cultural patterns, and material goods up the Nile valley, south along the Great Lakes, and westward into the savannah. East African coastal societies had already been shaped by transoceanic commercial migration and exchanges, slave trading, and the expansion of Islam.[9] The latter was marked by the birth of Islam in the seventh century;

Muslim occupation of the Iberian peninsula in the eighth century, and the "expansion of Islam from Arabia to India and across northern Africa and Spain to the Pyrenees (by 719 C.E.) . . . and the conquest of much of northwest Africa by the Berber Muslim Almoravid dynasty in the eleventh century."[10]

The enslavement and trading of Africans was global, crisscrossing Africa, Asia, Europe, North America, and South America. And it reflected the political, economic, and cultural expansions of the time. As noted by David Brion Davis, the "enslavement of foreign and alien peoples was a fundamental part of the remarkable expansion of Islam and the later expansion of Christian Europe."[11]

European expansionism and its emerging system of capitalism articulated with different systems of production in Asia, Africa, and the Americas, giving rise to a new economic formation. This looming capitalist system was characterized by an insatiable thirst for labor. In today's terminology, the shipment of enslaved Africans around the world was multinational, involving American, Brazilian, Cuban, Danish, Dutch, English, French, German, Italian, Portuguese, Spanish, and Swedish traders. It also required the complicity of continental African merchants and middlemen of various ethnicities, including newer identities such as Afro-Portuguese and Afro-Arab blacks, the leading slavers of the Islamic East.[12] Nathan Irvin Huggins captures the significance of this contradiction brilliantly:

> The twentieth-century Western mind is frozen by the horror of men selling and buying others as slaves and even more stunned at the irony of black men serving as agents for the enslavement of blacks to whites. Shocking though it is, this human barter was truly the most stark representation of what modernism and Western capitalist expansion meant to traditional peoples. In the New World, people became items of commerce, their labors, and their produce thrown into the marketplace, where their best hope was to bring a decent price. The racial irony was lost on African merchants, who saw themselves as selling people other than their own.
>
> . . .
>
> [T]he world of the African merchant allowed him to see only his limited involvement [and not] the enormous wealth that was to be produced by the hands of those he traded.
>
> . . .
>
> The Europeans, with whom they traded, however, had a different calculus of value . . . they made a distinction between a simple thing and one that produces other things, that creates wealth.
>
> . . .
>
> So the Europeans traded guns, ammunition and powder, pots and pans, beads and cloth, to the African merchants, receiving in exchange men, women, and children, who had

within them the capacity to produce wealth. . . . It was a bad trade no matter how much they received, for after the rum, the powder, and the bullets had been spent, they found themselves dependent upon their European trading partners for additional supplies. . . . It was much too late before the African tradesmen learned the first principle of the African market-women: it is not important what the thing you hold is worth to you; you must know what its real value is to the person who wants to trade for it.[13]

Much of the rest of this story is covered in depth elsewhere in historical work on the subject.

Today, dispersed communities of African descent are located in every region of the world and in most countries. In some Caribbean countries, such as Antigua, Barbados, Barbuda, Dominica, Haiti, Jamaica, Martinique, and St. Vincent, descendants of Africa are the majority population and have been present in large numbers since the early centuries of New World colonization and settlement. Elsewhere in the Caribbean region, especially in former Spanish colonies such as the Dominican Republic and Puerto Rico, the African presence is historically and demographically significant.

In South America the largest numerical concentration of African people outside of continental Africa reside in Brazil.[14] Identifiable and distinct communities are located in other parts of the continent, especially in Colombia, Ecuador, Peru, Uruguay, and Venezuela. The same observation can be made of Mexico and in Central America, where you find long-term settlements of both Spanish-speaking and English-speaking communities in countries such as Belize, Costa Rica, Honduras, Nicaragua, and Panama.

In the wealthier European-dominated metropolitan centers of North America and Western Europe the presence of the African diaspora is an indisputable reality. There is also a long history of migration and settlement of African peoples in Russia, the Eurasian Republics, and Central/Eastern Europe. With the arrival of new immigrants and refugees throughout Europe and Eurasia their numbers and settlements continue to increase.

Less well known are smaller settlements of African peoples in the Middle East and Asia that have persisted for centuries. Established settlements and enclaves can be found in Aden, Bangladesh, China, India, Indonesia, Iran, Iraq, Japan, Malaysia, Pakistan, Palestine, Saudi Arabia, Sri Lanka, Timor, Turkey, and Yemen, among others. Some notable examples are the Siddis (Sidi, Siddhis, Sheedis, Habshis) of India, who reside in a number of states including Andhra Pradesh (formerly the Kingdom of Hyderabad), Gujarat, Kerala, Karnataka, Maharashtra (formerly Bombay State), and West Bengal. Within and beyond India, there are also the Kafira/Kafara of Diu and the Saheli of Daman (former Portuguese areas of India); the Sheedis, Afro-Baluch, and Makranis of Pakistan; the Siddis of Bangladesh; the Ceylon Kaffir of Sri Lanka; the Turks of African ancestry in the Antalya region of Turkey; and African-Iranians in the Kerman, Jiruft, and Bandar Abbas regions of Iran.[15] These peoples are of diverse African origins, and many of their histories date from the seventh and eighth centuries; the spread of Islam and subsequent dynastic developments; the movements of peripatetic African merchants, traders, and soldiers; the East African slave trade; and, more recently, refugees and stateless peoples fleeing strife, hunger, and civil wars especially in the south, east, and Horn of Africa. A notable contemporary example of the changing global demographic morphology of the black African diaspora is the organized airlifting and resettlement of Ethiopian Jews (Beta Israel) in Israel that began in the mid 1980s.

The African diaspora is a demographic reality in terms of numerical population distributions and geosocial emplacements, patterns of movement and settlement, and social definitions. From a global perspective, most reside in the "Third World," their settlements often linked to localities where their ancestors—free, enslaved, and/or colonized—engaged in primary agricultural production, pearl diving, mining, ranching, crafts and skilled trades, shipbuilding, military service, and urban service work in households. Some were self-employed, but the vast majority were laborers for institutions of the colonial state, church, civil society, and commerce power complex. These localities of forbearers and descendants are the places where collective and individual histories are deeply embedded in material and symbolic spheres of social life.[16]

SOCIAL IDENTITY AND STRUGGLE: CHANGE AND CONTINUITY

A common experience throughout the age of the African diaspora has been the persistence of oppression, racialization, prejudice and discrimination, political disenfranchisement, and hostile social environments. Just as common, however, have been contestations of the ideologies, practices, and structural inequalities shaping this experience. Experience as "the site of subject formation" is also a "site of contestation; a discursive space where different and differential subject positions and subjectivities are inscribed, reiterated, or repudiated."[17] All global African peoples have struggled to be subjects of their own history; to establish places and spaces of meaning and material survival; to create institutions that offer venues for and visions of a just society, by which and in which to live their lives. These social experiences and relations inscribing processes of collective identity reformation are the "historical and contemporary trajectories of material circumstances and cultural practices which *produce the conditions* for the construction of group identities."[18] Thus, diaspora cultural identities are embedded in ongoing political struggles to define individual and collective selves in distinctive ways within historical contexts of displacement, oppression, and social inequality.[19]

A people can only be understood within the context of their historical specificities and the associated meanings and valuations thereof. As Anthony Smith argues, there is always some sense of historical continuity between the experiences of succeeding generations. There are shared memories of specific events and personages cited as turning points within a collective history, and there is a sense of common destiny on the part of the collectivity sharing those experiences. Social definitions and constructions of identity include "those feelings and values in respect of a sense of continuity, shared memories, and a sense of common destiny of a given unit of the population which has had common experiences and cultural attributes."[20] However, *continuity* should not be interpreted to mean *fixed*. Collective identities are contested, negotiated, conflictual, and dynamic. They are paradoxical and contradictory, generating internal "differences that themselves need to find a political voice."[21] Thus, we deliberately use terms such as social identities, social identity formations, and social identifications to emphasize that the significance and meaning of group membership are both ongoing and transient, relational to others and therefore comparative.

Fundamentally, a people can exist only in relationship to other people. The existence of a "we" implies the existence of a "they." Even the extent to which the mobilized actions of a people can be conceptualized as "acts for itself" implies a contradiction: people stand (act) in opposition to the forces that have conditioned their existential reality and material circumstances. Moreover, who people *are, have been,* and *may become* can be negotiated and can exist on many levels of social life. Neither sameness nor unity is implied. At the general and specific levels of African diaspora formation, there is variation by geographical location, by generations, by material and institutional conditions, and by socio-economic and demographic patterns. Of major interest are the "crosspoints," "active sites," and contradictions within a social system that not only facilitate the emergence and development of a collective "we" but also effectuate major dynamics within and among people of the diaspora.

THE GLOBAL AFRICA LANDSCAPE

While the "new" global political economy brings people and places into an integrated economic space, it has been accompanied by an acceleration of political and cultural conflicts and fragmentation among people within nation-states or among stateless people seeking nationhood. Global Africa is today part of "the landscape of persons who constitute the shifting world in which we live: tourists, immigrants, refugees, exiles, guest workers [athletes, entertainers, students, and scholars], and other moving groups and persons constitute an essential feature of the world, and appear to affect the politics of and between nations to a hitherto unprecedented degree."[22]

Who are these people, and how do they see themselves? How, after so many centuries, do settlements, enclaves, and communities continue to persist materially and symbolically?[23] How can we explain the social facts of their transformations and persistence, whether they are a majority population in a particular country, are a numerical minority elsewhere, or have (re)created settlements in distant lands and transnational spaces? How are global forces differentially experienced within different diaspora communities and, conversely, how might one town or collectivity impact an external world, and what are the processes and dynamics that make the difference?

What are the mechanisms and processes by which people produce and reproduce themselves over long periods, and what are the common connections and historical experiences among the culturally diverse peoples of the African diaspora? And in this context, what are the roles of the states, their policies and legal apparatuses? Why, for instance, are the Siddis of Karnataka, India, and other Afro-Asian peoples still living in settlement enclaves after centuries of existence in these localities? What internal and external factors contribute to these patterns? The Siddis have their own self-help organizations. What is it about the agency of people acting for themselves and the nature of social relations, constituted at local, national, regional and transnational levels, that contributes to the (re)shaping and transformation of a global African social identity?

Given the historical specificity and diversity of diaspora peoples, what are the systemic social relations, processes, and mechanisms that facilitate their interconnectedness and web of social networks? Among diaspora peoples, is there evidence of interest in preserving their historical and cultural distinctiveness? To what extent can collective cultural identity be a force for change in the distribution and location of African diaspora peoples in specific places and (trans)localities? These exemplary questions inform our work.

Four components have been useful in providing ADRP researchers with a way of rethinking how to build a macro conceptual framework with micro implications for analyzing the historical and contemporary experiences, relationships, and African diaspora identity formations. These components frame the discussions for the other essays in this volume and others in this series.

DEFINING AFRICAN DIASPORA SOCIAL FORMATIONS

As a modern diasporic social formation, the African diaspora can be conceptualized as a global aggregate of actors and subpopulations, differentiated in social and geographical space, yet exhibiting a connectedness based on a shared history of common experiences, conditioned by and within a dynamic world ordering system. The latter consists of political, economic, and socio-cultural forces linked to the emergence and growth of capitalist means of production and social relations, and its articulation with other modes of production over vast territories. Over time and space, these developments have major implications for the social construction of African diaspora peopleness and social identifications.

Based on field research, site visitations, analysis of primary and secondary sources, and advances in conceptual developments related to diaspora studies, four major components are advanced: geosocial mobility and displacement (the circulatoriness phenomenon); diaspora-homeland and transnational diaspora relations, social inequality and oppression (relations of domination and subordination); and endurement, resistance, and struggle (communities of consciousness and agency). As conceptual categories, these four components are neither exhaustive nor discrete. They overlap in theory and in fact provide greater explanatory value through the analysis of their interrelatedness. For example, the forceful displacement of Africans from their homelands is both a mechanism of oppression and domination and an example of geosocial mobility. These four components and their differential aspects are thus dialectic unities whose relationships are recognized to be uneven, contested, and even contradictory. Under various conditions they interpenetrate and transform each other. As relational modes and experiences they may coalesce and inter-join in disparate ways at various points in time to form distinctive structural and symbolic configurations. Moreover, at junctures in time, a particular experience and/or pattern of relations may emerge as the dominant feature or mode of an identity formation at local, national, regional, and/or transnational levels.

As articulatory practices, these components in their linkages and interconnections create the bases for the reformation, recreation, and redefinition of African diaspora social identity. In essence, articulation is "any practice establishing a relation among elements such that their identity is modified as a result of the articulatory practice."[24] Thus, the defining components should be understood as articulated cross points, active sites, and social fields of actions, effectuating the dynamics for social change, conflict, and transformation.

GEOSOCIAL MOBILITY AND DISPLACEMENT: THE CIRCULATORINESS PHENOMENON

The geosocial mobility of peoples of the diaspora, or circulatoriness, must be understood within the context of broader social, political, and economic transformations. Although individuals may make decisions to move, it is the emergent streams and patterns of passage that suggest major processes of structural change are contributing to the redistributions of populations. Qualitatively and quantitatively, geosocial mobility engenders shifts in worldwide localities of population concentrations, age and gender distributions, redefinitions of ethnicity and nationality, and changing structures and cultures of racialization.

Geosocial mobility is not just a physical movement but also a complex social process to be understood within the historical context of the larger collective experiences. The so-called brain drain, labor migration, and legal or illegal migration deal with forms of flows. Yet it is the historical conditioning that underlies the configuration of events and circumstances, which constitutes the experiences and relations to be fully analyzed. The challenge is to capture the central significance of the historical flows and movements as conditioned by various social forces and in relationship to the forms, patterns, and directions of the flows.[25] Within the matrix of the colonial institutions' power complex, it is no surprise that the state and its apparatuses were instrumental in displacing enslaved and free people to serve their interests and workforce requirements. Wherever and whenever there were geographical redistributions within the domain of colonial rule, all property, including enslaved Africans, moved. For instance, with the conquest of Peru by Spain in 1513, colonial settlers in Panama made an exodus to the new territory. This depopulation included the majority of the Spaniards, enslaved Africans, and indigenous people.[26]

This type of circulatoriness can be gendered in terms of the movements of men and women across time and space. During the *maafa*, for example, the preferential cargo were young males of working age, which established a pattern of male-dominated circulatoriness that prevailed for much of the period. Now women are leading the passages. The feminization of diaspora migration is indicative of the changing division of labor within a new global economy that is dominated by exporting and trading services. It is women who largely fill the poorly remunerated jobs in various service sectors such as tourism, entertainment, information, and communications. Women dominate the low-level service sector jobs, ranging from low-paid secretaries to sweatshop seamstresses, housekeepers, nannies, cooks, and waitresses. For immigrant women, entry into these jobs is not necessarily related to education and experience; it is the process by which they are incorporated into the global division of labor.[27]

The Proliferation of Departures

From its inception as a modern diaspora up to the present day, the geosocial movements of African diaspora people have been continuous. From the fifteenth to the late twentieth century, we can talk about a proliferation of departures across time and space, conditioned by and within a changing global cultural and political economy.[28] For purposes of this discussion we can think of these departures as primarily falling into three types: involuntary (e.g., slave trade, exile, expulsion); semi-voluntary (e.g., economic dispossession, labor recruitment, indenture); and voluntary (self-actualization, the search for decency and betterment). The first two tend to be more externally generated, while the latter seems to be more a result of the agency of the people themselves.

This proliferation of departures began with the direct (involuntary) physical force of stealing, capturing, and selling millions of African peoples as the principle commodity of exchange in terms of labor across the Atlantic and Indian Oceans and the Arabian Sea. For over four centuries, until the end of slavery in Brazil in 1888, there were continuous worldwide movements, with significant departures of Africans within and between the Dutch, British, French, Portuguese, and Spanish empires.

This was also a period in which men, women, and children fled their places of enslavement to establish *palenques* or maroon villages in isolated locations in mountains and jungle-like terrains. Most notable is the Kingdom of Palmares, established in 1670 in Brazil and comprised of some twenty thousand inhabitants, many of them former slaves from Angola. This confederation of villages withstood Portuguese attacks for several decades until their leader, Zumbi, was captured and killed in 1695. The surviving inhabitants were shipped as slaves to distant regions in Brazil, reflecting another chapter of the proliferation of involuntary departures. Many Africans during these four centuries took flight into "enemy" colonial empires, for example, from Jamaica (British) to Puerto Rico (Spanish). Often they secured their freedom and land from the competing empire because of the ongoing need for labor in the various colonies.

Numerous examples can be advanced to demonstrate the circulatoriness of global Africa in the earliest formation of New World empires, the antecedents of latter-day passages of African people to every part of the globe.

Military

Prior to the colonization of the New World, military slavery was well established in the Islamic East. Many of the earliest streams of Africans to the region were recruited into "slave armies" by rulers who felt safer under the protection of outsiders.[29] "A ruler could better trust a slave, his own property, than members of the local society with kinship ties and personal interests different from his own. Slave armies were common in the Muslim world—in Ottoman Turkey, in Egypt, and in Morocco, where slave soldiers from across the Sahara were used extensively in the eighteenth century. Because these slaves were valued as strangers, that value declined after the first generation, and successors had to be recruited beyond the frontiers of Islam."[30] Under different circumstances, the deadly competition among Europeans for land and resources required substantial manpower that could not be fulfilled by recruitment from the homeland. Thus, in 1795 Britain formed an army of black soldiers, under the command of white officers, known as the British West India Regiments (BWIR).

BWIR soldiers served in the war between Britain and France in the West Indies, which lasted from 1793 to 1815, quelled slave revolts, and fought in British colonial wars in West Africa, including the British war against the Ashanti in 1823. Recruits came from British West Indian Islands, especially Jamaica and Barbados; from the Dutch Islands; and from Africa. Those from the Caribbean consisted of New World–born creoles and recent arrivals born in Africa. Moreover, after the British government outlawed slave trading in 1807, they "established a vice admiralty court at Sierra Leone to which all illegally transported or condemned slaves captured by Royal Navy ships or privateers along the African coast were to be taken for adjudication."[31] These "liberated" or recaptured African men and boys were generally recruited directly into the BWIR. Free Africans from Sierra Leone and other regions along the West African coast also volunteered for service. Among the African ethnicities recorded were Ibo, Congo, Hausa, Coromantee, Mandingo, Yoruba, and Popo. Because of different methods of calculations, the estimates of total numbers who served in the BWIR range from 2,500 to 12,000.[32]

When the regiments were disbanded, resettlement areas were specific. "Some of the soldiers were permitted to remain in the Caribbean, but only in Trinidad or in the remote Honduras territory. The third area selected for settlement was Sierra Leone. Creole soldiers and those brought from Africa at an early age were to remain in the West Indies; the remainder would be removed to Sierra Leone."[33]

Beginning in 1831, Africans were recruited into the Dutch East-India Army. The first African soldiers (even before the colonization of Africa) were drawn from Ashanti (Ghana) and arrived in Java, Indonesia, in 1833. After agreement with the Asantahene, paramount chief of the Ashanti, their numbers increased rapidly. As many as three thousand Africans reinforced the Dutch East-India Army and fought in many expeditions, with more than seven hundred men still engaged as late as 1872. In the Malay language they were know as Belanda Hitam (Black Dutchmen). Stationed in special quarters in Java, some of them remained after their contracts were terminated, usually settling down near Semarang or Purworedjo and concentrated in special quarters and *kampongs*. Others returned to their home port in Elmina, located by the Dutch castles and fortifications near Cape Coast, Ghana. Many returnees settled close together on Java Hill, which remains part of the city of Elmina.[34]

Maritime Connections

Before chattel slavery was in full stride, Africans sailed along their own commercial waters and became expert seamen on Dutch and Portuguese crafts into Japan and other Eastern ports. At least a couple of centuries before the American Civil War, blacks in the United States worked as seamen traveling across much of the world. This merchant marine tradition continued through the mid twentieth century.[35]

Black seamen were critical to colonial maritime trade within imperial domains. West Indians and Africans, British and French, served on vessels and in ports throughout the world. A number of West Indians worked in Cape Town, South Africa, where some eventually settled. As Alan Cobley confirms, black seamen formed the nuclei of diaspora communities in British ports such as Cardiff, Liverpool, Bristol, London, and Glasgow.[36] These seamen were important diaspora cultural workers, and they brought news and information to those along their routes of passage, connecting others to the wider world they experienced.

Multifunctional Imperial Domains

The geosocial spaces taken and controlled by imperial states were multifunctional. They were sources for accessing, mobilizing, and deploying a vast array of black labor power (enslaved, re-captive, free) for multiple uses (agricultural, industrial, clerical-technical, domestic service, military, and so on). These spaces were also loci for religious proselytizing and missionary work, and for relocating and exiling those who could not be contained, such as rebellious slaves, maroon leaders, defiant African chiefs, and other activists.

Acting in their interests, people of the diaspora perceived and defined the same spaces as sites of contestation and rebellion, freedom and refuge, travel and adventure, job acquisition, and in general loci of access to a range of opportunities both within the limits placed on freedom and perceptions of life's possibilities beyond. Exemplary are the eight thousand Central and West African indentured laborers who immigrated to Jamaica in the mid nineteenth century. There were also "larger movements to Trinidad, Guadeloupe, Martinique, and the two Guianas, as well as smaller migrations to Tobago, St. Lucia, St. Vincent, St. Kitts, and Grenada."[37]

In the late eighteenth and early nineteenth centuries, laborers constituting free immigration originated in two areas of Africa. They came from the Kru coast (eastern Liberia and the western Ivory Coast) and Cabinda (northern enclave of Angola).

> These two regions began to provide European ships with crew, stevedores, and lighter-men [workers on flat-bottomed barges]. The Cabindans also emerged as important builders, owners, and operators of ships in their own right, sometimes crossing the Atlantic with loads of slaves. . . . The Kru-Cabinda "frontier" lay roughly between modern Cameroun and Gabon, although there was much overlap. Having acquired an excellent reputation as ship labor, it was natural that they should have been solicited for other work overseas, . . . urban employment, plantations, and public works.[38]

There remains much to learn about how those engaged in these passages empowered themselves as they interpenetrated and transformed one another while creating separated and interrelated spaces for contesting and ending their oppression.

Six centuries ago the African diaspora came into existence as a result of global forces including European expansionism and an emerging capitalist system. The diaspora remains integral to larger structural changes and social dynamics, changing as it is changed, transforming relations as it is in turn transformed. All of the above mentioned historical forces and social changes have had particular salience for African diaspora geosocial mobility and circulatoriness. Two cases are illustrative: Caribbean circulatoriness and changes in migration and displacement from Africa since the late twentieth century.

Caribbean Circulatoriness and Cultural Identity

Circulatoriness captures the experience of ongoing and continuous geosocial mobility and displacement of peoples of the diaspora. This historical, multidirectional process varies by quantity and scale, form and content, direction and rate. Circulatoriness itself can become a mode of "dwelling," in which "the wanderers of this world, those who live through, 'in transit,' the true homeless/rootless, are created."[39] The Caribbean has been more deeply and continuously affected by international migration than any other region of the world. It therefore seems appropriate to use it here as an example.

The flow of goods, natural resources, and people from the Caribbean was vital to industrialization in Europe and North America, and their areas of control in Central and South America, Africa, and Asia. Inter-territorial migration in the Caribbean region was directly impacted by global conditions that determined "the magnitude and timing of the movements." In the last decades of the nineteenth century, Dominicans (Dominica) went to work in the gold fields of Venezuela, as did Afro-Colombians; many Barbadians left for Surinam and St. Croix (Virgin Islands); and significant dispersions flowed from the Eastern Caribbean Islands to British Guiana (Guyana) and Trinidad.[40]

The "reserve army of West Indian laborers" was recruited to build the Panama Canal (1850–1914), to work for an American mining company in the Choco region of Colombia, to work on industrial projects in Brazil, and to construct railroads and docks in Costa Rica and other parts of Central America.[41] Given the bleak economic forecasts and lack of adequate earning power for themselves and their families, these men viewed labor migration as an avenue of social and economic opportunity. Their labor power was purchased at the lowest possible costs by British and U.S. commercial and industrial enterprises, one of which was the United Fruit Company and its "banana economy." The fact that these men were English speakers was value added since the alternative was to hire Spanish-speaking peasants of the region.

In the early twentieth century, West Indians migrated to Bermuda, the men entering the construction industry, building docks and military installations, and the women engaging in domestic service for European families. Many of these same men and women joined Haitians and other Caribbean islanders in the cane fields of the Dominican Republic. Between 1900 and 1930 significant numbers of Caribbean labor migrants engaged in this annual seasonal trek to work the January to July harvest period.[42] Over the next three decades the search for work led many Jamaicans to Cuba, Bahamians to Miami, and other West Indians to the United States.[43] The U.S. occupation of Cuba, the Dominican Republic, and Haiti in the early twentieth century greatly facilitated expanded sugar production in the first two locations and led to Haitian laborers becoming central to sugar cane production.[44]

The circulatoriness phenomenon was integral to labor migration, because many work opportunities were temporary and seasonal and, in a region subject to ecological and natural disasters, workers returned home or pursued employment in other locations. Bonham Richardson notes that state control "at either end" contributed to "back and forth" labor migration, although regulations were not very effective. The government of the Dominican Republic, for example, "imposed varying and changing rules about health certificates, deposit money, and immigrants' credentials . . . Similar constraints at home impeded a free emigration, taxing further the persistence of the potential emigrants."[45] The study of the circulatoriness phenomenon, whether in these particular instances or others, demands that students of the field assess the significance of state controls and policies and the relationships between the state, commercial enterprises, and their agents.

Within the United States, the period coinciding with World War I was also the beginning of the great migration from the rural South to cities and urban centers of the South and the North. "Going up North" continued well into the 1950s. During this same time period, however, West Indians continued to move regionally, with workers from Curacao, Trinidad, and Barbados finding work in the Venezuelan oil fields, as did Afro-Colombians from the Cauca region. When Shell Oil Company established a refinery in Curacao in 1915 a (re)circulation of British West Indians and other foreigners was imminent.[46]

After the U.S. occupation of Haiti from 1915 to 1934, other civilian leaders came to power; but the 1957 election of Francois "Papa Doc" Duvalier resulted in new routes and passages for Haitians. Many political elites opposing the regime of Duvalier and his private militia (Tonton Macoutes) fled to the United States, especially New York, Boston, and Chicago; others went to Canada, mainly Montreal.

In the 1950s, as the tourist industry expanded in the Bahamas along with related land development and building construction, Haitians were central to the low-wage labor market. As the need for Haitian labor lessened, Bahamians were less welcoming, and Haitians were expelled in various "clean-up" and "crackdown" campaigns. Around the early 1970s, continuous flows of Haitians left the Bahamas seeking asylum in Florida, giving rise to the "Haitian Boat People."[47] The struggles of Haitians to attain asylum and refugee status in South Florida continue with far too many in-between nowhere, others detained in prison waiting for asylum decisions, and most deported to Haiti.

During the immediate post–World War II period and into the last half of the twentieth century, Caribbean Islanders migrated in various streams to urban areas of

Britain, France, the Netherlands, the United States, and Canada. The reconstruction of Europe after World War II and the shifting need for workers in the expanding industrial and service sectors contributed to increased passages of men, women, and children.

Creoles and Maroons from Suriname and West Indians from the Netherlands Antillean islands of Curaçao, Aruba, and Bonaire increased their presence in the Netherlands between 1960 and 1980; some also migrated to the United States and Canada. During the same period, many residents of Guadeloupe, Guyana, and Martinique departed for France. As Overseas Departments (*departements d'outre-mer* or D.O.M.), they were considered citizens of France with the right to enter the mainland without restrictions. Similarly, residents of independent Commonwealth nations had free entry into Britain until restrictions were imposed by the Commonwealth Immigration Act of 1965. By 1974 the population from the D.O.M. in France was around 700,000.[48] The numbers of British Caribbean Islanders in Britain reached nearly 260,000 by 1962, and in the United States there were more than 1.2 million between 1960 and 1980.[49] According to Frances Henry, the West Indian population of Canada increased significantly during the 1960s, but especially in the 1970s, reaching around 320,000.[50]

The number of Puerto Rican–born residents living on the U.S. mainland grew exponentially after World War II, and between 1960 and 1981 Dominicans (from the Dominican Republic) arrived in large numbers. Once the United States and Canada changed racialized immigration policies in the mid 1960s, residents of Guyana, Haiti, Jamaica, Trinidad and Tobago, and other islands of the Caribbean broadened the diaspora presence in North America.[51]

Among the things many immigrants share are the processes and modes of their incorporation into urban centers of the metropoles. Immigrants, even those who may have held white-collar and professional positions in the Caribbean, are heavily concentrated in manual occupations and unskilled jobs. Job relocation at the bottom does not necessarily mean permanence for individuals. On the one hand, there are subjective goals and creativity of individuals, as well as the availability of support networks. On the other are the obstacles and barriers designed to maintain the hierarchies of power and privilege by which the dominant groups, civil and state, regulate access to political and legal rights and structures of opportunities such as jobs, education, and income.

The Caribbean has been more deeply and continuously affected by international migration than any other region of the world. Its experience since 1500 is extraordinary, and in the twentieth century there are few, if any, parallels in other world regions. One scholar argues that, more than any other region, Caribbean countries experience simultaneous emigration and immigration; those who leave represent a broader cross-section of the home societies than other sending countries; Caribbean states and governments have played a major part in promoting migration compared to other areas of the world; and most of the emigration is voluntary.[52]

These historically conditioned migration experiences have resulted in the creation of cultural and "symbolic patterns to give some minimum human support, if not comfort, to their condition. There is an instinctive drive to create, however minimally, symbolic patterns to give meaning and to guide action." The circulatoriness phenomenon is integral to identity formation and the "imagined communities" of "West Indianness" or "Caribbeanness." Caribbean cultural production and symbols reflect the dialectic of migration and the idealized quest for home, which is deeply embedded in literature, cultural artifacts, and ritualized social relations.[53] Social identity thus can develop within the process of the proliferation of passages, and the passages between time and place are indeed meaning-creating experiences.[54]

African Diaspora Connections: Myths and Realities of Homeland Relations

Homelands are socially constructed spatial representations embedded in economic, political, and cultural relations and processes. They may be neither geographical "facts" nor legally defined political or national territories. The "African homeland" is a case in point. Africa is a continent. There is no country-specific "African homeland." The nature of the dispersion process and the culture of violence associated with enslavement and colonialism is such that there are multiple diasporic identifications with Africa that do not necessarily coincide with legal/political boundaries linked to specific nation-states, past or present. As a place, Africa in the diaspora is part of a collective memory, a reference for tradition and heritage. Its symbolic and material significance lies within changing relations and ideas of homeland and diaspora—a dialectical relationship between and within Africa and its diaspora, defined by an ongoing proliferation of passages and marked by the impermanence of place and home.

For many of the diaspora, the African homeland is an emotional attachment, for others it is a distant past, and for yet others a concrete present. Ways of thinking about the homeland are mitigated by time and conditions of departures over long and short spans of time. For very recent African exiles such as the Beta Israel, for example, there are attempts to recreate an image of the homeland in the new settlement. Thus, "out of a need to recreate in exile an image of the sacred place of dwelling . . . the mirror of the Place becomes the unspoken symbol of Hope where hope [may] no longer [exist]."[55]

For messianic and millenarian groups such as the Rastafarians of Jamaica, the homeland is illustrated by way of symbolic voyages to Africa. The Rastafarian movement emerged during the world depression of the 1930s, and was based on the notion that there would be an eventual return or repatriation of black people to Africa. Members of the religion, now widely diffused throughout the world, still look toward Ethiopia as their promised land and to their Messiah, Ras Tafari, Negus Negust, the conquering Lion of Judah, Haile Selassie (the late deposed emperor of Ethiopia).[56]

An exemplary expression of physical return is the establishment of black settler colonies, the most resilient of which are the so-called Americo-Liberians of Monrovia and the Krios of Freetown, Sierra Leone. Growing out of colonization movements between the eighteenth and nineteenth centuries, for African returnees colonization largely meant the quest for the decent society, while for Europeans it was the solution to the "Negro problem."[57]

These colonization movements, on the one hand, symbolize positive aspects of black consciousness—the constructive attempts among diaspora peoples to extricate themselves from the bonds of oppression. On the other hand, they point to structural inequalities and negative aspects of the relationship between the diaspora and its homeland. Returnee and indigenous relations, for example, are implicated in both the 1980 coup and subsequent carnage in Liberia and the mid 1990s civil war and continuing undercurrents in Sierra Leone. The kinds of relations that have prevailed within these settler states require critical and objective analysis of the changing social, political, and economic relations and contradictions internal to these societies.

Much of the organized returns occurred during the nineteenth century, guided by strong currents of Pan-African nationalist consciousness and the support of major institutional networks established by black churches and mutual-aid societies. Return-to-Africa schemes continued into the twentieth century, however, with perhaps the most famous of which being the Garvey movement, which organized under the banner "Africa for the Africans at home and abroad."[58] Also evident are small but steady flows of persons back-to-Africa for a variety of reasons. During the early sixties, for example, many Afro-Americans went to Ghana and to the Republic of Guinea, often attracted to the ideologies and programs of Kwame Nkrumah and Sekou Touré, in particular. This interest also extended to Zambia, but especially to Tanzania and Julius Nyerere's notions of Ujamaa.

As St. Claire Drake points out, the "myth of the return" has always been an important aspect of the African-diaspora connection in both symbolic and concrete terms.[59] The "myth of the return" suggests that for its diaspora, Africa is a concept, an aspect of the symbolic and meaning construction process germane to the black cultural experience. The degree and extent of its significance varies over time and space among different actors and subpopulations of the diaspora. As a focus on "African heritage," it epitomizes the dialectical relationship between old, new, and emerging "roots," and is therefore an essential element in understanding the emergence and development of the diaspora as a social formation.

Settlement, demographic, and migration patterns, as well as processes of incorporating the labor and production of global Africa into the world economy, have been, and continue to be, directly impacted by the economic dominance of Europe and North America and the "white" Euro-elite bridgeheads of Latin America. It is within the context of a global system in which Euro-American power is hegemonic that African diaspora connections are symbolically and materially shaped and transformed. This situation is no different in cultural spheres such as religion and education, language, and sport, or in terms of ideologies and values. Dominant institutional practices and ideological systems condition not only what is known but the processes of controlling and channeling knowledge and information. Hence, knowledge of global Africa has been socially constructed by and within an unequal world ordering system.

The writings of Hegel, Darwin, Herbert Spencer, Count Arthur de Gobineau, Stewart Chamberlain, and others removed Africa and its diaspora from history, denying both movement and development.[60] European cultural ideologies, systems of social thought and representation, put Europe at the center of the world to reinforce claims of European universality. European ideas, art, representation, and imagery thus followed an imperial framework, a "hierarchical logic," that "remained basically unaltered into the twentieth century," in which the "myths of Africa and other continents correlate with a myth of Europe itself."[61]

In the nineteenth and early decades of the twentieth centuries a small but powerful group of African and diaspora intellectuals and scholars developed counteranalyses. Edward Blyden, William Wells Brown, W. E. B. Du Bois, and Alexander Cromwell were among those who contributed to the restoration of Africa and its diaspora to world history. In the 1920s and 1930s an organized movement of francophone African and diaspora intellectuals introduced *negritude*, which was paralleled among English speakers by the writers of the Harlem Renaissance of New York. Smaller scale but no less significant were *indigeniste* intellectuals of Haiti and *negritud* writers in Spanish-speaking South America. Collectively, these writers reaffirmed black African and diaspora cultures and rejected values associated with racial superiority, discrimination, and economic exploitation.[62]

It was not until the post–World War II era, however, that U.S. and European anthropologists sought to show in a scientifically conclusive way that "the New World Negro did in fact have both a determinate past and a distinctive culture."[63] Much of this theoretical and empirical work focused on African heritage and was guided by an emphasis on perceived sets of relatively stable and patterned relationships in which the predominant connection between Africa and its diaspora was conceptualized in unidirectional or asymmetrical terms: as socio-cultural flows and links from Africa to the diaspora. Thus, within various communities of the African diaspora the search has been for organizational patterns and institutions inherited from Africa, such as economic and family structures, and cultural and ideological survivals, including linguistic patterns, belief systems, religious rituals and symbols, music, and dance forms. This mode of theorizing directs attention to the consequences of African survivals, of "Africanisms," for the adaptation and adjustment of black people in the New World. Africanisms are interpreted as contributions from the Old World to the New World, exemplified in Melville J. Herskovits's query "What has Africa Given America?"[64]

While leaving a legacy accompanied by much controversy regarding the social identities and problems of the so-called New World Negroes in the Americas, these traditional conceptual paradigms have yielded basic data and insights regarding continuities and linkages between the diaspora and the African past.[65] They were also important for their attempt to counter the prevailing belief of mainstream Eurocentric scholarship that Africa had contributed little to world civilization. Yet their analyses reflect a limited view and understanding of the complexities of relationships between the dispersed peoples and the homeland. The interactions between the diaspora and Africa are changing dialectical relationships altered by internal dynamics, as well as by transformations in the global geopolitical system.

Interactive relations are based on social dynamics, not on asymmetrical relations or static conditions. This means the conditions of formation and historical development of both continental Africa and its diaspora are crucial to understanding the dynamic of their relationship to each other and to the world. The changing location of African and diaspora blacks in the world economic, political, social, and cultural division of labor is therefore a major explanatory variable.

The emergence of independent African states in the 1960s, for example, inaugurated new levels of interaction with and symbolic links to the diaspora. More direct diplomatic, economic, and cultural relationships ensued between African states, black countries, and subpopulations in the Americas. In the economic arena, representatives of African countries have increasingly expressed interest in developing more extensive business ties with Afro-American entrepreneurs. A greater cross-section of the African diaspora in the Americas (especially West Indians and U.S. blacks) has valorized the African past. This became most apparent during the era of the civil rights and black power movement, as is evidenced by hairstyles and dress, the African names assumed by adults or given to children, and increased tourism to the African continent.

During the past several decades, political developments within U.S. black communities have made possible new avenues of support for Africa, such as the interest of the Black Congressional Caucus in legislation and policy issues with implications for Africa. However, this kind of solidarity is not new. In the 1930s urban blacks in the United States and in the Panama Canal Zone demonstrated to protest the Italian Fascist incursion in Ethiopia. More recently, South Africa became the focus mobilizing the diaspora throughout the Americas to achieve investment boycotts.

As early as 1889 there was extensive contact between Africans and the traditionally black colleges and universities in the United States, with famous sons of Africa such as Kwame Nkrumah and Hastings Banda products of this association.[66] Currently, Howard University in Washington, D.C., symbolizes the changing contours of this historical alliance, often serving as a point of contact between Afro-Americans and African heads of state visiting the nation's capital. In 1979 the department of history at Howard hosted a historic scholarly conference, "The African Diaspora from a Changing Global Perspective."[67] A follow-up conference was held in 1981 at the University of Nairobi.

Finally, in the realm of popular culture, particularly music and dance and to a lesser extent films, the interaction has been extensive. Jazz, soul, and reggae have become an integral part of the African experience, with much cross-pollination. Taking advantage of new technologies as they have emerged, various elements of New World black culture, such as dress and speech patterns, have been popularized among young people in African cities and towns.

These selected examples are indicative of the changing bases and levels of interaction between Africa and the diaspora. The Africa of the diaspora's inception and the Africa of today are radically different worlds. Likewise the diaspora of the twentieth century and that of the fifteenth century are significantly different phenomena. What does this mean for Africa-diaspora relations? What are some of the conditions and processes that have been significant in mitigating the interactive relations? What have been some of the consequences? What might be expected in the future? More work on the Afro-Asian or trans–Indian Ocean connection would not only add to the knowledge base but would no doubt delineate different patterns and networks.

POWER, DOMINATION, INEQUALITY: STRUCTURATIONS OF BLACK DISPOSSESSION

Expansionism and conquest created social inequality and hierarchies of social difference, as well as fueled the emergence of a capitalist world system. For five centuries Europeans conquered, enslaved, and colonized peoples of color. In the process they institutionalized race, class, and gender divisions of labor throughout the mines, ports, plantations, towns, and commercial centers in the Americas, Asia, and Africa. The social order became a matter of power, and power a matter of control and force. A constellation of institutions, ideas, and practices enabled Europeans to achieve and maintain power and privilege through control and exploitation.[68]

To this day, attributes of power are associated with European states (colonial and independent), a major exception being Japan. Power, which implies potential force and the ability to get others to do one's bidding, is difficult to acquire, and those who have it seldom, if ever, relinquish it voluntarily. It is indeed the object of opposition. The forces that have caused such profound social change and disruption in peoples' lives and identities have not disappeared: "Two of the most glaring facts about this world [are] the tremendous inequality, within and between nations, in almost all aspects of human living conditions, including the power to decide over those living conditions; and the resistance of this inequality to change."[69]

It is within this context that the most pernicious and persistent experiences of the African diaspora must be assessed. Global Africa has existed and persisted in hostile, socially oppressive situations and conditions, and it continues to do so. While race is the indexical term in assessing the diaspora experience, racialization cannot be disentangled from the manifold axes of difference that constitute diasporic experience, access to opportunity, and the social identification and meaning of black collectivity.

Diasporic Axes of Difference: Race, State, Nation, Class, Gender, Empire

Racial distinctions can be based on somatic norms, "biological remembrances" and color, parental ancestry, place of origin, or even immigrant status. These and other principles of selection are used by a dominant group to place others in a hierarchy of relative social worth; they are also used as indicators of behavior and attitudes and as "discrete organizing principles of human consciousness and conduct."[70] The multiracial New World colonial societies were organized along a racial division of labor in every sector of the economy and social life. Initially, there were Europeans, Indians, and Africans. Later, Chinese, Japanese, and East Indians entered. Over three centuries (the fifteenth to the seventeenth), new peoples were created in the Americas. In Spanish and Portuguese colonies of the New World the term *castas* was used to define the offspring of interracial unions, and the *regimen de casta* was an explicit mechanism for racially and culturally identifying children who were the product of miscegenation. Catholic priests, as agents of the state, were instrumental in creating detailed classificatory schemes and categories of degradations in primary blood or *limpieza de sangre* (clean blood).

As a numerical minority, the Spanish colonialists used the system to protect their prestige and status, to maintain control over material and nonmaterial resources. One's classification determined access to benefits, jobs, business and educational opportunities, property rights, and enfranchisement. The situation became more acute as the new and invented social groups incorporated some free people of African descent. In fact, around the seventeenth and eighteenth centuries, this latter group was on the rise numerically. Moreover, it became an interstitial socially defined group and served as a buffer between Europeans and the large number of Africans at the bottom of the hierarchy. The middle group also posed a challenge to some Europeans for jobs and social status, which prompted more exclusionary laws and restrictions.[71]

What is intriguing is the elaborate ideology that emerged to rationalize the hierarchy of social race and racial inequality. Stigmatization and racial labels were integral to this process, but more important was the idea of "racial cleansing," the ideological drive toward drawing persons of color nearer to a white normativity, which to this day remains an important factor in socio-racial identification.

In most Latin American countries, for instance, a premium is placed on the European aspect of cultural heritage and identity. The guiding principle is that of *blanqueamiento*—that is, lightening or whitening to improve the race, as whiteness stands as the aesthetic marker of moral and social worth. *Mestizaje,* the symbolic explanation of racial mixing, becomes the nationalistic ideology of racial culture.[72] More important, ideology is put into practice in everyday life. The named identity people carry, such as chombo, moreno, mestizo, negro, trigueno, and mulatto, has an effect on their consciousness, how they see themselves, how they are seen by others, and what they believe others think of them.

African diaspora peoples were present at the formation of the first nation-states in the Americas and indeed in the modern world. Recruited as part of South American revolutionary and military leader Simón Bolívar's campaign and struggle for independence, they were even promised freedom in return for their efforts. They were deeply engaged in the Revolutionary War in the United States, fighting on both sides (as Patriots and Black Loyalists), seizing the opportunity not only to be free but also to be part of the new social experiment of creating independent nations. As these nations emerged, the white Creole leadership had specific ideas about what the new entity would look like and which people should comprise it. Immigration laws were used in every country in South, Central, and North America to exclude people of color, explicitly Africans, Chinese, and Japanese, from cultural, political, and institutional participation in social life.

In the late nineteenth and early twentieth centuries, Latin America became more integrated into the new era of industrialization and multinational corporations that exploited land and mineral resources worldwide. Labor remained a problem, and companies were allowed to use temporary workers from the West Indies, the southern United States, China, and Japan. These people built the railroads, worked the mines, and developed the agricultural sector in countries like Costa Rica, Panama, and Brazil. West Indians were brought in to build the Panama Canal. Yet, all were unwelcome strangers. Most were settled in segregated enclaves on company property. They were expected to return home when their job was completed, but they did not. As noted by George Simmel, the man who comes today and stays tomorrow is the "stranger." The stranger who refuses to go eventually calls the appropriated place home. The circulatoriness phenomenon brought diaspora "strangers" into direct confrontation with the centripetal, homogenizing state.[73]

Given the racialization of the immigrant, diaspora people were denied citizenship, restricted to particular territories, and subjected to stigmatizing labels. According to Zygmunt Bauman, the national state collectivizes friends and even enemies, but they also are "designed primarily to deal with the problem of strangers."[74] Then, as now, states seek to exercise taxonomical control over differences, and the relationship between state and nation is everywhere embattled.[75] Given the transitoriness of diaspora people and the significance of race as a factor in the definition of nations, this will continue to be a battleground for political and cultural identity.

With the modern era came the globalization of racism or the racialization of the world system. The meanings underpinning the problematics of race remain socially relevant because of the psychological, cultural, and political significance attributed to it. As the contours of the modern world system crystallized, a particular significance was placed on race. The very struggle of creating a new world order imposed upon race enormous meaning and prominence in distinguishing fundamental characteristics of people arranged in a hierarchy of human qualities. The issue of race became particularly important as a powerful rationalizing ideology based upon quasi-scientific validation and as a mechanism of social selection.

Race remains a central defining factor in the experience and historical memory of African diaspora people. For this reason, the primary experience of being defined in racial terms, articulated within these discourses of devalued social worth, is pertinent to the processes of subject formation. Racial definitions have constituted a fundamental reality imposed upon the African diaspora and have informed their fate within a racially structured world system. Racialist principles of selection have been overriding determinants in maintaining and compounding subordinate social positions.

The manner in which people interact with nature and sustain themselves materially also must be considered part of the historical process by which they become distinctive. An institutional structure that significantly divides individuals and groups, particularly in terms of political and economic organization, allows the possibility of creating different people. The general position of the African diaspora in the global system of production and distribution, the international division of labor, should be considered a significant factor in black identity formation. The empirical question revolves around the extent to which their general class position constitutes a fundamentally different experience from that of other groups. Moreover, is the cumulative nature of this experience a major factor in the making of their general and specific levels of black collectivity and subject formation—of peopleness?[76]

Much has been said and written about the growing black underclass in the United States and the increasing impoverishment of blacks in metropolitan centers and rural areas. There is disproportionate representation of blacks in subordinate positions within the income and occupational hierarchy and in the unemployed and underemployed economic categories. Diaspora communities in the Caribbean provide dramatic illustrations of how the class position of a people may be viewed within the framework of a global division of labor. Primary commodity specialization with a concentration on cash crop exports, such as sugar, coffee, and fruits, imposed a particular kind of experience on plantation societies. Presently, there is still little economic diversification other than an increasing hypertrophy in sectors that provide few or low-paying jobs: tourism, banking enclaves, runaway insurance companies. In a world context, these communities are "lower class," characterized by foreign control of major primary and extractive industries, a mono-economy that largely extracts fixed value, and low median SES among the population and high unemployment across all age cohorts. The consequences are seen in the poor quality of life and high levels of structural violence, which lead to high infant mortality, high crime rates, and low life expectancy. In addition, as suggested by their history of geosocial mobility and circulatoriness, these countries have had a highly exploitable labor force within the global framework, and economically driven "passages" have largely been limited to occupational areas, lower-level service jobs, and unskilled work.

While the means of production, technology, and organizational factors have changed, the qualitative position of African diaspora people in the global system has remained relatively constant. Such a pattern is directly related to the law of cumulative hierarchy, that is, "the present structure (and any past or future ones) is the result of the process of accumulating control opportunities . . . The structure becomes a set of control layers, the more recent ones imposed on the past; but without abandoning subordinate layers."[77]

The concern is with how the cumulative class position of diaspora people contributes to identity formation and the sense of shared memory. As pointed out by Julio Ortega, "the events themselves occurred at the origin, but the transformations unleashed by them have not ceased. We are living through the change itself, the drama of its madness that has no denouement." We live in a global political, social, and economic ordering system that continues to undergo change, yet structural inequalities still exist today because they are historically conditioned. Nation-states, trans-local affiliations, racial and ethnic formations are processual, always forthcoming enactments. Indeed, "we live in the imminent condition of peoples that [are] still being created, in which some standards are favored and others devalued, alternating in their exclusivity."[78] Today, therefore, many of the practices, ideas, and lived experiences of people in various places reflect the deep roots of protracted structural inequalities, which no doubt will continue well into the next millennium.

It is my contention that, in addition to being the first modern diaspora, African peoples for the most part constitute an oppressed racialized class subject in a world context. This is reflected in structural and cultural violence, specifically and generally, and in the direct violence and pathos faced by diaspora people in everyday life. One aspect of the cumulative experience of diaspora people relates to their place in other people's history and to the fact that they have historically existed in hostile, socially oppressive states and nations. The primary issue here is power and the driving interest of those who hold it to preserve their position of domination and social privilege. Class, gender, nationality, sexuality, and race have been major forces in shaping life experiences and social identity within the diaspora. They also have generated oppositional forces geared toward redistributing power and changing the hierarchy of inequality in the ongoing search for a decent society.

AGENTS OF RESISTANCE: DIASPORIC IDENTITIES AND COMMUNITIES OF CONSCIOUSNESS

While peoples of African descent have been the objects of oppressive social, political, and economic structures, the complete picture requires that we understand them as subjects of their history. To paraphrase Ralph Ellison, life for black people is a discipline, just as any human life that has endured so long is a discipline, teaching its own insights into the human condition, its own strategies for survival.[79] Africa's descendants are products not only of their economic and socio-political conditions but also of their interaction with those conditions and efforts to develop their own sense of who they are and what they want to be, to deal with life in particular ways, and to live life as they transform life.

People are not simply reactors but creators, devising their own mechanisms of survival, their own ideological tools and social networks, their own vehicles of struggle over time and space. This is what constitutes the cultural process, a dynamic and creative expression of all the relationships characterizing physical and historical reality. Culture is the continuous synthesis of a people's experiential knowledge, beliefs, values, and norms that *express* and *derive* from the conflicts at each stage of their development in the search for survival and progress.[80] Culture, then, is the fruit of a people's history and a determinant of that history, not fixed in the past but an ongoing interaction between past and present.

Looking broadly across time and space, it is possible to think of diasporas as communities of consciousness. This is the translation of their experiences in cultural terms, a field of social and political thoughts, behaviors, and actions. It is a consciousness itself, as well as a politicized or "oppositional" consciousness.[81] All consciousness, group and individual, is social and formed within the context of the group's historical experiences. This plane of social action may be reflected in the ordinary ways in which people act, think, and live their lives; it may include personal and individual practices, ritualized celebrations affirming the collective memory and difference, definitions of success and failure, or even the meanings of life and death. Worldviews manifest themselves in a number of forms, reflecting the obvious complexities of individual and social differentiation, but they may include popular culture, lifestyles, linguistics, and symbolic behavior. Consciousness emerges from a process of "perceiving and experiencing cultural differences and diversity, the singularity of one's own traditions opposed to those of the other, dominant society."[82]

African peoples in the Americas have received much attention from cultural anthropologists, who have studied in depth many of their syncretic traditions, ranging from religion to modern dance. Many of these cultural elements have been retained from the past, but they also include elements appropriated from the dominant group as well as other diaspora people who share their temporal and social spaces. People celebrate their difference and create systems of affirmation and valorization. In many instances the process idealizes that which may have been stigmatized and devalued by the other.

People create fictitious identities or invent new ones as means of empowerment and self-creation. For example, in November 1995 Afro-Brazilians celebrated the death of Zumbi of Palmares, promoted as the "tercentenary [of] Brazil's primary African hero." Leaders of the event said: "Our goal is to transform Zumbi into a hero of the Americas, the earliest great black hero of the Americas."[83] This invented tradition is in keeping with the emergence of submerged identities, suppressed along with those of other communities during the long reign of vicious military dictatorships in Brazil and other parts of the Americas. Afro-Brazilians are attempting to retrieve not only their history but also that of global Africa. The idea is to use a person or an event to commemorate and ascribe some historical significance to the Afro-Brazilian/Brazilian reality. In this way they can remember and celebrate events and persons that are part of their cultural history and identity.

Two issues are important here. First, how people *forget* or how they *remember* can be determined by social and political circumstances, and these can change. For example, prior to racial democratization, a great deal of Afro-Brazilian scholarship focused on religion rather than race, because there was a tacit policing of race studies, while religious inquiries were deemed politically safe. Identity can be lost or even elided because political and social conditions may threaten people's existence, physically, culturally, or psychically. The socio-political context and social practices have a direct effect on the form and content of collective remembering and forgetting, on how people perceive their past.[84]

Second, for populations throughout the diaspora, new and old traditions, myths, and fictitious or even borrowed identities can not only restore dignity, but also reconstruct connections among people long divided by class, race, and color— as is the case in Brazil, due to the ideologies of racial democracy and *mestizaje*. Thus, by inventing traditions and connectedness, "not only is the sense of bonding intensified, but a reversal of collective status is achieved, at least on the cognitive and moral levels. It is the start of a moral and social revolution through the mobilization of hidden collective energies."[85]

Cultural and Political Consciousness and Agency

Historian Robert Hill, in an attempt to capture some of the dynamics and relationships among peoples of African descent, refers to the diaspora as a "field of action."[86] This notion may be further interpreted to mean that, in socio-spatial terms, the diaspora is an active site of cultural and political action and struggle. As Aldon Morris has suggested, systems of domination give rise to political consciousness, which is comprised of cultural beliefs and ideological expressions that realize and maintain group interests and that continuously shape and influence concrete social and political struggles. Moreover, this political consciousness becomes "oppositional consciousness" for subordinate groups who struggle to dismantle systems of domination that prevent them from realizing their interests.[87] Black African diaspora identity politics or the politicization of culture embodies processes of symbol and meaning construction in terms of active social and physical planes of action, the range of political activities, and the solutions engendered to resolve the conflicts that characterize each phase of diaspora history. The pervasive manifestations of African diaspora oppositional consciousness and actions relate to the forms of political expression and struggle reflected in the various strategies of liberation, resistance, and rebellion. This ranges from slave revolts and the ebb and flow of worker militancy to urban insurrections of more recent years; from the Haitian revolution of the late eighteenth century to the Grenada revolution of the late twentieth century; from flight or the formation of maroon communities (*palenques, quilombos, cumbes*) to the planned emigration settlements, back-to-Africa movements, and black Utopias in Canada.[88] There have been clearly orchestrated Pan-African movements, such as the congresses in 1919 (Paris), 1921 (London), 1923 (London and Lisbon), 1927 (New York), and 1945 (Manchester), as well as the All-African Peoples Conference in Accra in 1958.[89]

Throughout history, there have been "shifting centers of historical gravity" within the diaspora.[90] The places, people, and events that seem to represent or embody the most active sites of conflict and change vary over time and space. These diverse fields of action are interrelated and tend to represent acts of deliberate cross-fertilization and interpenetration. They also represent a people's realization of its own potential to engage in the transforming and rebuilding process of society, a conscious force acting for itself.

The dispersed peoples of African descent, separate and interrelated, are "communities of consciousness" engaged in an ongoing quest for human dignity and collective self-actualization. This notion encompasses the cumulative and shared endeavors to make themselves the kind of people they imagine themselves capable of being, to make their own development, to realize their humanity in their own terms, and to deny their status as simply social objects—as slaves or wage laborers in some other people's development process. To struggle for human dignity and social decency and to maintain some dynamic concept of human freedom are formative experiences that shape the cognitive landscape and social infrastructure of a people. The challenge is to discern how this shared experience and consciousness are crystallized and transformed into various forms and relations within a geosocial and institutional framework and within the historical content of that framework at different times.

Toward a Non-Essentialist View of Diasporic Similarity: Contradictions and Abutments of Culture

To recognize the existence of common and particular features does not imply cultural unity or the existence of only one culture of the black diaspora.[91] Circumstances can restrict the extent to which people can embody various elements of their culture and history. The degree to which a group moves toward a common recognition of itself as distinctive is in part directly related to the degree to which certain ideas and values are cognitively internalized. The issue is one of identity, which in the framework of the cultural process means "at once the affirmation and denial of certain attributes defining individuals or sub-populations in relation to others at any point during their development."[92]

In *Black Skin, White Masks* Frantz Fanon illuminates the problem of how a subordinated people may be culturally and psychologically penetrated by their dominators. Using language as an example, he contends that "every colonized people . . . finds itself face to face with the language of the civilizing nation; that is, with the culture of the mother country. The colonized is elevated above his jungle status in proportion to his adoption of the mother country's cultural standards. He becomes whiter as he renounces his blackness, his jungle."[93] This observation points to the need to elaborate and uncover many of the contradictions and conflicts within the diaspora revolving around competing forms of identification, including class, color, nation, and religion.

The ongoing struggle of the black diaspora for human dignity and liberation is a creative process. It embodies contradictory crosscurrents and conflicts, such as the dialectical relationship between creativity and action, travail and reaction. It is essential to recognize that culture is an expanding and developing phenomenon. No culture is ever a complete, perfect, finished whole. The elements of culture are comprised of strengths and weaknesses, positives and negatives, stagnation and growth, regression and progress. Moreover, among peoples of the African diaspora, the quantitative and qualitative levels of cultural action and practice vary significantly.

Finally, it should be emphasized that to learn about the persistence, endurance, and struggles of people of the African diaspora is to be conscious of their value in the context of a human universality. We must compare their historical experiences and realities with those of other people, not with a view to deciding superiority or inferiority but to determine, in the general framework of human progress, what contributions they have made and can make and what kinds of support they can and should receive. To understand people as subjects of their history is to help retrieve, preserve, and provide a more objective and meaningful interpretation of that history within the universal context.

NOTES

1. ADRP research staff have come from Ethiopia, Ghana, Kenya, Nigeria, Algeria, Brazil, Panama, Costa Rica, Mexico, Trinidad, the Dominican Republic, Puerto Rico, Canada, the United States, France, India, and Taiwan. Research in African diaspora places and spaces has been conducted in the Bahamas, Brazil, Canada, Costa Rica, Dominican Republic, Ecuador, Germany, India, Israel, Mexico, Nigeria (Lagos-Brazilians), Panama, Puerto Rico, Sierra Leone (Krios), Trinidad, and Venezuela. Site visits and conferences have occurred in Brazil, Colombia, Cuba, England, Honduras, and Peru. For details, see *The African Diaspora Research Project: A Report on Progress 1986–1993* (East Lansing, Mich.: The African Diaspora Research Project, Michigan State University, 1993).

2. Because a great deal has been written about diaspora experiences of peoples of African descent in the United States, few examples of this are used in this chapter. This should not be interpreted as a lessening of the importance of the diaspora in the United States, but rather as an effort to broaden knowledge of the scope of the worldwide diaspora.

3. Etymologically, *dia* means through or part and *spora* means to sow, as in scattering seeds that will take root and grow. Thus the term *diaspora* refers to the scattering of a people and their subsequent settlement in other places.

4. Robert E. Park, "Introduction," *Negroes in Brazil: A Study of Race Contact in Bahia*, ed. Donald Pierson (1942; Carbondale: Southern Illinois University Press, 1967), lxxxii.

5. James Clifford, *Routes: Travel and Translation in the Late Twentieth Century* (Cambridge, Mass.: Harvard University Press, 1997), 254.

6. Note this descriptive statement of *Diaspora: A Journal of Transnational Studies:* "The journal welcomes essays exploring the underpinning of terms such as 'nation,' 'exile,' 'transnational,' 'multicultural,' 'ethnic,' . . . [and] aspects of the infranational and transnational phenomena now challenging the homogeneity of the nation-state, including nomadic ideas, works of art, and mass media productions that traverse frontiers and borderlands" (1, no. 1 [spring 1991]: 124).

7. For the African diaspora, the following works are relevant: Michael Bradley, *The Black Discovery of America: Amazing Evidence of Daring Voyages by Ancient West African Mariners* (Toronto: Personal Library, 1981); Chester S. Chard, "Implications of Early Human Migrations from Africa to Europe," *Man*, no. 152 (August 1963); Yu M. Kobishchanow, "On the Problem of Sea Voyages of Ancient

Africans in the Indian Ocean," *Journal of African History* 6, no. 2 (1965): 137–41; Martin Bernal, *Black Athena: The Afroasiatic Roots of Classical Civilization*, vol. 1: *The Fabrication of Ancient Greece 1785–1985* (New Brunswick, N.J.: Rutgers University Press, 1987); *Black Athena: The Afroasiatic Roots of Classical Civilization*, vol. 2: *The Archaeological and Documentary Evidence* (New Brunswick, N.J.: Rutgers University Press, 1991); Legrand H. Clegg, "The Beginning of the African Diaspora: Black Men in Ancient and Medieval America?" *A Current Bibliography on African Affairs* (November/December 1969), "Ancient America: A Missing Link in Black History," *A Current Bibliography on African Affairs* (May 1972), and "The Olmec Puzzle: A Challenge of Pan-African Historians," *A Current Bibliography on African Affairs* (spring 1974); Joseph E. Harris, *The African Presence in Asia* (Evanston, Ill.: Northwestern University Press, 1971); Susan Raven, *Rome in Africa* (New York: Longman, 1984); Ivan Van Sertima, *They Came Before Columbus: The African Presence in Ancient America* (New York: Random House, 1976); Ivan Van Sertima, ed., "African Presence in Early Europe," *Journal of African Civilizations* (New Brunswick, N.J.: Transaction Books, 1985), "African Presence in Early America," *The Journal of African Civilizations* (New Brunswick, N.J.: Transaction Books, 1987), and "Black Women in Antiquity," *The Journal of African Civilizations* (New Brunswick, N.J.: Transaction Books, 1988); J. A. Rogers, *Sex and Race*, vol. 1: *The Old World* (New York: Helga M. Rogers, 1967).

8. *Maafa*, a Kiswahili word, means a major event or even series of events causing great suffering, misfortune, upheaval, or trauma. Many thanks and credit goes to former ADRP graduate research assistant Maria Pease for introducing and making *maafa* part of our nomenclature.

9. Dirk Hoerder, *Cultures in Contact: World Migrations in the Second Millennium* (Durham, N.C.: Duke University Press, 2002), 139–42.

10. David Brion Davis, "Slavery—White, Black, Muslim, Christian," *The New York Review* (July 5, 2001): 51–52. Also consult E. A. Alpers, *The East African Slave Trade* (Nairobi: East African Publishing House, 1967); David Brion Davis, "A Big Business," *The New York Review* (June 11, 1998): 50–53; William Gervase Clarence-Smith, ed., *The Economics of the Indian Ocean Slave Trade in the Nineteenth Century* (London: Frank Cass and Company, 1989); Harris, *The African Presence in Asia*; John Hunwick, "Black Africans in the Mediterranean World: Introduction to a Neglected Aspect of the African Diaspora," *Slavery and Abolition: A Journal of Comparative Studies, Special Issue: The Human Commodity: Perspectives on the Trans-Saharan Slave Trade*, ed. Elizabeth Savage, 13, no. 1 (April 1992): 5–38; Graham W. Irwin, *Africans Abroad: A Documentary History of the Black Diaspora in Asia, Latin America, and the Caribbean During the Age of Slavery* (New York: Columbia University Press, 1977); and Ronald Segal, *Islam's Black Slaves: The Other Black Diaspora* (New York: Farrar, Straus and Giroux: 2001).

11. Davis, "Slavery," 51.

12. Segal, *Islam's Black Slaves*, 49.

13. Nathan Irvin Huggins, *Black Odyssey: The African American Ordeal in Slavery* (1977; New York: Vintage Books edition, 1990), 20–22.

14. "President George W. Bush surprised Brazilian President Fernando Henrique Cardoso by asking, 'Do you have blacks, too?' Condy [Dr. Condaleeza Rice, national security advisor to Bush] (who's paid to know things) rescued her boss by aptly observing that Brazil 'probably has more blacks than the U.S.A'" ("News of the Week in Review," *The Nation* [July 1, 2002]: 7).

15. Harris, *The African Presence in Asia*; Stanley Lane-Poole, *Mediaeval India Under Mohammedan Rule* (A.D. 712–1764) (New York: Haskell House, 1970); William Gervase Clarence-Smith, ed., *The Economics of the Indian Ocean Slave Trade in the Nineteenth Century* (London: Frank Cass and Co., 1989); Abdulaziz Y. Lodhi, "African Settlements in India," *Nordic Journal of African Studies* 1, no. 1 (July 1991): 83–87; R.R.S. Chauhan, *Africans in India: From Slavery to Royalty* (New Delhi: Asian Publication Services, 1995); Research sponsored by the ADRP (Ruth Simms Hamilton and Vandana Kohli); Professor Jean-Pierre Angenot, International Research Project Network: The African

Diaspora in the Indian Subcontinent, 2003.

Professor Sabir Badalkhan calls attention to the Afro-Baloch population of Balochistan and Sind, especially those living around the Karachi area. "Some estimates has it that they make more than 30 per cent of the total population of about half a million on coastal Makran and more than half of the total Baloch population of Karachi, estimated at more than one million."

16. Because the scope of this paper is limited, Africa before the age of the diaspora is not addressed. This should not be interpreted as a reflection on its importance. It should be a major factor in the development of programs of research, study, and curriculum development in the field.

17. Avtar Brah, *Cartographies of Diaspora: Contesting Identities* (New York: Routledge, 1996), 116.

18. Ibid., 118.

19. James Clifford states that "Diaspora is a signifier not simply of transnationality and movement but of political struggles to define the local, as distinctive community, in historical contexts of displacement" (James Clifford, *Routes: Travel and Translation in the Late Twentieth Century* [Cambridge, Mass.: Harvard University Press, 1997], 252).

20. Anthony D. Smith, "Towards a Global Culture?" in *Global Culture: Nationalism, Globalization and Modernity*, ed. Mike Featherstone (Newbury Park, Calif.: Sage Publications, 1990), 179.

21. William E. Connolly, *Identity/Difference: Democratic Negotiations of Political Paradox* (Ithaca, N.Y.: Cornell University Press, 1991), 93.

22. Arjun Appadurai, "Disjuncture and Difference in the Global Cultural Economy," in *Global Culture: Nationalism, Globalization and Modernity*, ed. Mike Featherstone (Newbury Park, Calif.: Sage Publications, 1990), 297.

23. Moreover, due to long-term patterns of immigration and resettlement in new locations, near and far, many aspects of these communities are (re)created temporally and (trans)spatially.

24. Ernesto Laclau and Chantal Mouffe, *Hegemony and Socialist Strategy: Towards a Radical Democratic Politics* (1985; New York: Verso, 1994), 105.

25. See Alejandro Portes and John Walton, *Labor, Class, and the International System* (New York: Academic Press, 1981); Saskia Sassen, *The Mobility of Labor and Capital: A Study in International Investment and Labor Flow* (New York: Cambridge University Press, 1988).

26. Robert C. Murphy, "The Earliest Spanish Advances Southwest from Panama along the West Coast of South America," *Hispanic American Historical Review*, no. 21 (1944): 16.

27. Benjamin R. Barber, *Jihad vs. McWorld: How Globalism and Tribalism Are Reshaping the World* (New York: Random House, 1995), 78–79; Saskia Sassen, *The Global City: New York, London, Tokyo* (Princeton, N.J.: Princeton University Press, 1991), and "Analytic Borderlands: Race, Gender and Representation in the New City," in *Re-Presenting the City: Ethnicity, Capital, and Culture in the 21st Century Metropolis*, ed. Anthony D. King (New York: New York University Press, 1996), 183–202.

28. The term *proliferation of departures* is borrowed from Francesco Pellizzi, "To Seek Refuge: Nation and Ethnicity in Exile," in *Ethnicities and Nations: Process of Interethnic Relations in Latin America, Southeast Asia, and the Pacific*, ed. Remo Guidieri, Francesco Pellizzi, and Stanley J. Tambiah (Austin, Tex.: A Rothko Chapel Book distributed by University of Texas Press, 1988), 155–71.

29. See chapters by Alpers and Thornton in this volume for further insights.

30. Philip D. Curtin, "Africa and Global Patterns of Migration," in *Global History and Migrations*, ed. Wang Gungwu (Boulder, Colo.: Westview Press, 1997): 63–94, 70.

31. Roger Norman Buckley, *Slaves in Red Coats: The British West India Regiments, 1795–1815* (New Haven, Conn.: Yale University Press, 1979), 130.

32. Ibid., 131–32, and Alan Cobley, "Migration and Remigration between the Caribbean and Africa," in *The African-Caribbean Connection: Historical and Cultural Perspectives*, ed. Alan Cobley and Alvin Thomas (Bridgetown, Barbados: Department of History, University of the West Indies, Cave Hill, and the National Cultural Foundation, Barbados, 1990), 60.

33. Buckley, *Slaves in Red Coats*, 136.

34. Dr. W. T. Kroese, *The Origin of the Wax Block Prints on the Coast of West Africa* (Hengelo, Netherlands: NV Uitgeverij Smit Van 1876, 1976), chap. 5. On 15 February 2003 the Elimina-Java Museum was opened in Ghana, founded by "Dr. Thaddeus Ulzen, a Ghanaian, whose great-great-grandfather was one of the first 44 freeborn Africans to sail to the East Indies." Six descendants of the Belanda Hitam from Holland and the United States were among those present. Hulskamp writes of his great-grandfather, Willem Nelk, who was recruited in 1862 at the age of twenty-four to serve in the Dutch East-Indies. In 1880, after eighteen years of service in Indonesia, he returned to Elmina to live out his life. See Richard Hulskamp, "We Met in Elmina, Ghana," International Scientific Research Network: The African Diaspora in Asia (TADIA) 21 July 2003, agenot@gm-net.com.br.

35. See Jeffrey Bolster, *Black Jacks: African American Seamen in the Age of Sail* (Cambridge, Mass.: Harvard University Press, 1997); Carla Davidson, "Found at Sea," *New York Times Book Review* (July 20, 1997): 12–13.

36. Cobley, "Migration and Remigration,", 62–64.

37. Monica Schuler, *"Alas, Alas, Kongo": A Social History of Indentured African Immigration into Jamaica, 1841–1865* (Baltimore: Johns Hopkins University Press, 1980), 10.

38. W.G. Clarence-Smith, "Emigration from Western Africa," in *European Expansion and Migration: Essays on the Intercontinental Migration from Africa, Asia and Europe,* ed. P. C. Emmer and M. Morner (New York: Berg Publishers, 1992), 208.

39. Pellizzi, "To Seek Refuge," 157.

40. Dawn Marshall, "A History of West Indian Migrations: Overseas Opportunities and 'Safety-Valve' Policies," in *The Caribbean Exodus,* ed. Barry B. Levine (New York: Praeger Publishers, 1987), 19.

41. See Vera Lucia Benedito, "West Indian Migration to Brazil" (master's thesis, Michigan State University, 1990).

42. Bonham C. Richardson, *Caribbean Migrants:* Environment and Human Survival on St. Kitts and Nevis (Knoxville : University of Tennessee Press, 1983), 118–22;, and Peter Wade, *Blackness and Race Mixture: The Dynamics of Racial Identity in Colombia* (Baltimore: Johns Hopkins University Press, 1993), 104.

43. Marshall, "A History of West Indian Migrations," 22.

44. Alex Stepick, "The Haitian Exodus: Flight from Terror and Poverty," in *The Caribbean Exodus,* ed. Barry B. Levine (New York: Praeger Publishers, 1987), 131–51.

45. Richardson, *Caribbean Migrants,* 130.

46. Marshall, "A History of West Indian Migrations," 23–24.

47. Stepick, "The Haitian Exodus," 135–37.

48. Gary Freeman, "Caribbean Migration to Britain and France: From Assimilation to Selection," in *The Caribbean Exodus,* ed. Barry B. Levine (New York: Praeger Publishers, 1987), 187.

49. Oswald Sephuinus Warner, "In Search of a Better Life Abroad: An Exploratory Case Study of the Perceptions and Responses of Afro-Trini Immigrants to their Economic Incorporation Experiences in the Greater Toronto Area, Canada" (draft Ph.D. dissertation, Michigan State University, 2001), 355, 352.

50. Frances Henry, "Caribbean Migration to Canada: Prejudice and Opportunity," in *The Caribbean Exodus,* ed. Barry B. Levine (New York: Praeger Publishers, 1987), 215.

51. See Barry B. Levine, "The Puerto Rican Exodus: Development of the Puerto Rican Circuit" and David B. Bray, "The Dominican Exodus: Origins, Problems, Solutions," in *The Caribbean Exodus,* ed. Barry B. Levine (New York: Praeger Publishers, 1987), 93–105, 152–70.

52. Aaron Segal, "The Caribbean Exodus in a Global Context: Comparative Migration Experiences," in *The Caribbean Exodus,* ed. Barry B. Levine (New York: Praeger Publishers, 1987), 44–64.

53. Orlando Patterson, "Migration in Caribbean Societies: Socioeconomic and Symbollic Resource," in *Human Migration: Patterns and Policies,* ed. William H. McNeill and Ruth S. Adams (Bloomingont: Indiana University Press, 1976), 128.

54. Victor Turner, *Dramas, Fields and Metaphors: Symbolic Action in Human Society* (Ithaca, N.Y.: Cornell University Press, 1974) and *The Forest of Symbols: Aspects of Ndembu Ritual* (Ithaca, N.Y.: Cornell University Press, 1962); Benedict Anderson, *Imagined Communities: Reflections on the Origin and Spread of Nationalism* (New York: Verso, 1991).

55. Pellizzi, "To Seek Refuge," 157.

56. Leonard Barrett, *The Rastafarians* (Boston: Beacon Press, 1977), 80–86.

57. The following materials provide black views on emigration and colonization: Howard H. Bell, "The Negro Emigration Movement, 1849–1854: A Phase of Negro Nationalism," *Phylon* 9 (summer 1959): 132–42, and "Negro Nationalism: A Factor in Emigration Projects, 1858–1861," *Journal of Negro History* 47 (January 1962): 42–53. There are two papers on planned emigration to Haiti in the nineteenth century by James Theodore Holly and J. Dennis Harris in *Black Separatism and the Caribbean, 1860,* ed. Howard H. Bell (Ann Arbor: University of Michigan Press, 1970). See also Martin Robinson Delany, *The Condition, Elevation, Emigration, and Destiny of the Colored People of the United States* (Philadelphia: privately printed, 1852); Martin Robinson Delany and Robert Campbell, *Search for a Place: Black Separatism and Africa, 1860* (Ann Arbor: University of Michigan Press, 1969); Floyd J. Miller, *The Search for a Black Nationality: Black Emigration and Colonization, 1787–1863* (Urbana: University of Illinois Press, 1975). For White-proposed solutions to the race problem see Walter H. Fleming. "Historic Attempts to Solve the Race Problem in America by Deportation," *Journal of American History* 4, no. 2 (1910): 197–213, and Henry Noble Sherwood, "Early Negro Deportation Projects," *Mississippi Valley Historical Review* 2, no. 4 (March 1916): 484–508.

58. Tony Martin, *Race First: The Ideological and Organizational Struggles of Marcus Garvey and the Universal Negro Improvement Association* (Westport, Conn.: Greenwood Press, 1976).

59. St. Claire Drake, "Diaspora Studies and Pan-Africanism," paper prepared for presentation at the Institute on Diaspora Studies, Howard University, August 25–28, 1979 and published in *Global Dimensions of the African Diaspora,* ed. Joseph Harris (Washington, D.C.: Howard University Press, 1993).

60. For overviews, see Ivan Hannaford, *Race: The History of an Idea in the West* (Washington, D.C.: Woodrow Wilson Center Press, 1996) and David Theo Goldberg, *Racist Culture: Philosophy and the Politics of Meaning* (Oxford, U. K: Blackwell Publishers, 1993).

61. Jan Nederveen Pieterse, *White on Black: Images of Africa and Blacks in Western Popular Culture* (New Haven, Conn.: Yale University Press, 1992), 20, 22.

62. Marvin A. Lewis, *Afro-Hispanic Poetry 1940–1980: From Slavery to "Negritude" in South American Verse* (Columbia: University of Missouri Press, 1983), 3. For an introduction to the intellectual movements, see Michel-Rolph Trouillot, *Haiti State Against Nation: The Origins and Legacy of Duvalierism* (New York: Monthly Review Press, 1990), chap. 4; Richard Jackson, *The Black Image in Latin American Literature* (Albuquerque: University of New Mexico Press, 1976); Ellen Conroy Kennedy, ed., *The Negritude Poets* (New York: Viking, 1975); Nathan Irvin Huggins, ed., *Voices from the Harlem Renaissance* (New York: Oxford University Press, 1995); and Lilyan Kesteloot, *Black Writers in French* (Washington, D.C.: Howard University Press, 1991).

63. David Scott, "That Event, This Memory: Notes on the Anthropology of African Diaspora in the New World," *Diaspora* 1, no. 1 (winter 1991): 277.

64. Melville J. Herskovits, *The New World Negro* (Bloomington: Indiana University Press, 1966), originally published as "What Has Africa Given America?" in *New Republic* 84, no. 1083 (1935).

65. Critical assessments regarding the conceptual and methodological approaches, along with research findings, patterns, and exceptions, are discussed in a substantial body of literature. See Sandra T. Barnes, *Africa's Ogun: Old World and New* (Bloomington: Indiana University Press, 1989); Roger Bastide, *African Civilizations in the New World* (New York: Harper and Row, 1971) and *The African Religions of Brazil: Toward a Sociology of the Interpenetration of Civilizations,* trans. Helen Sebba

(Baltimore, Md.: Johns Hopkins University Press, 1978); Jacob Drachler, ed., *Black Homeland: Black Diaspora* (Port Washington, N.Y.: National University Publications/Kennikat Press, 1975); Joseph Harris, ed., *Global Dimensions of the African Diaspora* (Washington, D.C.: Howard University Press, 1982); Melville J. Herskovits, *The Myth of the Negro Past* (1941; Boston, Mass.: Beacon Press, 1969); Joseph E. Holloway, ed., *Africanisms in American Culture* (Bloomington: Indiana University Press, 1990); Irwin, *Africans Abroad*; Joseph M. Murphy, *Working the Spirit: Ceremonies of the African Diaspora* (Boston, Mass.: Beacon Press, 1994); Walter F. Pitts Jr., *Old Ship of Zion: The Afro-Baptist Ritual in the African Diaspora* (New York: Oxford University Press, 1993); George Eaton Simpson, *Black Religions in the New World* (New York: Columbia University Press, 1978); Robert Farris Thompson, *Flash of the Spirit: African and Afro-American Art and Philosophy* (New York: Vintage Books, 1984); Lorenzo D. Turner, *Africanisms in the Gullah Dialect* (1949; Ann Arbor: University of Michigan Press, 1973); Sheila S. Walker, ed., *African Roots/American Cultures: Africa in the Creation of the Americas* (Lanham, Md.: Rowman and Littlefield Publishers, 2001); and Norman E. Whitten and Arlene Torres, *Blackness in Latin America and the Caribbean: Social Dynamics and Cultural Transformations*, vols. 1 and 2 (Bloomington: Indiana University Press, 1998).

66. Kenneth James King, *Pan-Africanism and Education: A Study of Race Philanthropy and Education in the Southern States of America and East Africa* (Oxford: Clarendon Press, 1971).

67. The conference has become known as the First African Diaspora Studies Institute. The proceedings appeared in Joseph E. Harris, ed., *The African Diaspora in Global Perspective* (Washington, D.C.: Howard University Press, 1982).

68. See Robert Blauner, *Racial Oppression in America* (New York: Harper and Row, 1972) and Zygmunt Bauman, "Modernity and Ambivalence," in *Global Culture: Nationalism, Globalization and Modernity*, ed. Mike Featherstone (Newbury Park, Calif.: Sage Publications, 1990), 163.

69. Joan Galtung, "A Structural Theory of Imperialism," *Journal of Peace Research*, no. 2 (1971): 81.

70. Marci Green and Bob Carter, "'Races' and 'Race-makers': The Politics of Racialization," *Sage Race Relations Abstracts* 13 (May 1988): 6.

71. See Michael Hanson, "Twoness: The Mixed Race Body in Scopic Regimes," *Body & Society*, forthcoming.

72. Norman E. Whitten Jr. and Arlene Torres, "Blackness in the Americas," Report on the Americas, *NACLA* 25 (February 1992): 18.

73. Bauman, "Modernity."

74. Ibid., 153.

75. Appadurai, "Disjuncture," 303.

76. E. Thompson, *The Making of the English Working Class* (London: V. Gollancz, 1980). Thompson observed that the English working class of the nineteenth century was so different in way of life that it was viewed as a people, not just a source of labor. Similarly, Karl Marx contends that a *Klasse un sich* by its consciousness can become a *Klasse für sich*. The point is that a group can come to recognize its own common identity, and that recognition can be a factor in the mobilization of political and cultural agency.

77. Helge Hveem, "The Global Dominance System: Notes on a Theory of Global Political Economy," *Journal of Peace Research* 10, no. 4 (1973): 324.

78. Julio Ortega, "La cultura peruana: experiencia y carencia," *Escritura* 11, no. 3 (January–June 1977), as quoted in Stefano Varese, "Multiethnicity and Hegemonic Construction: Indian Plans and the Future," in *Ethnicities and Nations: Processes of Interethnic Relations in Latin America, Southeast Asia, and the Pacific*, ed. Remo Guidieri, Francesco Pellizzi, and Stanley J. Tambiah (Austin: Rothko Chapel, 1988), 60.

79. Ralph Ellison, *Shadow and Act* (New York: Signet Books, 1966), 119–21.

80. Amilcar Cabral, "National Liberation and Culture," in *Return to the Source: Selected Speeches of Amilcar Cabral*, ed. Africa Information Service (New York: Modern Reader, 1973), 41–42.

81. There is a large body of disparate work addressing the conditions for the possibility of resistance under the circumstance of domination and marginality. The early subcultural studies of the Centre for Contemporary Cultural Studies at Birmingham, the "weak weapons" of James Scott, the quotidian practices of Michel DeCerteau, the subaltern postcolonial interventions from South Asia, and the post-capital elaborations of Antonio Negri provide some examples of the elaborations of oppositionality that are easily incorporated into thinking through black diasporic political imaginations and resistance.

82. Varese, "Multiethnicity," 69.

83. James Brooke, "From Brazil's Misty Past, a Black Hero Emerges," *New York Times*, November 30, 1994, A4.

84. David Bakhurst, "Social Memory in Soviet Thought," in *Collective Remembering*, ed. David Meddleton and Derek Edwards (Newbury Park, Calif.: Sage Publications, 1990), 203–4.

85. Smith, "Towards a Global Culture," 182. Also see Eric Hobsbawm and Terence Ranger, *The Invention of Tradition* (London: Cambridge University Press, 1983), 1–14.

86. Robert Hill, "The Changing Balance of Forces within the African Diaspora from the Haitian Revolution to the Present," lecture presented at Michigan State University, November 18, 1976. Hill is on the faculty at the University of California, Los Angeles.

87. Aldon D. Morris, "Political Consciousness and Collective Action," in *Frontier in Social Movement Theory*, ed. Aldon D. Morris and Carol McClurg Mueller (New Haven, Conn.: Yale University Press, 1992), 362–63.

88. Howard H. Bell, "The Negro Emigration Movement, 1849–1854: A Phase of Negro Nationalism," *Phylon* 9 (summer 1959): 132–42, and "Negro Nationalism: A Factor in Emigration Projects, 1858–1861," *Journal of Negro History* 47 (January 1962): 42–53. There are two papers on planned emigration to Haiti in the nineteenth century by James Theodore Holly and J. Dennis Harris in *Black Separatism and the Caribbean, 1860*, ed. Howard H. Bell (Ann Arbor: University of Michigan Press, 1970); see also Martin Robinson Delany, *The Condition, Elevation, Emigration, and Destiny of the Colored People of the United States* (Philadelphia: privately printed, 1852); Martin Robinson Delany and Robert Campbell, *Search for a Place: Black Separatism and Africa, 1860* (Ann Arbor: University of Michigan Press, 1969); Floyd J. Miller, *The Search for a Black Nationality: Black Emigration and Colonization, 1787–1863* (Urbana: University of Illinois Press, 1975); and William H. Pease and Jane Pease, *Black Utopia: Negro Communal Experiments in America* (Madison: State Historical Society of Wisconsin, 1963).

89. George Shepperson, "Pan-Africanism and 'Pan-Africanism': Some Historical Notes," *Phylon* 23 (winter 1962): 346.

90. Hill, "Changing Balance," 1979.

91. This discussion draws heavily upon Cabral, "National Liberation," 39–56.

92. Hussein Abdilahi Bulhan, "Black Psyches in Captivity and Crises," *Race and Class* 20, no. 3 (1979): 246.

93. Frantz Fanon, *Black Skin, White Masks* (New York: Grove Press, 1967), 18–19.

The African Diaspora in the Northwestern Indian Ocean: Reconsideration of an Old Problem and New Directions for Research

Edward A. Alpers

ORE THAN A QUARTER CENTURY AGO JOSEPH E. HARRIS PUBLISHED HIS pioneering study, *The African Presence in Asia: Consequences of the East African Slave Trade.* His hope "to stimulate Eastern and Western scholars and professional writers to devote some of their energies to the reconstruction of the African heritage in Asia" has been largely unfulfilled.[1] Harris has steadfastly pursued his goal in a series of essays and more detailed studies to the present,[2] but, with rare exception, others have failed to follow his lead. As he noted a decade ago on the occasion of the 150th anniversary of the abolition of slavery in Mauritius, "one must acknowledge that the African diaspora in the East has not received the study it deserves. . . . Until serious, more up-to-date studies appear, hopefully by Asians, on the Asian dimension of the African diaspora, we will remain grossly uninformed about the scope and impact of the global dimension of the African diaspora, which clearly has been an important factor in the Western world and Africa."[3]

To be sure, the call has not gone entirely unheeded, but for the most part what we know is limited to several examples of the African presence in Asia and to efforts to quantify the dimensions of the slave trade as part of the larger continental project in order to understand its demographic consequences. In this work I review this literature, with particular attention to the northwestern region, and then suggest some lines of inquiry for further research that may lead to a more humanistic understanding of this very important but too little appreciated aspect of the diaspora. I begin with a few cautionary words about defining the region under study.

The Northwestern Indian Ocean
from an African Perspective

There is no question that the northwestern Indian Ocean has been a critical cultural as well as commercial corridor for northeastern Africa. For the Nile Valley and the Sudan, the Ethiopian highlands, and the lowlands of the Red Sea and Somali coasts, we can document a long history of trade, cultural exchange, and demographic movement that even precede pharaonic times. The dominant language family of this region is known as Afro-Asiatic. The rise of Islam in the seventh century, which in so many ways made the Indian Ocean world with which we are familiar, enhanced these ancient connections. It also created a new set of cultural dynamics by drawing together in increasingly intimate relationships the world of Islam and Africans and Indians outside that world. Viewed from eastern Africa, by which I mean the coast south of Mogadishu down to Sofala and much of the interior, as well as the offshore islands that became integrated into coastal Islamic society, such intimacy dates only from the rise of Islam, the evidence of pre-Islamic commercial contacts notwithstanding. These connections reached a peak during the first half of the second millennium, and under Omani hegemony they were strongest from the mid-eighteenth century until the imposition of European colonial rule at the end of the nineteenth century.

The influence of the Indian Ocean on eastern Africa extends well beyond the northwestern corridor and the cultural dominance of Islam, however. At the farthest remove historically stands the fundamental presence of Indonesia in the making of Malagasy society, not to mention the still incompletely appreciated Indonesian influence on the continent itself. Closer to our era, and concomitant with the period of Omani hegemony over the coast north of Cape Delgado under the Busaidi dynasty, is the forced migration of Africans to the islands of the Indian Ocean. Thus, the pre-Islamic experiences of these two vast regions of the African continent, while tenuously connected, are actually quite distinct with respect to the Indian Ocean, and the African diaspora in the more recent precolonial past cannot be properly understood without including the southwestern and northwestern Indian Ocean in the mix. Finally, even in the context of eastern Africa in the nineteenth and twentieth centuries we must necessarily expand our definition of the region to include Indonesia, since influences on popular Islam often derived from there through the Hadrami diaspora, which connected Indonesia, western India, the Persian Gulf, and eastern Africa.[4] I do not by any means seek to unbundle the working notion of the northwestern Indian Ocean; rather, I want only to recall that we need to be flexible in pursuing an understanding of this historically complex cultural milieu.

The Literature about the African Diaspora in the Indian Ocean

Joseph Harris was not the first scholar ever to acknowledge the African presence in Asia, but he certainly was the first to focus attention on this phenomenon. Despite the encompassing title, *The African Presence in Asia* concentrates on the slave trade in the nineteenth century and on the settlement of Africans in India. Harris based most of his research on the slave trade on official British archives and published sources; he used a wide range of scattered sources in English as well as a number of interviews and personal observations on these communities from India to inform his discussion on the settlements. In what I regard as the key chapters of the book, he concentrates on specific communities, such as the Sidis of Janjira, the Habshis of Gujarat, and the Sidis of Hyderabad in India, and on the most prominent of all Africans in Indian history, Ethiopian-born Malik Ambar, who ruled the Muslim state of Ahmadnagar from 1607 to 1626. Harris is also especially sensitive to the assimilation of Africans in India, and he laments what he sees as the "slow and agonizing process of racial and cultural oblivion" that confronted these Afro-Asian communities, a process that greatly complicated "the problem of reconstructing this aspect of Afro-Indian history."[5]

Although new books about the African diaspora continue to appear regularly with little or no recognition of the Asian or Indian Ocean element of this movement,[6] some scholars have heeded Harris's call. As early as 1977 Graham Irwin included in his documentary history of the diaspora a major section on Africans in Asia. Covering some of the same ground as Harris, but extending the coverage both geographically and temporally, Irwin's intelligent introductory essays to translations of some of the principal primary sources on the African presence in Asia provide a very useful complement to Harris's more focused short study.[7] A much briefer contribution that situates the African presence in Asia and the Indian Ocean in its widest context is the chapter by Devisse and Labib for volume 4 of the UNESCO *General History of Africa*.[8]

A major problem in the study of the African diaspora in general has been establishing its dimensions; for the centuries before our own, this meant a focus on the magnitude of the slave trade. However heated the debate surrounding the Atlantic trade, the evidential and methodological problems confronting historians of the Indian Ocean commerce, where the forced migration of African labor was not exclusively in Euro-American hands and record keeping was even more haphazard than for the Atlantic trade, are considerably more daunting, and any hopes for precision are much more dim. For our purposes, this challenge also involves weaving together fragmentary evidence and contrasting reconstructions for northeastern and eastern

Africa, which most historians treat as distinct precolonial commercial trading regions. In the vast literature on the slave trade, many early examples from the colonial period reflect a strong abolitionist bias in their tendency to exaggerate both the numbers and the antiquity of the trade on the eastern side of the continent. These works need not detain us here.[9]

The first serious attempt to quantify the nineteenth-century Arab slave trade in eastern Africa was published by Esmond B. Martin and T. C. I. Ryan in 1977, and Abdul Sheriff also has contributed significantly to clarifying the numbers.[10] But without question the most persistent scholar working in this difficult field is Ralph A. Austen, who in a series of works has sought to arrive at a consolidated figure for the entire Islamic slave trade from both eastern and northeastern Africa in the nineteenth century.[11] Briefly, Austen demonstrates that the Gulf of Aden was the principal source of slaves for the Red Sea trade, but only about one-third of those exported from the Swahili coast actually left Africa, most being absorbed by Zanzibar or its coastal domain. For the entire century he suggests total exports of slightly fewer than 500,000 from the Red Sea and somewhat more than 300,000 from the Swahili coast, with annual exports fluctuating significantly by decade and port.[12] As Austen notes, his latest estimates are conservative and do not stand unchallenged. To this I would add that the debate on numbers focuses on the Islamic trade in the nineteenth century and does not attempt to address either the earlier periods of that trade in either region or the trade to Portuguese Asia in the sixteenth and seventeenth centuries; it also tells us nothing about the European trade in the eighteenth century, which played an important catalytic role in the slave trade of the southwestern Indian Ocean.[13] It does serve to remind us, however, how recent was the heyday of the slave trade that created a visible African diaspora in the northwestern Indian Ocean.

Localized studies on the African diaspora in the northwestern Indian Ocean mainly concern India. The earliest was published by D. R. Banaji in 1932 on the relationship between the Sidis of Janjira and the British at Bombay. It is, as Harris notes, essentially a political history, but it remains a useful reconstruction from traditional, primarily British colonial, sources.[14] Preceding Harris in recognizing that the topic is of significance was Richard Pankhurst, who drew upon scattered references in the *Cambridge History of India* for his brief overview.[15] Two shorter contributions that possibly reflect a somewhat broader interest in Afro-Indians at about this time were published by Indian scholars D. K. Bhattacharya and Vasant D. Rao. Both mention highlights of Afro-Indian history, but their main concern was to bring attention to the impoverished condition of these communities as they found them a quarter century ago.[16] In a work published in the same year as Harris's book, G. S. P. Freeman-Grenville sought to identify as mainly Swahili a word list that Richard Burton collected randomly among the Sidi population of Sind in the mid-nineteenth century.[17] Although his was only an exploratory effort, Freeman-Grenville does establish that this particular population was much more recently introduced from Africa than was that of Janjira.

Two brief essays by African travelers deserve mention. The earlier, by Ayodeji Babalola, recapitulates Harris's theme that "it is negligent to ignore African history made in the Asian diaspora," while also reiterating the general impression of poverty among present-day Afro-Indian communities.[18] The more recent, by Abdulaziz Y. Lodhi, suggests greater ethnic consciousness among some groups of Afro-Indians, which I will discuss later.[19]

At least two detailed socioeconomic studies of different groups of Sidis have been undertaken, one in the early 1960s by T. C. Palakshappa, the other three decades later by T. B. Naik and G. P. Pandya of the Tribal Research and Training Institute of Gujarat Vidyapith. Both involved extensive periods of field research and meticulous household surveys.[20] In the 1980s, Vandana Kohli, who trained at Michigan State University as part of the African Diaspora Research Project, undertook a sociological study of Afro-Indian communities.[21]

Finally, a collection of essays edited by Indian Africanist Anirudha Gupta on various immigrant groups on the western coast of India includes a very general overview of African communities by Jayanti Patel as well as brief essays on the Habshis and Sidis by the editor. The latter piece is noteworthy for its description of an important ritual dance, to which I will return later.[22]

Another category of work focuses on Malik Ambar (also spelled Amber), who according to some was the most important Indian political leader of the seventeenth century. Although unquestionably an African by birth, he acted as much as a Deccani as an African leader in India. His presence must not be ignored in studies of the diaspora, but his story tells us as much about the social, political, and cultural system into which he was taken as a slave, not to mention his personal attributes, as it does about African communities in India or even Indian attitudes toward Africans. In addition to several biographies dating from the 1930s, various representations of Malik Ambar appear in Deccani and Mughal paintings of the period.[23]

Still another group of specialized studies concern former Portuguese India. C. R. Boxer made scattered references in his fundamental works, but the first historian to draw focused attention to this topic was Ann M. Pescatello, who provides a broad qualitative survey of the extent of African slavery and the uses to which the captives were put throughout Portuguese India, primarily during the sixteenth and seventeenth centuries, the heyday of their importation. Pescatello indicates that the main source of supply was Mozambique and that the main use was in domestic servitude;

large numbers of Mozambique domestic servants were sought as a matter of prestige by the Portuguese.[24] Other sources note the extent to which Africans served as both soldiers and sailors throughout the Estado da Índia, a role in which they acted as important bearers of African culture in the Indian Ocean world.[25] More recently, Jeanette Pinto has devoted an important small book to this topic. It is based on much more extensive primary research than previous efforts, although her findings serve mainly to underscore the general points made by Pescatello. Much of Pinto's work is descriptive and rather sentimental, which suggests to me that there is considerable room for further analysis of these same sources before we are fully informed about African slavery in Portuguese India.[26] Other, more restricted studies that indicate renewed interest in the African slave trade to Portuguese India have recently appeared from other scholars working at Goa.[27] Finally, an important critique of the quantitative aspects of the work by both Jeanette Pinto and Celsa Pinto was made by Rudy Bauss, who argues that "both have failed to answer the question of how many slaves entered Portuguese India and have also avoided estimations of the dimensions of the trade" during its declining years.[28] In time it will be important to integrate his work in the larger debate on the dimensions of the Indian Ocean slave trade.

Compared to research on Africans in India, there is much less scholarship on Africans in the Arabian Peninsula and the Persian Gulf. Since the early 1980s this situation has begun to be remedied, although much remains to be done. There is, of course, literature on ancient connections between Ethiopia and southern Arabia that enables us to appreciate the pre-Islamic roots of an African presence in the region, but much less work has been done on more modern periods.[29] Bernard Lewis provides a useful introduction and overview to the broader place of Africans as slaves throughout the region since the rise of Islam, but he does not address the topic systematically and almost completely ignores the Hadramaut and Oman.[30] Among earlier Arabists, the prolific writings of R. B. Serjeant on southern Arabia are peppered with occasional references to Africans, but only two very idiosyncratic short pieces directly address their presence in the region.[31] Much more stimulating is the work of anthropologist Fredrik Barth, whose well-known study of Sohar includes an important discussion of the significance of African descent and slavery that suggests lines of investigation that might be pursued among other diaspora communities throughout the region.[32]

In the past decade, historians have begun to pay more attention to Africans in Arabia. An interesting essay on slaves as political actors in the Yemen to the late eighteenth century, by Husayn ibn 'Abdallah al-'Amri, provides a nice parallel to the role of African slaves as military and political leaders in India, although it tells us little about African communities.[33] Drawing upon the compulsive record keeping that characterized British India and was extended to Aden after the British seizure of that strategic port in 1839, I have attempted to reconstruct the history of its Somali community in the nineteenth century, when Somalis comprised about 15 percent or more of the total population.[34]

The 1987 School of Oriental and African Studies (SOAS) workshop on the economics of the Indian Ocean slave trade resulted in a publication with two important papers that address this topic. The essay by Albertine Jwaideh and J. W. Cox, which establishes very clearly the importance of exploring the Turkish archives for studying the African diaspora, suggests strongly that Turkish Arabia was not a major receiver of slaves during the nineteenth century and that "the numbers of black slaves which were imported into this region have been grossly overestimated."[35] It is just as clear, however, that the small but significant communities of African origin throughout that region are similar in size to such groups elsewhere in the northwest Indian Ocean, and there was a large community in Kuwait. Indeed, the work of Jwaideh and Cox provides a model for continuing this sort of archival and library research; it also helps identify possible living communities, although access to them is often difficult if not impossible, as in southern Iraq. In the same collection, Thomas M. Ricks recognizes the weakness of the available data but tries to demonstrate an increase in the volume of slaves imported into the Persian Gulf and southern Iran in the nineteenth century and argues for a significantly expanded role for male slaves during this century.[36]

Finally, Janet Ewald is currently working on an important new project that looks at forms of African labor migration in the western Indian Ocean during the nineteenth century. Early evidence indicates that by linking the slave trade to postemancipation forms of coerced and "free" African labor migration, she will contribute an important dimension to our appreciation of the African diaspora in this part of the world. Among Ewald's contributions is her poignant conclusion that "the heritage of forced mobility and the hard struggle to find a place for themselves . . . ultimately separated slaves and freedmen from other migrant workers, who returned to their homelands or maintained ties between diaspora communities and homelands."[37]

This observation provides a convenient transition to a related aspect of the topic: Diasporas, in general, include recognition of the fact that the origins of an individual or a community lie somewhere else. Although irredentist movements and sentiments have not flourished in the Indian Ocean region as they have among Africans in the Americas, a few studies of returnees deserve mention in this context. As part of his research on British Protestant missions in Kenya, Arnold Temu first drew attention to the so-called Bombay Africans, who were liberated in India primarily by the Church Missionary Society and then returned to help proselytize the faith on the Mombasa coast in the last quarter of the nineteenth century.[38] A decade ago Joseph

Harris produced a major study of this interesting group.[39] By virtue of their mission education and European sponsorship, however, the Bombay Africans were an elite group and clearly atypical among Africans in Asia. Their unique experience tends to bear out the general distinction suggested by Ewald.

More tantalizing, perhaps confounding, is the continuing research by anthropologist Francesca Declich among the Zigua community of southern Somalia, significant numbers of whom have sought refuge from the chaos of civil war in that country by returning to their home territory in northeastern Tanzania, from whence their ancestors were sold as slaves in the nineteenth century.[40] Declich's extraordinary success in both identifying such consciousness of a specific African identity and studying this kind of community return seems unlikely to be repeated in the Indian Ocean context. Nevertheless, field workers should remain alert to such possibilities once they gain the confidence of the communities in which they are living and studying.

I would like to close this review with a look at a wide-ranging essay on the slave trade in the Indian Ocean by Hubert Gerbeau, which was presented in Haiti in 1978 to the UNESCO meeting of experts on the African slave trade. Gerbeau made three important observations regarding future research that deserve mention because of their resonance with what I understand to be the trajectory of the Stockhom University project. First, Gerbeau explicitly acknowledges that "the Indian Ocean is not the Atlantic," with all the attendant research problems that this poses, including regional specialization and the need for multiple language skills. Second, he asks whether it is possible to "write the history of silence," a very prescient postmodern question to have raised in 1978.[41] Third, he urges scholars to not reduce the study of the slave trade "to a paragraph in commercial history but place it at the level of a history of civilization."[42] Accordingly, suggests Gerbeau, the historian must employ a variety of unfamiliar tools.

> It will no longer suffice to date the cargoes and count the men and piastres; he must think in terms of cooking, religion, magic, dancing, music, population, social organization, agricultural practices and cultural themes. The historian will have to be an archaeologist, an ethnologist, a specialist in oral tradition, a biologist, a linguist and perhaps a psychiatrist.
>
> Even where there are no texts concerning a slave-trade phenomenon the historian can s[t]ill proceed with his work. He will have to go to the spot himself, i.e., to the land whence the slaves departed and to the one where they arrived. It is essential for him to glean information from the local inhabitants, to search their memories and their land. His archaeology should extend to the sites inhabited by the Maroons. Perhaps then we shall understand better how far the slaves, and more particularly the rebel slaves, have

kept Africa alive in the "Indian Ocean" area. The absence of studies does not necessarily mean the absence of a subject requiring study.[43]

Allowing for Gerbeau's gendered language and his traditional assumptions about what constitutes the usual sources for reconstructing history, his prescriptions establish an important agenda for future research on the African diaspora.

New Directions for Research

There are many directions in both time and space in which one might undertake research on the African diaspora in the northwestern Indian Ocean. Let us accept Gerbeau's challenge to push beyond the boundaries of conventional historical evidence as a first step toward a more complete appreciation of the African experience and possible influence in Asia. At the same time, I want to try to bring some balance to our notion of the possible by exploring some of the evidence for Africans in Arabia and suggesting possible research among those communities. Both these lines of inquiry focus on cultural manifestations.

What I have to say may be new for diaspora historians in the Indian Ocean who have concentrated on the political, military, economic, and social history of Africans, but it is certainly not for their colleagues in the Atlantic. To take only a single example: in a provocative and controversial study of the role played by Africans in the making of the Atlantic world, John Thornton states:

> In order to understand the process of cultural maintenance, transformation, and transmission, one must first understand something about what is meant by culture and particularly cultural dynamics. Anthropologists define it as a total lifeway for a society, including among other things kinship, political structure, language and literature, art, music and dance, and religion. But all these elements are not equally fixed. Some are highly sensitive to conditions in a particular area and might change rapidly; others are much more fixed and change slowly.[44]

Thornton suggests that whereas family structure and kinship can be highly variable, other characteristics, like language, are much more stable. He then observes that "between these two extremes of stability and changeability of culture are a wide range of other possibilities," such as religions and philosophies. He also includes in this middle range "principles of aesthetics (including art, music and dance, literature, decoration, and even cooking)," as well as "material culture, broadly speaking." Correlations among these different traits, he contends, "do not hold together well in circumstances of change over time or migration." Some survive more or less intact, others are transformed, still others are lost. Thornton relates these ideas to the past study of African cultures and Africanisms in the Atlantic diaspora; explores the evidence for language, social structure, and aesthetics; and discusses African religions and Christianity in the Atlantic world.[45] This last topic serves as a useful reminder of how very different are the worlds of the Atlantic and Indian Ocean, but differences between Islam or Hinduism and Christianity or the Old and New World should not mislead us into thinking that we have nothing to learn from such comparisons. In fact, this kind of thinking may be one reason Africans have for so long remained relatively invisible in the Indian Ocean world. To be sure, there are indeed very great differences between the Atlantic and Indian Ocean diasporas, but we can learn much from the rich body of scholarship on the Atlantic diaspora as we pursue our quest.

An example of the kind of aesthetic integration of which Thornton speaks emerged in my research on nineteenth-century Mogadishu, in which I argued that various dances now claimed to be "traditional" were introduced to Somali society and popularized by slaves imported from elsewhere in eastern Africa. By 1974 an official Somali government booklet includes Beebe (one of these dances; the name derives from Swahili *pepo,* a kind of spirit dance, but also the generic word for spirits) in a listing of "ritualistic Somali dance," without any apparent recognition of its foreign, slave-introduced origin.[46] I concluded that short article by discussing an account of African slave dances performed at the end of Ramadan, written by a mid-nineteenth-century American traveler to Oman, because it suggested to me that the Somali example was not isolated. Indeed, it most certainly is not.

In 1852, after having spent considerable time at Zanzibar, Salem merchant Joseph Osgood found himself at Masqat, where he noted a substantial African population. On the occasion of 'Id al-Fitr, on the plains outside the city walls, he first witnessed a long display of Omani horsemanship by the sultan and his followers. After a couple of hours the elite Arabs left the space for the slaves, who "clustered together for a dance, called by them 'Gooma.' When they were arranged I counted ten different groups, each consisting of between twelve and fifty men and from two to thirty women." Although Osgood claims that the groups were so similar in dress and movement that he could see no point in detailing more than a few of them, what he has left us is remarkably detailed for its time and deserves to be quoted in its entirety.

> In the first set were twelve men in a circle, to whose legs were attached many wooden globes filled with pebbles. They wore native costume. Two others wore monkey skin

waist bands, and head dresses three feet in diameter, made of colored feathers. The singular costume of this doublet was completed, *a tergo*, by a horse's tail fastened at a small angle with the waist. They balanced within the circle, moving their limbs in lazy gesture for a moment or two, when they dropped upon their hands and knees, and prancing hither and thither like infirm quadrupeds, shook their heads spitefully, and ended by butting them forcibly together, barking like dogs, or bleating like goats during the performance. Meanwhile three masked women were dancing around them, singing wildly and fanning with a diligence becoming Spanish ladies in a fandango. The twelve men kept up a rattling gallop in their outer sphere. The music by which the dance was timed emanated from three huge log drums, whose goat skin heads were beaten with right good will by perspiring negroes squatting like toads beside them.

In another set twelve men, wearing but a waist cloth and wooden balls upon their legs, danced with six women to the noise of four drums and a crescent shaped horn.

A third set of fifty men, some carrying swords and others sticks in their hands, ambled round singly in a circle, chanting solemnly like mate-bereaved blackbirds, though not with such graceful sonorousness. While keeping up their uninterrupted course they dispensed with instrumental accompaniments.

In a fourth company twenty men were arranged in a line opposite as many women. Each of the men was provided with two sticks of hard wood, which were repeatedly clashed together, while the happy dancers sang in concert with the din of seven drums. Opposite couples of this set danced forward and back, and then joined hands in a grand swing round.

Other groups were waltzing and dancing fanciful figures, each distinguished by different ear-distracting noise machines, such as single and two-headed drums, gourd shells and boxes filled with pebbles, rude harps, wooden whistles, trumpets, cymbals, and notched bamboo canes rubbed upon sticks, while the whole grand symphony was mollified by frequent vociferations from healthy lungs. The zeal and energy of the actors in this amusement were truly surprising. Several women fainted from too violent exercise in so heated an atmosphere; but they again resumed their toil of pleasure as soon as they were restored by hydropathic treatment, snapping their joints and violent rubbing. The women wore cotton gowns and masks, so that only their eyes, hands and feet were exposed. Such is what they call sport at Muscat.[47]

Although Osgood provides the kind of detail (offensive language notwithstanding) one needs in order to begin to sort out the various dance and musical traditions that were evolving at Masqat 150 years ago, what is missing (with the exception of *ngoma*, Swahili for drum and by extension the generic term for any dance or music) are the kind of language markers I found so helpful in my work on Mogadishu, for which I was able to check the Somali names of dances against Swahili dictionaries. But with careful attention to the evidence and working with ethnomusicologists who specialize in both African and Arab music and dance traditions, I believe there is much to build on here. Osgood's testimony is also useful because it indicates the adoption of Omani dress by these women, even though the dances were clearly of African origin, which again reminds us of the complexity of cultural transformation.

At least one other traveler was alert to cultural manifestations of Africans in Oman in the nineteenth century. J. R. Wellsted, who spent a considerable amount of time there in 1835–36, describes a baggala, a large sailing vessel characteristic of the Persian Gulf:

> African negroes . . . compose the greater part of the crew, which may amount in number to one hundred and fifty men. For their encouragement and recreation, whenever work is going on, about ten of their number are selected to sing to the remainder. A boy, with a sharp tenor voice, usually leads the concert, and to him his comrades reply in a deep, bass cadence, accompanying their voices with several rude instruments of music, and joining in a wild and picturesque sort of dance.

Wellsted indicates that the instruments included a tom-tom, tambourine, and even cooking dishes. On another occasion, when being entertained by the young sheikh of the Beni Abu Ali tribe, Wellsted comments: "One of the slaves kept pounding coffee from the time they first arrived. The pestle on these occasions is made to strike the sides and bottom of the mortar in such time and manner as to cause it to resemble the chiming of bells, and the slave usually accompanies it with a song."[48] Although he does not state that the slave was African, in the context of Omani society such identification seems almost certain.

Later in his sojourn, Wellsted declares that the Arabs have no musical instruments of their own, but he then mentions as being Arab an earthenware drum and a long curved horn. "They however neither object nor refuse to listen to slaves playing as such as they use, which are brought from Africa; the principal one being a rude guitar possessing six strings, which pass across a piece of parchment, spread over a wooden bowl, and produces notes by no means unpleasing." Finally, he describes a dance he observed at 'Id al-Fitr: "Two lines form at the distance of ten or fifteen yards, and approach each other to the sound of a drum, beaten by two slaves stationed midway between them. They proceed at a slow and measured pace, until within about two yards from each other, and then either party, after simultaneously bowing their heads, retreated to the same distance as before"; this pattern was repeated until he retired for the evening.[49] This dance is clearly different from those described by

Osgood at the same celebration more than a decade later, and Wellsted does not claim that its provenance is African, but it provides another opportunity to be explored.

Wellsted also furnishes some additional clues as to the ethnic origins of the considerable slave population that he witnessed at the Masqat depot. He identifies three major categories of slaves and sources of supply: The Towáylee (probably a corruption of Swahili) come "from the Zanzibar coast," and "are known by having their teeth filed, sometimes to a point, and sometimes in notches like those of a saw. They have also some perpendicular notched incisions on either cheek, made with a penknife when the children are five or six years of age. The scars which remain denote the tribe to which they belong." This kind of description, while not alone sufficient for specific identification, indicates a likely southern Tanzania or northern Mozambique origin, which is what one would expect, since the overwhelming majority of all slave exports through Zanzibar came from Kilwa. The other two sources of supply Wellsted indicates are Nábí (Nubi) and Galla (probably including both Oromo and other peoples from southwest Ethiopia).[50]

The question remains as to whether any traces of African cultural traditions can be identified in Oman today. Barth, who is very explicit about what he calls "the stigma of slave admixture" and negative color discrimination in Sohar, is not encouraging. Although he identifies a bundle of cultural features that distinguish the former slave population, including the performance of "acts that are regarded as dishonorable by others," noting specifically that "men play music in public for money; and the women sing as public entertainment at weddings," he concludes that "the number of distinctive African survivals in the assemblage that composes their subculture seems small, despite a temporally close and ethnographically fairly homogeneous connection with Zanzibar and the East African coast." For Barth, future research should focus on "the factors in the host society responsible for imposing or inducing patterns and conceptions of local origin," and he suggests the significance of comparative studies with the New World.[51] I think Barth reveals precisely the kind of scholarly myopia I am seeking to redress. He is not asking the wrong questions; they are legitimate and important. Rather, by staying within his disciplinary boundaries, he does not look seriously at what Thornton calls aesthetics. Fortunately for us, others have.

In 1985 the government of Oman hosted a major international conference on the country's traditional music. This was the culmination of an effort to document the musical arts of Oman, a project that has yielded a remarkable archive of materials that to the best of my knowledge have only begun to be explored. Several papers presented on that occasion specifically discussed African influences on Omani music and point the way toward future collaboration with nonmusicologists who are studying the African diaspora. For example, among the four major categories of Omani drums is the ms-ondo group, which "has its origins in Africa, where the Omani Empire extended to the East Coast and its adjacent islands." There are apparently three types of ms-ondo, long, short, and sitting, "covered by ox hides, either with or without hair."[52] The name of the instrument comes directly from the Swahili, although in East Africa it generally is applied only to a large, long drum, so there has clearly been some adaptation in the Omani context over time.[53]

Again, in a catalog of professional arts troupes in Oman, one finds Afro-Omani performers in all regions of the country except the south, while Sur "is the richest in numbers of Afro-Omani arts." This group "specializes in types of singing and dance that came from the east coast of Africa, and its adjacent islands, and in the past its types were associated with magic arts and leger-demain, although most of its types have been transformed, during this period of blessed renaissance, into arts for entertainment and pastime." Five kinds of arts are listed: *al-mikwarah, at-tanburah (an-nuban), ash-sharh, al-maidan,* and *az-zar,* as well as seven different performing troupes with their specialties.[54] Two of these arts—*at-tanburah (an-nuban)* and *az-zar* —derive from northeastern Africa, which we know was a source of slaves for Oman in the nineteenth century, although these performance styles may also have entered Oman from Zanzibar.[55] Even in the southern region of Zofar, Moustafa mentions "the Hadid bin Shamsah troupe in Mirbat, which specializes in *ar-rabubah,* the negro dancing," a name that belies its Sudanese origins; *rababa* is a local name for the lyre that is the quintessential expression of *tumbura,* as it is known in the Sudan.[56]

Moustafa concludes his inventory by emphasizing the importance of these art troupes and performance itself as cultural repositories:

> The chiefs of troupes which perform, professionally, some types of traditional music and dance in Oman, are among the most important human sources for collecting and documenting the arts, as they both learn and transmit them, in a hereditary way, over the generations. The members of incoming (imported) arts, the Afro-Omani and Asio-Omani arts, preserve with great care the texts of these types, which to some of them are looked upon as texts possessing talismanic and magical potential. This belief, though foolish and lacking any logical or scientific roots, is still currently held by many who practice these arts—especially the Afro-Omani, secretly, as in the *zar* for example.[57]

The same general principle holds for performance of *at-tanburah (an-nuban),* which has been described recently by Ali Jihad Racy as being performed at Dubay, in the United Arab Emirates. Racy gives us further insight into specific elements of

African cultural influence in the Persian Gulf.[58] He states that this ritual, which is connected with spirit possession and healing, is associated with an African instrument, the lyre, that it has Sudanese roots, and that is inherited matrilineally.[59] The lyre, *tanburah,* is the medium that helps contact the world of spirits; it is also considered to be female, and individual instruments are given women's names. The ritual he studied involves a pantheon of spirits, with names like *mashaykh, sawahli,* and *habshi,* each with specific associated herbs, such as aromatic woods or frankincense. There are also foreign words embedded in the songs performed, which Racy suspects may be of African origin. In addition, he indicates that an Arabized version of *tanburah* has been adapted to a Sufi form of performance, which suggests the need to look beyond Afro-Arab communities for such influences over time.

Racy's analysis of *tanburah* is paralleled by Olsen's earlier description from Bahrain. Olsen suggests that the dance may have been introduced from the Bendadir coast of southern Somalia, although "I think the music is Sudanese," and in addition to the lyre and drums, the performance he observed included "a large belt of sheep's hooves called 'manjour' worn by a dancer."[60] On a more technical note, he adds that this music was the only example of pentatonic scale in all the field recordings he made in the Gulf and is characterized by unusual rhythms and polyrhythms.[61] Finally, the people who shared their performance of *tanburah* with Racy do not identify themselves as Africans but as local Arabs. If we return to Barth's observations, which also emphasize the importance of patrilineal descent for determining hereditary slave status in Sohar, I think the ethnomusicological research of Olsen and Racy makes it evident that there may be much more room for recovering African survivals in the Indian Ocean diaspora than we have previously appreciated, especially when we consider that many of the peoples who were sent as slaves to the Persian Gulf from Zanzibar were torn from matrilineal societies, as Declich has documented for riverine Somalia.[62]

To complete Moustafa's survey of Omani musical forms, it is worth mentioning his inventory of the specific songs that accompany the various tasks of sailors, which constitute what he calls "the Arts of the Sea." Although Moustafa does not indicate that these are in any way associated with Afro-Omani arts, Wellsted's testimony that significant numbers of Omani crews in the 1830s were African, an observation verified a century later for Kuwaiti crews by Alan Villiers, surely suggests that this is another potential source for investigating African cultural influence in the Persian Gulf area.[63] In fact, Villiers vividly describes the musical setting of the entry into a crowded Zanzibar harbor from Mombasa of the Arab *boom* on which he sailed from Kuwait:

in the brief lull of our own sailors' lusty singing we could hear the songs of their sailors careening them, and all the tumult of the harbor–Suri drums, Omani feet-stampings, Swahili songs, Lamu fiddles, Batina triangles. . . . Meanwhile our sailors continued to sing, and there was such a banging of drums as I had never heard before. The serang [boatswain] was leading them, an expression of ecstasy on his Negroid face. They sang and sang, banging on tambourine and drum. They sang so much that they could hear no orders. Thus sang our score of mariners, to the accompaniment of loud banging on all the ships drums and ecstatic whoops and cheers from Mohamed the serang. . . . At last the serang saw that the sail must be lowered and, leaping up, he led half the mariners to that job while the others still sang and banged the drums. . . . Down came the yard, creaking and protesting; on rushed the ship. Still drums banged and songs came from somewhere underneath the sail.[64]

In fact, there are at least two modern analyses of an Omani popular dance that is unambiguously connected to this tradition. In a work rich with references to the kinds of African cultural influences that I am suggesting have flourished in Oman for at least a century and a half, Ruth M. Stone describes a dance called lewa that is performed at both Sohar and Zanzibar, two of the critical ports in the Omani-African maritime connection. At Sohar, lewa is danced by men to the accompaniment of a mizmar, a kind of double-reeded oboe that is ubiquitous throughout the Islamic world, drums, and a conch; the musicians are surrounded by the dancers, who "hold herding sticks in their right hands . . . [and] perform a slow stately dance of dips and turns" as they move counterclockwise around the musicians. The mizmar player leads the group, often in a call-and-response pattern with the chorus of dancers, who also sing. According to Stone, lewa "customarily precedes the dance *sabats* and then *boom*, the latter named after the large ships that sailed to Africa and on whose decks this was danced by sailors."[65] Clearly, lewa was not a work-related dance, but its connection to sailing, at least at Sohar, suggests just how much cultural exchange undoubtedly occurred through maritime activity on the Indian Ocean. Stone's analysis also highlights many examples of explicit African influences. Reminiscent of Racy's comment on the link provided to the spirit world by certain instruments, Stone records that "Omanis believe that the *mizmarist* possesses a kind of supernatural power when he performs. Coming to his role by family inheritance, he must not be touched while playing or the offending person will die."[66]

In Christensen's less detailed description of lewa, which he observed at a coastal village in Sohar district, the mizmar (also identified as *zamr al-lewa*) player was not a regular member of the group, and Christensen says nothing about any supernatural danger connected with the performance. Yet, Christensen identifies all members of the lewa group as *khuddam,* or descendants of slaves, and he notes that the instruments they used included the African musundu (*msondo*) and a conch trumpet, burgham, "also known under its Swahili name *gum.*" He notes, further, that "it is the sound of the *lewa* drums that is said to induce trance."[67]

More certainly, African influences are identified by Stone in the song lyrics of lewa and the "layered polyrhythms" that lead her to assert that "the percussion is African in flavour or essence."[68] Apart from an Arabic reference in the song lyrics to Mombasa,[69] what is interesting about the song texts is that words Stone identifies as Swahili are by no means standard Swahili or, I would suggest, necessarily Swahili, as opposed to East African Bantu. *Se se ya Lambo,* which she translates as "Catch well, Lambo," does not recall anything in Swahili, while her claim that *marumbu* is "the Swahili word for corn" is quite wrong. To be sure, *chesa mana chesa,* "play too much play," gets closer to the mark, but her identification of the two closing phrases of the text as "calling a man with a Swahili name, Miyasa" is also off target.[70] This certainly refers to a general African identification of someone who was brought as a slave from east central Africa to the coast, that is to say, a *Mnyasa.* Nevertheless, texts such as this one unquestionably hold much promise for future research and emphasize the importance of not ignoring the cultural dimensions of the diaspora, a criticism that Christensen specifically makes of Barth's work.[71] As Stone observes, "the *musundu* drum, percussion rhythms, and Swahili texts then evoke the most striking characteristics of elements African."[72]

Olsen has described lewa as performed in Dubay and Bahrain in strikingly similar terms, although he identifies the reed instrument as *surnay* rather than *mizmar.* Olsen comments particularly on the call-and-response pattern of the drummers, which he relates to a type of war dance—called *ardha* at Bahrain and *ayala* along the neighboring coast—that he singles out for uniquely reflecting African rhythmic influence in an otherwise Bedouin form of music. Olsen notes further that "the *lewa* can become a *zar:* when someone is possessed, the *surnay* player as well as all the others present gather around him to free him from the evil spirit: the dancing becomes more agitated but the music remains the same" (translation mine). Finally, Olsen expresses some surprise that he was able to identify thirty-six different melodies among the seven performances of lewa that he recorded, with distinctions between those heard at Dubay and those at Bahrain, and he wonders if such variation might possibly reflect different African origins or only local variation.[73]

This raises an aspect of the complex cultural intermingling so characteristic of the Indian Ocean littoral: language. The old assumption was that Islam and Arabic were so absorptive that other cultures and tongues disappeared. In the late 1930s, however, Villiers noted that "the sailors used many Swahili, Hindustani, and Persian words, all of which are more simple than Arabic, and their daily language also included some curious distortions of English," although the crew of his *boom* was entirely Arabic-speaking.[74] More recently, Phillips echoed this observation:

> There is little uniformity in the Arabic spoken in Muscat and neighbouring villages such as Sidab. Long intercourse with Zanzibar and East Africa has had its influence on the local dialect. One individual may speak like a desert nomad, using vocabulary, phrases and sentence structure which are akin to the classical language, while another may use idioms, simplifications and pronunciation resembling the colloquial dialects met around the northern end of the Persian (Arabian) Gulf. In general, however, their language is full of pidgin English and pidgin Hindustani and has a flavour which belongs to Muscat alone.[75]

This kind of research is extremely demanding and will probably not attract the attention of most students of Arabic, but its importance should not be underestimated, particularly as this situation is not restricted to Oman.

Serjeant mentions that in Aden the Jabarti, whose origins may be traced to Ifat and the Zeila region of the Horn of Africa, "speak pidgin Arabic," and those inhabiting the Wadi Risyan between Zabid and Ta'izz in south Yemen have a "curious dialect."[76] He also writes about the linguistic complexity of the Tihamah districts of Yemen and Saudi Arabia, which he describes as having a "large black population," an area noteworthy both for its deep historical connections to northeast Africa and for more recent infusions of African slaves. A further hint of the kind of research that may be possible is found in an encounter that Charles Doughty had in the mid-1870s with a group of "negro bondsmen" returning from the fields outside of Mecca. When Doughty asked them in Arabic where their home country was, "they began to chat between them in their African language." And when he was held for many months at Khaybar, "the Hejâz negro village" or "an African village in the Hejâz," to the north of Medina, he stayed with two Galla who spoke either different languages or mutually unintelligible dialects, so they communicated in Arabic. "Though brought as slaves to the Hejâz in their childhood," he states, "they forgot not there their country language: so many are now the Gallas in Mecca and Medina, that *Hábashy* is currently spoken from house to house."[77] These clues, while few and far between, indicate the potential value of both historical linguistic research and more contemporary linguistic analysis for understanding the place of African language influences in Arabia, especially in the south.

Other observations on African influences in Saudi Arabia and Yemen go well beyond linguistic possibilities. Abyssinian female slaves were so greatly admired and desired in Arabia that among Hadrami poets a standard metaphor for describing a beautiful woman was to say that "her tresses are Abyssinian black."[78] In the Tihamah plains, Serjeant noted three decades ago that the material culture of the black population was "closely similar to what I have seen on the west bank of the Red Sea, notably the 'Tukul' huts in which they live, but also the leather work and pottery."[79] In fact, a visitor to this coast in the early nineteenth century could have seen the same style of domestic architecture in the Somali village outside the town walls of Mukha, where there had been a Somali settlement since before the last quarter of the eighteenth century.[80] Farther north, at a settlement called Imbarak, on the road to Jiddah from Mecca, Doughty passed "the beehive-like cottages of straw and palm branches (made in Abyssinian wise), which are common in this country," and at Abu She'ah in the Wadi Fatima he noted "that village is most-what of the beehive-like dwellings— which are called *'usha*—made of sticks and straw," adding that these were reputed to last fifty years.[81] One wonders if any traces of these African-derived building styles persist today.

Once again, music and other forms of entertainment emerge as an area of African influence and cultural transformation in the nineteenth century. At Khaybar Doughty briefly notes evening sword dances to the beat of "the great tambour" and accompaniment of "their double pipe of reeds, *mizmàr.*"[82] At Mecca, according to Snouck Hurgronje, African music was a visible part of public culture in the late nineteenth century.

> From Thursday afternoon to Friday morning they hold festival, regaling themselves with their national music, with song and dance. . . . The negro-orchestra consists of the six-stringed *tumburah* (which word is also used for the whole orchestra) and of some drums (*tubûl*). Besides, a slave wears a rattling girdle of sheep's hoofs wherewith he dancing and nervously shaking his whole body makes a great noise. . . . Within the circle two or more slaves dance round with long sticks in their hands, and make movements as it were of fighting.[83]

At Aden, according to Sergeant's informant, the Jabarti "are famous for their *tumburah*, a sort of harp, which they play with drums called *dirmamah*, dancing to the music of these exuberantly, the dance being called *dirmamah*. They work themselves into a state of excitement, called *gadbah* in Arabic, and fall to blows with each other." More generally, he remarks, "in most of the Arabia I know, perhaps all Arabia, for a tribesman to beat the drum is a shaming act (*'ayb*), so drumming is a function of socially inferior groups. . . . Slaves or descendants of slaves form the drummer bands of the chiefs and petty sultans of districts like the Tihamah."[84]

Perhaps the most vivid description of an informal occasion on which African dancing took place comes from Serjeant, who seems often to have found himself at the right place at the right time:

> At the port of Bal-Haf [well east of Mukalla on the Gulf of Aden] in November 1947, the *qaim* invited a number of seamen whose ships lay in the anchorage at the time, to his house, and we were also present. The men, Omanis, Hadramis, Yemenis, some Somalis and others, a thorough mixture of types, sat in a sort of square round the walls of the room. With the feeling of a holiday and the strong *Humumi* tobacco, the air was electric with excitement. The principal singer was a Tamimi from one of the villages near Tarim, and he sang Egyptian, 'Umani, Aden, and Hadrami songs. The singing was loud and intense, beautiful, one might almost have said fervent, had it not been an evening of pleasure, and the room was hot though late in the year. The music commenced with a light strumming on the harp (*zamzamiyah*) and two pottery drums heated over a charcoal fire in a pottery brazier to make the skin top tight. There was clapping to the music with a peculiar timing, performed by all. As the company grew more excited, two African-looking types, Swahilis or Somalis, perhaps, began to do a hip-waggling dance, holding the turban ('*imamah*) as in Fig. 2 (q.v. Diagram, from above, of a dancer holding the turban ['*imamah*] round the body just over the hips, or round the hips, when performing *lawk*). Coarse remarks were flung at the dancers, artists in this form of dance, by the seamen. The waggling or rather, shaking, of the hips is called *lawk* (vb. *lak, yluk*), while to shake the shoulders is *ra'ash* or *an'ash*. At one point, someone shouted in admiration, to the dancers, '*Allah yilawwikak!* (God shake you!)'"[85]

There are many leads and much that needs more careful scrutiny in sources like this, but there can be scarcely clearer evidence of the complex and cosmopolitan intermingling of cultural influences in the Indian Ocean world than Serjeant's description of this evening's entertainment on the Hadramaut coast half a century ago.

As for other forms of entertainment, Doughty reports that Galla slaves (among whom at least some could distinguish Gurage) had introduced a card game from Africa to the Hijaz.[86] Snouck Hurgronje associates drinking an intoxicating beverage called *bûzah* with the dancing of *tumburah*, but half a century before Burckhardt wrote that the wives of African pilgrims at Mecca "prepare the intoxicating liquor made from durra, and called *bouza*, of which the meaner inhabitants are very fond."[87] In fact, *dhurah* is included in a fourteenth-century Arab compendium on grain cultivation in Yemen, which recognized that "its origin is from the land of the Blacks [al-Sudan], and it has several varieties." Later, in a lengthy description of these several varieties, the author suggests that one of these may come from Abyssinia, and "in a negro language it is called H s b." For his part, Serjeant confesses, "I have so far not traced this word, but it could also conceivably be from a dialect of the Tihamah people of mixed African blood."[88] Millet beer, while a time-honored African beverage, presumably is no longer readily available in Arabia, but it would be interesting to learn more about its history and the suppression of its brewing.

Another potential indicator of African presence or connections can be found in place names. At Aden, the Jabartis lived "in a street of their own called Shari' Hafat al-Gabart." Separate slave quarters existed at Mukalla and Tarim, the latter of which (*Hafat al-'Abid*) was organized like other quarters with a headman (*mukaddam*) and a unique *tansurah,* "a kind of rallying-song or theme special to each quarter, and doubtless each with its special tune," that was used by men on special occasions. Each quarter also had a particular, formulaic call for help, that for slaves was quite different from that for all others.[89] Serjeant mentions a place named Jidfarat al-Zinji in Hadramaut; traveling five decades ago on the road east of Aden, van der Meulen remarked on "the pleasant village of Zanjubar the name of which made us think of ancient slave trading contacts with the African Zanzibar."[90] I wonder if the route poetry about which Serjeant writes, in which each village has its nicknames and appropriate response, very much like the cries for help just noted, might reveal something about the African presence in Arabia.[91]

If van den Berg is correct then, we may also learn something from personal names. He noted a century ago that slaves in Hadramaut "almost never bear the ordinary first names of Arabes, but some special names, such as Faradj, Mabrouk, Murdjân, 'Obaid, Josur, Amân, Naçîb, Sa'd Allâh, Sâlimîn, etc. Similarly, female slaves are named Rahmah, Za'farân, etc." (translation mine). Similarly, slaves often were given surnames like "the tall" or "the short" instead of family names.[92]

One further aspect of African influence in this part of the Arabian peninsula concerns magic. I have already noted the influence of spirit possession in association with Afro-Omani dance, and the presence of *zar* at Mecca is documented as well. Serjeant mentions the specific fear of Jabartis at Aden and, more generally, the association of magic across southern Arabia with Africa, "as for instance the spirit taking possession of women in the *zar* is sometimes distinguished as being a Habashiyah."[93] More curious and less direct is his observation that "many Hadramis come back from East Africa (1954) and seem mad and bewitched until they return there. The African name for this spell, 'Ugangah' [The Swahili word meaning "medicine charm"] is quite well known in Hadramawt. After their return to East Africa these men become quite normal again."[94] Here we have evidence for the way in which contact with Africa and Africans had worked its way into a Hadrami culture that bears the stamp of more than a century of diaspora across the breadth of the Indian Ocean.

I want to return briefly to the issue raised by Ewald on the distinction between slaves/freedmen and free-born migrant laborers in this part of the world. On the one hand, Doughty states that although Galla in Arabia had an idyllic recollection of their home, a Galla companion at Kheybar told him that few Gallas ever returned to their land after they were freed.[95] Similarly, in the late 1930s at Mukalla, Ingrams chanced upon one of the 250 slave soldiers in the sultan's army. "He was a Mgoni from southern Tanganyika who knew Lake Nyasa and spoke fluent Swahili. He told us he had come to Mukalla as a boy. He was married here and no longer desired to go home."[96] On the other hand, the experience of the Somali at Mukalla, who traveled back and forth between Arabia and their homeland, provides evidence of the mobility of free diaspora Africans.[97] In about 1960, decades before emancipation, van der Meulen and von Wissman were impressed by the system of rotating labor migration established by the hundred or so slaves of the then impoverished, old, and blind governor (*muqaddam*) at Qasam, near Tarim: "In turn they go in groups to their paternal country on the African coast or elsewhere to earn something by trading or by manual labor and then they return to their old master, to share the money that they have saved, with him and their fellows."[98] If their description of this system of mutual support is at all reliable, then it indicates an interesting pattern of temporary return migration among African slaves in the early twentieth century that adds an extra wrinkle to Ewald's generally sound conclusion, while the report of Ingrams suggests that memories of African homelands may have remained more vivid than we sometimes credit.[99]

Many of these same themes can be taken up for the African diaspora in India, but I will try to limit my comments to a few examples of cultural survivals. The last nineteenth-century *Gazateer* for Bombay Presidency includes a number of notes about the Sidis, sometimes called Habshis, that recall cultural manifestations we have previously noted for Africans in Arabia and possibly shed new light on some of them.

They are African negroes of different tribes chiefly from the Somali coast, who have been brought to India as slaves. They form two classes, newcomers *wilaitis* [clearly from *wilayat* or district in Arabic] and countryborns *muwallads*. They speak a broken Hindustani and sometimes among themselves an African dialect, probably the Somali known as Habashi or Abyssinian. [Note: This dialect is not Abyssinian but Somali.] . . . In north Gujarat they sometimes build round hovels about ten feet in circumference, the walls of earth, roof circular and of grass.

Except professional players, Sidis are the only Gujarat Musalmans who are much given to dancing and singing.

On marriage and other high days men and women together dance and sing in circles to the sound of the drum *dhol* and a rough rattle *jhunjhuna*. [Note: Their fiddle made of gourd with a stiff catgut string is surmounted at the end with a bunch of peacock feathers and ornamented with odd glass beads and shells as charms to prevent the evil eye from bursting it. It is played with a bow or stick, one end of it laden with a coconut shell in which stones rattle. The Sidis hold their musical instruments in great veneration, never touching them unless they are ceremonially pure. They call the *jhunjhuna* or rattle the instrument of Mama or Mother Misrah, and their big drum that of a leading male saint. If he is careless in touching the instruments when sexually impure Mother Misrah or Father Ghor is sure to punish the offender.][100]

Here we have a parallel to the Habshi spoken at Mecca, a description of *tukuls* in all but name, recognizable distinctions between older and more recently imported African populations, and a distinguishable African musical tradition that embodies the same kind of spirit power we have seen from Oman and elsewhere in Arabia. In this case, however, the names of the instruments are associated with the most important African Muslim saint (*pir*), Bava Gor, reputedly an Abyssinian trader who probably pioneered the renowned agate industry of Gujarat in the fourteenth century with his eldest sister.[101]

Gupta provides an interesting brief description of the annual celebration at Jambur devoted to this Muslim saint, which is called the *Urs*-Sharrif of Bava Gor and features walking on a pit of burning charcoal by many Sidis after imbibing "enchanted water." On this occasion, among others throughout the year, the Sidis also perform the dance known as dhamal.[102] Gupta confirms the ceremonial sanctity of the instruments used in this dance and the danger connected with sexual impurity. The instrumentation for the dance includes different drums, among them

> *mugaram*, which is the biggest drum, standing above 3½ feet high, and the *mushiro*,
> which is slung from the shoulder. *Selani* is a fiddle-like instrument with a dried gourd
> having a stiff catgut string and a bunch of peacock feathers mounted on one end and
> shells as charms to ward of[f] evil. It is played with a stick held with a coconut shell in
> which loose pebbles rattle. The latter is wrapped up in silken cloth, and is also known as
> *jhunjhuna* or *mai misra* after their goddess and can be played as a solo instrument also.

This description very closely parallels that from the Bombay *Gazateer*, but Gupta notes further that "drums and shouts dominate the performance, as the rhythm, rather than the tune, sets the pace of the dance." Conch shells, horns, and another drum, *dhamama*, are also identified among instruments played by participants in the dance.[103] Songs, called *jikar*, accompany the dancing, which symbolizes "the theme of the hunter and the hunted," according to Gupta. Peacock feathers are sometimes used to represent that bird in the dance. Over time, dance participants "appear to be almost hysterical and are calmed only by a glass of holy water." Songs are said to honor various Muslim saints or praise their own tribe, but the only text Gupta reproduces is "The Siddi child is like a lion."[104] Bhattacharya states, however, that "they sing about their forefathers who came from the high seas and propitiate them" and that "the main dancer smears white colour all over his body and face and wears cowree shells on his gown." He also enters a trance by the end of his performance. Finally, Battacharya provides additional detail on instrumentation by indicating that the coconut-shell rattles, which he names *ulka*, contain cowrie shells.[105] Despite the many common features, not to mention some intriguing parallels with some of the African dances recorded for Arabia, dhamal evidently has certain variations that are reflected in these different descriptions and need to be sorted out more systematically.

Harris has noted the survival of another African performance art, the "savage and superbly rhythmical war dance of the African Bodyguards of the Nizam of Hyderabad," as it was ethnocentrically reported in the Indian press after the 1953 India Republic Day celebrations at New Delhi, almost a century after the bodyguards were originally organized by the Nizam (and five years after the forcible incorporation of Hyderabad into India).[106] Another record of African dance in India from a military source comes from Diu, where in the late 1940s the Portuguese governor witnessed a *batuque*, the usual Portuguese designation for an African (or Afro-Brazilian) dance, performed outside the walls of the fortress by a platoon of soldiers from Mozambique, who he identified as Landins, a term broadly and not very precisely applied to peoples from the area around Maputo. He also observed that the local Indians quite enjoyed these performances and that at Dwarkar, near Junagadh, "there still exists a village of Africans, brought some time ago expressly from Zanzibar to entertain the Nabob with their spears."[107] Although Pinto makes passing reference to the importance of "slave folklore as reflected in slave song," she mentions only a local folk song from Daman that "tells of the physical characteristics of the negroes who hailed from different African regions" according to their hair styles.[108]

On another front, these references to Somalis and Africans from Zanzibar in Gujarat remind us of the need to follow up on Freeman-Grenville's suggestive article on Sidis and Swahili. Bhattacharya mentions that "local Gujarati claim to find African words in their vocabulary, but no linguist has so far confirmed this"; Sud reports that "the language spoken by the Sidis of Karnataka has . . . traces of Swahile"; and Lodhi indicates that the Sidi in Daman and Diu "speak Gujarati with many Swahili/Bantu words and phrases." He notes further the special tribal names for the different Sidi communities, such as "the Tai of Saurashtra, the Shemali of Jambur Village near Madhapur (probably of Somali origin), the Kafara of Diu (probably from southern Mozambique and/or South Africa) and the Saheli of Daman (probably from the Kenya-Tanzania coast)." The Kafara (from Portuguese *cafre*), he adds, "have maintained some of their African customs and a few linguistic items."[109] Naik and Pandya confirm these tribal names, and they include those of twenty-four exogamous clan names among the 281 families covered by their study. Some of these seem clearly to derive from local Hindu castes, but others reveal probable African origins. Those that I am confident about identifying as African are Mazgul (Zigula from Tanzania); Musagara (Sagara from Tanzania); Makwana (Makuana section of Makua from Mozambique, although Naik and Pandya think this might be an example of Rajputization); Nobi (Nubi from Sudan); Miyava (Yao from Mozambique); and Makwa (Makua).[110] In addition, some of the kinship terminology they report would seem to reflect the influence of Swahili, such as *mamaji* and *kakaji*, which they define as "spouse's mother's brother" and "spouse's father's brother," respectively.[111] Careful linguistic analysis may be able to sort out the precise nature of these linguistic survivals as well as the kinds of cultural retentions and influences they reflect among both the Sidis and, if Bhattacharya is correct, their neighbors.

The research by Kenneth Jackson on Indo-Portuguese Creole reveals clear evidence of African musical influence as well as unambiguous textual references to Africa. Drawing upon the rich literature on this former lingua franca throughout maritime Asia, developed from the Afro-Portuguese Creole and brought by Portuguese crews when they entered the Indian Ocean at the end of the fifteenth century, Jackson's study focuses on a unique nineteenth-century manuscript and the living communities of so-called Portuguese Mechanics at Batticaloa and Trincomalee, on the east coast of Sri Lanka.[112] Working in a very multidisciplinary way, Jackson provides a rich analysis of a cultural tradition that has apparently survived at least as successfully in Sri Lanka as in India, where the Portuguese presence lasted considerably longer. Its African components can be traced to the introduction of East African soldiers through Goa as part of the Portuguese imperial presence on the island in the first half of the seventeenth century, later reinforced by the introduction of fresh African troops by the British in the nineteenth century.[113] The Kaffirs, as they were called locally (*kapiri* or *kapili* in Sinhala), "were frequently employed in regimental bands, there being some 700 stationed in Columbo in 1807."[114] They survive as a very small minority, although their cultural influence has been disproportionately great.

Jackson identifies two reflections of African influence in Indo-Portuguese Creole culture. The first involves African references in song and verse; the second focuses on a dance called kaferingha (also cafferina and other variants). The textual references fall into two types: those that refer to characterizations of Africans and those that mention African place names. For example, some of the nineteenth-century songs are written "as quizzical dialogues with a *negraenya* (Ptg. *Negrinha*), or black woman," a form that is also recorded for Portuguese India. These references contain multiple allusions to the sexuality of African women, a theme we recognize from the Americas as well.[115] One type of song noted from the same period that indicates African origin in its title was called *Velinda Mozambiqu,* also called *Villona de Mozambieu,* while the ethnic name "Macua" was included in a musical performance Jackson attended in 1982.[116] Jackson's research also unearthed various songs in this tradition from Diu and Daman that reflect similar African influence, including "lyrics and melodies performed traditionally by the negroes at St. Benedict's feast in Damão" that were published by A. F. Moniz in 1925. The verse of one ends: "That's a kaffir from Inhabano" (Inhambane, in southern Mozambique), while other verses "name Macuane and Somaliz as the Kaffirs' places of origin."[117] Considering both the tribal and clan names recorded for Sidis in Gujarat, these references should come as no great surprise, although in fact I suspect they do for most of us. Finally, Jackson indicates that both the kaferingha and another African-derived dance revealingly called the Chikothi (from *chicote,* whip) have had such a significant influence on popular culture in Sri Lanka that their musical forms are "now incorporated into popular Sinhalese *baila* music."[118] There are many more subtle references to African performance and influence that can be identified as a result of Jackson's work, but even this synopsis should serve to reinforce my point about the value of looking well beyond traditional historical sources for tracking the African diaspora in the Indian Ocean.

CONCLUSION

By design, I have raised more questions than I have answered. Much evidence—some solid, some more problematic perhaps—exists for reconstructing the history of the African diaspora in the Indian Ocean. Indeed, I do not believe that I have by any means exhausted all the possible published sources of information available that bear upon African cultural traditions and influences in the diaspora, quite apart from archival sources and other unpublished materials, as well as fieldwork. What I hope to have established, however, is the value of taking a very broad geographical, interdisciplinary approach to this topic, just as scholars of the Atlantic world have done. Only by breaking the boundaries of accepted disciplinary discourse and examining the work of those whose particular academic fields may be far from our own, and our own expertise, can we begin to see some patterns in the experience of Africans in the Indian Ocean diaspora. I believe that such an approach, especially in the culturally and linguistically complex world of the Indian Ocean, also calls for team projects that join scholars from different disciplines, with different language and methodological skills, as well as from different parts of the world, in pursuit of common or complementary intellectual goals.

To achieve such a vision, I am convinced that we will need significant cooperation from the governments of the region that we hope to study, which means that they (as represented by both their universities and their ministries of culture and education) must be prepared to acknowledge the importance of documenting the African experience in their lands. In the case of India, of course, the category of Scheduled Tribe creates an official recognition by the state that facilitates the preservation and academic study of minority cultural heritage. Compare, for example, the situation of the Sidis of North Kanara, "where there is no attempt on the part of the Siddhi either now or in the past to retain their distinctive characteristics," with that of the Sidis of Gujarat, whose tribal structure is supported by the institution of the *jamat* or *jamayat* (caste association), through which "they ensure the continuity of traditional customs, rules and norms of the society."[119] In the latter case, as well, specific welfare associations exist, such as Bhavnagar's Negro Welfare Board, which issues the *Sidi Samachar Patrika*, "in which news concerning Sidi Society, and articles on Sidis' ancestors, social rules and regulations, are regularly published."[120] I also want to recognize the role played by Oman in supporting the comprehensive ethnomusicological project that was inaugurated a decade ago. Indeed, elsewhere in the Indian Ocean, bilateral cooperation between nations has begun to support a framework for this kind of endeavor, as the Cultural Agreement between Mauritius and Mozambique that was signed in 1987 vividly indicates, with its specific recognition of Mozambique as a principal source during the era of the slave trade for Africans in Mauritius.[121] With the right conditions, then, there is no reason the African diaspora in the Indian Ocean cannot assume a more prominent place in Indian Ocean scholarship, African studies, and the burgeoning field of diaspora studies.

NOTES

I would like to thank L. Lloys Frates for research assistance in the preparation of this paper. An original version of this paper appeared as Edward A. Alpers, "The African Diaspora in the Northwestern Indian

Ocean: Reconsideration of an Old Problem, New Directions for Research," *Comparative Studies of South Asia, Africa and the Middle East* 17, no. 2 (1997): 62–81. Copyright 1997, CSSAAME. All rights reserved. Reprinted by permission of Duke University Press.

Significant advances have been made in the historiography of the African diaspora in this part of the Indian Ocean since 1997. Recent works of which readers should be aware include R. R. S. Chauhan, *Africans in India: From Slavery to Royalty* (New Delhi: Asian Publication Services, 1995); Shanti Sadiq Ali, *The African Dispersal in the Deccan from Medieval to Modern Times* (Hyderabad: Orient Longman, 1996); Shihan da Silva Jayasuriya and Richard Pankhurst, eds., *The African Diaspora in the Indian Ocean* (Trenton, N.J.: Africa World Press, 2001).

1. Joseph E. Harris, *The African Presence in Asia* (Evanston, Ill.: Northwestern University Press, 1971), xv. An important exception is the African Diaspora Research Project at Michigan State University. Harris is a member of the African Diaspora Research Project's International Advisory Committee.
2. See, for example, Joseph E. Harris, "The Black Peoples of Asia," in *World Encyclopedia of Black Peoples*, vol. 1 (St. Clair Shores, Mich.: Scholarly Press, 1975), 264–72; Joseph E. Harris, "A Commentary on the Slave Trade," in *The African Slave Trade from the Fifteenth to the Nineteenth Century* (Paris: Unesco, 1979), 289–95; Joseph E. Harris, "A Comparative Approach to the Study of the African Diaspora," in *Global Dimensions of the African Diaspora*, ed. Joseph E. Harris (Washington, D.C.: Howard University Press, 1982), 112–24, esp. 117–20; "The African Diaspora in the Old and New Worlds," in *General History of Africa*, vol. 5, ed. B. A. Ogot (Berkeley: University of California Press, 1992), 113–36, esp. 128–36; Joseph E. Harris with Slimane Zeghidour, "Africa and Its Diaspora since 1935," in *General History of Africa*, vol. 7, ed. Ali A. Mazrui (Berkeley: University of California Press, 1993), 705–23, esp. 720–21; Joseph E. Harris, "The Dynamics of the Global African Diaspora," in *The African Diaspora*, ed. Alusine Jalloh and Stephen E. Maizlish (College Station: Texas A&M Press, 1996), 7–21; and Joseph E. Harris, "African Diaspora Studies: Some International Dimensions," *Issue: A Journal of Opinion* 24, no. 2 (1996): 6–8.
3. "The African Diaspora Connection," in *Slavery in the South West Indian Ocean*, ed. U. Bissoondoyal and S. B. C. Servansing (Moka, Mauritius: Mahatma Gandhi Institute, 1989), 5.
4. Edward A. Alpers, "'Ordinary Household Chores': Ritual and Power in a Nineteenth Century Swahili Women's Spirit Possession Cult," *International Journal of African Historical Studies* 17, no. 4 (1984): 685.
5. Harris, *African Presence*, chaps. 6–8, quoted at 127, 114.
6. See for example, Ronald Segal, *The Black Diaspora* (New York: Farrar, Straus and Giroux, 1995). Although Segal acknowledges there was a "substantial" trade in slaves in the Islamic world and includes a chapter on blacks in Britain (xiv, 263–86), Segal's nod in this direction excludes much of the Indian Ocean world and all the rest of Europe. Indeed, he makes only passing reference to the presence of Africans in Spanish America in his coverage of the Atlantic world. The attractive pictorial work by Chester Higgins Jr., *Feeling the Spirit: Searching the World for the People of Africa* (New York: Bantam Books, 1994), gives the impression of being completely unaware of these other dimensions of the African diaspora.
7. Graham W. Irwin, *Africans Abroad: A Documentary History of the Black Diaspora in Asia, Latin America, and the Caribbean during the Age of Slavery* (New York: Columbia University Press, 1977), 39–176.
8. J. Devisse and S. Labib, "Africa in Inter-Continental Relations," in *General History of Africa*, vol. 4, ed. D. T. Niane (Berkeley: University of California Press, 1984), 635–72, esp. 653–59.
9. For earlier reviews, see Edward A. Alpers, *The East African Slave Trade* (Nairobi: East African Publishing House for the Historical Association of Tanzania, 1967) and Bethwell A. Ogot, "Population Movements between East Africa, the Horn of Africa and the Neighbouring Countries," in *The African Slave Trade from the Fifteenth to the Nineteenth Century* (Paris: Unesco, 1979), 175–82. Both focus on eastern Africa.

10. Esmond B. Martin and T. C. I. Ryan, "A Quantitative Assessment of the Arab Slave Trade of East Africa, 1770–1896," *Kenya Historical Review* 5, no. 1 (1977): 71–91; and Abdul Sheriff, *Slaves, Spices & Ivory in Zanzibar: Integration of an East African Commercial Empire into the World Economy, 1770–1873* (Athens: Ohio University Press, 1987), 35–41.

11. Ralph A. Austen, "The Nineteenth Century Islamic Slave Trade from East Africa (Swahili and Red Sea Coasts): A Tentative Census," in *The Economics of the Indian Ocean Slave Trade in the Nineteenth Century,* ed. William Gervase Clarence-Smith (London: Frank Cass, 1989), 21–44; note that article includes a complete listing of Austen's earlier works.

12. Compare the discussion of numbers in Patrick Manning, *Slavery and African Life: Occidental, Oriental, and African Slave Trades* (Cambridge: Cambridge University Press, 1990), 50–53, 72–81.

13. See, for example, Edward A. Alpers, "The French Slave Trade in East Africa (1721–1810)," *Cahiers d'Études Africaines* 10, no. 37 (1970): 80–124; J. M. Filliot, *La Traite des Esclaves vers les Mascareignes au XVIIIe siècle* (Paris: ORSTOM, 1974); José Capela and Eduardo Medeiros, *O Tráfico de Escravos de Moçambique para as Ilhas do Índico 1720–1902* (Maputo: Núcleo Editorial da Universidade Eduardo Mondlane, 1987); and Gwyn Campbell, "Madagascar and the Slave Trade, 1810–1895," *Journal of African History* 22, no. 2 (1981): 203–27; and "The East African Slave Trade, 1861–1895: The 'Southern' Complex," *International Journal of African Historical Studies* 22, no. 1 (1989): 1–26.

14. D. R. Banaji, *Bombay and the Sidis* (London: Macmillan, 1932).

15. Richard Pankhurst, "The Hapshis of India," *Ethiopia Observer* 4, no. 10 (September 1960): 347–52. I located this article, as well as several others on Africans in India, in the Fowler Museum of Cultural History Library, Arnold Rubin Collection, Indian Files, at UCLA. I am grateful for permission to work with and reproduce these materials to Director Doran Ross, and to Betsy Quick, Elizabeth Cameron, and Monica Sahagun for their assistance. Rubin, an Africanist art historian, spent the academic year of 1983–84 in India as a senior Fulbright scholar in search of African cultural survival. For an interview with him during this period, see K. N. Sud, "Brought in Chains Centuries Ago," *Overseas Hindustani Times*, March 24, 1984, 8. This article also refers to the work of Professor Anirudha Gupta, whose work is mentioned below. References to Afro-Indians are also included in appropriate volumes of the *New Cambridge History of India*, e.g., 2/4, Stewart Gordon, *The Marathas 1600–1818* (Cambridge: Cambridge University Press, 1993), 64, 65, 68, 123–24 on the Sidis of Janjira.

16. D. K. Bhattacharya, "Indians of African Origin," *Cahiers d'Études Africaines* 10, no. 40 (1970): 579–82; and Vasant D. Rao, "The Habshis: India's Unknown Africans," *Africa Report* 18, no. 5 (September–October 1973): 35–38. The latter includes some interesting photographs, as does D. K. Bhattacharya, "Anthropometry of a Negro Population: Siddis of Gujarat," *Zinruigaku Zassi—The Journal of the Anthropological Society of Nippon* 77, nos. 5–6 (1969): 70–75, which includes some significant misinformation on slave sources from eastern Africa, quite apart from my general disinclination toward anthropometry.

17. G. S. P. Freeman-Grenville, "The Sidi and Swahili," *Bulletin of the British Association of Orientalists,* New Series, 6 (1971): 3–18, republished in his *Swahili Coast, Second to Nineteenth Centuries* (London: Variorum Reprints, 1988), xvii. I am grateful to Jeremy Prestholdt of Northwestern University for drawing my attention to this article. One of only two modern references to Afro-Pakistanis that I have discovered so far is, appropriately, in Harris, "African Diaspora Studies," 8n.1, where he calls them Sheedis.

18. Ayodeji Babalola, "The Siddis: African Descendants in India," *Massife* 1, no. 1 (1984), unpaginated, reprinted from *Network Africa Magazine.*

19. Abdulaziz Y. Lodhi, "African Settlements in India," *Nordic Journal of African Studies* 1, no. 1 (1992): 83–86. I thank Mr. Lodhi for sending me a copy of his article, which I might not otherwise have seen.

20. T. C. Palakshappa, "*The Siddhis of North Kanara (India),*" (working paper, Department of Sociology, University of Waikato, Hamilton, New Zealand, 1973); and T. B. Naik and G. P. Pandya, *The Sidis*

of Gujarat (A Socio-Economic Study and a Development Plan) (Ahmedabad: Tribal Research and Training Institute, Gujarat Vidyapith, 1993).

21. See brief reports of Kohli's work in Conexões 1, no. 1 (1989): 4, 6–7, and 2, no. 1 (1990): 9.

22. Jayanti K. Patel, "African Settlements in Gujarat," in Minorities on India's West Coast: History and Society, ed. Anirudha Gupta (Delhi: Kalinga Publications, 1991), 17–24, and Appendix A, "Habshis of India," and Appendix B, "Siddi: A Negroid Tribe of Gujarat," 203–22, as well as comments in the editor's introduction, i–xix, in the same volume.

23. On his life, see sources indicated in Harris, African Presence, 144–45, as well as B. G. Tamaskar, Life and Work of Malik Ambar (Delhi: Idarah-i Adabiyat-i Delli, 1978). For differences regarding representations of Malik Ambar, see Karl Khandalaval and Moti Chandra, "Identification of the Portraits of Malik Ambar," Lalit Kala 5, nos. 1–2 (1955–56): 23–32; and Mark Zebrowski, Deccani Painting (Berkeley: University of California Press, 1983), appendix to chap. 1, "Malik Ambar, Dictator of Ahmadnagar (1600–26)," 36–39.

24. Ann M. Pescatello, "The African Presence in Portuguese India," Journal of Asian History 11, no. 1 (1977): 26–48.

25. See King to Viceroy of India, Lisboa, February 23, 1608, in Documentos sobre os Portugueses em Moçambique e na África Central 1497–1840, vol. 9 (Lisboa: National Archives of Rhodesia and Nyasaland/Centre de Estudos Historicas Ultra Marinos, 1989), 116–17, noting that slaves from Mozambique should be sent to the royal galleys, "since they alone serve for the work of the oars as they are strong and there is usually a shortage of galley-slaves" (I thank Jeremy Prestholdt for alerting me to this reference). In addition, see G. V. Scammell, "Indigenous Assistance and the Survival of the Estado da India, c. 1600–1700," Stvdia 49 (1989): 105, 109–11; and B. S. Shastry, "Slavery in Portuguese Goa (A Note on the Nineteenth Century Scene)," a paper presented at a workshop on the long-distance trade of slaves across the Indian Ocean and the Red Sea in the nineteenth century (School of Oriental and African Studies, University of London, December 17–19, 1987).

26. Jeanette Pinto, Slavery in Portuguese India 1510–1842 (Bombay: Himalaya Printing Press, 1992).

27. See Teotonio R. de Souza, "French Slave-Trading in Portuguese Goa (1773–1791)," in Essays in Goan History, ed. Teotonio R. de Souza (New Delhi: Concept, 1989), 119–31; and Celsa Pinto, Trade and Finance in Portuguese India: A Study of the Portuguese Country Trade 1770–1840 (New Delhi: Concept, 1994), 163–71.

28. Rudy Bauss, "The Portuguese Slave Trade from Mozambique to Portuguese India and Macau and Comments on Timor, 1750–1850: New Evidence from the Archives," Camões Center Quarterly 6/7, nos. 1 and 2 (1997): 21–26 and "A Demographic Study of Portuguese India and Macau as well as comments on Mozambique and Timor, 1750–1850," Indian Economic and Social History Review 34, no. 2 (1997): 199–216. I am most grateful to Dr. Bauss for sharing these papers in draft with me.

29. See, for example, Sergew Hable Sellassie, Ancient and Medieval Ethiopian History to 1270 (Addis Ababa: United Printers, 1972), 26–34, 126–32, 145–58; H. de Contenson, "Pre-Aksumite Culture," in General History of Africa, vol. 2, ed. G. Mokhtar (Berkeley: University of California Press, 1981), 341–61, esp. 343–55; F. Anfray, "The Civilization of Aksum from the First to the Seventh Century," in General History of Africa, vol. 2, ed. G. Mokhtar 362–78; and Walter Raunig, "Yemen and Ethiopia—Ancient Cultural Links between Two Neighbouring Countries on the Red Sea," in Yemen: 3000 Years of Art and Civilisation in Arabia Felix, ed Werner Daum (Innsbruck: Umschau-Verlag, 1987), 409–18.

30. Bernard Lewis, Race and Slavery in the Middle East: An Historical Enquiry (New York: Oxford University Press, 1990).

31. R. B. Serjeant, "South Arabia and Ethiopia—African Elements in the South Arabian Population," in Proceedings of the Third International Congress of Ethiopian Studies (Addis Ababa, 1969), 25–33, and "Some Observations on African Slaves in Arabia," a paper presented at a workshop on the long-distance trade in slaves across the Indian Ocean and the Red Sea in the nineteenth century

(School of Oriental and African Studies, University of London, December 17–19, 1987.)

32. Fredrik Barth, *Sohar: Culture and Society in an Omani Town* (Baltimore: John Hopkins University Press, 1983), 42–49, 98–99.

33. Husayn ibn 'Abdallah al-'Amri, "Slaves and Mamelukes in the History of Yemen," in *Yemen: 3000 Years of Art and Civilisation in Arabia Felix,* ed Werner Daum (Innsbruck: Umschau-Verlag, 1987), 140–57.

34. Edward A. Alpers, "The Somali Community at Aden in the Nineteenth Century," *Northeast African Studies* 8, noṡ. 2–3 (1986): 143–68.

35. Albertine Jwaideh and J. W. Cox, "The Black Slaves of Turkish Arabia during the Nineteenth Century," in *Indian Ocean Slave Trade,* ed. Clarence-Smith, 56.

36. Thomas M. Ricks, "Slaves and Slave Traders in the Persian Gulf, Eighteenth and Nineteenth Centuries: An Assessment," in *The Economics of the Indian Ocean Slave Trade in the Nineteenth Century,* ed.William Gervase Clarence-Smith (London: Frank Cass, 1989), 60–70. Other contributions to the Clarence-Smith collection of special interest for the Red Sea zone are by Janet Ewald, "The Nile Valley System and the Red Sea Slave Trade 1820–1880," 71–92; Abdussamad H. Ahmad, "Ethiopian Slave Exports at Matamma, Massawa and Tajura *c.* 1830 to 1885," 93–102; and Timothy Fernyhough, "Slavery and the Slave Trade in Southern Ethiopia in the Nineteenth Century," 103–30; see also Clarence-Smith's far-ranging introduction, "The Economics of the Indian Ocean and Red Sea Slave Trades in the Nineteenth Century: An Overview," in *Indian Ocean Slave Trade,* ed. Clarence-Smith, 1–20.

37. Janet Ewald, "Crossers of the Sea: Slaves, Freedmen, and Other Migrants in the Northwestern Indian Ocean, c. 1750–1914," *American Historical Review* 105, no. 1 (2000): 69–91. I am very grateful to Professor Ewald for sharing a pre-publication draft of this paper with me.

38. A. J. Temu, "The Role of the Bombay Africans (Liberated Africans) on the Mombasa Coast, 1874–1904," in *Hadith* 3, ed. Bethwell Allan Ogot (Nairobi: East African Publishing House, 1971), 53–81.

39. Joseph E. Harris, *Repatriates and Refugees in a Colonial Society: The Case of Kenya* (Washington, D.C.: Howard University Press, 1987).

40. Francesca Declich, "Coming Back from Southern Somalia to 'Zigualand' in Tanzania: What Matri-Kin Group Do I Belong to?" paper presented at the Thirty-eighth Annual Meeting of the African Studies Association, Orlando, Florida, November 5, 1995. For references to the slave trade in Uzigua, see James L. Giblin, *The Politics of Environmental Control in Northeastern Tanzania, 1840–1940* (Philadelphia: University of Pennsylvania Press, 1992).

41. Compare Teotonio de Souza, "The Voiceless in Goan Historiography: A Case for the Source-Value of Church Records in Goa," in *Indo-Portuguese History: Sources and Problems,* ed. John Correia-Afonso (Bombay: Oxford University Press, 1981), 114–31.

42. Hubert Gerbeau, "The Slave Trade in the Indian Ocean: Problems Facing the Historian and Research to be Undertaken," in *African Slave Trade from the Fifteenth to the Nineteenth Century* (Paris: Unesco, 1979), 184.

43. Ibid., 186, 203.

44. John Thornton, *Africa and Africans in the Making of the Atlantic World, 1400–1800,* 2nd ed. (New York: Cambridge University Press, 1998), 206.

45. Ibid., 207–9.

46. Edward A. Alpers, "Dance and Society in Nineteenth Century Mogadishu," in *Proceedings of the Second International Congress of Somali Studies,* vol. 2, ed. Thomas J. Labahn (Hamburg: H. Buske, 1984), 134–35.

47. Joseph B. F. Osgood, *Notes of Travel or Recollections of Majunga, Zanzibar, Muscat, Aden, Mocha, and other Eastern Ports* (Salem: G. Creamer, 1854), 106–8.

48. J. R. Wellsted, *Travels in Arabia,* vol. 1 (London: J. Murray, 1838), 28–29, 63–64.

49. Ibid., 345–47.

50. Ibid., 388–89. For a twentieth-century example of Hadrami categorization of slave origins, see R. B. Serjeant, "Forms of Plea: A Saf'i Manual from al-Sihr," (written in 1955) in his *Customary and Shari'ah Law in Arabian Society* (Hampshire: Variorum, 1991), 11: 6: "I was told that in relatively recent times, three categories of slaves were distinguished: al-Biharah, i.e. slaves from al-Sawahil; Tulud (S. Talid), slaves born and raised in Hadramawt; and Nubah, Nubians."

51. Barth, *Sohar,* 45, 48–49, 99.

52. Youssef Shawki Moustafa, "Traditional Musical Instruments of Oman," in *The Complete Documents of the International Symposium on the Traditional Music in Oman,* October 6–16, 1985, ed. Issam el-Mallah (Wilhelmshaven: Florian Noetzel Verlag, 1994), 1: 53–54. I am indebted to my colleague at UCLA, Ali Jihad Racy, professor of ethnomusicology, for sharing his copy of this important publication with me.

53. Frederick Johnson, *A Standard Swahili-English Dictionary* (London: Oxford University Press, 1939), 304.

54. Moustafa, "Collecting and Documenting the Traditional Music in Oman," 2: 18–19. Note that these names are not translated in the original source and are not, in any case—strictly speaking—in Arabic. Rather, they represent the Omani incorporation of different regional names for African-derived music and dance forms. Thus, *at-tanburah* is derived from both the musical instrument (lyre) and ritual called *tanburah* (with many variants) in the Sudan; *an-nuban* (not, by the way, Nubian, as the Nubians and Nubas are different people in different regions of the Sudan) is simply an ethnogeographical variant on the same musical-ritual form. Similarly, *az-zar* takes its name from the music and ritual associated with possession by *zar* spirits (which derive from Ethiopia and the Horn). *Ar-rubabah,* which occurs later in this same paragraph, takes its name from the Beja (a people of the Eastern Sudan) name for the lyre.

55. There is a rich literature on *zar* possession in northeastern and eastern Africa as well as in Arabia; see, for example, I. M. Lewis, Ahmed al-Safi, and Sayyid Hurreiz, eds., *Women's Medicine: The Zar-Bori Cult in Africa and Beyond* (Edinburgh: Edinburgh University Press, 1991), which includes an excellent select annotated bibliography, and Alpers, "Ordinary Household Chores," 688 and sources cited therein. I thank Shahram Khosravi of Stockholm University for drawing my attention to a reference to *zar* possession among the African peoples of coastal southern Iran: Kaveh Safa, "Reading Saedi's Ahl-e Hava," *Culture, Medicine and Psychiatry* 12 (1988): 85–111.

56. Moustafa, "Collecting and Documenting," 18; Pamela Constantinides, "The History of *Zar* in the Sudan: Theories of Origin, Recorded Observation and Oral Tradition," in *Women's Medicine: The Zar-Bori Cult in Africa and Beyond,* ed. I. M. Lewis, et al. (Edinburgh: Edinburgh University Press, 1991), 89–91, and G. Makris and Ahmad Al-Safi, "The *Tumbura* Spirit Possession Cult of the Sudan, Past and Present," in *Women's Medicine: The Zar-Bori Cult in Africa and Beyond,* ed. I. M. Lewis, Ahmed al-Safi, and Sayyid Hurreiz (Edinburgh: Edinburgh University Press, 1991), 122–23.

57. Moustafa, "Collecting and Documenting," 19; see also page 26, where he notes that in Sur, *sharh,* one of the five types of art performance, "designates a type of art which is believed by those who practice it to free a sick man from a *ginn* spirit that has dominated him, causing his illness." It is worth mentioning that this is only one of four localized meanings for *ash-sharh,* which demonstrates the need for close collaboration with local scholars and performers who are capable of making these distinctions. Finally, Moustafa notes the kinds of occasions on which Afro-Omani arts are performed (30–31).

58. Ali Jihad Racy, "Africa and Arabia: Performance Traditions from the Arab Gulf Region," illustrated lecture delivered at the Symposium on African Music, UCLA, February 23, 1996. The following account is based on my lecture notes.

59. The same association with the lyre and women is observed in *zar,* according to a comment by Lois Anderson following Racy's presentation. It is important to note that Professor Racy has also done

research in the Sudan. For a broader perspective on this instrument and its Sudanic origins in the Gulf area, see Racy, "The Lyre of the Arab Gulf: Historical Roots, Geographical Links, and the Local Context," *Al-Ma'thurat Al-Sha'biyyah* 27 (1992): 7–17.

60. For *tabura* (sic) in southern Somalia, see Gustavo Pesenti, "Canti e ritmi arabici, somalici e suaheli" (1910), 1422–24 (unattributed reprint in author's possession). *Mangur* or *manjur* is the name given to this ceremonial belt in the Sudan, where it is an integral part of *tumbura;* see Constantinides, "History of *Zar,*" 89–91; and Makris and Al-Safi, "The *Tumbura* Spirit Possession Cult," 123, 128.

61. Paul Rovsing Olsen, "La musique africaine dans le golfe persique," *Journal of the International Folk Music Council* 19 (1967): 28–29, 36. Habib Hassan Touma, "The Fidjri, a Major Vocal Form of the Bahrain Pearl-divers," *World of Music* 19, nos. 3–4 (1977): 122, also mentions *tanburah* in passing at Bahrain. When I met with Racy on December 10, 1996, he confirmed Olsen's point about pentatonism and rhythms and also mentions a girdle of sheep or goat hooves in *tanburah* at Dubay.

62. Francisco Declich, "Identity, Dance and Islam among People with Bantu Origins in Riverine Areas of Somalia," in *The Invention of Somalia,* ed. Ali Jimale Ahmed (Lawrenceville, N.J.: Red Sea Press, 1995), 191–222.

63. Compare Touma, "Fidjri," 121–27. Although Touma does not identify any aspect of *fidjri* as African, he includes references to connections in instrumentation and performance in the Sudan. Jwaideh and Cox, "Black Slaves," 53, also report that the small African community at Kuwait had "its own club and peculiar sky-signs, where they frequently danced to their own music through the night."

64. Alan Villiers, *Sons of Sinbad* (New York: Charles Scribner's Sons, 1940), 201–3. For the observation that "an astonishingly high proportion" of the nearly ten thousand "qualified deep-sea sailors" at Aden in 1939 were "of Negro origin," see Villiers, "Some Aspects of the Arab Dhow Trade," *Middle East Journal* 2, no. 4 (1948): 406–7.

65. Ruth M. Stone, "Oman and the African Diaspora in Song, Dance and Aesthetic Expression," in *The Complete Documents of the International Symposium on the Traditional Music in Oman,* 6–16 October 1985, ed. Issam el-Mallah (Wilhelmshaven: Florian Noetzel Verlag, 1994), 3: 58–59. Stone transliterates *lewa* as *leiwah;* I have chosen to adopt the form used in both Moustafa, "Traditional Musical Instruments" and Dieter Christensen, "Music Making in Sohar: Arts and Society in al-Batinah of Oman," both in *The Complete Documents of the International Symposium on the Traditional Music in Oman,* October 6–16, 1985, ed. Issam el-Mallah Wilhelmshaven: Florian Noetzel Verlag, 1994), vol. 2.

66. Stone, "Oman," 59. She also identifies the *musundu* as a drum of African origin, "with African looking incisions in the wood."

67. Christensen, "Music Making," 76–77. Christensen may be mistaken here, since Moustafa identifies *burgham* as "an animal horn," of the type noted by Osgood, for example, at Muscat in the 1850s, and as distinguished from sea conches. *Gum,* however, would seem to be derived from either Swahili *kome* or *kombe,* a generic term for univalve and bivalve shells; see Johnson, *Dictionary,* 218–9.

68. Stone, "Oman," 59–60.

69. Jihad Racy has commented that some of the songs he heard in Dubay contain similar African geographical references, in his case to Port Said. Personal communication, 10 December, 1996.

70. Stone, "Oman," 59–60.

71. Christensen, "Music Making," 69.

72. Stone, "Oman," 61. There are bound to be recognizable African elements in certain Omani dances as well, although the one paper at the 1985 symposium that addresses this topic is not particularly helpful; see Hazel Chung-Hood, "Afro-Omani Reciprocal Influences in the Traditional Dances of Oman," in *The Complete Documents of the International Symposium on the Traditional Music in Oman,* October 6–16, 1985, ed. Issam el-Mallah (Wilhelmshaven: Florian Noetzel Verlag, 1994), 3: 97–102.

73. Olsen, "La musique africaine," 30–36. Touma, "Fidjri," 122, mentions *lewa* at Bahrain as well, and

Racy does likewise for Dubay. See also Zubaydah Ashkanani, "*Zar* in a Changing World: Kuwait," in *Women's Medicine: The Zar-Bori Cult in Africa and Beyond*, ed. I. M. Lewis, Ahmed al-Safi, and Sayyid Hurreiz (Edinburgh: Edinburgh University Press, 1991), 219–29.

74. Villiers, *Sons of Sinbad*, 28.

75. Wendell Phillips, *Unknown Oman* (Beirut: Librarie du Liban, 1971), 10–11.

76. R. B. Serjeant, "South Arabia and Ethiopia" and "South Arabia" in his *Studies in Arabian History and Civilisation* (London: Variorum Reprints, 1981).

77. Charles M. Doughty, *Travels in Arabia Deserta*, 3rd ed. (New York: J. Cape and the Medici Society, 1923), 2: 491, 76, 77, 84–85.

78. R. B. Serjeant, *Prose and Poetry from Hadramawt* (London: Taylor's Foreign Press, 1951), 11.

79. Serjeant, "African Slaves in Arabia," 3; also see his "South Arabia and Ethiopia," 27, where he includes the tantalizing note that these huts were owned by women in the northern Yemen village of Mashaf. At Mukalla in the 1830s, Wellsted says that the blacksmiths "are principally natives of Zanzibar" (*Travels*, 2: 428). It would be interesting to see if any vestige of their craft survives today. For a photograph of a slave, obviously African, making bread at El Tanem in the Tihamah in 1912, see Andrew Wheatcroft, *Arabia and the Gulf: In Original Photographs 1880–1950* (London: Kegan Paul International, 1982), 135. This volume includes other photographs that depict African retainers of various Arab dignitaries, as well as a frequently reproduced photograph from C. Snouck Hurgronje, *Mekka in the Latter Part of the Nineteenth Century*, trans. J. H. Monahan (Leiden: E. J. Brill, 1931), of an African nursemaid and eunuch, c. 1886 (121).

80. Osgood, *Notes of Travel*, 193; and Robin Bidwell, *Travelers in Arabia* (London: Hamlyn, 1976), 45, reproducing a plan from J. Bellin, *Le petit atlas maritime* (1764), vol. 3, map 20, according to a letter to the author dated December 5, 1985, from Charlotte Dean of Newnes Books, Feltham, Middlesex, U.K.

81. Doughty, *Travels*, 2: 533, 535.

82. Ibid., 118.

83. Hurgronje, *Mekka*, 11–12, which also includes four bars of a repeated sequence of notes.

84. Serjeant, "South Arabia and Ethiopia," 32. Serjeant also comments: "Tamburah is a word also known in al-Bahrein where it seems to mean an African dance" (n. 25), which provides still another Persian Gulf manifestation of this dance. In note 26 he writes that *gadbah* derives from classical Arabic *jadhb* and cites C. de Landberg, *Glossaire datinois* (Leiden: E. J. Brill, 1920–42), 272, "where *jadhabh* is described as a sort of dance executed at the *mawlid* of a saint," which seems to confirm Racy's information on the sacred transformation of this musical performance. For drumming, see Serjeant, "African Slaves in Arabia," 3.

85. Serjeant, *Prose and Poetry*, 18–19. The setting detailed by Serjeant recalls Touma's description of the special house, called *dar*, which he likens to a pearl-divers' club, where the men "drink tea, smoke, tell stories, eat, sing and dance." In the nineteenth century, there were more than a hundred *dar* scattered along the Bahrain coast, but only twelve remained in 1977. See Touma, "Fidjri," 123–24, which also reproduces a photograph with a ship painted on the wall from inside a *dar*.

86. Doughty, *Travels*, 1: 536; for the Gurage reference, see Hurgronje, *Mekka*, 14.

87. Hurgronje, *Mekka*, 12; and John Lewis Burckhardt, *Travels in Arabia* (Beirut: Librarie du Liban, 1972 [1829]), 112, 257, 384. I have not yet been able to identify the etymology of this term.

88. R. B. Serjeant, "The Cultivation of Cereals in Medieval Yemen" (written in 1984) in *Farmers and Fishermen in Arabia*, ed. G. Rex Smith (Aldershot: Variorum, 1995), 7: 45, 52, 71 n. 165.

89. Serjeant, "South Arabia and Ethiopia," 32; "The Quarters of Tarim and Their Tansurahs," *Le Muséon*, 58, nos. 3–4 (1950): 277, 279, 283–84; and D. van der Meulen and H. von Wissman, *Hadramaut—Some of Its Mysteries Unveiled* (Leiden: E. J. Brill, 1932), 16–17 plate 3.

90. For the former, see Serjeant, "Some Irrigation Systems in Hadramawt" (written in 1964), in *Farmers and Fishermen in Arabia*, ed. G. Rex Smith (Aldershot: Variorum, 1995), 8: 58; for Zinjibar, as it

appears on modern maps, see D. van der Meulen, *Aden to Hadramaut: A Journey in South Arabia* (London: J. Murray, 1947), 21. Both Serjeant and van der Meulen provide some explicit indications of where and where not in south Arabia one was most likely to find African communities at the time of their travels.

91. Serjeant, *Prose and Poetry*, 9–10.

92. L. W. C. van den Berg, *Le Hadhramaut et les Colonies Arabes dans l'Archipel Indien* (Batavia: Imprimerie du Gouvernement, 1886), 70.

93. Serjeant, "South Arabia and Ethiopia," 32–33.

94. Serjeant, "Sex, Birth, Circumcision: Some Notes from South-West Arabia" (written in 1962), in his *Customary and Shari'ah Law in Arabian Society* (Hampshire: Variorum, 1991), 14: 195.

95. Doughty, *Travels*, 2: 156–66, 168.

96. Harold Ingrams, *Arabia and the Isles* (London: J. Murray, 1942), 154 n. 1, 155–56.

97. Wellsted, *Travels*, 2: 431. Van den Berg, *Le Hadhramaut*, 69, notes that there were also significant numbers of Somali slaves in the Hadramaut.

98. Van der Meulen and von Wissman, *Hadramaut*, 150.

99. See Abu'1-Qasim Afnan, *Black Pearls: Servants in the Household of the Báb and Bahá'u'lláh* (Los Angeles: Kalimat Press, 1988), xxi, 41–42.

100. Reprinted in Irwin, *Africans Abroad*, 165–66.

101. Compare Sud, "Brought in Chains"; Thomas H. D. La Touche, *A Bibliography of Indian Geology and Physical Geography*, part 1 (Calcutta: Office of the Geological Survey of India, 1917), 1: 153; Bhattacharya, "Indians of African Origin," 580; and Gupta, *Minorities*, 216–17. There is much conflicting genealogical and geographical evidence about Bava Gor that needs resolution.

102. Gupta, *Minorities*, 219–22, for the following paragraph and its quoted passages.

103. Naik and Pandya confirm the names of some of these instruments and add one or two others in a paragraph on "Material Culture of Religion" They note, too, that these instruments are kept in the Bava Gor mosque at Ratanpur in Bharuch District (*Sidis of Gujarat*, 20, 88).

104. The part of Gujarat inhabited by many of the Sidi community today is near the Gir Forest, the only place in India where lions remain in the wild. See Bhattacharya, "Anthropometry," 70.

105. Bhattacharya, "Indians of African Origin," 581–82. Again, Naik and Pandya confirm that dhamal dancers paint their bodies, while adding that they dress in skins as well as feathers (*Sidis of Gujarat*, 89).

106. Harris, *African Presence*, 112. For what appears to be a more recent similar public performance, in 1987, see Austen, "The Nineteenth Century Islamic Slave Trade," 42 n. 23: "BBC reports of Benazir Bhutto's wedding celebration in Pakistan singled out the role of local African-descended communities."

107. Miguel de Noronha de Paiva Couceiro, *Diu e Eu* (Lisboa: Agência-Geral do Ultramar, 1969), 137.

108. Pinto, *Slavery in Portuguese India*, 94. This sounds very much like a gloss on Moniz's account of St. Benedict's Feast celebrations as reported by Kenneth David Jackson in *Sing Without Shame: Oral Traditions in Indo-Portuguese Creole Verse* (Philadelphia: J. Benjamin, 1990), 74.

109. Bhattacharya, "Indians of African Origin," 581; Sud, "Brought in Chains"; and Lodhi, "African Settlements," 83–84. Afro-Indian place names are well known as markers of Sidi and Habshi communities: see, for example, Rao, "The Habshis," 35.

110. Naik and Pandya, *Sidis of Gujarat*, 6, 48–50, 74–79. Another possibility found among clan names represented by spouses of their families, Varanga, may derive from the Karanga of the Zambezi valley.

111. Ibid., 53.

112. Jackson, *Sing without Shame;* see also, among others, M. H. Goonatilleka, "A Portuguese Creole in Sri Lanka: A Brief Socio-linguistic Survey," in *Indo-Portuguese History: Sources and Problems*, Teotónio de Souza (Bombay: Oxford University Press, 1981), 147–80; and Ian R. Smith, *Sri Lanka*

Creole Portuguese Phonology (Vanchiyoor, Trivandrum: Dravidian Linguistics Association, 1978); and Dennis B. McGilvray, "Dutch Burghers and Portuguese Mechanics: Eurasian Ethnicity in Sri Lanka," *Comparative Studies in Society and History*, 24, no. 2 (1982): 235–63.

113. For a passing reference in a contemporary Sinhalese poem to "Kaffirs and Abyssinian" in the Portuguese army that invaded Sri Lanka in the seventeenth century, see Edmund Peiris, "An Interesting Ethnical Group from Mannar," *Ceylon Historical Journal* 3 (1953): 16, quoting *Kustantinu Hatana*, v. 96. This reference to African troops should also remind us that the slave trade was not the only source for the African diaspora in the Indian Ocean.

114. Jackson, *Sing without Shame*, 75.

115. Kenneth David Jackson, *"Canta sen vargonya:* Portuguese Creole Verse in Sri Lanka," *Journal of Pidgin and Creole Languages*, 2, no. 1 (1987): 39–41.

116. Jackson, *Sing without Shame*, 64, 75, 84.

117. Ibid., 74.

118. Jackson, *"Canta sen vargonya,"* 32. *Baila* (from Portuguese *bailar,* to dance) itself reflects still another external cultural influence in that society.

119. Palakshappa, *Siddhis of North Kanara*, 59; and Naik and Pandya, *Sidis of Gujarat*, 60.

120. Naik and Pandya, *Sidis of Gujarat, 63;* see also page 93, which reproduces a 1979 resolution published by this journal declaring that they alone "be included in the administration of the tomb of Bava Gor." Harris, "Africa and Its Diaspora," 720–21, also notes that a delegation of Sidis visited East Africa in 1973 to learn about the continent and "explore areas of possible cooperation."

121. Armoogum Parsuraman, *From Ancestral Cultures to National Culture—Mauritius* (Moka: Mahatma Gandhi Institute Press, 1988), 62–64. The author was minister of education, arts and culture.

The Diaspora in Yemen

Tim Carmichael

T HE TRAVEL TO EASTERN AND NORTHEASTERN AFRICA OF YEMENI MERCHANTS, religious leaders, and immigrants is well documented, but there is little knowledge about Africans in the Arabian peninsula aside from studies on slavery and its institutions. Middle East scholars have neglected African communities and cultural continuities or influences, as well as the Africans who went to Arabia to pursue education, to trade, or to live. Africanist understanding of the ties between the southern Gulf and east Africa, on the other hand, is better developed. For example, the excellent book on the Swahili coast by Randall Pouwels and an article by B. G. Martin discuss, among other topics, the integration of foreign Muslims into Swahili society and their influences on it, and recent years have witnessed a surge in interest in the Indian Ocean region, including east Africa. While the Horn has received less attention, Haggai Erlich outlines the history of Muslim discourse—both positive and negative—about Ethiopia, and A. Nizar Hamzeh and R. Hrair Dekmejian examine the rise to religious and political leadership of Ethiopian émigrés to Lebanon. Together, their work points to the Ethiopia-Yemen connection as a potentially rewarding focus.[1]

Relations between Ethiopia and Yemen are ancient. Commercial exchange has taken place for at least two millennia, and over the centuries each has successfully invaded/colonized the other. By the thirteenth century Ethiopian emperors were sending mail to Cairo through Yemen, whose rulers were asked to endorse and forward the correspondence.[2] During the sixteenth century many Yemenis came to

Ethiopia to fight on the side of Ahmad bin Ibrahim al-Ghazi, the local Muslim commander of a war against the Christian kingdom.[3] In the seventeenth century Khodja Murad was sent as a Yemeni ambassador of sorts, in an attempt to foster warmer relations between the two governments.[4] Throughout the nineteenth century many Yemeni merchants traveled to Ethiopia, and oral traditions in Ethiopia's ancient Islamic city of Harär emphasize that Yemen was one of the most important destinations for Haräri traders when they went abroad. Most European travelers to Ethiopia during the 1800s first went to Aden (Yemen), where they made plans, obtained supplies, and acquired practical and political information before continuing their journey.[5]

In the early twentieth century there was increased emigration of Yemenis to Ethiopian trade centers, such as Harär and Dire Dawa. Owing to British fears of pan-Islamism and Ottoman influence, Foreign Office records before and during World War I report the visits of foreign Muslims, including Yemenis, to Ethiopia. Contacts between the two countries continued throughout the century. During the Yemeni civil war informal talks were held in Ethiopia in 1958; in the early 1960s Aden's trade was heavily dependent upon Ethiopian goods; and during 1974–91 many Ethiopians sought to escape the Marxist-Socialist dictatorship by traveling to Yemen. It is noteworthy that both countries claim the Queen of Sheba as well as the geographical origins of both coffee and qat.[6] During my research on Harär, it became clear that the city's historical orientation (in economic and socioreligious terms) has been toward Yemen rather than the central highlands of Ethiopia.[7]

It is useful to think in terms of a two-way diaspora. On one side are the Hadhrami commercial and religious networks and social structures and the history of the Hadhrami diaspora in the Indian Ocean, Red Sea, and Swahili coast regions.[8] On the other are Africans in Yemen, such as Somalis in British-controlled Aden,[9] and African elements in southern Arabia.[10] Because we know much less about Africans in the Middle East than in other regions, scholars need to grapple with "serious issues related to defining the African diaspora and understanding the complexities associated with the study of the dispersion of Africans and people of African descent *throughout* the world."[11]

A closely related topic is transnationalism, an emerging field critical of received ideas about space and place within the social sciences and roughly divided into two branches, one dealing with migration and one dealing with cultural studies. Both aspects are relevant to the history of Ethiopians and other Africans in Yemen and elsewhere.

A general problem with the transnational migration literature is that it continues to focus overwhelmingly on movements of people, capital, and ideas between

"Third World" and "First World" nations.[12] In a global context, however, movements within developing countries, although less visible, may well be equal in intensity, frequency, and daily economic importance to those between the developing world and Western or Northern countries.[13] Even though the capitalist profits involved in intra–developing country migration may be less than those related to other movements, they are still significant for many local and family economies, and any truly holistic theory of transnationalism must attend to such networks. Yemeni-African relations comprise only one possible arena for study, but the political, economic, social, and religious diversity in the Horn of Africa and southwest Arabia make the region a particularly promising one on which to focus.

So little is known about the details of migration in the region that the wider scope of transnational cultural studies may be the best way to begin. For example, Arjun Appadurai delineates several interrelated and overlapping spheres of sociocultural, economic, and political interface, which he labels "scapes," prefaced by ethno-, media-, techno-, finance-, and ideo-. He explores various ways in which these spheres overlap and influence one another.[14] Although his larger model remains more structuralist than he perhaps intended, its strength is that it charts a wide variety of possible mechanisms and processes that link, both materially and via assorted imaginaries, the global, the national, and the local. Drawing on such an approach, more case studies throughout different regions of the world, particularly such neglected ones as Northeast Africa and Southwestern Arabia, not only would provide rich historical and ethnographic detail but also would improve our understanding of the linkages between local, national, and global movements everywhere, as opposed to just within the West or between the West and the rest.

During travels in Yemen in 1997 and 2001, I met with numerous Ethiopians and "mixed" Ethio-Yemenis (*muwalladin*)[15] in different parts of the country. Despite many indications of acculturation into Yemeni life, the Ethiopians and Ethio-Yemenis cook and eat primarily Ethiopian cuisine, though they supplement it with Yemeni/Middle Eastern dishes. Nearly all the women I met spoke Amharic well, in addition to Arabic, but many of the men spoke Amharic only with difficulty and often with serious grammatical mistakes and pronunciation and accents that aroused women's teasing scorn.[16] In Sana'a, the capital, I learned that as recently as the 1970s Ethiopians encountered social difficulties because of their skin color, but the situation slowly improved through the 1980s, and social acceptance is much better since the Därg government in Ethiopia fell in 1991. ·

According to my contacts, as larger numbers of Africans arrived, Yemenis became more accustomed to seeing darker-skinned residents, particularly in Sana'a. Also, the Africans' social support networks improved and facilitated further their compatriots' entry into Yemeni society. For example, during the 1970s new arrivals were advised not to sport huge afro hair styles or to wear bell-bottomed jeans and tee-shirts, which were unacceptable by local standards.[17] I was also told that many more Ethiopians came after 1991 not to escape from the new regime at home but because it was suddenly much easier to be issued a passport. At that time a number of new Ethiopian restaurants appeared around Sana'a and were frequented not only by Ethiopians and Ethio-Yemenis but also by Arab Yemenis, many of whom apparently like Ethiopian food.[18] Thus, food, language, skin color, and clothing are markers of sameness or difference, both within the Ethio-Yemeni community and between it and the rest of Yemeni society. Furthermore, oral testimonies clearly situate certain practices and personal experiences within specific politico-historical contexts, even in the recent past, which underscores the importance of historical context to studies of culture and society.

Edward A. Alpers charts some of the source material terrain for studying the western Indian Ocean region generally. Concentrating on "nonconventional" evidence, he argues that various aesthetics, including music, dance, and song, promise to reveal much about Africans, in terms of both their cultural heritage and their influences on other societies.[19] Other avenues of inquiry that are worth pursuing are historical patterns of travel and (im)migration, intermarriage, and government relations, as well as how Yemeni authors at different periods have written about Ethiopians or East Africans and vice versa. We know far less about Yemeni-African connections than we do about other regions of the world, and it would be useful to consider how various local discourses related to the tenor of political or economic relations prevailing at the time.

The study by Engseng Ho of *muwalladin* (primarily Indonesian, but also African) in the Hadhramaut region of Yemen is an exemplary work that blends literary and textual research with interviews and analyzes each source within its temporal, geographic, and cultural context.[20] Ho concentrates on individuals who were born abroad and later came to Yemen, but what about *muwalladin* born and raised in Yemen? How do their life trajectories compare to those of *muwalladin* born abroad? Work along these lines may find that the country of parentage, its economic prospects, and an individual's family or other contacts are important factors in distinguishing various *muwallad* experiences. According to Walters,

> Yemeni society would . . . not be characterized by many as racist. Despite constitutional
> and Islamic egalitarian ideals, Yemen's rigid social hierarchy is based on birth and occu-
> pational status rather than race. However, implicit in the categories that Yemenis use to
> identify themselves and others are racial and ethnic ideologies. Yemenis with known

African ancestry, ex-slaves (*'abid*) and Yemenis with reputed African origins (*akhdam*) are relegated to the bottom of the social scale. Moreover, Yemeni servant groups with no known or presumed African ancestors (*khaddam*) are considered black and thereby racialized.[21]

In addition to *muwalladin,* there are *'abid,* who are descendants of former slave communities in the south, and *akhdam,* who are believed to have African ancestry, perhaps predating the rise of Islam, but who are "deprived of a tribal ancestral genealogy" and thus are "denied the benefits of respectability in their society."[22] It did not strike me as a complementary label under any circumstances, but I met an Ethiopian (immigrant) *shaykh* in Zabid who seemed to be well respected, lived in a nice house, and attracted an impressive social circle, yet he was referred to as *akhdam* by Yemenis.[23]

More recently,[24] I met several cleaning women in guest houses, language institutes, and business offices who spoke to me in Amharic after overhearing my conversations about Ethiopia with others. Their job seemed "appropriate" to *akhdam,* but they referred to themselves as *muwalladin.* When I asked them about the Arabic term *akhdam,* they invariably launched into diatribes about how even *muwalladin* are "treated" as *akhdam* on occasion.[25] I also met a number of *muwalladin* who held jobs considered to be quite good even by Arab Yemenis, and they claimed—between violent criticisms of the social racism they often endure—that as well-employed *muwalladin* they were not unique.[26]

Clearly, issues related to race are relevant to daily life in Yemen, as elsewhere, but further work is needed on the usage and meanings of various terms. What words are used by Yemenis and Africans to refer to themselves, one another, and others? When, why, and how? It would be interesting to know whether usage differs with region and how different persons interpret these terms. Do class, education, employment, background, gender, or region (both of origin and of residence) influence such interpretations? Also, do meanings or nuances depend upon the language being spoken (e.g., Arabic, Amharic, Somali, Swahili) or the context of conversation? This sort of investigation might generate a host of related issues for further research.

Another question is whether northern Sudanese, who occupy a liminal conceptuo-racial space between Africa and the Arab world and who speak Arabic as their first language, are judged differently from other Africans in Yemen. Have Yemeni views of them changed because of the influx of other Africans in the recent past? Does their presence affect local attitudes toward other blacks? The relationship between "racial appearance" and linguistic abilities should be examined. Compounding the complexities of such phenomena is the large number of northeast African refugees who have arrived in Yemen in the past few years and the ways their presence affects local attitudes toward other blacks.

Ethiopians and other Africans as well as African-descent populations in Yemen are relevant to diaspora studies, work on transnationalism, African and Middle East studies, and the emerging field of Indian Ocean research. Knowledge about these groups may open or reify creative links between and among these areas of study, but the research will not be easy. Alpers reiterates the formidable linguistic skills necessary for comprehensive work on the history of the African diaspora in the Indian Ocean region.[27] In the case of Yemen (as well as Oman and a few other countries) and Eastern/Northeastern Africa, at the very least a knowledge of Arabic and one African language is required. A growing number of East Africanists speak Arabic and Swahili, and they may pioneer the next generation of scholarly work on the region.[28] A perspective that incorporates the Horn (Ethiopia, Somalia, Somaliland, Djibouti, and Eritrea) would require other languages, such as Afar, Amharic, Oromo, Tegreñña, and Somali.[29] When scholars who have such skills turn their attention to the topics discussed here, among others, our understanding of the African diaspora will be greatly enriched.

N O T E S

1. Randall Pouwels, *Horn and Crescent: Cultural Change and Traditional Islam on the East African Coast, 800–1900* (Cambridge: Cambridge University Press, 1987); B. G. Martin, "Arab Migrations to East Africa in Medieval Times," *International Journal of African Historical Studies* 7, no. 3 (1975): 367–90; Haggai Erlich, *Ethiopia and the Middle East* (Boulder, Colo.: Lynne Rienner, 1994); A. Nizar Hamzeh and R. Hrair Dekmejian, "A Sufi Response to Political Islamism: Al-Ahbásh of Lebanon," *International Journal of Middle East Studies* 28, no. 2 (1996): 217–29. See also Ahmed Hussein, "A Brief Note on the Yemeni Arabs in Ethiopia," paper presented to the Seventh History Department Seminar, Addis Ababa University, Jimma, Ethiopia, 27 March 1997.

2. Mahar Hammarah Muhammad, *al-Wathaiq al-Siasiah wa al-Adariah lil-'asra al-Maluki 656/922–1258/1516: Darasah wa Nasus* (Beirut, 1980), 468–70, 496–98.

3. Shihab al-Din, *Tuhfata al-Zaman aw Futuh al-Habashah* (Cairo: 1974/1394); French version: Rene Basset, trans., *Histoire de la conquête de l'Abyssinie (XVIe siècle)* (Paris: Leroux, 1897–1901).

4. E. van Donzel, *Foreign Relations of Ethiopia, 1642–1700: Documents Relating to the Journeys of Khodja Murad* (Istanbul: Nederlands Historisch-Archaeologisch Instituut, 1979).

5. Gordon Waterfield, *Sultans of Aden* (London: John Murray, 1968), 143–49.

6. Qat is a leaf chewed in various forms (and sometimes drunk as a tea) to produce semi-narcotic effects. No scientific studies have established that it is physiologically addictive, as opposed to psychologically habituating, but in the United States—where it is consumed primarily by African and Yemeni immigrants—it is now illegal, classified as a Schedule I drug.

7. The Haräris have long been urban-based, even when agriculture was the primary basis of their

economy. They refer to themselves as "the people of the town," to their ways as "the culture of the town," and to their language as "the tongue/language of the town." Over the past few centuries at least, their primary socio-cultural identification has centered on their city. Owing to religion and trade, their "outside view" has been toward Yemen (via present-day Somaliland) rather than to the west (central Ethiopia).

8. R. B. Serjeant, "The Hadrami Network," in *Society and Trade in South Arabia*, ed. G. Rex Smith (Aldershot, Hampshire: Variorum, 1996); Ulrike Freitag and W. G. Clarence-Smith, eds., *Hadhrami Traders, Scholars and Statesmen in the Indian Ocean, 1750s–1960s* (Leiden: Brill, 1997).

9. Edward A. Alpers, "The Somali Community at Aden in the Nineteenth Century," *Northeast African Studies* 8, nos. 2–3 (1986): 143–68.

10. R. B. Serjeant, "South Arabia and Ethiopia: African Elements in the South Arabian Population," in *Proceedings of the Third International Conference of Ethiopian Studies*, vol. 1 (Addis Ababa: Institute of Ethiopian Studies, Haile Selassie I University, 1969).

11. Carlton Wilson, "Conceptualizing the African Diaspora," *Comparative Studies of South Asia, Africa and the Middle East* 17, no. 2 (1997): 118, emphasis added.

12. For example, Linda Basch, Nina Glick Schiller, and Cristina Szanton-Blanc, *Nations Unbound: Transnational Projects, Postcolonial Predicaments and Deterritorialized Nation-States* (New York: Gordon and Breach Publishers, 1994); Linda Basch, Nina Glick Schiller, and Cristina Szanton-Blanc, "Toward a Transnational Perspective on Migration: Race, Class, Ethnicity, and Nationalism Reconsidered," in *Transnationalism from Below*, ed. Luis Eduardo Guarnizo and Michael Peter Smith (New Brunswick, N.J.: Transaction Publishers, 1998); Louisa Schein, "Importing Miao Bretheren to Hmong America: A Not-So-Stateless Transnationalism," in *Cosmopolitics: Thinking and Feeling Beyond the Nation*, ed. Pheng Cheah and Bruce Robbins (Minneapolis: University of Minnesota Press, 1998); Robert C. Smith, "Transnational Localities: Community, Technology and the Politics of Membership within the Context of Mexico and U.S. Migration," in *Transnationalism from Below*, ed. Luis Eduardo Guarnizo and Michael Peter Smith (New Brunswick, N.J.: Transaction Publishers, 1998).

There are notable exceptions, but they fall more into intra-"First World" movements, such as Aihwa Ong, *Flexible Citizenship: The Cultural Logics of Transnationality* (Durham: Duke University Press, 1999). Additionally, while many transnationalism scholars have limited their work to the late twentieth century, Nina Glick Schiller has recently delineated historical phases in order to highlight similarities and differences in migration experiences between the late 1800s and the late 1900s ("Transmigrants and Nation-States: Something Old and Something New in the U.S. Immigrant Experience," in *The Handbook of International Migration: The American Experience*, ed. Charles Hirschman, Philip Kasinitz, and Josh DeWind [New York: Russell Sage Foundation, 1999]).

13. In "Conceptualizing the African Diaspora" Wilson raises the difficult issue of intra-African migration, which is certainly pertinent to my point here (119).

14. Arjun Appadurai, *Modernity at Large: Cultural Dimensions of Globalization* (Minneapolis: University of Minnesota Press, 1996), 33–36.

15. *Muwallad* (sg.) literally means "half-caste," although in Sana'a it usually seems to carry fewer negative connotations than its translation conjures in the United States. Here, I use it primarily in terms of Arab-Africans, but the term extends to non-African mixed-race persons, too. For discussion of the broader meanings, see Engseng Ho, "Hadramis abroad in Hadhramaut: The *Muwalladin*," in *Hadhrami Traders, Scholars, and Statesmen in the Indian Ocean, 1750s–1960s*, ed. Ulrike Freitag and W. G. Clarence-Smith (Leiden: Brill, 1997), 131–32.

16. The men spoke Amharic only because I was there and my Arabic was not as proficient as my Amharic. At one social gathering I finally had to tell an Ethio-Yemeni man, who was speaking Amharic, that I could hardly understand anything he was saying. My statement sent all the women into peals of laughter, and one shouted "Neither can we!" Afterward we had a brief discussion about language, which provided me with more questions to pose later to other people I met.

I hypothesize that two interrelated factors account for what I observed. First, it is more common for Yemeni men to marry Ethiopian women than for Ethiopian men to marry Yemeni women. Second, Yemen's gendered socialization means that young males spend enough time with their mother and other women to learn their language(s), but later spend most of their time with other boys and men, whose primary spoken language is Arabic. As they grow up, therefore, they speak less and less Amharic (or any other "mother's language"), and although they still hear it and maintain the ability to understand it, their verbal skills become rusty.

17. For a more recent example of a Kenyan *muwallad* who encountered problems for similar reasons in a different region of the country, see Ho, "Hadhramis abroad in Hadhramaut," 144.

18. Many of the Ethiopian restaurants in Sana'a later closed as a result of Yemen's economic problems following the first Gulf War, when the government sided with Iraq and about a million Yemeni workers were expelled from Saudi Arabia and elsewhere.

19. Edward A. Alpers, "The African Diaspora in the Northwestern Indian Ocean: Reconsideration of an Old Problem, New Directions for Research," *Comparative Studies of South Asia, Africa and the Middle East* 17, no. 2 (1997); see also Edward A. Alpers, "Recollecting Africa: Diasporic Memory in the Indian Ocean World," *African Studies Review* 43, no. 1 (2000): 83–99.

20. Ho, "Hadhramis abroad in Hadhramaut," 131–46.

21. Delores M. Walters, "Women, Healthcare and Social Equality in Yemen," in *Feminism and Antiracism: International Struggles for Justice*, ed. France Winddance Twine and Kathleen Blee (New York: New York University Press, 2001), 73.

22. Ibid., 75. For more on this terminology, see also Delores M. Walters, "Perceptions of Social Inequality in the Yemen Arab Republic" (Ph.D. diss., New York University, 1987).

23. Of possible interest to Horn scholars is that the *shaykh* was Afar and claimed not to know any Amharic. Also, at least in my presence, he clearly identified far more closely with "Islamic" Yemen than he did with "Christian" Ethiopia.

24. I am grateful to the American Institute of Yemeni Studies for its funding and support of this fieldwork, which was cancelled in progress.

25. I also met many "black" women in various markets throughout Sana'a who were of Ethiopian descent and spoke Amharic. The brevity and public nature of our encounters made in-depth conversation difficult, but they referred to themselves as *muwalladin*. I conjecture that *muwalladin* as a self-referent may signify certain class or other social aspirations.

26. A woman in Sana'a, the sister of a good friend of mine in Ethiopia, recounted that a man had thrown a lit cigarette through her car window as she drove by. She had no idea whether he was hostile because she was a woman driver (driving alone) or obviously of African descent, or a combination of the two.

27. Alpers, "The African Diaspora in the Northwestern Indian Ocean."

28. Among them are Eric Gilbert (Arkansas State University), Scott Reese (Northern Arizona University), Matthew Hopper (UCLA), Andy Ivaska (University of Michigan), and Thomas McDow (Yale University). Ned Bertz (University of Iowa) adds Hindi to his Swahili.

29. Scholars who know Arabic and at least one Horn of Africa language include Hussein Ahmed (Addis Ababa University), Alessandro Gori (Istituto Universitario Orientale), Mohamed Haji Mukhtar (Savannah State College), Ali Jimale Ahmed (Queens College/City University of New York), Abdalla Omar Mansur (Universita di Roma), and Jonathan Miran (Michigan State University). Italian scholars probably lead the field here, but I am unable to provide a reliable listing.

Historicizing the African Diaspora

Joseph E. Harris

A MAJOR DEVELOPMENT IN THE HISTORY OF AFRICANS AND PERSONS OF African descent dispersed around the world occurred in 1965 when the First Congress of African Historians convened in Tanzania to discuss emerging themes in African history, which at that time had not gained recognition as a legitimate academic field of study. The old characterization of Africa as inferior and having no history as promoted by the philosophers David Hume and George Hegel, historians Trevor Roper, U. B. Phillips, and William Dunning, anthropologists C. G. Seligman and Samuel G. Morton, and many others in various disciplines and professions still held sway among most European and American scholars.[1] Thus, by including the African diaspora as a theme in the emerging field of African history, the Tanzania Congress reinforced the status of the history and culture of Africans and their descendants as legitimate fields of study. The subsequent UNESCO publication of the eight-volume *General History of* Africa, which included several discrete chapters focusing on the diaspora, also helped to legitimize black history and culture globally.

Fourteen years after that historic conference in Tanzania, the First African Diaspora Studies Institute convened at Howard University in Washington, D.C., at which more than 120 scholars, writers, and others from twenty English- and French-speaking countries in Europe, Africa, and the Americas gathered to assess the state of studies on Africans and their relationship to people of African descent abroad. The follow-up Second African Diaspora Studies Institute convened in 1981 at the University of Nairobi, in Kenya, with the same agenda. Three significant results of those conferences were the development of courses on the African diaspora or African American history at several universities in Africa, the infusion of the African diaspora concept and methodology in black or African American studies programs in the United States, and the publication of papers presented at those institutes.[2] Thus, by the turn of the twenty-first century several other U.S. colleges and universities had joined the historically black colleges and universities in offering diaspora conceived courses. In addition, the African diaspora label had become widely used by public personalities and public-policy makers in government, business, and other areas. This latter development is especially significant because of its positive impact on public awareness and discourse about Africans and their descendants.

Although historically the term *diaspora* has been applied most frequently to the Jewish dispersion, in recent years it has become a common label for studies of Chinese, East Indian, and other groups of people outside their ancestral homelands. Several precursor studies have made significant contributions not only to our understanding of specific dispersed groups but also to the concept and methods of diaspora research in general. W. E. B. DuBois wrote in this tradition when he described the "double consciousness" of African Americans, and William H. Shack and Elliott P. Skinner expanded the "stranger concept" as a way of comprehending diaspora peoples in Africa. Skinner also has assessed the complex and dialectical contradictions between African diaspora people and their original homeland. Although DuBois's work related to African Americans and Shack and Skinner's "strangers" were Africans, both works are relevant to studies of other dispersions and the effect of diaspora people on domestic and foreign policies.[3]

The study of diasporas received added momentum with the fragmentation of a number of countries and the separation of ethnic groups in Eastern Europe, especially the Soviet Union; in Africa, notably Ethiopia, Eritrea, and Somalia; and in Southern and Southeast Asia, particularly India, Vietnam, and Cambodia. But, unlike those developments, the African diaspora resulted from unique historical developments, namely, the global slave trades conducted for centuries primarily by Arabs and Europeans, and the Berlin Conference of 1884–85 that partitioned Africa and set boundaries that continue to divide ethnic groups and inspire irredentism. Both the slave trades and the Berlin Conference continue to have a significant impact on the African diaspora, the former because of its global dispersion, accompanying stereotypes, and the sustained identification of blacks with Africa, and the latter because it shares with the former the inspiration for return movements and because the partition led to separation of families and ethnic groups, and changes in country names and borders, thus complicating the memory and identification of diaspora blacks with Africa.[4]

Since ancient times, African merchants, seamen and soldiers, missionaries for Islam and Christianity, entertainers, and adventurers have established a global presence that was greatly enhanced by the slave trades. Arab slave traders took Africans from the northern and eastern regions of the continent to southern Europe, the Middle East, and Asia; and from the fifteenth century onward European and European-American traders took them from all areas of the continent to Europe, the Americas, and parts of Asia.

During the colonial era, Africans from the continent and the diaspora gravitated to and settled in cities in several European countries: Senegalese, Malians, Ivoriens, Algerians, Congolese (Brazzaville), Moroccans, Tunisians, Haitians, Martinicans and Guadeloupeans in France; Egyptians, Sudanese, Ghanaians, Nigerians, Kenyans, South Africans, Jamaicans, Trinidadians, Guyanese, and Barbadians in England; Angolans, Mozambicans, Cape Verdians, and Brazilians in Portugal; Surinamese in the Netherlands; Congolese (Kinshasa), Burundis, and Rwandans in Belgium; Ethiopians, Eritreans, Libyans, and Somalis in Italy; and Rio Mundis and Peruvians in Spain. Africans from virtually all parts of the continent settled in the United States during the colonial era and after World War II.

An important aspect of the older (slave-based) diaspora up to the 1880s is that it occurred before the partition of Africa, and thus manifested a consciousness of the continent as a whole and not as reflected by contemporary boundaries and new country labels. Most of the African descendants abroad at that time, therefore, remained essentially un-free and "stateless," without a common country, language, religion, or culture. Their strength as a people was their collective memory of a common African origin, a common and transformative socioeconomic condition abroad, a legacy of return efforts, and a transnational network affirmative of them as a people, all of which continue to shape their identity in the diaspora.

Descendants of Africans abroad developed their cultural and political bonds as they evolved into people with nationally competitive occupational and communication skills, social and economic status, and access to decision-making bodies in their adopted countries. The degree to which the local political system was decentralized and allowed Africans abroad and their descendants to exert pressure at different levels in that system affected the extent of their influence. In the United States, for example, political and economic power came slowly for African Americans for well-known historical reasons. Racial discrimination and segregation, personal and institutional, were designed to limit the influence of blacks. Nevertheless, the Pan-African movement led by Henry Sylvester Williams of Trinidad, W. E. B. DuBois of the United States, Marcus Garvey of Jamaica, and others established an international framework for and promoted a consciousness of both national and global mobilization of African peoples, and it provided a sense of pride and the opportunities for participation in state-oriented structures and environments.

Italy's invasion and occupation of Ethiopia enhanced a global Pan-African sentiment that spurred a number of less well-known organizations and leaders in Pan-African movements abroad that deserve to be better known for the important roles they played in that international effort. In the United States key players in those efforts included the Ethiopian Research Council and the Ethiopian World Federation, led by Malaku Bayen of Ethiopia and William Leo Hansberry of the United States, which published the *Voice of Ethiopia*, a Pan-African cultural and political publication; the Council on African Affairs, led by Max Yergan (who had spent over fifteen years in South Africa and continued to represent the All African Convention as its secretary of external affairs), W. E. B. DuBois, and Paul Robeson; and the National Association for the Advancement of Colored People and its publication, the *Crisis*. In France, the Society for African Culture, led by the Senegalese Alioune Diop, published *Presence Africaine*, and an affiliated organization, the American Society for African Culture in the United States, led by John A. Davis, published the *African Forum*. In England, the International Friends of Ethiopia was organized by the Trinidadian C. L. R. James, and the Pan-African Publishing Company was organized by the Guyanese Ras Makonnen; Makonnen also joined James, Peter Abrahams of South Africa, Isaac Wallace-Johnson of Sierra Leone, and Kwame Nkrumah of Ghana to form the Pan-African Federation that convened the historic Fifth Pan-African Congress in 1945. These and other entities and individuals paved the way structurally and ideologically for the emergence of many subsequent organizations, including TransAfrica, the major lobby for African and Caribbean issues in the United States. Indeed, many of these groups, well and less-well known, served as training grounds for Africans and their descendants, enhanced their knowledge of world affairs, reinforced their language skills, provided experience in financial arrangements and the media, and influenced the organization of their political parties and ultimately the Organization of African Unity (now the African Union), thus legitimizing their legacy as a force in world politics for Africa and its diaspora.

The dynamics of the black nationalism in the African world during the latter part of the twentieth century transformed the meaning of identity in the African diaspora. Whereas the older slave-derived diaspora was essentially "stateless" and relied primarily on an Africa remembered for its identity, the era of African independence from the late 1950s created a consciousness of new nations, symbols, names, and ideologies. The older diaspora was and still is often challenged to make hard choices between conflicting interests, not only within the global diaspora community but also between the diaspora and particular African countries or governments. Moreover, before the 1960s, continental Africans dealt with the diaspora through nongovernmental organizations, whereas after independence African and Caribbean leaders have had to negotiate their strategic political and economic interests through governments and their representatives, thereby significantly limiting diaspora influence. To some extent, the Congressional Black Caucus in the United States has asserted its influence in a number of instances (the Africa Growth and Opportunities Act, for example) and thus demonstrated how a diaspora constituency can have impact on foreign policy.

Meanwhile, two significant developments have broadened our consciousness of the scope and importance of the African diaspora. First, although the focus of the African diaspora has been on Europe and the Americas, communities of African descent in Asia are gaining increased attention. An African Pakistani, Mohammad Siddiq Mussafar, wrote about the slave experience in Pakistan and discussed enslavement in the United States. He identified Frederick Douglass and Booker T. Washington as *shidis*, the term that defined him and others of African descent. He also referred to Tuskegee Institute (University) as a model for Pakistanis of African descent. That book had a limited circulation and is now rare.[5]

From 1971, when *The African Presence in Asia: Consequences of the African Slave Trade* was published, no other book of that scope and type was published until 1995, when two books were published by Indian researchers—*The African Dispersal in the Deccan*, by Shanti Sadiq Ali, and *Africans in India: From Slavery to Royalty*, by R. R. S. Chauhan. In 2006 The African Diaspora in Asia (TADIA) convened with UNESCO the first regional conference of Siddis (descendants of Africans), at which scholars and other researchers from around the world gathered to assess the status of and discuss ways of assisting the diaspora in Asia. TADIA has produced a long list of researchers, Siddi communities and their leaders, as well as a substantial bibliography. TADIA also is in the process of organizing itself as a sustaining international network, and plans to hold its second conference in Mozambique in 2008.[6]

The second development is the initiative of the African Union (AU), which has established the Conference of Intellectuals in Africa and the Diaspora (CIAD) to broaden mutual understanding and foster greater cooperation in the development of African and diaspora countries. In this regard the AU seeks "continuous, sustained and constructive engagement of intellectuals and policy makers." The first of these conferences convened in Senegal in 2004 and the second met in Brazil in 2006. The CIAD's "Strategic Plan, 2004–2007" calls for the mobilization of "all segments of the African population" and recognizes that the "Diaspora is a particularly important and vital segment in this regard." It therefore appeals to this constituency to provide "the requisite scientific, technological and financial resources and expertise for the successful management of the programmes of the African Union Commission."[7]

These developments constitute major challenges for Africa and its global diaspora, especially in view of the contemporary demographics of that diaspora which continues to expand and practice its ethnic cultures as manifested in ethnic-language newspapers, journals, ceremonies, and social organizations. These increasingly provide the older diaspora with perspectives of the new Africa and facilitate links to it. These two diasporas, old and new, confront the continuing transformative process of socialization in their adopted countries. In addition, the new diaspora is acquiring greater recognition and influence in its original homeland with remittances to families in Africa as well as support to agencies and organizations in the diaspora. However, the older diaspora still holds sway because of its larger numbers, pool of expertise, institutions of higher education, and other historically black-oriented organizations committed to freedom and human rights.

While some of these initiatives are embryonic, all of them are extensions of the Pan-Africanism stemming from the legacy of Williams and DuBois and could become the twenty-first century's greatest challenge for the global African diaspora.

NOTES

1. Edith R. Sanders, "The Hamitic Hypothesis: Its Origins and Functions in Time Perspective," *Journal of African History* 10, no. 4 (1969), remains a valuable source for this subject. See also Joseph E. Harris, *Africans and Their History*, rev. ed. (New York: Meridian, 1998), ch. 1.

2. Joseph E. Harris, *Global Dimensions of the African Diaspora*, rev. ed. (Washington, D.C.: Howard University Press, 1988).

3. W. E. B. DuBois, *Souls of Black Folk* (New York: Fawsett, 1961); William H. Shack and Elliott P. Skinner, *Strangers in African Societies* (Berkeley: University of California Press, 1979); Elliott P. Skinner, "The New African Immigrant and United States Foreign Policy," *The Ambassadors Review* (fall 1998): 116–23.

4. For the global slave trades from Africa, see Joseph E. Harris, The African Diaspora Map-1, 1990. A. I. Asiwaju, *Partitioned Africans: Ethnic Relations Across Africa's International Boundaries,1884–1994* (New York: St. Martin's Press, 1985), is highly recommended for an analysis of contemporary issues stemming from the Berlin Conference of 1884–85.

5. Mohammad Siddiq Mussafar, *An Eye-Opening Account of Slavery and Freedom* (Pakistan, 1954), written in Sidhi and translated for me by my late colleague at Howard University, Dr. Mohammed Feroz.

6. Joseph E. Harris, *The African Presence in Asia: Consequences of the East African Slave Trade* (Evanston, Ill.: Northwestern University, 1971). Although the following two books focus on only India, they represent major contributions to the literature on the diaspora in Asia: Shanti Sadiq Ali, *The African Dispersal in the Deccan* (New Delhi: Orient Longman,1995) and R. R. S. Chauhan, *Africans*

in India: From Slavery to Royalty (New Delhi: Asian Publication Services, 1995). For TADIA, consult its Web site, www.TADIA.org.

7. Commission of the African Union, "Strategic Plan of the Commission of the African Union, Strategic Framework," vol. 2, 2004–2007, the seventh key idea, p. 25.

African American Studies in Libraries: Collection Development and Management Priorities

Howard Dodson

I N DECEMBER 1916, A GROUP OF BLACK BIBLIOPHILES GATHERED AT THE WASHING-ton, D.C., residence of John Wesley Cromwell to explore the feasibility of establishing the Negro Book Collectors Exchange. The occasion was the annual meeting of the American Negro Academy, an association of African American "men of Science, letters and art or those distinguished in other walks of life" founded in the nation's capital in March 1897. The academy's purpose was to encourage research, writing, and publication of scholarly works dealing with the global African experience. Its members were also encouraged to develop an archive of materials by and about peoples of African descent. Cromwell, a bibliophile and amateur historian, was a founding member of the academy, and its first meeting had been held in his home.

The book exchange would have a more limited goal: "to centralize all literature written by colored people." In attendance were bibliophiles John Edward Bruce, Henry Proctor Slaughter, the Reverend Charles Douglass Martin, Dr. Jesse F. Moorland, Daniel Alexander Payne Murray, and Arturo Alfonso Schomburg. To achieve their objectives, members proposed to ask all the known "Negro book collectors" to register themselves as well as the titles and authors in their collection with the exchange. Equipped with this master database, which we would call a worldwide union list of books by and about people of African descent, the exchange would then serve as a comprehensive clearinghouse of information on black-related material as well as a vehicle to facilitate the trading of duplicate copies among its members. There is no evidence that the Negro Book Collectors Exchange ever met again, much less formally carried out its ambitious agenda. Informally, members continued to exchange information about their collections and to assist one another in acquiring copies of fugitive titles, including duplicates, from their respective collections.[1]

Those of us who have inherited these collections or are responsible for continuing to collect and preserve materials documenting the African experience still have not solved the communications problem that impeded the efforts of our predecessors. Informally, we continue to share information about recent acquisitions. Occasionally, we make duplicate copies of rare books available to sister institutions. The publication and dissemination of our respective catalogues have helped us inform ourselves and the library world of the nature of our holdings. Membership in cooperative bibliographic services, such as the Research Library Information Network (RLIN) and the Online Computer Library Center (OCLC), has extended access to our most recent acquisitions. Although most of us participate in these networks, there still is no organized, systematic program for development and preservation among the major research libraries and special collections with primary responsibility for collecting black-related materials. As a consequence, we are not prepared to respond to the research, information, and technological challenges of the twenty-first century.

Our collection development strategies run the risk of being trapped in a paradigmatic framework that is rapidly losing its centrality if not usefulness in defining the field of African American studies. Even as we have become parts of cooperative networks, we have continued to function as though we believe that each of our collections could, if we work hard enough to this end, become self-sufficient repositories of publications and information on the black experience, capable in and of themselves of addressing the research and information needs of our respective clienteles. Furthermore, escalating costs and shrinking budgets notwithstanding, we continue to expend scarce revenues duplicating certain holdings or competing for rare and unique items (thereby escalating the costs). A modern version of the Negro Book Collectors Exchange would likely help us begin to address the latter problems. The issue of an outmoded framework, however, requires some fundamental rethinking of our mission and the scope of our development, preservation, and access responsibilities.

A publication by Ruth Simms Hamilton, "Toward a Paradigm for African Diaspora Studies: Research Questions and Strategies,"[2] brought me face-to-face with the realization that most of the material contained in research libraries and other repositories that have been documenting the black experience over the past half century or so was collected, managed, and preserved to respond to the political and intellectual problems of a different age. Those priorities and strategies require radical revisions in light of contemporary research questions raised by Dr. Hamilton and the African Diaspora Research Project. Stated more bluntly, her proposed paradigm necessitates more comprehensive and collaborative development, management, and documentation strategies than were required at any previous stage of research on the global African experience. I will review the dominant intellectual and political frameworks that have informed our collecting activities. I will then contrast these with those that are implicit in the new paradigm. I will conclude by suggesting some of the ways that technology can help us prepare to meet the challenge of the twenty-first century.

THE EARLY COLLECTIONS

It is likely that the bibliophiles who organized the first exchange shared the philosophy of collection development articulated in the constitution of the Negro Society for Historical Research. Founded in 1911 by John E. Bruce and Arturo Schomburg, this society sought "to collect useful historical data relating to the Negro race, books written by or about Negroes, rare pictures of prominent men and women, letters of noted Negroes or white men friendly to the Negro, African curios of native manufacture etc." The society's purpose was "to show that the Negro race has a history which antedates that of the proud Anglo Saxon race." Its founders were committed to collecting books, manuscripts, and other historical data to support their claims regarding the antiquity of the Negro race and its contributions to world civilization.[3]

St. Clair Drake, a professor of anthropology at Stanford University and a longtime student of the African diaspora, frequently referred to the development of the "vindicationist school" of black intellectuals that emerged during the late-nineteenth century in the United States. Through their research, writing, and publications, these authors sought to defend people of African descent against charges of racial inferiority and historical and cultural insignificance. Selectively drawing evidence of black people's intellectual and social development and their contributions to world civilization from published sources, photographs, art, and other documentary resources, the vindicationists helped establish the tradition of black scholarship as a resource in blacks' struggle for freedom and human dignity.

By the turn of the twentieth century, another network of vindicationist collectors had emerged in the African American community. The bibliophiles who attended the first exchange meeting were active members of this network. Two aspects of their collecting activities are significant for our purposes. First, all of them collected globally, although selectively. Their aim was to acquire and preserve the best publications and art produced by black people and the most significant evidence of black achievement worldwide. Second, the collections of several of these individuals were the foundations on which most of today's major black research libraries and special collections in the United States were built. Daniel Alexander Murray's collection became one of the bases for the Africana holdings at the Library of Congress. Jesse Moorland's collection laid the foundations for the Moorland-Spingarn Research Center. The black holdings at Atlanta University include the Slaughter collection. And, of course, the materials gathered by Arturo Schomburg and John E. Bruce provide the foundations for the Schomburg Center for Research in Black Culture in New York.

Of equal significance, the early development of these collections, which consisted primarily of books, was guided by a concern for correcting the impression that black people were inferior to whites. Over the years, all the collections have expanded their scope to include a wide array of material (both positive and negative) by and about people of African descent. But the dominant paradigm, a product of late-nineteenth and early-twentieth-century intellectual and political concerns, has remained intact.

The closest thing to an alternative approach was established by the field of Afro-American studies as defined and interpreted by Melville J. Herskovits during the 1940s.[4] His principal concern was to document the presence of Africanisms in the New World and the processes through which African, European, and Native American cultures exerted mutual influence on one another in this hemisphere. Unlike the dominant paradigm, the new Afro-American studies discipline was based in anthropology rather than history. Interdisciplinary and comparative in approach, its method was ethnohistory. As such, unlike the dominant approach, it was as concerned (perhaps more) with black mass-based social groups as it was with black leaders and elites in various fields of human endeavor. Collections developed to support research in this field included published literature, but photographs, artifacts, sound recordings, film, oral history interviews, and other forms of documentation were also gathered from both sides of the Atlantic.

Initially concerned with establishing the historical derivation and forms of African diasporan cultures, Afro-American studies introduced such research concepts as retention, reinterpretation, and syncretism. In so doing, it pointed up the dynamic quality of African-derived cultures in the Americas. Among the principal questions the field placed on the research agenda were the causes of the diversity of African people in the hemisphere. How did Africans accommodate themselves to their new environments during slavery? How did this process work out in different parts of the Americas, where differing ecological settings, basic industries, and

cultural orientations prevailed? How did class differentials influence the accommodation process?[5] Herskovits and his colleagues raised these questions in the 1930s
and 1940s and worked on many of them until the 1950s, when Herskovits turned his
attention to the study of Africa. These kinds of questions would not be taken up
again until the late 1960s, with the renewed interest in comparative studies of slave
societies in the Americas.

AFRO-AMERICAN STUDIES AND THE NEW AFRICAN DIASPORA PARADIGM

I am a part of that generation of the 1960s and 1970s that raised fundamental questions about the adequacy of what we then called "Negro history" for addressing the
intellectual and political needs of the post–civil rights phase of black Americans'
struggle for freedom and human dignity. The development of "black history" as a
critical alterative to "Negro history" paralleled the development of black studies or
Afro-American studies programs and departments at U.S. colleges and universities.
Rejecting Negro history's liberal, integrationist political outlook, this new black history also posed questions of the black American and American experience that had
not been on the agenda of Negro history or vindicationists. The new black history,
we maintained, had to be expansive enough to accommodate the experiences of the
masses of black people as well as the political and social elite—men and women of
achievement. Women and children as well as men had to be included. The class and
ethnic diversity of African Americans needed to be reflected. Of greatest significance,
black people, like all human beings, needed to be viewed as history- and culture-
makers in their own right, rather than mere participants in or objects of established
definitions of American historical and cultural processes. The new black American
history was seen as a critique of the traditional approaches to the study of both Negro
and American history. Firmly committed to developing new insights into the
processes of historical and cultural transformation that characterized the black
American particularity, it was also committed to contributing to the process of
redefining and rewriting American history. Its separatist agenda was both a means
to an end and an end in itself. Undergirding these formulations was the assumption
that black American and American history were part of a broader, dynamic, global
process of development and underdevelopment, transformation and change.

What is attractive to me about the African diaspora paradigm is that it applies
many of these same principles to the study of diasporan social formations around

the globe. It establishes a framework in which both the historical and contemporary dynamics of the diverse diasporan communities can be viewed. It provides a paradigm for comparative study of these communities as a means of discerning the areas of commonality and difference that exist among people of African descent worldwide.

By viewing African peoples in diasporan settings as actors and subjects in history- and culture-making processes, criteria are established for measuring both the change occurring within the diaspora and the economic, political, cultural, and social influence of the diaspora on the communities and nations in which people of African descent reside. Recognizing this experience as a global phenomenon, the paradigm seeks to analyze the historical, cultural, social, and contemporary thought and behavior of diaspora peoples in the context of the world political economy.[6]

This new framework combines the very best elements of black American history with the questions about group formation and change that informed Herskovits's concept of Afro-American studies at the peak of its development. Whereas the earlier research paradigms (and the collections they engendered) were consciously elitist and relatively limited in scope because of their explicit or implicit political agenda, the new approach must, of necessity, be more expansive and comprehensive. Studying the inner dynamic of African diaspora communities requires documentation and analysis of all the social subgroups that compose them. Social and cultural change are viewed as interactive processes in which all elements of the social formation are participants. Whereas the vindicationists focused on elites and the Afro-Americanists concentrated on sectors of the masses, the new paradigm requires that both of these as well as their gender, class, and color elements be treated as part of the analysis.

Relations between African diaspora communities and their host society as well as the broader global political economy also require more expansive and comprehensive documentation strategies and conceptual frameworks than was the case in the vindicationist and Afro-Americanist models. This is especially true if we are to reach new understanding of the consequences of the diaspora's economic, political, and social action on itself and its sociopolitical environment. The points of intersection between diaspora peoples and the host society in key areas of political and social action require much more sophisticated documentation strategies than anything we have known in the past. Whereas both the vindicationists and Afro-Americanists were content to identify evidence of the "contributions" blacks had made to American and world society, the new paradigm insists that we go beyond a notion of positivist contributions and seek to understand the consequences—both intended and unintended—of the purposive action of African diaspora peoples.

Documenting the internal and external dynamics of the diaspora's historical and cultural development poses major challenges to our traditional collection development strategies. Focusing on the diaspora experience in the Western Hemisphere and its relationship to the development of Afro-American studies, I will now consider some of the short-term implications for libraries.

IMPLICATIONS FOR LIBRARIES

Libraries are challenged to develop more comprehensive and more balanced collections on the African diaspora experience. Of special urgency is the need to intensify our collecting of retrospective book titles on that experience, especially on blacks in Latin America and the Caribbean. We need to begin to think of our collections in hemispheric terms. Certainly, high on our acquisitions lists should be anything and everything we can find on the Afro-Brazilian experience. Brazil has the second-largest black population in the world (exceeded only by Nigeria). In the Western Hemisphere, Brazil was the first major importer of African slave labor; it also was the largest importer (accounting for about 40 percent of the estimated ten million brought to the New World) and had the oldest and longest running slavery system until abolition in 1888. It remains one of the most vibrant centers of traditional African culture in the Americas, and virtually every aspect of Brazilian culture bears the stamp of the African presence.

The Caribbean, the center of the sugar plantation economy and the hemisphere's second-largest importer of enslaved Africans, also merits greater attention in our collection development and preservation priorities. The French, Spanish, and Dutch colonies established on these islands and along the coasts of the Caribbean Sea are virtual laboratories for the comparative study of the processes of cultural transformation that occurred in the Americas. Moreover, the migration of residents of the Caribbean basin to Central and South America, the United States, and European metropolises both during and after slavery has had an extraordinary influence on the cultural landscape and economic and social processes of the receiving societies. Works documenting both aspects of this Caribbean diasporan phenomenon should be added to our collections, and courses on these subjects should become part of our curricula.

Finally, the Afro-Hispanic experience should receive greater attention than it has in the past. Works documenting the historical and cultural roles of African peoples in colonial Spanish America are available in greater abundance than for any previous period of diaspora history. These materials should be collected comprehensively to the extent that budgets and other resources allow. As is the case in Afro-Brazilian studies, works on the Afro-Hispanic experience tend to focus on the slavery period. The post-emancipation diaspora experience in the Americas has, with a few noteworthy exceptions, been sorely neglected by scholars. While the foundations of diaspora culture in the Americas were laid during slavery, it was during the period after emancipation that the greatest change occurred. We are challenged, then, to collect and provide access to as much of this information as is available. It is likely that many of the retrospective materials needed to fill the void are out of print and unavailable. Should this prove to be the case, we may have to rethink our relationship to the collections of research repositories (especially comprehensive research libraries) and the major on-line bibliographic services.

The Schomburg Center, for example, is currently involved in a survey project to identify African diaspora and African-related materials in the collections of the other research centers of the New York Public Library. They were founded before the Schomburg Center and have been collecting black-related materials on other parts of the hemisphere since the library's inception. In many instances, the collections on Latin America and the Caribbean or general holdings pertaining to these areas contain a substantial amount of relevant material. More often than not, it was not catalogued in such a way as to provide subject access to its black-related content. Most comprehensive research libraries with large retrospective collections do not have plans to initiate large-scale retroconversion or recataloguing in the immediate future. In the interim, projects can identify and recatalogue discrete black-related segments of such retrospective holdings, providing better subject access to them, and enter them into the national on-line databases. The overall objective of the Schomburg's project is to do just that.

Collecting, preserving, and providing access to serials on these subjects poses a different set of problems. Newspapers, periodicals, newsletters, and other serials have been published by people of African descent throughout the hemisphere at least since the nineteenth century. The Historical Society of Wisconsin, which currently houses one of the largest collections of African American newspapers published in the United States, recently initiated a project to establish a national union list of holdings in this area. The project should go a long way toward filling the gaps in our knowledge about how many of these kinds of materials have survived and are available for research purposes. A long-term objective of the society apparently is to issue microform editions of the most significant bodies of these materials so they can be distributed more widely.

I am not aware of any comparable project for serials published by blacks in Latin America and the Caribbean. As daily, weekly, or monthly chronicles of black thought and behavior in these parts of the diaspora, such publications are invaluable resources for the study of history and culture. The Schomburg Center recently acquired what is likely the only extant complete run of the *Panamá Tribune*, the voice of the West Indian community there during most of this century. Every aspect of West Indian life in Panamá is covered by this newspaper. Publications of longer and shorter run for all the Caribbean islands as well as Brazil and other South and Central American countries need to be identified, collected, preserved, and disseminated as comprehensively as possible.

Nowhere is the need for collaborative approaches more obvious (or possible) than in the area of current serials. The duplication of effort in the collection and preservation of these materials is likely enormous. Acquiring and preserving serials is a huge drain on our budgets, but we have not yet taken any serious steps toward developing collaborative initiatives. The time is right to do just that. With a minimal level of planning and coordination among the dozen or so research libraries and special collections that systematically acquire serials relevant to the African diaspora, we should be able to develop a comprehensive joint strategy. Each participant would assume responsibility for a selected or assigned area. Either microform copies could be made available to collaborating members at cost, or facsimile copies of articles could be provided on demand.

The Schomburg Center has initiated a project to catalogue and recatalogue all its retrospective serials holdings. We also are reevaluating our serials acquisition and preservation policies. We would welcome the opportunity to meet with sister institutions that collect in these areas to see how best we can tackle these nettlesome (and costly) problems.

The major challenge facing libraries and the field of African American studies in documenting the diaspora experience in the Americas lies in identifying, preserving, and providing access to the primary research resources that are essential to new scholarship in this field. The preservation and documentation problems are at least hemispheric in scope. I say "at least" because significant bodies of primary materials exist in the libraries, museums, and national, colonial, and religious archives of the major European colonizers. This suggests that, in addition to a collection development strategy, we may need a comprehensive strategy for identifying and providing access to a massive but as yet relatively inaccessible corpus of manuscript and archival records, organizational records, personal papers, photographs, prints, and ephemera. These may either lie buried in repositories in this hemisphere and in Europe or be stored in at-risk environments—attics or basements in old buildings, churches, monasteries, private residences, and offices—where they are not receiving proper care and are not accessible to researchers. In addition, as in the case of books and serials in existing repositories, records in general collections on countries with a significant African diaspora population need to be revisited and updated to provide improved subject access to black-related items.

The magnitude and complexity of identifying and preserving an adequate record of the African diaspora in this hemisphere suggests the need to develop a comprehensive documentation strategy. This generally is defined as a local, state, regional, national, or international plan to ensure the adequate documentation of ongoing multi-institutional issues, activities, functions, or subjects.[7] As noted above, primary research materials on the diaspora experience in the Americas are likely to exist in provincial, state, and national archives throughout the hemisphere as well as in European repositories (especially colonial archives). Finally, significant resources are probably to be found in the records of religious and secular organizations. The documentation strategy should include at least five major components: identification and preservation of relevant research materials in existing repositories; dissemination of microform copies of the most significant of these records; identification of relevant materials not currently housed in an archive or other preservation environment; development of a hemispheric union list of all relevant materials; and establishment an ongoing cooperative program among various organizations to ensure the continued documentation of the diaspora phenomenon.

COLLECTIONS MANAGEMENT AND ACCESS

In the past, libraries and archival institutions defined themselves primarily in terms of their holdings and saw themselves as relatively self-sufficient entities. The information explosion over the past two decades and the technological advances in information science that are occurring almost daily suggest, however, that all libraries and repositories will be forced to rethink their identity, mission, and approaches if they are to fulfill their public service responsibility to their clientele. Since few institutions can any longer consider themselves comprehensive repositories on any subject, the challenge to libraries is to carve out areas of specialization, refine collection scopes and levels, and position themselves within a network of complimentary institutions that can provide them and their clients with access to materials that they do not collect. Libraries of the future likely will be more defined by the access they can provide to information requested by clients than by the specific materials they house. The challenge of the moment is to establish access to bibliographic records on given subjects and enter into cooperative arrangements with complimentary institutions that can provide access to information.

Among the institutions documenting the diaspora experience in the Americas, the Schomburg Center for Research in Black Culture of the New York Public Library and the Moorland-Spingarn Research Center at Howard University have the strongest and most comprehensive collections. Libraries responsible for supporting African American studies programs and departments on college and university campuses are not likely to have comparable resources. Yet, students and scholars working in the field need access to the collections of these two research centers, as well as to those of the Library of Congress, the National Archives, the Smithsonian Institution, and other major collecting entities.

A small percentage of the holdings in these repositories is being disseminated widely in microform. The National Archives has pioneered in this area and continues to issue on microfilm major manuscripts on African American themes. The Schomburg Center also has been aggressively publishing and disseminating microform editions. To date, its Dictionary Catalog, a selection of pre–twentieth-century books, its clipping file, and about a dozen of its manuscript holdings are available in microfilm or microfiche.

It is likely, however, that other means of dissemination will have to be put in place if African American studies programs and departments are to have access on campus to the collections of these major repositories. It appears to me that this is technologically possible by relying more heavily on the on-line bibliographic services; by taking greater advantage of CD-ROM technology for providing access to fugitive materials within the collections; and by using telefacsimile technology to supply copies of documents, published records, photographs, and other materials.

As of 1994, about 90 percent of the Schomburg Center's processed collections had been catalogued in the RLIN and OCLC databases. A retrospective conversion project is currently transferring our pre-1972 records to electronic formats. A special collections access project is cataloguing manuscript and archival records, sheet music, playscripts, photographs, prints, artwork, sound recordings, motion pictures, videotapes, and oral history materials for the RLIN database. These records will then be downloaded into OCLC. All member institutions of these bibliographic services will thus have access to records on 90 percent of our holdings.

Two CD-ROM products are being planned. The first, the *Kaiser Index to Black Resources: 1948–1986*, is a selected bibliographic guide to serials records and ephemera at the Schomburg Center. We are currently equipped to provide copies of these materials. The second is a cumulative electronic version of *Black Studies*, a bibliographic guide to the center's acquisitions from 1973 to 1992. The added advantage of the CD-ROM formats is the rapid subject access they provide.

Finally, the Schomburg Center is exploring the feasibility of establishing formal relationships either with African American studies programs directly or with their supporting libraries. The intent is to provide ongoing access to the center's collections using various technologies as they become available and applicable. The collection management challenges facing libraries in support of African American studies in university settings are manifold.

NOTES

1. See Elinor Des Verney Sinnette, *Arthur Alfonso Schomburg: Black Bibliophile and Collector* (Detroit: Wayne State University Press, 1989), 73–74, for a discussion of the origins of the Negro Book Collectors Exchange.

2. Ruth Simms Hamilton, ed., *Creating a Paradigm and Research Agenda for Comparative Studies of the Worldwide Dispersion of African Peoples* (East Lansing: African Diaspora Research Project, Michigan State University, 1990), 15–26.

3. See Sinnette, *Schomburg*, 43.

4. See Melville J. Herskovits, "Problem, Method and Theory in Afroamerican Studies," *Afroamerica* 1 (1945): 5–24, and "The Present Status and Needs of Afroamerican Research," *Journal of Negro History* 36, no. 2, reprinted in *The New World Negro*, ed. Frances S. Herskovits (Bloomington: Indiana University Press, 1966), 23–41, 43–61.

5. Ibid.

6. Hamilton, *Creating a Paradigm*.

7. For a discussion of documentation strategies in libraries and archives, see Helen Willa Samuels, "Who Controls the Past?" *American Archivist* 49 (spring 1986): 109–24; and Larry J. Hackman and Joan Warnow-Blewett, "The Documentation Strategy Process: A Model and Case Study," *American Archivist* 50 (winter 1987): 12–47.

Two Academic Programs in the African Diaspora: Afro-Brazilian Studies and U.S. Africana Studies

Milfred C. Fierce

THIS DISCUSSION HAS THREE INTERRELATED PURPOSES. THE FIRST IS TO describe Afro-Brazilian studies programs at four universities in Brazil.[1] The second is to stimulate thinking about the evolution of Africana studies programs in the United States and in Brazil. In a larger sense, this touches on the dynamics of race and race relations in the two countries. The third purpose is to observe developments in these programs in the two countries outside Africa with the largest black populations, in the context of the African diaspora.

There are three reasons for focusing on Brazil. First, because of the enormous black and mulatto population, the influence of African culture, especially on religion, is pervasive in Brazil. Second, U.S. Africana studies have largely ignored this major center of the African diaspora. Third, Brazil often is perceived as a European-dominated vacation paradise in which blacks are either nonexistent or invisible, but this view is much too simplistic. In this extremely complex multicultural community, the subject of race relations has enjoyed no fruitful internal debate.

This study combines the historical method (the U.S. component) with empirical research through on-site interviews (in Brazil). In both countries, documents, books, college catalogs, and ephemera were consulted.

Finally, the term *African diaspora* requires some comment, since its meaning varies widely among scholars. Some see it as an extension of African history and heritage. Others minimize the centrality of Africa and emphasize the uniqueness of the diaspora experience. Professor John G. Jackson dedicates his book, *Introduction to*

African Civilization, "to all people of African descent, the entire human race." Quarrels will continue among specialists over the best definition, and it is not the intention of this essay to engage in or settle that debate.

BRAZIL AND THE UNITED STATES: SIMILARITIES AND DIFFERENCES IN RACE RELATIONS

Brazil and the United States are the two best laboratories in the world for the study of relations between blacks and whites. Historically and today they offer the best examples of large groups of these populations living together. Slavery was abolished in both countries in the second half of the twentieth century, in 1865 in the United States, and in 1888 in Brazil. A brutal and bloody civil war brought emancipation in the United States, whereas abolition came grudgingly but without war in Brazil. Early in their respective histories, Brazil was dominated by the Portuguese and the United States by the British, heritages that still manifest in the language and much of the national culture of the two countries. The legacy of slavery continues to intrude upon many aspects of Brazilian and U.S. society—economic, political, and social.

Although race relations have taken different paths in the United States and Brazil, both countries are experiencing an ongoing challenge to end discrimination. In the United States, the early decades of the past century were characterized by widespread racial segregation, but during World War II, when industrial employment opportunities increased for African Americans, many of the previous racial barriers began to break down. After the war, inspired by the ideals of freedom expressed so eloquently by W. E. B. DuBois, Winston Churchill, Franklin D. Roosevelt, and others, black organizations accelerated the pace of African American confrontation with bigotry and racism. Further inspiration was provided when the nations of Africa and the Caribbean shook off the yoke of colonialism in the 1950s and 1960s, realizing a degree of their own self-determination and liberation. In the mid-twentieth century, black leaders, organizations, and people in the United States drew the attention of the world to the nation's civil rights revolution. From it came government-enforced equal employment opportunities and, later, affirmative action policies in the public and private sectors.

In Brazil, official government policy was to deny the existence of race prejudice and promote the image of an idyllic, color-blind society. Beginning in 1964, the leaders of the military regime persistently repressed the efforts of Afro-Brazilians to raise consciousness about socioeconomic conditions and racial discrimination. As a result, the myth of a Brazilian society free of racism was reinforced. The idea of "racial democracy" prevailed until the late 1970s, when its ideological superstructure was eroded by its factual base. By 1979, probably inspired by the U.S. civil rights movement and following the end of military rule, the people of Brazil began to enjoy new freedom of expression in a changing climate of democratization. One consequence was the re-emergence of Afro-Brazilian consciousness groups focused on the common problems of the nation's black community.

Seventy to eighty million blacks and people of mixed race make Brazil the country with the world's largest population of people of African descent. The depressing socioeconomic profile of this population virtually ensures a movement to gain equality sooner or later, roughly comparable to the one that occurred in the United States. In 1980, the first Brazilian census in thirty years to include race categories provided preponderant evidence of racial discrimination. The illiteracy rate among Afro-Brazilians was more than twice that of whites. Among the 4 percent of Brazilians who were college graduates, 0.6 percent were black. Average annual income for white males was double that of black men. Black workers were generally and disproportionately working jobs that required the least skills and paid the lowest salaries, such as domestic services, farm work, and construction labor. In May 1988, the *Washington Post* reported that the wealth of the top 1 percent in Brazil equaled that of the poorest 50 percent; those in the latter category were overwhelmingly black. In 1989, seven of the 559 members of the Brazilian congress were black, and half of the black members eschewed issues and problems related to race. No blacks are large landowners or generals in the military. The urban violence of the early 1980s in Brazil has been characterized as a civil war pitting unemployed black youths against middle-class whites.[2]

Too much can be made of comparisons between blacks in Brazil and those the United States. Measuring the progress of one, or the lack thereof, against the other misses the point. To explain existing disparities, more useful comparison is made with others in the same society, subject to a relatively common set of historical, governance, and other experiences. For example, in the United States, some analysts identify real gains in the past twenty-five years, pointing to black caucuses in Congress and state legislatures, a black governor in Virginia, black mayors in major cities (including New York, Los Angeles, and Chicago), black cabinet officers, and black pacesetters in arts, entertainment, the media, and academia. General Colin Powell, the first black to chair the Joint Chiefs of Staff, and Jesse Jackson, who made credible runs for the Democratic presidential nominations in 1984 and 1988, bear witness to a sea change in U.S. race relations in the space of a single generation.

Critics note that the gains in the United States have not trickled down to the larger black community. For example, in 1990 the National Urban League reported that family poverty was three times greater for blacks than for whites, and that at the current rate of change it will be 169 years before the gap is closed. Drugs, AIDS, homelessness, poor health care, limited educational opportunities, and underemployment and unemployment plague U.S. blacks disproportionately compared to whites. A frequently cited variation on Henry Ford's famous dictum about the U.S. economy captures the view of many: When America sneezes, blacks catch pneumonia. Equality and parity, the twin goals of the civil rights crusade, are still generations away from being realized.

Apologists for Brazil's glaring inequities maintain that the problems are grounded in class, not race. Reminiscent of the "growth hypothesis" advanced first in South Africa, this line of argument contends that economic growth will bring expanded opportunities, and race-based discrimination will fade. From this standpoint, the mobilization of individuals and organizations around race and black solidarity as a "legitimate means of collective identity and political action" is criticized. Indeed, blacks who do mobilize are viewed as troublemakers and racists. Such a perception relieves the government and whites generally from partial responsibility for the condition of Afro-Brazilians.

The topic of race is perhaps more complicated and controversial in Brazil than anywhere else in the world. There has been little significant national debate about race in Brazil, in part because its importance in social mobility has long been denied, and also because widespread racial mixing has rendered the term "black" imprecise and suspect. It is reported that one Brazilian survey used 125 different colloquialisms for "blacks." In common usage are such categories as mulatto, light mulatto, medium mulatto, and dark mulatto. There is a dearth of documentation on the disadvantaged position of Afro-Brazilians and of information and analysis on race. Scholars have been discouraged from examining the issue due to the unavailability of research funds and the inherent political risks. Most are not interested in an unpopular subject that is unlikely to bring them peer respect, job security, or promotion. More will be said about the academic climate for such work in Brazil after an examination of the U.S. situation.

U.S. Africana Studies

In U.S. universities, Africana studies refer to examination of the history, politics, culture, and current socioeconomic status of Africans and people of African descent throughout the world. Geographic emphasis may vary considerably from one campus to another. Greatest focus ordinarily is placed on Africa, the United States, the Caribbean, and, to a lesser extent, Brazil. Ideally, Asia, the Pacific Islands, Europe, and anywhere else diaspora peoples are found are included.

Modern Africana studies exploded onto the landscape a generation ago in response to black student and faculty demands at predominantly white universities. The grudging reaction in many cases was to establish a unit labeled black, Afro-American, African American, ethnic, or minority studies. These ranged from fully autonomous tenure-granting departments to tenuous, ill-conceived, and poorly defined centers. Black students and faculty played an unprecedented role in recruitment, retention, and promotion and in university governance and life generally.

The term *black studies* is limited and descriptive. It is also ambiguous. Does black refer to skin color, phenotype, ideology, culture, or something else? Should such a label include individuals or groups other than those of African descent? The descriptions Afro-American studies and African American studies are popular, but they are parochial. Presumably they refer to people of African descent in the United States, but this notion is rejected by many, especially in other areas of the Americas, who argue that they, too, are Afro-Americans.

Africana studies is likewise a confusing and complicated term. Nevertheless, it is used, warts and all, to convey the Pan-African or international dimension in the intent or orientation of many programs. Broad yet definitive, it links diaspora descendants with Africans and the homeland. The term is sometimes confused with Afrikaner, the former ruling white minority in South Africa, especially when it is spoken. Furthermore, many libraries have Africana collections or sections, and these sometimes include items from only continental Africa, though in other cases they include materials from the diaspora, as well. It may be a while before consensus is reached on the most accurate and appropriate label for programs referred to here as Africana studies.

A separate and discrete terminology is African studies, a movement that originated in the United States just after World War II. Officials in the U.S. Department of State and others became concerned about the general lack of knowledge regarding African affairs and what soon were to be independent African nations and especially with the inadequacy of African language instructors. Between 1948 and 1971, nine Title VI National Resource Centers were established in African studies, at Boston, Howard, Indiana, Michigan State, and Northwestern universities, as well as the universities of California at Los Angeles, Florida at Gainesville, Illinois at Urbana, and Wisconsin at Madison. The major professional organization in this field is the African Studies Association (ASA), which publishes the *Journal of African Studies* and is currently headquartered at Emory University in Atlanta, Georgia. The primary concern of the field is with events and policies related to the continent and its fifty or so countries.

Africana studies originated earlier, in the first and second decade of the twentieth century, with the initiatives of W. E. B. DuBois, Carter G. Woodson, and others. These efforts resulted in the Association for the Study of Negro Life and History (ASNLH), the name of which was changed in the early 1970s to the Association for the Study of Afro-American Life and History, (ASALH). Such publications as the *Journal of Negro History* and the *Negro History Bulletin* were established early on; later, the *Journal of Black Studies* was initiated. A watershed in Africana studies occurred in 1969, when a group of "Africanists," several of whom were prominently associated with the black studies movement, after having disagreed with the leadership and direction of the ASA for several years, broke away and formed the African Heritage Studies Association (AHSA). The National Council of Black Studies (NCBS), ASALH, and AHSA are the three major professional organizations for Africana scholars in the United States.

A very important point is that the field of African studies has been led and controlled by whites, whereas Africana studies for the most part are dominated by blacks. Many scholars are active in both, and the relationships between the two programs, ranging from cooperation to tension, differ from one campus to another and sometimes from one department to another. Several campuses have both programs, offering similar courses and competing for the same students and resources. The strain is greatest when faculty and students in either program feel the need to protect their "turf." There also may be conflict over an Afrocentric versus a Eurocentric orientation, and such differences are not easy to iron out.

On the surface, programs that overlap or duplicate seem an enormous waste of precious resources, but the Africana studies movement needs to be understood in the context of the civil rights crusade of the 1960s as well as U.S. race relations in general. Three decades ago there was significant distrust of white scholars and administrators who had failed to provide learning experiences considered relevant by many black faculty and students. Consequently, the latter felt it was necessary to take control of these programs where possible on predominantly white campuses, and because of the long-standing mistrust behind this they are reluctant to relinquish that control.

In summary, the Africana studies movement in the United States has produced an identifiable group of scholars dedicated to teaching and research related to the black experience. Although located under different rubrics and auspices, they are found on almost every campus in the country. This has not happened in Brazil.

AFRO-BRAZILIAN STUDIES

Comprised of twenty-three states, Brazil is a country with many universities. Some are supported by federal or state governments, and some are privately sponsored by the church or others. Only five universities in three states (Bahia, Rio de Janeiro, and São Paulo) are analyzed here, but academics in Brazil indicate that the situation at these institutions is at least comparable to that of others in the country, if not more advanced or progressive. One major difference between Afro-Brazilian studies programs and Africana studies programs in the United States is that the former do not grant degrees, hire and tenure faculty, or participate in university affairs to nearly the same extent.

Another glaring difference is the absence of discernible, phenotypical black professors and students in Afro-Brazilian studies. The small number of black faculty in the field, which means there are few role models, is indicative of the situation in all professions and helps explain the slow and questionable development of Afro-Brazilian studies. Presumably, black professors would be the likely catalysts, and black students would be the natural constituents for such studies. Competition is very keen, however, for college admission, and the public schools that most blacks attend are inferior; blacks are rarely successful in obtaining a university education. The lack of opportunity restricts their chances for upward mobility and feeds the vicious cycle. The small number of black students and faculty in Brazilian academia portends a long wait for the maturation of a Brazilian version of Africana studies.

At the instigation of the Ford Foundation, in the summer and fall of 1986 two meetings of Brazilian scholars interested in Afro-Brazilian studies were held to explore the feasibility of establishing programs on university campuses. The July meeting led to agreement among participants that black Brazilian history and culture were increasingly underemphasized. In addition, it was concluded that larger numbers of black students in universities would increase the demand for Afro-Brazilian studies. It was felt that such studies have "low prestige" in the social sciences, and black groups in Brazil need more, better-informed, and better-trained individuals in order to confront the unique and subtle brand of racial bigotry that exists there.

The follow-up meeting at the State University of Campinas in São Paulo State, attended by a dozen Brazilian historians, anthropologists, and sociologists, resulted in a plan to formulate an undergraduate course in Afro-Brazilian Studies. The course was to be offered in 1987 at the home institution of participants, to stimulate interest in the topic and improve teaching techniques. These specialists then were to visit other campuses, lecturing about and generating interest in Afro-Brazilian studies.

Eventually, the program would attract more students, especially blacks, both filling a substantive void and promoting a stronger black student and faculty presence on Brazilian campuses. The components of this multidisciplinary course, which in essence defined Afro-Brazilian studies, were the slave trade and slavery, the transition to free labor, black culture (especially religion), race relations, and the socioeconomic condition of blacks. These plans were never implemented because the campus audience for such a program was so small, despite the large number of blacks in the general population. Furthermore, the consciousness raising that has played so important a part in the United States has not yet moved beyond the activist community in Brazil. In sum, the time is not yet ripe, although it may not be far off, for the establishment of bona fide programs in Afro-Brazilian studies. The case studies that follow illustrate the situation.

Federal University of Bahia

The Federal University of Bahia (FUB) is in Salvador, the capital of the state. Located in northeastern Brazil, Bahia has the largest concentration of people of African descent in the country. FUB is the state's major institution of higher education, serving approximately 18,000 students. There are very few phenotypically black professors. An important program at FUB is the Center for African and Oriental Studies (CEAO), directed by Dr. Pessoa de Castro. This is not a program in Afro-Brazilian or Africana studies; it was founded in 1959 with the aim of "providing opportunities for study, teaching, research and exchange in the realm of African and Asian culture, as well as their presence in Brazil and of Brazil's presence in those cultures." The center's mission later was expanded to "carry out the program of cultural cooperation between Brazil and the African countries and the development of Afro-Brazilian Studies." Nevertheless, the center has concentrated more on interaction between continental Africa and Brazil than on the history and culture of the Afro-Brazilian population.

Courses in language (Japanese, Yoruba, and others) and other subjects (literature, linguistics, geography, anthropology) are offered at the center but are mainly "extramural," that is, not for university credit. An exception is a selection of history courses, which are accepted for credit by arrangement with the department of history. Courses ranging from three months to six months or one year are available to anyone who is interested. There is also a library and documentation division at CEAO, a museum, a program that coordinates projects carried out by Brazilian and foreign researchers, and a translation service for theses, essays, and monographs. The center publishes a monthly newsletter, *Informativo CEAO*, and a journal, *Afro-Asia*.

U.S. scholars, including some Africana studies professors, have visited the center from time to time, but none for sustained periods or to do research. CEAO has no linkage arrangement with a U.S. Africana studies program, but does receive students on a regular institutional exchange program between Brown University in Providence, Rhode Island, and FUB. The Afro-American studies program at Brown participates in the exchange, which is promoted by Professor Anani Dzidzienyo, a Ghanaian and frequent visitor who specializes in Afro-Brazilian history and culture; he holds a joint appointment at Brown in the Center for Portuguese and Brazilian Studies and the Afro-American studies program. About fifteen to twenty students per semester participate. FUB students rarely go to Brown because of the cost and language barriers.

A two-way exchange program between FUB and the University of the West Indies in St. Augustine, Trinidad, involves five to ten students on each side and is coordinated in Brazil by Dr. Barbara Lala, head of the department of linguistics. This initiative was developed by Dr. Pessaa de Castro, when she was cultural attaché at the Brazilian Embassy in Trinidad, from 1986 to 1988. There is also a one-way "exchange" between FUB and Obafemi Awolowo University in Nigeria, coordinated by CEAO. By the end of 1989, although several Nigerian students had visited Brazil, only one FUB graduate student had gone to Awolowo.

Affiliated with the FUB is Programa de Estudo do Negro na Bahia (PENBA), coordinated by anthropologist Dr. Julio Braga. PENBA's objective is interdisciplinary research and student training in Afro-Brazilian studies. A group of graduate students under the supervision of faculty do research on black cultural traditions, race relations, and blacks in labor and the workplace, all in Salvador. Professor João Reis of the Department of History, a member of the PENBA group, teaches Afro-Brazilian history at FUB and wrote a well-received book on an 1837 slave uprising in Bahia that debunked the notion of passiveness among Brazilian slaves. Another historian and PENBA researcher, Professor Ines de Oliveira, also does research on Brazilian slavery. Braga and his anthropology colleague, Vivaldo da Costa Lima, are interested in the religious practice of candomblé. PENBA receives funding from the Ford Foundation.

University of São Paulo

The University of São Paulo (USP) is a very prestigious university in the city and state of the same name. Because it is a public institution with an excellent academic reputation, it attracts the best students and is highly competitive. The Federal University in the state has a less important presence than USP. There are few black faculty or students at USP, and there is no program in Afro-Brazilian or Africana studies. The two black professors are relatively unfamiliar with the workings of Africana studies in the United States, although they accept the idea. There is a greater preoccupation among blacks generally with what is considered pervasive racial discrimination in São Paulo—city, state, and university. The lack of Afro-Brazilian or Africana studies is a bit surprising in a city where the United Black Movement (Movimento Negro Unificado [MNU]), a militant protest organization, was formed in the 1970s and attracted a wide following. MNU inspired the creation of several other black organizations in São Paulo following the relaxation of government repression after 1978.

The Center of African Studies at USP concentrates exclusively on continental Africa. It offers a full menu of programs and activities comparable to similar centers and has a consistent and ambitious publications series, including the journal *Africa*.

Pontifical Catholic University

Sponsored by the Catholic Church, Pontifical Catholic University (PUC) has campuses in several Brazilian cities including São Paulo, where 17,000 students are enrolled. For the past decade or so there have been so-called Negro groups at PUC, that is, students and faculty with a strong interest in the condition of Afro-Brazilians. Fortunes have ebbed and flowed for the Afro-Brazilian Studies and Research Institute (IPEAFRO), founded at PUC in the early 1980s under the leadership of Abdias do Nascimento. It was one of the many institutes that proliferated at PUC then, and it apparently had little contact or interaction with university academic programs. According to some faculty members at PUC, the main reason for IPEAFRO's slow development is the perception that an interest in blackness is a drawback for students concerned about upward mobility. Anani Dzidzienyo has referred to this as the "etiquette" of race relations in Brazil. Another factor, it is claimed, is that racial mixing has blurred the lines between racial groups; this has encouraged the propaganda and pre-eminence of being simply Brazilian rather than "hyphenated," which discourages militant Afro-Brazilian advocacy. What credence these arguments now deserve is uncertain.

Some PUC faculty have interesting theories about the comparative development of Africana studies in the United States and Brazil. Brazil was an "exploitation colony," where domination was accepted, but the colonial United States resorted to revolution. Thus, Brazil evolved into a culture of accommodation, while the United States established a tradition of protest and confrontation. From this perspective, the demand for Africana studies in the United States is consistent with the national tradition, but Brazilians have no precedent for "storming the Bastille" to resolve conflicts, racial or otherwise.

Some anthropologists at PUC espouse the view that their discipline has been in the forefront of race studies in Brazil because it has always been more radical and experimental than other fields. History and sociology are more preoccupied with maintaining tradition and investigation in safe areas than with journeying into uncharted waters. Medical doctors, they observe, conducted the earliest studies of "minorities" and soon were overtaken by anthropologists, the first to ask: Who are these black people? What should be done with them? And so on. To this day, they maintain, for better or worse, it is in anthropology that the most exciting research is being done in Afro-Brazilian studies and race relations.

Scholars in the social psychology graduate faculty are engaged in research on various aspects of race discrimination in labor and the workplace. Similar pioneering work on inequalities in the Brazilian school system is being conducted by faculty in the school of education. History faculty at the University of Campinas (one of the three state universities in São Paulo state) have held annual seminars re-examining central issues in Brazilian slavery as part of a wave of revisionism in this area.

FEDERAL UNIVERSITY OF RIO DE JANEIRO

At the 3,000-student Federal University of Rio de Janeiro (UFRJ), one of the most exciting research projects in Brazil is being carried out by Professor Yvonne Maggie, an anthropologist in the department of social science and the Institute of Philosophy of Social Science (IFES). The objective is to coordinate a formal cluster of several colleagues within her department into a "laboratory of social research," called a "nucleus of black studies." These clusters are fairly common in Brazilian universities, and the one at UFRJ is likened to FUB's PENBA. Roughly translated, the project is entitled "The Place of Black Representation in Brazilian Society."

Undergraduate students, many of them black, do empirical and archival research under Professor Maggie's supervision and form discussion groups around their findings on such topics as black representation in beauty contests or the media and Portuguese perceptions of blacks during the colonial era. One hypothesis of the project is that black culture is distinctively different from white culture in Brazil, whereas emphasis in the United States has been on equality and integration. (Apparently, there is a lack of information or understanding about the position of

U.S. black "militants" and others on this subject.) Some of the students go on for graduate study.

Professor Maggie believes that several courses in the social science division alone at UFRJ might be called black studies, such as "Race and Culture," "Inter-Ethnic Relations in Brazil," and "Perceptions of Blacks in Brazilian Social Thought since the 19th Century." She recalls required courses on Afro-Brazilians, indigenous Indians, and other groups, and that these requirements ended with the advent of military rule.

The Center for Contemporary Interdisciplinary Studies (CIEC), in the school of communications at UFRJ, undertook a series of activities related to the centenary of abolition in Brazil. The ambitious project involved publishing, cataloging, video collections, archive development, and seminars. In 1988 a major set of programs dealt with emancipation, and the project is now involved in rigorous and productive follow-up. Directed by Dr. Carlos Perreira, Muniz Sodre, former head of the School of Communications, CIEC benefits from the participation of key Brazilian scholars. Among them are Dr. Maggie, who prepared a comprehensive report of the abolition centenary; Dr. Julio Braga of PENBA, the highly regarded writer and historian; and Dr. Joel Rufino dos Santos and Dr. Caetana Damaseno of the Institute of Religious Studies.

Along with Dr. Abdias do Nascimento (now retired), Dr. Lelia Gonzalez occupies a special place among black scholar-activists in Brazil.[3] She now teaches in the department of anthropology at PUC in Rio but has been on the faculty at other universities. Coauthor with Dr. Carlos Hasenbalg of the acclaimed study, *Lugar do Negro* (1982), she is a founding member of the MNU. Recognized as one of the country's leading intellectuals by Brazilians as well as Africana scholars in the United States, she and Dr. Nascimento have been more involved in U.S. Africana studies than any other Brazilian academics. Dr. Gonzalez has attended meetings of the AHSA and regularly visits the United States; U.S. Africana studies scholars who have visited Brazil (the list is short) have consulted her.

There is currently no black studies nucleus at PUC–Rio, but one is being organized by Dr. Gonzalez. It will be the second of its kind led and organized by a black person (preceded by Dr. Abdias do Nascimento at PUC–São Paulo). The objectives are to develop curriculum, stimulate sensitivity to the widespread discrimination in Brazil, promote Pan-Africanism and the dignity of black culture and identity, and inaugurate linkages with Africana studies programs in the United States and with universities in Africa and the Caribbean. Dr. Gonzalez has introduced a new term into the lexicon, Amefrican Studies, which she prefers over Afro-Brazilian or Afro-American (people of African descent in the Americas) because it is more Afrocentric and is original; there is a uniqueness, she believes, about people of African descent that requires a different name. She feels they are neither hyphenated Brazilians nor Africans but instead combine the better elements of both cultures, a notion best captured by Amefrican.

Worthy of mention is the work of Dr. Nelson do Valle Silva, although he is on the periphery of academia in the strictest sense. A Ph.D. from the University of Michigan, he heads the department of information and documentation, national computer science laboratory, in the ministry of science and technology. He is a sociologist and demographer who was a Fulbright scholar for one year at the University of Florida. His current research, on race and social mobility as it relates to social stratification and inequality, finds that blacks and mulattoes are close together and far behind whites in socioeconomic circumstances. In such social relations as marriage, discrimination is not as pronounced—that is, socioeconomic distance does not hold in social relations. In other words, the huge gaps between blacks and whites in terms of labor, education, and income, for example, are not as clear or great in marriage. The fact that there is less discrimination against mulattoes marrying whites than in employment or income distribution, says Dr. Silva, creates a dichotomy.[4] He is a member of the editorial board of *Estudos Afro-Asiaticos,* the journal of the Center for Afro-Asian Studies at Candido Mendes University. That institution has no Afro-Brazilian studies program as such, but Silva points out that *Estudos Afro-Asiaticos* prints many articles on Africa and blacks in Brazil, such as "Racial Miscegenation in Brazil" (March 1989), "Contemporary Black Brazilian Literature" (September 1987), and "Black Territories in Brazilian Cities" (September 1989).

CONCLUSION

Brazil and the United States, the two largest population centers in the African diaspora, are not at comparable stages in the development of Afro-Brazilian and Africana studies. In the United States there are highly sophisticated and productive programs as well as weak and undernourished ones. In Brazil, where formal structures for Africana or Afro-Brazilian studies do not yet exist, one is more likely to find individuals in mainstream departments engaged in research and teaching on these topics. Full examination of the reasons for this difference exceeds the limit of this essay. Suffice it to say that the foundation laid by the U.S. civil rights movement and the national consciousness raising that accompanied it established a political climate that inspired if not provoked the modern Africana studies movement in the United States. This factor is crucial in understanding its emergence and expansion.

There has been no equivalent development in Brazil. Whether or not it will take a similar social revolution to produce an aggressive Afro-Brazilian studies movement is impossible to know. It appears that it will require at least an organized and mobilized black academic/intellectual community (including students and faculty in substantially increased numbers) with strong allies elsewhere in Brazilian society (such as the media, business, politics, and the church). It may take much more in the near term (the next twenty years), such as direct government intervention in university affairs, perhaps through the imposition of policies similar to U.S. affirmative action, to open academia fully to a segment of the population so long excluded. More important and certainly more difficult is the need to explode the myth of Brazil as a country in which there is equal opportunity for all citizens and where discrimination on the basis of race is insignificant. Brazilian universities have an enormous role to play in that challenge, with Afro-Brazilian studies helping to lead the way. This may be too great a responsibility to place on a fledgling movement. Nevertheless, in the light of Brazil's history, it will take nothing less than very bold initiatives to change the university landscape from white enclaves to plural learning centers that recognize the vital and widespread contributions of people of African descent in Brazil, alongside those of others in the country. The magnitude of the task cries out for Afro-Brazilian academics and Afro-Brazilian or Africana studies programs to coalesce with other enlightened and progressive forces and lead Brazilian universities out of their narrow, stagnant past into the new realities of the twenty-first century. Brazil—indeed, the world—will never again be what it once was.

NOTES

1. Information is drawn from a March 1990 report to the Ford Foundation, "Africana Studies Outside the United States: Africa, Brazil and the Caribbean," by this author. The extracts from it are used with the permission of the Ford Foundation.
2. *Economist* (10 May 1986), 42.
3. Dr. Nascimento has written several books on blacks in Brazil and Pan-Africanism. With Lelia Gonzalez he was a founding member of MNU in São Paulo. He served for a time as a congressman from Rio de Janeiro in the national legislature and formerly chaired the department of Puerto Rican studies at SUNY–Buffalo.
4. For an elaboration of his views, see Nelson do Valle Silva, "Updating the Cost of Not Being White in Brazil," in *Race, Class and Power in Brazil*, ed. Pierre-Michael Fontaine (Los Angeles: Center for Afro-American Studies, UCLA, 1985) and Nelson do Valle Silva and Carlos Hasenbalg, "Social Stratification, Mobility and Race," in *Estrutura Social, Mobilidade E Raca* (São Paulo: Epiçoes Vertice, 1988).

The Diaspora in Indo-Afro-Ibero-America

Jorge Silva Castillo

AFRICAN DIASPORA STUDIES HAVE COME A LONG WAY SINCE THE LATIN AMERI-can Association of Asian and African Studies (ALADAA) was formally consti-tuted in 1978. At that time it was more or less implicitly assumed that African studies in our association referred specifically to knowledge of Africa itself and did not include African descendants in Latin America. Moreover, an overwhelming majority of members were interested only in Asia. At our first international congress, held in Mexico in 1978, Africa was rather poorly represented—the focus of only nine out of more than eighty papers—and it was almost absent at the second congress held in Columbia in 1981.[1] It was not until we met in Rio de Janeiro in 1985 that Afro–Latin American issues made their entrance as a legitimate concern; they were the subject of seventeen of the almost one hundred papers, compared to fifteen focus-ing on Africa and another ten on Latin American relations with the continent. The Brazilian lesson was definitive for us; in Latin America, studies on Africa should not be separated from those on Afro–Latin Americans, and Afro-American issues cannot be fully understood without their deep African dimension.

Since then, our meetings have included both aspects of this reality. Using the titles of papers presented as one indicator of the thinking within ALADAA, three main areas in Afro–Latin American studies emerge: history, broadly speaking (45 percent), anthropology and folklore (30 percent), and religion (10 percent). Also represented are sociology and politics (5 percent), art and literature (5 percent), and others (5 percent).[2] If we assume that religion, art, and literature very often show an anthropological approach, we find that history and anthropology are dominant by far. This is probably because Latin American sociologists or political scientists, unlike their North American colleagues, generally suppose that Afro–Latin American issues are not their concern. This is an important point. If we examine the focus among scholars of Afro-Americans in the United States, for example, we find a picture in sharp contrast to the one above. The topics most frequently treated may be summarized as follows: social (30 percent), civil and human rights (28 percent), political (22 percent), historical (10 percent), and others (10 percent).[3]

Of course, different situations and conditions of African diaspora people in North America and Latin America may at least partially explain such divergence. In general, one difference lies in the degree of self-identity and cohesiveness, which is greater in the north than in Latin America, although the situation varies in the latter.

Due to high mortality, massive participation in the wars for independence and subsequent conflicts, and racial mixing, black people have virtually "disappeared" in many places, such as Argentina and Uruguay. In Mexico, people of African descent have mixed with other ethnic groups, and residual physiognomic features are not perceived by them as indicators of their origin. Even in La Costa Chica, in the state of Guerrero, on the Pacific Coast, where some almost purely black people can be seen, the inhabitants consider themselves indigenous to the region, darker—they argue—because the sun there burns too much. Only in the state of Veracruz do some people self-identify as *negritos* and maintain certain oral traditions, such as the famous story about Yanga, a *cimarron* who challenged the colonial army until he obtained the right to found a free black village (San Lorenzo do los Negros). In this way, and through contacts with the Caribbean region, people in the area are conscious of their origins, although they do not constitute a socially cohesive group along ethnic lines.

In Colombia, where the Indian labor force was less abundant than in Mexico, African slaves were concentrated in plantation and mining areas. Therefore, cases similar to that of La Costa Chica are much more numerous, and traditions of African origin are very easily identifiable. Self-identity with African roots is perhaps the strongest in Cuba and Brazil, where the number of African descendants is large. Such cultural features as religion, language, music, dance, and literature reflect those roots and have been kept alive in both rural and urban areas. Moreover, in Brazil, the economic marginalization of most people of African descent who live in industrialized urban areas puts them in a condition somewhat similar to that of blacks in the United States. If Brazilian social protest movements have failed in the past, this may be due to the ephemeral life of political parties, according to Franklin W. Knight.[4]

One wonders, however, whether a more fundamental reason may lie in another point raised by the same author:

> Where Afro-Americans form a majority of the population and where they have [one would say, rather, "share," which is implied by the context of the author's argument] political power, race seems to be a less important consideration than color, social status, and economic position. This is the meaning of the Caribbean and Brazilian phrase: money whitens. . . . In the Caribbean and in Latin America, Afro-Americans form a part of all the social strata. Afro-Americans share every occupation and every status—even if they predominate in lower-skilled, low paying, jobs.[5]

The intermingled and complex situation of blacks in Latin America prevents them from forming a cohesive group with common aims, common problems, and common feelings. Afro–Latin Americans are not a group that cuts across all economic strata of society; black peasants would identify with all other peasants, black workers with all other workers, that is, with those sharing similar problems of social class rather than along racial lines.[6] Whitened mulattos in the upper economic class prefer to perceive themselves as part of the group of mestizos or whites at the same economic level.[7] This may change, and already it is changing in Brazil because of the current economic crisis, which strikes the lower strata of society the hardest. Quite possibly, however, the situation will remain unchanged in countries where Afro-American self-identity is not as strong.

It is not surprising that scholarly activity reflects the differing presence of African diaspora people in Latin America. Where that presence is less visible, as in Argentina, only historical and some folkloric studies are carried on.[8] Where mostly rural and village populations are involved, as in Mexico, anthropological studies predominate, together with historical research.[9] The greater demographic importance of black people in Colombia is reflected in a richer bibliography, including work in the areas of fiction, poetry, history, anthropology, and sociology.[10] In Brazil, where black urban groups are very numerous, historical, anthropological, folkloric, and sociopolitical studies on people of African descent are more developed than in any other Latin American country.[11] In Cuba the official egalitarian policy of the socialist government has had an unexpected effect; tensions have been controlled by the regard of any racial conflict as antirevolutionary, and some activists consider this a means of whitening Cuban society.[12]

As we move into the twenty-first century, we need to be aware of such diverse currents in order to advise our students. On the one hand, they should engage in realistic and useful research according to the local circumstances. On the other hand, they should try to go beyond the limits of what has been done and have a clear idea of their objectives.

Although it is not true that Latin America is free of racial discrimination, prejudice exists against all nonwhites, and it is all the more insidious and difficult to fight because it is less open. Prejudices are rooted not only in memory of slavery but also in disdain for and ignorance about Africa. That is why knowledge of Africa itself has been conceived very consciously as the basis for building self-reliance among Latin American blacks and respect among nonblacks.

In Mexico, a group of young scholars interested in issues concerning black people, some of whom are involved in sociopolitical movements, are taking courses on Africa at El Colegio de México as a way to prepare themselves for academic or social work among people of African descent. Recently, a team of social anthropologists was formed to do fieldwork in Oaxaca, Guerrero, and Veracruz with the aim of dignifying the contribution of people there to Mexican culture. This program, *La Tercera Raiz*, views African culture, together with the Indian and the European, as one of the three roots of Mexican culture. The first step for many on the team, before going into the field, is to take a course about Africa.

Knowledge of Africa implies knowledge of African history. If students can deeply understand the African past, then they will also understand the positive contribution of black people to our material and spiritual culture. In addition, the ethnic history of diaspora people will be enriched, and we will have a more positive insight into our own past. Anthropological and folkloric studies also must continue, since they are one way to identify African origins in the customs, attitudes, and values of black people, which are their more evident contributions to our culture. But we also should try to develop more acute socioanthropological insights about groups of African descent in order to open the path for deeper sociological research in this area. It is of the utmost importance to evaluate scientifically the degree of self-identity with African origins among blacks and mulattos, that is, the extent to which they see themselves as blacks, as a different group of peasants among all peasants, or workers among all workers, in order to be sure about the reliability of our assumptions on this relevant issue. Such study would provide a solid ground for guiding students toward their objectives in research or social work.

Furthermore, ALADAA should try to interest sociologists and political scientists in our association. These disciplines can provide fresh perspectives on issues related to Afro–Latin Americans. Finally, it would be useful to review what has been done in each country where our association has members, such as the initiative that resulted from the first symposium on blacks held in Colombia in October 1983.[13] This may be a suitable starting point for developing, in a rational and coherent way, programs adapted to the needs of each country. The theme for ALADAA's seventh international congress, held in Mexico in 1992, was "Encounters in Chain," meaning that the relevance of Christopher Columbus was his role in starting a dynamic, pluridirectional chain of cultural encounters on our continent. The new perception in Mexico about the plural nature of Latin American culture recently was captured by the famous novelist Carlos Fuentes in the term "Indo-Afro-Ibero-America."[14] This fortunate expression contains a whole program, which in time it is hoped will be understood throughout Latin America. The commemoration of the fifth centennial of the European discovery of America offered the occasion to begin working toward that end.

NOTES

1. The proceedings of the first and third congresses were not published, but the papers are available in the files of ALADAA. The only article on Africa from the second congress is by J. M. Turner and A. Dzidzienyo, "Relaciones entre Africa y Brasil," published in *Asia y Africa en América Latina* (Tunja: Universidad Pedagógica y Teconológica de Colombia, Ediciones La Rana y el Aguila, 1983), 237–58.

2. The figures are from the programs of the third international congress of ALADAA (Rio de Janeiro, 1985); the second (Jalapa, 1985) and third (Puebla, 1987) national congresses of the Mexican section; and the first national congress of the Venezuelan section.

3. Figures were obtained from the 276 titles found in *Bibliographical Guide to Black Studies* (Boston: G. K. Hall, 1978), under the heading "Afro-American" (9–16). They must be considered indicators of broad tendencies.

4. Franklin W. Knight, *The African Dimension in Latin American Societies* (New York: Mcmillan, 1974), 90–91.

5. Ibid., 135.

6. Octavio Ianni, "Race et Classe au Brésil," *Présence Africaine*, no. 53 (1965): 102–19.

7. Richard L. Jackson, *The Black Image in Latin American Literature* (Albuquerque: University of New Mexico Press, 1976), 5–6.

8. See George Reid Andrew, *Forgotten but Not Gone: The Afro-Argentines in Buenos Aires* (Madison: University of Wisconsin Press, 1978).

9. The pioneer is Gonzalo Aguirre Beltrán, two of whose works are justly considered classics: *La Población Negra en México*, (Mexico: FCE, 1958) and *Cuijla* (Mexico: FCE, 1958).

10. See *El Negro en la historia de Colombia—Fuentes Escritas y Orales*, Primer Simposio sobre bibliografía del negro en Colombia, Fondo Interamericano do Publicaciones de la Cultura Negra en la Américas–UNESCO (Mexico: F.C.I.F., 1983).

11. Florestan Fernandes's *The Negro in Brazilian Society* (New York: Columbia University Press, 1969) offers not only pertinent content for our purposes but also an excellent bibliography, which bears witness to the rich material on the subject (63–69).

12. See R. Fermoselle-López, *Black Politics in Cuba* (Washington, D.C.: American University Press, 1972). Jackson, *Black Image*, 15–16. Knight, *African Dimension*, 99–100, does not agree with Jackson's interpretation.

13. Proceedings of the symposium entitled "El Negro en la Historia de Colombia" were published in *El Negro en la historia de Colombia*.

14. Carlos Fuentes, "¿Desaparece la Nación?" *La Jornada/Semanal,* 15 June 1990, 22.

African Diaspora Passages from the Middle East to East Asia

Michael C. Thornton

Islam and the Diaspora

The geographical proximity of Africa to Asia is most evident as one looks eastward from the Horn, out across the Red Sea. Because at this narrow point it seems almost possible to reach out and touch Yemen from Djibouti—Ethiopia and Yemen are separated by less than one hundred miles—it is not surprising that there has been an African presence in western Asia for many thousands of years. While the evidence is sporadic, the historical record is dotted with many signs of Africans in Asia. African involvement in the region was such that "the infiltration of Negro blood, which spread to all parts of the peninsula and seems destined one day to change the race completely, began in very early antiquity."[1] Some go as far as to say that the "Entire Arab people, reportedly including the Prophet, is mixed with Negro blood." Evidence from the sixth century reveals that Ethiopians conquered Yemen and later brought Christianity there. "Yemen was a Negro Ethiopian colony and remained so until the birth of Mohammed." The African influence runs deep in other ways as well. According to Arab historians one of the major artifacts of Islam was created by an African: "Mohammed had an ancestor, Ishmael, son of Abraham and Hagar the Egyptian (an African female), who constructed the sacred stone, *Kaaba*."[2]

A hero of central Arabia during the sixth century was Antar Ibn Shadda, poet and warrior, described as a "raven of the Arabs."[3] His mother, Zabuba, was an

Ethiopian slave, and his father an Arab soldier.[4] His chief poem is contained in the *Mocallakat.* Writing in 1890, Lenormant said of him:

> Antar, the romantic hero of pre-Islamic Arabia, is a mulatto on his mother's side. Nevertheless, his thoroughly African face does not prevent his marriage to a princess of the tribes proudest of their nobility, so habitual had this black-skinned Melanian admixture become.[5]

Two other influential sons of Africa during the period were Zaid Bin Harith, a slave who became one of the Prophet's foremost generals,[6] and Hadzrat Bilal Ibn Rahab, an Ethiopian who was the first high priest and treasurer of the Mohammedan empire.[7]

The most extensive evidence relates to the African presence in what is present-day Iran. Toward 2300 B.C.E., the plains of the Tigris and Anzan-Suskinka were ruled by a dynasty of black kings.[8] The inhabitants of Sushan have been described as "Aryano-Negroids" corresponding to the ancient Sushans who for the most part were blacks, a race of short "Negroes."[9] Cheikh Diop claims that before the Jews and Syrians (Canaanites) occupied Phoenecia (present-day Syria), Palestine, Ethiopia (Kush), and Egypt (Ham, Mesraim), and before the Arabs occupied Arabia, those lands were inhabited by blacks, who had for thousands of years created a civilization in the area.[10] In Phoenecia, Diop suggests, they were "the Canaanites, descendants of Canaan, brother of Mesraim, the Egyptian, and Kush, the Ethiopian, sons of Ham"[11]; then, "after many ups and downs, the Canaanites and the white tribes . . . blended to become in time the Jewish people of today."[12]

Xerxes built a hall that depicted twenty-three groups of representatives greeting the Shah on the occasion of the Norooz festivals, usually begun on the first day of spring. The twenty-third group consisted of three Africans from Ethiopia, one of whom carried an elephant tusk.[13] These carvings, made about 2,500 years ago, show that blacks were present in Iran, contributing to and recruited into the Persian armies, even serving with Xerxes against the Greeks.

Dating from around 470 B.C.E. is a bas-relief on the eastern stairway of the Apadana Hall at Persepolis (in present-day Iran, near the city of Shiraz), capital of the Achaemenian kings of Persia, depicting a "Negroid delegation from south of the Sahara."[14] As noted by Joel Rogers, Darius the Great (522–486 B.C.E.), "whose capitol city was Susa [northwest Iran, near the Iraqi border], had wives of many races and may have been a mulatto or a black."[15] During Darius's reign, Persia held dominion from the Danube to the Indus River, including most of north and northeast Africa (Libya, Egypt, parts of the Sudan, and Ethiopia).

Black Slavery and the Rise of Islam, Seventh to Fifth Centuries

There are three histories of the African presence in Asia corresponding to regional differences. The first is the African influence in the area traditionally called the Middle East. The second consists of South Asia (primarily India and Pakistan). And the third is East Asia (including China and Japan). In this section we write of the first two histories; East Asia will be addressed later in this chapter.

THE MIDDLE EAST

The largest and most widely dispersed number of Africans entered this region following the rise of the Islamic empire during the seventh century.[16] Most came as non-Muslim slaves, but most became converts and were freed.[17] The slave trade permeated the whole of western Asia, from Saudi Arabia to Oman to Iraq. There was a long-standing trade in East African slaves to the Persian Gulf area. In the ninth century a large number of black slaves were found in the Euphrates Valley, and during the eleventh century the princesses of Bahrain (Persian Gulf area) were said to possess 30,000 black or Abyssinian slaves, who were employed in agriculture and gardening,[18] while numerous slaves were brought from the Sudan and Ethiopia to serve many roles.[19]

African men had a major influence on Turkish history. According to Halideh Ebib, a former minister of education in Turkey, several black eunuchs occupied the position of Kizlar Agasi, that is, chief of the harem. As far back as 602–610 there is mention of Nicephorous Phocus, a black Arab and ruler in the Byzantine empire.[20] Tarik-Ibn-Ziad, one of the most famous Africans in Islam's history, was born a slave but later became a great general. Jebel-u-Tarik (the mount of Tarik), that is, Gibraltar, is named after him. Other Africans were patrons of art and literature and were well educated.[21]

The list of notable Africans in Turkish history continues. For example, Hassan of Oulubad, a Sudanese soldier, was a hero in the capture of Constantinople by the Turks in 1453; Hafiz Beheram, another Sudanese, was the Grand Eunuch of Turkey in 1877, which meant he was second-in-command after the sultan. But if becoming a eunuch in Turkey was like it was elsewhere, achieving such social heights was doubly daunting: "A gentleman has informed us, that of 200 African boys emasculated at Judda, only ten survived the cruel operation."[22] Leaders of eunuchs were themselves eunuchs.

Although slavery differed structurally and ideologically in the Islamic and Western worlds, it was intolerable for those in both societies. Revolts were frequent in the Islamic empire. Especially violent were the uprisings of 689–690 and 694–695, and the main Zanj (name given to slaves from East Africa in the Persian Gulf area) revolt in Iraq, an insurrection so serious that it endangered the caliphate, lasted from 868 to 883.[23] In southern Iraq, rich landowners possessed large tracts on which sugarcane was cultivated by the Zanj, who lived in wretched conditions. In 868 a man named 'Al' Ibn Muhammed, who claimed to be of 'Alid origin (a sect of Shiism), led the rebellion, which was initially successful in part because canals in the area hampered military activity. The Zanj pillaged Basra (southeast Iraq near Kuwait) and intercepted trade between Basra and Baghdad. The caliph eventually razed their stronghold at Man'a, a fortress the Zanj had constructed south of Basra.[24]

Africans were also used as infantry in both Iraq and Egypt. In a tradition that was paralleled in U.S. military policy during the nineteenth and twentieth centuries, Africans were used in only certain branches of Iraqi and Egyptian armies because it was believed their temperaments made them suited for specific purposes.[25]

Although social mobility was possible, it was the exception and not the rule for Africans in the Middle East of this era, whether because of their color, paganism, or their slave origin. Islamic literature of Africans often explains or justifies their subordinate status; many of the negative views parallel ideas that are familiar even today. Some researchers suggest the derisive attitudes held of Africans echoed traditions learned from others in the western world, such as the Greeks.[26] The literature speaks of blacks possessing specific qualities: kinky hair, broad noses, sharp teeth, and a certain size of genitals. That they also embraced music and dance indicated that the "love of entertainment preoccupies the mind of the black man and his intellect therefore becomes feeble." In a broader sense, it appears that there was seen to be a substantive difference between blacks and Arabs, for the former were situated at the bottom of a racial/color hierarchy, following whites (including Arabs) and "yellows." One thing that could redeem individuals despite their color was their achieving some religious status, such as becoming close to the Prophet or becoming the chief scholar of Arabia.[27]

Though more was written about the inadequacies of African men, African women were not ignored:

> their bad qualities are many, and the blacker they are the uglier their faces and the pointed their teeth. They are of little use and may cause harm and are dominated by their evil disposition and destructiveness. . . . Dancing and rhythm are instinctive and ingrained in them. Since their utterance is uncouth, they are compensated with song and dance. . . . They have the cleanest teeth of all people because they have much saliva, and they have bad digestions.[28]

Other evidence also suggests that many in the region did not consider Africans their social equals. It would have been unthinkable for an Arab, Turk, or Persian to marry his daughter to a black, although marriages between African female slaves and Arab men did occur. One literary passage suggests:

> Black man, why waste your time on falling in love?
> Stop courting the white girls if you have sense.
> A man like you, an Abyssinian black,
> Has no chance to consort with the likes of them.[29]

In the following passage from Charles Doughty, who traveled in Ṣaudi Arabia in the late 1800s, we see the racial and social hierarchy reiterated in this meeting with a man named Zeyd, who was:

> a swarthy nearly black sheykh of the desert, of mid stature and middle age, with a hunger-bitten stern visage. So dark a colour is not well seen by the Arabs, who in these uplands are less darkish brown than ruddy. They think it resembles the ignoble blood of slave races; and therefore even crisp and ringed hair is a deformity in their eyes. We may remember in the Canticles, the paramour excuses the swarthiness of her beautiful looks, "I am black but comely, ye daughters of Jerusalem, as the booths of the Beduw, as the tent cloths of Solomon"; she magnifies the ruddy whiteness of her beloved. Dark, the privation of light, is the hue of death (*mawt el-aswad*) and, by similitude, of calamity and evil; the wicked man's heart is accounted black (*kalb el-aswad*). According to this fantasy of theirs, the Judge of all the earth in the last judgment hour will hold an Arabian expedite manner of audit, not staying to parley with every soul in the sea of generations, for the leprosy of evil desert rising in their visages, shall appear manifestly in wicked persons as an horrible blackness. In the gospel speech, the sheep shall be sundered from the goats—wherein is some comparison of colour—and the just shall shine forth as the sunlight. The Arabs say of an unspotted human life, *kalb-hu abi'th*, white is his heart: we in like wise say candid.[30]

While the views expressed about Africans were perhaps little different from those found in the West centuries later, the Muslim world's view of slavery differed in significant ways. Certain tenets of Islam and the high demand for slaves allowed, and in fact encouraged, manumission. Although most blacks were not able to rise above menial labor, others, especially those of mixed parentage, reached positions of considerable importance.[31] While the Qur'an endorsed slavery, it also mitigated its effects: "Fear God concerning your slaves. Feed them with what you eat and clothe them with what you wear and do not give them work beyond their capacity. Do not cause pain to God's creation." Further, only certain populations could be enslaved: nonbelievers with whom Muslims held no nonaggression pact and whose territory had not been forcibly overrun by a jihad.[32]

The initial criterion was religious, not racial, and could be justified because pagans were offered the opportunity to learn the precepts of the true religion, convert, and attain Paradise. With time and increasingly diversified contact, Muslims began to define Africans as savage and to think of Africa as peopled with cannibals; this thinking allowed them to conclude that it was better for an African to be a "civilized" slave than a free savage.[33] What caused this metamorphosis in attitude? According to Bernard Lewis three developments were at the heart of this transformation. First, with the spread of Islamic power, the conquerors came to view their culture as superior. Second, conquests brought contact with blacks whose civilizations were not as advanced as the that of the Ethiopians with whom they had had much of their early experience. Finally, because of the slave trade, Arabs began to perceive blacks only in positions of servitude—doing only the most menial jobs—and thereby increasingly came to regard them as inferior.[34]

While the nature of slavery in the Islamic world was less strongly capitalistic and smaller in scale than in the West, in the final analysis, African people were subjugated and denied their freedom and, for the most part, there was a high correlation between the color of one's skin, being known as a slave, and placement on the social ladder in both worlds. However, one substantive difference persists despite the similarities: Africans were able to rise to the highest echelons of the Islamic world, an achievement that would not be matched in the West for a millennium.

South Asia

In western and eastern India, two hundred years before the first black slaves arrived in the Americas, Habshis (Africans from the Red Sea area) were found in Muslim territory from Delhi to present-day Sri Lanka.[35] Before the arrival of Europeans to the area, the Islamized Habshi were brought to India either as slaves purchased by Arabs from the Horn of Africa or as military troops from neighboring Muslim countries. Most were Abyssinians (Ethiopians), for Habshi means Abyssinian, although the term would later be applied to all blacks, even after Portugal arrived on the scene and most blacks in the region were Bantu or Sudanic in origin. Blacks entered the region in sizable numbers as early as the thirteenth century. They came as adventurers, clerics, bodyguards, policemen, bureaucrats, traders, concubines, soldiers, servants, and slaves. There is frequent mention of African involvement in civil and military life in

Gujarat (near the Gulf of Kachchh, western India) in the thirteenth century, as well as records of a time when Sultan Bahadur had 5,000 African slaves, many of whom were said to have been captured in battles against Ethiopia. Malik Sarwa, a Habshi eunuch, was appointed vizier to the sultan of Delhi and in 1394 became governor of the eastern provinces, with his capital at Jawnpur.[36]

In south central India, Habshis rose to influence in the fifteenth century. With the ascendancy of the Deccan party under Shah Amad I, a Habshi became governor of two of the sultanate's four provinces, and in 1480 a black served as minister of finance.[37] Farther east there was a report of 8,000 slaves in Bengal,[38] where Calcutta was a major center of the Arab slave trade.[39] In 1493 there was a successful revolt against the last Habshi ruler that resulted in the expulsion of these Africans from Bengal. Many went to the Deccan (the central part of the subcontinent) and to Gujarat.[40]

But perhaps the most famous African of them all in the history of India was Malik Ambar (born 1550). A former slave who became a soldier and administrator, he played an important role in the Ahmad Nagar dynasty with the Mughal emperor of Delhi, from whom he received the title of malik (lord). He is especially noted for his *rayotwari* (land revenue) system, based on the fertility of the soil and average rainfall, adopted by the British and used in India into the twentieth century.[41]

In contrast to the success stories noted thus far, records show that life was particularly hard for most Africans in India. In the Bombay area, during a five-year period, "the negro births were thirty-seven, and the deaths 754."[42] Ironically, other Africans, because they were such an integral part of the slave trade, were able to use their color to counter its disadvantage:

> Subjects of the Sultan of Muscat and Zanzibar were in the habit of bringing negro slaves from Africa for sale to Bombay, and of taking back Hindu females for the same purpose to Zanzibar. The male negroes were carried into port as part of the crew, and the females as their wives. As a large portion of the crew . . . was (and is) composed of negroes, it was extremely difficult . . . to ascertain whether the Africans on board were *bona fide* seamen, or brought for sale.[43]

The East African Slave Trade and the World Economy, Sixteenth to Nineteenth Centuries

By the second half of the eighteenth century there was a rapidly developing global economy. Europe's trading connections with Asia and the Americas were making important contributions to its prosperity. Manufactured goods were exchanged for exotic foods and materials, and by the 1770s France and Britain were doing as much business with India as with China. England's foreign commerce almost trebled, while France's increased eightfold. Trade flowed on Portuguese, English, French, and Dutch ships or traveled overland through Turkey and Russia toward China, India, and Indonesia.[44]

Certain European cities greatly prospered from this international trade. Liverpool rose rapidly to command the slave business. London became the preeminent sugar handler and monopolized Britain's Asian commerce. In France, Bordeaux drew ahead of the other Biscayne ports, although Nantes still had the largest slave trade. Lisbon and Cadiz dominated in Portugal and Spain, respectively. The need for ships to transport bulky goods over long distances for long-term credit and for large-scale capital investment made most of the great new fortunes of the period.[45] Only certain countries benefited, however, and many more were hurt, with devastating consequences for the future. Countless fortunes were built on the back-breaking labor and countless deaths of peoples of African and Asian descent.

THE MIDDLE EAST

While much of the rest of the trade in slavery was controlled by the West, that going to Asia found Arabs as the primary traders, particularly Oman, although such diverse groups as the Syrians, Copts, and Turks (not to mention Europeans) were also involved. Most countries in the modern Arab world at one time had slave ports or centers in them. In Oman the influx was so great that at one point its population of 800,000 was estimated to be approximately one-third black.[46] While there were always other sources of slaves during this period, such as those from central and eastern Europe (the "Slavs") and Central Asia (the Turks, Mongols, and Russian Georgians), the major source was Africa.[47] Such ports as Sawakin (northeastern Sudan), Dahlak (off the northern coast of Eritrea), Berbera (northern Somalia), and Brava (southern Somalia) were supplied from Ethiopia and the Sudan. The ports south of Brava (or Barawa, in Somalia) bought slaves from interior regions in the Rift Valley and along the Congo River. Entrepots such as Pate, Lamu, and Mombassa in Kenya, Kilwa in Tanzania, and Mocambique and Quelimane in Mozambique were among the many to which slaves were shipped and marched.[48]

Blacks were then taken to such ports as Al-Mukha in Yemen to be reshipped to Mecca, Jiddah, Cairo, Damascus, Baghdad, and other cities in the Middle East.[49] Some were shipped to Persian Gulf ports in Oman, Qatar, Bahrain, Kuwait, and Iraq before being sent inland. Most west coast Indian ports, such as Bombay, Goa

(Mumbai), and Kutch; east coast ports, such as Calcutta; and places along the Malabar coast (southwest) seem to have received slaves from the Persian Gulf or Al-Mukha.[50] "Thus East Africa became a huge reservoir from which flowed a constant stream of human cargoes to the Comorin Islands, Madagascar, Reunion, Mauritius, the Seychelles, Arabia, Turkey, Persia and even India."[51]

The extent of the slave trade in the Muslim world, beginning well before the seventh century and peaking in the eighteenth and nineteenth centuries, has been estimated to involve about ten million Africans.[52] They were exported across the Sahara, to the Red Sea, and then the Indian Ocean. Most were moved into the Arabian peninsula, north Africa, the Persian Gulf states, the Levant (Eastern Mediterranean Sea areas), Iran, Iraq, India, Pakistan, and Turkey; but the largest proportion stayed in the Middle East.

Slaves brought to the Middle East performed in a number of capacities, whether laboring in Iraqi mines or on the sugar plantations of Basra. They were used for pearl diving in Bahrain, as slave soldiers in Arabia, Iraq, and Persia, and as eunuchs in many areas, but particularly Mecca, Medina, and Turkey.[53] But, as is true for much of their presence in the Middle East, the evidence about the lives of Africans there is sparse.

The number of black slaves in Iran increased from the fifteenth up to the end of the nineteenth century. In addition to the conventional slave caravan routes and sea voyages, the British brought several thousand blacks to southern Iranian port cities to use them mainly as porters for loading and unloading British ships. But many young slaves worked in rich Iranian households as domestics, as assistants in the bazaars, and as laborers on farms and construction sites. Left behind, they settled mainly in Bandar-e Bushehr (southwest Iran), Bandar-e Abbas (southern Iran), and other smaller communities.[54] Several of these communities have been identified in the province of Kerman in south-central Iran.[55]

Some evidence suggests that in the last years of the nineteenth century "there were still between 25,000 and 50,000 slaves" in Iran. This figure does not take into account the number of freed blacks. There are no official statistics available on race or other ethnic characteristics in Iran. It is highly likely that about half a million blacks of African origin may be living in Iran. This estimate is based on the assumption that there were many free blacks living in Iran by the end of the nineteenth century, that their rate of growth has been either similar to or slightly higher than the national average, and that still more slaves entered the country in the twentieth century. However, due to isolation and the unequal distribution of resources, especially in more impoverished southeast Iran, blacks are likely among the lowest of income groups. That the situation for blacks in Iran is ambiguous invites further research.[56]

Iranian Black Santa Claus, Hajji Firooz

Iranian pilgrims were the major slave buyers during the Hajji season. They brought expensive carpets and turquoise stones to trade for black slaves. Each Hajji would buy slaves, and upon purchase Iranian Hajjis would give them names. Firooz (turquoise) was a popular name for slaves bought during the Hajji period.

Freed black slaves who stayed in the larger urban centers often wore clothes similar to that of Santa Claus during the weeks before the Norooz (the coming of spring) celebration. They were known as Hajji Firooz, "the messenger of the good news." The coming of spring is a symbol of happiness and freedom. Nowadays, it is not surprising to see nonblacks who paint their faces, dance, play their tambourines, and sing the lyrics of the good news in major Iranian cities before Norooz.

Some blacks in Iran found their way to royal courts and became well-known clowns. They would entertain the royal family by telling stories and performing practical jokes, a practice especially common during the Qajar dynasty (1796–1925). The performer was expected to make people laugh, chastise the king to be fair, and highlight the moral lessons of the plays. Blacks also would play the main character in popular plays, which required that they be among the funniest or most competent actors.

The discussion of Hajji Firooz is contributed by Mohammad Kamiar, an Iranian and a former research associate of the African Diaspora Research Project.

During the nineteenth century, when slavery was technically illegal in western Asia, Africans were brought to Turkey as slaves but mostly as eunuchs. Africans have appeared in Turkish judicial registries since at least the 1590s and were in great demand in the sixteenth and seventeenth centuries. Most of these Africans came from Sudan, by way of Cairo.[57] The eunuchs were called "*Kizlar Aghasi* (master of the maids), and *daru se ada laga* (lords of the abode of bliss), and [they] guarded the harems."[58] Their chief, known as the Kizlar Agasi, was one of the most powerful positions at the Ottoman court. The corps of eunuchs was about the only avenue by which a black could attain a high position in the Ottoman empire.[59]

The number of Africans in the household of the sultan varied over time, from 20 to 40 in the sixteenth century to more than 400 black eunuchs at the beginning of the nineteenth. For 400 to survive the operation to become a eunuch meant that 80,000 had died.[60] Other major employers of eunuchs were mosques in the two holy cities. In the 1850s, about 80 eunuchs worked at the Mecca mosque, and 120 at the Medina mosque.[61] The victims were usually between the ages of eight and ten years old. A eunuch could be sold at double the price after emasculation, and it was that increased profit that impelled "the owners, or rather usurpers, to have some of these wretches mutilated."[62]

From 30 to 60 black slaves entered Turkey monthly in 1868–69 and they were sent to such places as Scala Nuora, Sokia, Tirak, Manesia (Manisa), and Cassaba (now Turgutlu). In late 1869 and early 1870 approximately 2,000 black slaves were carried from Egypt to Turkey.[63]

Black marines are also known to have served in the Turkish navy in the middle nineteenth century. Bernard Lewis cites a naval report that says:

> They are from the class of freed slaves or slaves abandoned by merchants unable to sell them. . . . Those brought by the *Faizi Bari*, about 70 in number, were on their arrival enrolled as a Black company in the marine corps. They are in exactly the same position with respect to pay, quarters, rations, and clothing as the Turkish marines, and will equally receive their discharge at the expiration of the allotted term of service. . . . A negro Mulazim [lieutenant] and some negro tchiaoushes [sergeants], already in the service have been appointed to look after and instruct them. . . . No amount of ingenuity can conjure up any connexion between their condition and the condition of slavery.[64]

Generally speaking, slaves were not much in demand in the Islamic world as agricultural workers.[65] Land tenure was based on small holdings. With the Muslim acquisition of new areas, peasants were left in possession of the land. In the greater part of the Muslim world there were no vast tracts of land waiting to be opened as was the case in North America. The history of the nomadic heritage of the Arabs provided no motivation for agricultural settlement, and in general peasant life was looked on with contempt.[66]

However, during the nineteenth century greater numbers of slaves were diverted to plantation-like labor. In 1832 Sultan Said, the Amir of Oman, moved his capital to Zanzibar. That event marked an important period in the history of slavery, for it was then that the slave trade reached its zenith. Increasing numbers of slaves were exported to Arab and Muslim countries, many to be used on sugarcane and clove plantations, or to drain salt marshes. Sheriff argues that merchant capital was the mechanism that developed the slave mode of production in Zanzibar.[67] By this time, Arab traders not only controlled slave trade on the east coast of Africa, they also dominated the trans-Saharan slave trade and penetrated deep into central and west Africa. The end result is that the slave trade, particularly between the 1840s and the early 1900s, was "transformed into a ruthless, flourishing and well-organized business."[68]

South Asia

Africans on the western Indian coast were well established by the sixteenth century. The greatest number worked as domestics. It appears there were many Africans in India despite not having plantation economies. A European traveler, commenting on Abyssinians, noted that "there are many of them in India that are slaves and captives, both men and women which are brought out of Aeteopia."[69] He further observed, along with perpetuating the belief that Africans are the primary source of slavery, that:

> From Mosambique great numbers of these Caffares [black Africans] are carried into India, and many times they sell a man or woman that is growne to their full [strength] for two or three Ducats . . . the cause why so many slaves and captives of all nations are bought to sell in India, is, because everie ten or twelve miles, or rather in every Village and towne, there is a severall King, one of them not like another . . . are in warres, and those that on both sides are taken they keep for slaves.[70]

They came as soldiers, sailors, domestics, and dock and dhow workers. African soldiers made a particularly significant contribution during this era and were the backbone of armies in Egypt and India. They were predominant in the Gujarat (India) navies during the same period, both as commanders and as men-at-arms. In the sixteenth and seventeenth centuries in particular, the Portuguese used them to defend their Asian trading posts from Hormuz to Macao, as well as to man their ships.[71] There appeared to be so many black militia in India that there were frequent requests from other parts of the Portuguese empire for their services. For example, in 1651 the governor of Macao requested a squad of Africans as part of additional military support for the Macaense garrisons.[72] During many periods these slaves enjoyed a rather unusual position as a luxury and prestige element, and they were often highly regarded in relation to the indigenous populations of the places to which they were imported.[73]

Ann Pescatello suggests that one must understand the idea of the slave in the Indian context. Western and African notions of people as chattel had little basis in Indian social thought. According to international legal dictates and Iberian philosophical enquiries at the time, the concept of slave implied a social and economic rather than a racial subjugation. She concludes, "Thus it would appear that Africans who lived and labored in India, . . . were a type of 'slave' not related in status to the type of chattel laborer we associate with plantation workers . . . after the seventeenth century."[74]

The tentacles of the Arab slave trade reached southeastern Asia as well. From the thirteenth to the sixteenth century, Ceylon (now Sri Lanka) was a way station in the commerce with East Asia.[75] In the 1850s, Commodore Perry cited the presence of black people in Ceylon in a log he kept of his journey, noting "a singular mixture of black of all colors, from Negro black to dingy brown."[76]

When Ceylon colonizers opened up vast areas of land for coffee in the 1820s, the local population was unwilling to become wage laborers on the new plantations. Workers were sought in southern India, the original homeland of Ceylonese Tamils, and between 1841 and 1849, 70,000 (or 25 percent) of the immigrants died of malaria, malnutrition, and bad treatment. Though the Tamils are not described as black, many are,[77] and a significant number of people in southern India are of African heritage.[78] Also, Arab slavers had established trading posts on the island, so it can be assumed that at least some black slaves remained there as a result of this trade.

THE SIDDIS OF JANJIRA

By the seventeenth century Siddis had become the principal landowners on the island of Janjira, from which base they extended their power along stretches of the Indian coast. They had considerable historical influence, affecting the policies and actions of Great Britain, Portugal, and the Netherlands as well as local Indian states. A smaller Siddi state in Gujarat, Sachin, had some power, but its influence did not approach that of the Janjira blacks.[79] Siddi is derived from *Syed,* "man of a priestly calling or tendency." It is an honorific title given to African Muslims in western India. Siddis are also known as *Habshis,* a term derived from the Arabic word *El Habshis.*[80]

THE MAKRANIS OF PAKISTAN

The blacks in western Pakistan are called Makranis, apparently because the early slave trade centered around the Makran Coast (southwestern Pakistan), from where slave shipments also went to such places as Las Bela, Kharan, Kalat, and Karachi. The Karachi blacks, according to records of the day, came from Muscat and Kishan.[81] This infusion of Africans, discernible in the population of the Makran coast, led one British traveler to observe: "These people were quite different from [those] inland; many of them had almost black skins and seemed to come of African stock, with thick lips and broad noses."[82]

Blacks in the Arab World and South Asia
in the Twentieth Century

Although self-contained communities of peoples of African descent are identifiable today in Yemen, Saudi Arabia, Aden, Iraq, Iran, Pakistan, India, and elsewhere in Asia, little is known about these populations (for an exception, see Joseph Harris, *The African Presence in Asia*). Most of them live in poverty and have been integrated to a greater or lesser extent into local social and political structures, although prejudice against them remains.

THE MIDDLE EAST

Jonathan Derrick notes slavery continued well into the twentieth century in the Middle East, so many black communities there are a direct result of recent forced migration.[83] In 1934, the sultan of Al-Mukalla (Yemen) had a slave force of 250, "all of African origin."[84] In Iraq, the marsh Arabs had slaves who were retainers of the shaykh. In the Syrian desert, Seabrook discovered a black as the right-hand man of a tribal shaykh, whose word on behalf of the shaykh was considered law.[85] Many of the more recent arrivals (those arriving since the turn of the century) have been able to retain parts of their African heritage. Hence, in the 1950s most blacks in Oman, especially Masqat, though considering themselves Arab, formed a separate community at Salalah and retained African customs.[86]

Though the attitudes of Iranians toward people of African descent in Iran is an unresearched topic, the black communities there clearly developed as a result of migration and settlement by African merchants, as well as a consequence of the trade in slaves, and today live in several identifiable communities. E. Bastrani-Parizi[87] identifies several such areas in Iran: Zanjiabad ("village built by Africans"), Deh-Zanjian ("village of Africans"), and Gala-Zanjian ("castle of Africans"). The interior entrepot of Jiruft, which dealt in the slave trade, and which still has a black community near it, is thought to be comprised of descendants of African merchants and slaves. This also may be the case with some of the population around Bandar-e' Abbas.

According to J. Laffin, King Ibn Saud, who died in 1953, had 3,000 slaves of his own. Most of the recent slaves may have been smuggled into Arabia via Egypt and across the Red Sea to become servants, soldiers, and sex partners. Both Greenridge and Laffin associate the influx of oil revenues into Saudi Arabia and some other Arab countries with increases in demand for slaves.[88] It can be said, however, that slave labor has been transformed into migrant labor in most oil-producing Arab countries.

The pilgrimage to Mecca has been used as one of the few remaining means of promoting slavery. Some pilgrims have sold their servants to pay their travel expenses, thus, using human beings as living travelers' checks.[89] Buyers have profited by reselling the slaves in their countries, on their return from Mecca.

South Asia

It is known that many Africans arrived in Pakistan with the slave trade and migrated to Karachi, the capital, after the partition of India in 1947. While the origins of the population remain questionable, new dimensions continue to unfold. Most of the people of African descent in Pakistan are in the Makran district of Baluchistan. Early in the twentieth century they apparently constituted one-quarter of the total population.[90] In the 1951 census, about 80,000 Makranis were reported in West Pakistan.[91]

The Kharan district in Baluchistan also possesses a large group of blacks, who are called Sarozais and Longahis. Sayed Habib, writing of Kharan in 1907, maintained they were "the descendants of those captured slaves who were taken in battles with Iran and Afghanistan. Purdil Khan . . . is said to have brought 4,000 captives from Minab in southern Persia to the area" in the eighteenth century.[92]

The Gadras of Las Bela and Makran, whose ancestors came from Africa by way of Saudi Arabia, have mixed with slave peoples of a later period and appear culturally different from other blacks found in Pakistan. Some are quite educated and no longer speak the language of their country of origin. Despite the education some have obtained, most in Las Bela live off the streets. Vertical mobility is a very recent occurrence, and much of it is due to the great emigration of the Hindu and Sikh populations, which gave new opportunities to the Makranis. Karachi, as a capital, has augmented the possibilities. Not unexpectedly, what little economic mobility that has occurred did not necessarily mean status mobility. For example, intermarriage between Makranis and other groups remains the exception rather than the rule.

The descendants of Africans are still to be found in many parts of India, though they are concentrated primarily in three areas.[93] They are linked to their African heritage by language and physical appearance.[94] The largest number reside along the coastline at Janjira, long an important black center. Among them are descendants of army conscripts, many of whom make a living as rickshaw drivers. The blacks of Janjira speak the language of the state of Maharastra-Marathi. While a few of them have assimilated into Indian society, most maintain their indigenous customs and identity despite living in India for centuries. Their physical features suggest the presence of African heritage.[95]

In Hyderabad, black people are located in a section called *habshiguda* ("the black locality"). They speak Urdu.[96] Joseph Harris provides a striking account of this

African community. To some degree they retain various cultural aspects of their African heritage, in particular linguistic and artistic characteristics. Most are Muslims with little education and as of the 1970s worked as menial laborers and house servants.[97]

A study of North Kanara Siddis found strong community pride, although Siddis were assimilated into Hindu culture, and were situated in the middle of the local caste hierarchy. A researcher concluded of this group that "a stranger to [the] area would not be in a position to distinguish the Siddhis from other groups except through their racial characteristics. The Siddhis do not suffer from any sort of prejudice, either racial or cultural."[98]

A few Siddi also live in the state of Gujarat and particularly in Ahmadabad, its capital; their local area is called *Siddi Ganj.* A study commissioned by the Labour Social Welfare and Tribal Development Department, Government of Gujarat, found that Gujarat Siddis concentrate in the towns of Kutch, Broach, and Surat and in the Ahmedabad district. According to the 1971 census, Siddis numbered 4,482, an increase of 23 percent over 1961 census figures.[99] Unlike conditions for those in Kanara, Gujarat Siddis live in deplorable circumstances and in extreme poverty. Working mainly as agricultural, construction, and forest laborers, it is often difficult for them to find work, especially full-time.

In 1968 several Siddis in India organized the Siddi Welfare Association. As of 1975 they were unable to significantly alter their social and economic condition. However, they had taken an important first step—they had achieved a higher level of consciousness. After a trip through Africa, members of the association expressed a desire to establish direct contacts with black peoples worldwide.[100]

Conclusion

Though the diaspora permeated the Middle East in large numbers thousands of years ago, the communities that exist there today remain little understood, either because they are small or because records of their existence are rarely and poorly kept. What is available in the historical record indicates that, in the Middle East, Africans have been accepted into societies at uneven rates, in some areas achieving great fame and success, while in others the life as a worker remains their only obvious legacy. Whether because they learned it from others or because of their own ethnocentrism, documents indicate that most societies in western Asia also held mixed feelings about those with black skin. Whether this is still the case remains one of many great mysteries of the African presence in the Middle East.

The presence of Africans in East Asia stands in sharp contrast to that of the Middle East in large part because the numbers of Africans there have been relatively small. The smaller numbers suggest that actual communities of Africans are less likely to exist. In the next section we examine the African presence in East Asia from the fourth century to the present.

THE AFRICAN PRESENCE IN EAST ASIA

From the Fourth to the Twentieth Centuries

Among the countries of East Asia only in China and Japan did people of African ancestry appear in any measurable numbers before the nineteenth century. Chinese knowledge of Africans dates to the third century, and Japan's contact with Africa began in about the sixteenth century. A Chinese work of the third century, *Brief Accounts on the Wei Kingdom*, alludes to the City of Alexandria.[101] Commerce between the two areas developed early and soon involved human cargo. In China, dark-skinned Kunlun slaves were very popular, and there are references to them in the fourth and fifth centuries. In T'ang times, some Kunlun slaves were Africans imported by Arab traders.[102] There also is mention of slaves from Seng-chih, which probably is the same as T-seng-chi-I, a transliteration of Zanji, the general Arabic word for black Africans.[103]

Generally speaking, foreign slaves were called several names, including Kunlun. This term initially was confined to people from southwestern China and probably was applied specifically to negritos. It was later used for slaves from countries around the Indian Ocean, including black Africans.[104] An early record states "that most of the wealthy people keep devil-slaves. Their colour is black as ink, their lips red and teeth white. They are called K-un-lun slaves."[105] According to a document of the eighth century, "negro slaves were once again sent to the T'ang court in 724 A.D., coming from the kingdom of Palembang," and they appear to be Africans imported via Sumatra; other "negro slaves were also imported to China by way of the South Sea Islands."[106] Chinese attitudes are revealed in their terms for this population: "devil-slaves," "wild men," and "barbarian slaves."[107]

Although the number of Africans in China was never great, it was notable. T'ang (618–907) and Sung (960–1279) literature contains many references to black slaves, and they emerged in Chinese romances and fables.[108] By the thirteenth century their ownership was a measure of status: Important men in north China "were said not to be perfect gentlemen" unless they had a black servant. In 1382 "101 male and female Negroes" were sent as gifts to an emperor of the Ming dynasty (1364–1644).[109] Contact came to include diplomatic missions, and chronicles refer to envoys from East Africa with gifts of great interest to the Chinese. The *Pictorial Records of Foreign Countries*, published about 1430, contains a drawing of a zebra supposedly brought from Africa, and in 1444 an artist painted a giraffe purportedly given by an East African ruler to a king of Bengal, who then sent it to China. A giraffe brought directly to China from Malindi is also mentioned at an early period.[110]

Much of the early African slave trade to China was transacted by Arabs; later, the Portuguese also became a major influence. On a typical trip, a Portuguese ship left home in April or May; stopped in Africa, Goa, and Ceylon; called at Malacca, Singapore, Macao, and Canton; and went finally to Kyushu.[111] From China, "a ship starting . . . in mid-winter (the eleventh moon) would arrive at Lam-Li [Lamri, in northwestern Sumatra] in about forty days, where it would carry on trade during the summer. Then making use of the northeast monsoon of the following year, it would weigh anchor and reach the country of the Arabs in sixty days."[112] This journey of almost 10,000 miles as the crow flies was nearly twice that by sea, and a round trip could take almost a year.

Despite the distance, at one point Hainan became a very important Muslim colony, and the Arab merchants in Canton were powerful enough to start a rebellion and sack the city in the eighth century. By the sixteenth century, the Portuguese dominated East Asian trade and they brought Africans for sale to both China and Japan and used them as part of their imperialistic army and navy.

The far-flung Portuguese empire required a large number of men to maintain it, and the workforce available in such a small country was inadequate. The population was about 1.2 million in the sixteenth century, and an estimated 2,400 left Portugal annually for overseas territories, most of them young, able-bodied, unmarried males. Many died of illness en route or in Africa or Asia. The manpower shortage was so severe that mustering 1,000 white men for an expedition was difficult. Very few women emigrated to Asia; some ships carried up to fifteen, but most had none.[113]

Given the desperate need for seamen, Asians often served under Eurasian or white officers, and ships plying the Goa-Macao-Nagasaki route were sometimes manned entirely by Asians and blacks under a Portuguese captain.[114] European conquest owed much to persons of African and Asian ancestry, but we know little about those who served on the ships. As Arnold Rubin notes in his study of "Black Nanban": "One of the most tantalizing questions has to do with the remarkable degree of professionalism manifested by the Black sailors."[115] Were they placed in these positions to acquire on-the-job training, or did they have this expertise when they were enslaved?

The Portuguese also were forced to use African and Asian soldiers to protect their possessions. The example of Macao is instructive. Strategically located on lucrative trade routes, Macao was attacked by the Dutch in the 1620s, but the attackers were repulsed by black soldiers who fought so well that many of them were later liberated and settled in the area. Jan Coen, who had been sent to establish a Dutch base on the China coast, wrote about the slaves who served the Portuguese so faithfully: "It was they who defeated and drove away our people last year." A heroine of these campaigns was a black female who wielded a halberd with such effect that she was admiringly compared to a Portuguese heroine, a legendary woman of Alijubarrota, who slew seven Spaniards with a shovel. Many of these slaves were Bantu, primarily from southern Africa.[116]

Aside from their military importance, Africans contributed to the social composition of Macao:

> There was much intermixing of Portuguese, African, and Asian blood. In Macao, the admixture of Chinese blood in the course of the centuries came from cohabitation of masters with their *muitasi* [local female children sold by impoverished parents for domestic service], and was for many years less noticeable than the strain derived from other Asiatic races and African negresses.[117]

According to another source,

> in 1635, . . . it was said to contain some 7,000 inhabitants: 5,100 were slaves, and most of the slaves were African men and women. . . . Many were assigned to the hard, coarse labour of crewing the great trading carracks which sailed from Macao to Portugal's outposts in India and Japan. Others . . . were employed in the Jesuit residence, the charity hospital and the various private households.[118]

Some slaves evidently saw a chance for a better life in China than with the Portuguese, for a number fled from Macao and allied with Chinese commanders. Three hundred of them were organized into a bodyguard for Zheng Zhilong, a retired coastal pirate who accepted the job of suppressing other pirates on behalf of the failing Ming dynasty.[119]

In Japan, early evidence of a black presence comes mainly from art of the sixteenth and seventeenth centuries that focused on contact with foreign visitors. According to Charles Boxer, who has written much on the Portuguese involvement with the East, the *kurombojin* (blackamoors) are frequently depicted in popular Japanese glyptic and applied art.[120] *Nanban* (meaning southern barbarian; foreigners at the time always came from the south of Japan) paintings seem to have been made for *daimyo* (feudal lords) or wealthy Nagasaki merchants, as many were done in expensive gold-flecked paints. Only about sixty of these *byobu* (folding screens) survived the attempted cleansing of European influence after 1639. The *Nanban-byobu* that contain black subjects usually show a Portuguese ship disembarking passengers and crew, who are met by Japanese and some Europeans. Many of the screens depict "negro sailors in the ship's rigging and performing acrobatic feats,"[121] or "negro attendants carrying large parasols."[122] Rubin believes the *Nanban-byobu* show "that the Africans in question were quite aware of their specialized and pivotal roles. This seems to be communicated through the remarkable vitality, self-confidence, and sense of full participation" that characterizes the blacks on the screens. "Evidence in this regard ranges from the flamboyance of the retainers and attendants, to the briskly businesslike demeanor of black boatmen, stevedores and porters, to the breathtaking acrobatics performed by black sailors."[123]

The Portuguese are shown as tall, aquiline-nosed, aloof, pale, and imperious but with a degree of individualization. Those accompanying them range in skin color from gray to yellow to black, have less facial expression, and wear less elaborate costumes than the whites. Taken together, they are almost certainly representations of the Arabs, Gudjratis, Malays, and Africans upon whose labor and seamanship Portuguese enterprise in East Asia depended.[124]

While it does not appear often, evidence suggests that some encounters between Africans and Japanese were bloody. In 1615 a brawl in Nagasaki between a Portuguese foraging party and some Japanese ended in two or three of the latter being killed. When a *daimyo* demanded the surrender of the culprits, "four Negro slaves were handed over for execution."[125]

Many of these early visitors to Japan kept diaries of their trips. The accounts make a point of noting that the Japanese were especially impressed by the sight of Africans. In 1581 Bartolomeu Vaz Landeiro impressed the Japanese "as he went everywhere attended by a bodyguard of eight Muslim and Negro slaves."[126] When Alessandro Valiganao traveled to Kyoto in 1591, his procession included horses accompanied by an Indian groom "attired in gorgeous costume, and even the black slaves were dressed in velvet."[127]

Traditionally, most of these accounts reflect opinions and experiences of the privileged participants in historical events. We seldom obtain a view of how the masses feel, but a few accounts give us some insight. Most people seem to have been especially intrigued with African members of the Portuguese companies that visited during the seventeenth century. Africans were so interesting that the Japanese "would often come thirty or forty miles to see them and entertain them honorably for three or four days at a time."[128] Luis Frois, a Jesuit priest, wrote in April 1581 about this curiosity:

> The . . . population of Miyako [Kyoto] broke down the door of the Jesuit residence in their eagerness to inspect a negro slave and several were injured in the ensuing brawl. So great was their desire to see him that it was alleged that he would have earned at least 10,000 *cruzados* in a very short time if put on exhibition. All this aroused the curiosity of Nobunaga [a shogun] who summoned the man into his presence. He was so intrigued by the dusky fellow that he made him strip to the waist to satisfy himself that his colour was genuine. The ruler thereupon called his children to witness this extraordinary spectacle and one of his nephews gave the man a sum of money.[129]

Despite the role skin color plays today, the Japanese made little note of it during early contact with the West. In his account of the history of Japanese perceptions of skin color, Hiroshi Wagatsuma states that initially the Japanese were more impressed with the height, hair color, general hairiness, and large noses and eyes of the Europeans than with their coloring. Moreover, much of what the Japanese learned about how to fit Africans into their conceptual world—and into an increasingly important international context—was directly related to what they were told by Europeans. For example, one Japanese scholar wrote that his Dutch friends told him "these black ones" were by nature stupid; they had flat noses because they "tie their children's noses with leather bands to prevent their growth and to keep them flat." Moreover, he was told, "They are uncivilized and vicious in nature."[130] Others believed that the Africans' dark skin and frizzy hair resulted from living too close to the sun. The more enlightened Dutch informed the Japanese that Africans were impoverished Indians and were not monkeys.[131]

Evidence suggests that there were African slaves in the Philippines in the sixteenth and seventeenth centuries. The first archbishop of Manila petitioned for free passage for three African slaves "as have been given the other prelates in the Indies."[132] Most African slaves were purchased directly or indirectly from the Portuguese, although some apparently were born on the island. Given their status as slaves, and being so far from home, it is not surprising that they gave the Spanish much trouble. Africans were generally reported as being "of the worst kind" and "given to carousing, revolt, thievery and highway robbery," and "there were repeated requests to prohibit their importation or to remove those already resident—four or five hundred of them in 1636."[133]

People of African ancestry next appear in the Japanese historical record in the nineteenth century.[134] This was more than two hundred years after the closing of

Japan to the outside world and before Commodore Perry's 1853 visit, during the era of *sakoku* (foreign exclusion). In 1848 the American ship *Manhatten*, captained by Mercator Cooper, returned some shipwrecked Japanese home. Among the crew was Pyrrhus Concer, the steersman and probably the first black American to be seen in Japan. The Japanese initially were fearful of the white crew, but that feeling later turned to curiosity. Concer, however, was almost an immediate spectacle:

> Hundreds of the population came aboard both day and night to satisfy their curiosity. Everything, especially the woolen clothing of the men, was examined and marveled at. . . . One after another tried to rub off the black of his skin, stare at his marvelous white teeth and listen to him speak. They had never seen a black man before. Captain Cooper was asked where Pyrrhus and other black men came from. He was able to satisfy them by drawing a crude map of the United States and simply drawing a line across the map indicating whites came from one side and blacks from the other.[135]

One Japanese author suggests that Concer was considered the leader of the expedition because of his distinctive color.[136] Not long after this visit other black Americans followed.

In 1854, when Commodore Perry and his black warships forced the reopening of Japan to the West, at either side as he disembarked was an African American bodyguard, "two of the best-looking fellows of their colour that the squadron could furnish." In fact, they were specifically chosen for their imposing nature to impress the Japanese.[137] After an exchange of gifts, there followed entertainment derived from white American views of blacks—a minstrel show, with whites in blackface. The black faces, ragtime music, and strange dances and costumes probably were astonishing to the Japanese.[138] One can only speculate how Japanese views of Africans were influenced by a cultural exchange that highlighted stereotypical and racist notions about black Americans.

While the visits of Africans helped shape Japanese views about them, there were other sources of information as well. A Japanese delegation toured Africa and the United States on the eve of the American Civil War, a time when the separation of races was generally considered as for the good of (white) society. Some Japanese attitudes can be seen in diaries kept during the trip. The black condition is rationalized in several ways. According to one delegate, Yanagawa, "the laws of the land [United States] separate the blacks. They are just like our *eta* caste. But they employ the blacks as their servants. The whites are of course intelligent and the blacks stupid. Thus the seeds of intelligence and unintelligence are not allowed to mix." Another delegate,

Namura, blames Africans for slavery: "The Africans' industry has been for many years the sale of their children and relatives to other countries."[139]

Masao Miyoshi, who wrote a book about the diplomatic journey, suggests that the Japanese held ethnocentric and even racist notions about their own superiority, but their views of blacks and Africans were rarely based on direct contact. Thus, much of what they had learned came from others, most probably Europeans and Americans. When contact did occur, how it was interpreted often was filtered through the Western delegates who accompanied them, in this case William Preston, who had been U.S. minister to Spain. The following is from the diary of one Japanese delegate visiting the United States:

> Preston was a big man, around thirty-eight or thirty-nine years of age. He was proud as he pointed out the flags of the Rising Sun to me, saying "very good." As he singled out black women, he said they were the same color as the black wool suit he had on, and sneered at them, calling them ugly. He seemed very pleased with the white people and, whenever he saw white women, said "very good," and pointed them out to me.[140]

That kind of socialization would be used to help the Japanese explain, and rationalize, the racial hierarchy they found in the West, which placed Africans at the bottom.[141]

Afro-Asians in the Twentieth Century

The earlier views of Africans continued into the twentieth century, often reinforced by a continual flow of Western images and contact. There were four primary avenues by which Asians could learn about people of African descent: through the transfer of cultural artifacts from the West to Asia, foreign visitors, the interaction between the Chinese and African diasporas, and U.S. military involvement in Asia.

Cultural Artifacts

The Japanese learned much about blacks through American cultural artifacts and ideas that made their way to East Asia during the early twentieth century. For example, the stereotypical views of black Americans in *Uncle Tom's Cabin* and Stephen Foster's "Old Black Joe" were common staple in Japanese classrooms in the

1930s and 1940s. Other fare, such as the popular children's magazine *Adventurous Dankichi,* reinforced these attitudes. The main character in the magazine was a Japanese boy who grew up in the South Pacific. He consistently outwitted the black natives and eventually became their king (the stories mixed myths about the South Pacific and Africa). In these stories blacks were simpleminded souls, cannibalistic and warlike; once the boy tamed and educated them, they became loyal servants. Reflecting this view, popular caricatures of blacks would become marketing successes in the 1950s and 1990s (in the form of dolls that look like pickaninnies).[142]

Most Japanese, like most Americans, do not see themselves as prejudiced, but on closer inspection Japanese biases against blacks appear in a number of sources. According to Wagatsuma, who reviewed attitudes toward skin color throughout Japanese history, "the Japanese are unequivocally and unanimously negative toward the negroid features of Black Americans and Africans," find very negative connotations in black pigmentation, and hold sexual and animalistic stereotypes of blacks. These attitudes even extend to contemporary novels written by noted Japanese authors. Wagatsuma also found that among a number of ethnic groups, blacks were the least liked after Koreans.[143] A survey of Sophia University students in Tokyo in the 1960s revealed that many of them held images of blacks similar to the most bigoted opinions in the United States.[144] Most of the specific views of the Japanese about blacks resemble American attitudes. Considering that the Japanese have had little contact with Africans and black Americans, it appears that they have learned to mimic American racial attitudes, at least toward people of African ancestry.[145]

Foreign Visitors

The second source of information on people of African ancestry comes from visitors. There were not many in earlier eras, and they left few distinguishable descendants in East Asia. The blacks seen there today often came as students, diplomats, trade representatives, and in other capacities, as did Alex Quapong, former vice chancellor of the University of Ghana, who was appointed to head the United Nations University in Japan in the 1970s.

Many African students came to the People's Republic of China (PRC) because they were attracted to its liberation ideology and African policies.[146] Their feeling of kinship to this country is similar to that expressed by W. E. B. DuBois earlier in the century. He celebrated his ninety-first birthday there and called upon the people of Africa and all others who were oppressed to look toward China, which after long centuries has arisen to her feet and leapt forward. Africa arise, and stand straight, speak and think! Act! Turn from the west and your slavery and humiliation for the last 500 years and face the rising sun. Behold a people, the most populous nation on this ancient earth which has burst its shackles, not by boasting and strutting, not by lying about its history and its conquests, but by patience and long suffering, by hard, backbreaking labor and with bowed head and blind struggle, moved up and on toward the crimson sky.

She aims to "make men holy; to make men free." But what men? Not simply the rich, but not excluding the rich; not simply the learned, but led by knowledge to the end that no man shall be poor, nor sick, nor ignorant; that the humblest worker as well as the sons of emperors shall be fed and taught and healed and that there emerge on earth a single unified people, free, well and educated. Speak, China, and tell your truth to Africa and the world. What people have been despised as you have? Who more than you have been rejected of men? Recall when lordly Britishers threw the rickshaw money on the ground to avoid touching a filthy hand. Forget not the time when in Shanghai no "Chinamen" dared set foot in a park which he paid for. Tell this to Africa, for today Africa stands on new feet, with new eyesight, with new brains and asks: Where am I and why?[147]

Many Africans who have visited China would find fault with this view.

Beginning in the late 1950s, the PRC made a concerted effort to attract African visitors, mostly students. Many of them wished to make friends with the Chinese, but that was a time when casual friendship with foreigners was difficult. Most interactions were superficial. Many of the Africans were single males, which created additional conflicts, especially when they wanted to date Chinese women. One of the first clashes between Chinese and Africans is chronicled by Emmanuel Hevi, a Ghanian student who condemned the educational program offered by the Chinese. His account would be used to hasten the program's demise. It was revived in the 1960s in response to moves by rivals (especially the USSR) to create programs in Africa.[148]

Studies of reactions by the Chinese to African students during the 1970s and 1980s suggest that their prejudice was a mixture of racial, class, and cultural attitudes. Anti-African protests were a combination of nationalism fused with racial views and an effort to promote democratic reforms to strengthen China's national dignity. The roots of this prejudice, it is argued, developed over time and through contact with Africans. The Chinese saw themselves as white prior to the twentieth century, and lighter skin color was considered a sign of higher social status. When the Chinese met Africans in significant numbers in the twelfth century, they had developed few attitudes about them but saw them as both barbarians and embodiments of valor. "Chinese merchants and travelers made contact with Africans . . . during the Song Dynasty (1127–1279) and they recorded their positive impressions of Africans and their customs. When a delegation from a state on the East African coast went to China in the late eleventh century, its emissaries were treated with honour equivalent to ambassador status."[149] This image changed after the twelfth century with the arrival of Arab traders bringing African slaves. The idea of Africans as sub-humans became established and grew during the closing of China under the Ming dynasty. By then the world was conceptualized as consisting of two groups, the superior white and yellow races and the unhistorical races (such as Africans), who were regarded as China's backward past. The Chinese in the twentieth century especially did not want to be seen as Third World people with all that would imply about them as a player on the international stage.[150]

The Chinese Diaspora Intersects with the African Diaspora

The interaction between the African diaspora and the Chinese diaspora is exemplified by Eugene Chen, born in San Fernando, Trinidad, in 1878 to Chinese parents who had fled Taiping for political reasons. He was one of Trinidad's first Chinese solicitors, and on several occasions in the 1920s and 1940s he was foreign minister to the Chinese government. He died in 1944 in Shanghai under house arrest by the Japanese. His connection to the African diaspora lies in the fact that he married a Creole of African descent, Agatha Ganteaume, one of whose ancestors was Admiral Ganteaume of Napolean's navy.[151]

Of the eight children from this marriage, four survived to adulthood: Percy (born 1901), Sylvia (1905), Jack (1908), and Yolanda (1912). By the time their father was in his mid-thirties, he was wealthy enough to retire. He left a brother in charge of his law practice and took his children to England to be educated.[152] Percy went to University College School at Hampstead, London University, and Middle Temple to become a lawyer; Jack took much the same route and also became a lawyer. Sylvia studied dance and elocution.[153] Little is known about Yolanda.

When Eugene moved to England, China, and then Moscow, most of the children followed. While in England in 1915–16, Percy appeared in a movie, "Smooth Dick, The Gentleman Cracksman," with Gladys Cooper, a renowned beauty of the English stage. In the late 1920s, Yolanda, Percy, and Jack lived in China. They all moved to Moscow in 1927, where the elder Chen was in exile and where Percy worked for General Motors. Jack and a woman named Si-lan (perhaps Sylvia) are mentioned by

Paul Robeson on one of his many visits to Moscow; at the time, Si-lan was married to an American, Jay Layda.[154]

Jack, a journalist, married a Russian who died in 1948. In 1950 he went to China with their son. He worked for *People's China* and *Peking Review*. One of the few foreigners to take part in the Cultural Revolution, he left in 1971 with his son and his second wife, a Chinese woman.[155] Among some of his works are *A Year in Upper Felicity, The Sinkiang Story,* and *The Chinese of America.* Although Agatha Chen was of African descent, as were her children, not once in the autobiographical accounts of Percy and Jack is there mention of their color, despite the fact that Sheean alluded to their black heritage by stating that the Chinese strain seemed almost to have vanished.[156]

The U.S. Military and Creation of the Amerasian

A significant source of Afro-Asians came about through interaction between military personnel and Asian women. This began for the United States with the Spanish-American War and occupation of the Philippines in 1898, which resulted in a number of mixed-race children, often called Amerasians, who fit neither world and were often abandoned. It was the beginning of a major problem that continues to vex us. The Pearl S. Buck Foundation, one of the earliest organizations in the world to deal on any systematic level with problems faced by Amerasians, estimates that in the early 1980s there were up to 85,000 Amerasians in East Asia.[157] More recent figures are hard to find because the countries in which Amerasians reside do not keep good records of their numbers (if they keep them at all) and because many Amerasians are among those most difficult to count—they live in the streets or do not want to be found. Most of the figures mentioned are conjecture or educated guesses.

The majority of Amerasians were born after World War II. Exactly ten months after the first black American servicemen arrived to occupy Japan, the first brown-skinned child was born.[158] These births were not limited to any particular stratum in society, since one of the first half-black babies was the grandson of a former admiral in the Japanese navy. By 1951 there were 2,000 out-of-wedlock Amerasian children, although a like number may have been murdered by a parent at birth.[159] By 1967 there were an estimated 20,000, one-tenth of whom were half black. In the early 1980s the number was between 20,000 and 25,000, of whom about 3,000 to 4,000 were Afro-Japanese.[160] Statistics given by International Social Assistance Okinawa in 1972 showed 3,000 Amerasians. Of these, 89 percent had no father present; 60 percent were products of a white father, and just over 3 percent had black fathers.[161]

In Korea, in 1965, after fifteen years of contact, there were approximately 12,000 Amerasians.[162] In the 1980s there were between 1,800 and 3,000 black Koreans.[163] For the most part, these children resulted from the "yobo culture." *Yobo* is Korean for "honey" or wife, and is used by soldiers to describe a Korean prostitute who provides a live-in arrangement. Called ranching on Okinawa and bungalowing in Thailand, this culture left a serious sociological problem wherever troops were stationed. To address the problem in many cases, orphanages were set up with donations from GIs.[164]

Vietnam has the most extensive Amerasian population in Asia. Between 1961 and 1971, two million American men served there, and it is estimated that by 1971 there were from 5,000 to 400,000 Amerasian children there.[165] By 1975, anywhere from 1,500 to 120,000 could have been black, although official statistics claimed there were 500.[166] In 1980, the Vietnamese government reported 8,000 Amerasians in Ho Chi Minh City (formerly Saigon) alone.[167] These statistics represent children who have to cope, if they survive, with environs that are at best indifferent to them. Often their mothers are illiterate and unskilled, disdained for consorting with a foreigner, and unable to provide much of a future. One woman compared the French and Americans in Vietnam: Americans had five minutes of fun and forgot about the consequences; the Frenchman at least paid for his child's education.[168]

In Vietnam, dark skin is automatically viewed as inferior.[169] Among Amerasians, those who are part black encounter the most discrimination because their skin makes other Vietnamese suspicious of them, since their color is equated with the lower peasant class. Thus, their color affects marital possibilities and self-esteem.[170]

Some black soldiers claim that the military made it almost impossible for them to marry a Vietnamese woman and bring her home, even though she had already given birth to their child, whereas it was easier for white military personnel to do so. The same was said by black servicemen in Germany, England, Italy, and France after World War II and later in Korea and Japan. More than one black soldier was transferred after officers discovered a liaison with a local woman.[171]

In societies with a common culture and homogeneous population, mixed-race children are easily spotted and face extreme discrimination. A father is crucial in Buddhist and Confucian social structures, and he determines a child's citizenship. Because there is no "official" father, in some places Amerasians are technically citizens, counted for statistical purposes, but have no rights. In Thailand, for example, there have been attempts to deal with this problem, but most of the children remain stateless, with all the hardships that implies. In the 1980s, Okinawa alone had "at least six hundred of these stateless children."[172] The general problem is illustrated by the situation in Japan, where the civil code stated in the 1970s that nationality is determined by the father. In order to obtain a decent job, for example, one must be recognized, that is, have a family name, which is obtained through the father. Prospects are dim for an uneducated, part-black youth with no family connections, to whom only certain fields are open, such as boxing, which is stereotypically seen as black-dominated.[173]

The military occupation of Japan in 1945 may have played a role in shaping Japanese attitudes toward black Amerasians. During World War II, the U.S. military was still segregated. Black units were primarily under the command of whites, and blacks were assigned more menial tasks. The Japanese usually saw blacks in these subordinate positions. Japanese society is very hierarchical,[174] and it is more than likely that blacks were considered in much the same way as Japanese view Ainu, *eta* (cultural and ethnic outcasts), and Koreans in their society, as low in the social order. It is clear that prejudicial attitudes increased with the influx of blacks into Japan after 1945, since a film genre on this social problem developed. One movie, *Yassa Massa*, produced by Japan's leading film company, starred a black American sailor,[175] and like others in the genre it depicted the hardship of black Japanese children and their parents.[176]

Studies on Amerasians find several factors that predict high distress: not living with the biological mother, low formal education, and being black.[177] Black Amerasians exist in a social and cultural twilight zone, and they live doubly hard lives due to disenfranchisement because they do not have a father at home and are scorned because they are black.[178] They encounter discrimination in the Asian culture into which they are born and rarely are granted U.S. citizenship, which can only be viewed as an extension of the historic pattern of racial exclusion in the United States. Abandoned by their father and often by their mother, as well as by the U.S. military and government, those who do not die as infants often grow into angry and despairing adults. Emotionally insecure and often harboring self-hate, many have serious psychological problems.

Teresa Williams examined a group of forty-three Amerasians living in Japan during the late 1980s. Among her black informants, few had developed a fully positive Afro-Asian self-image, a situation confounded by conflicting messages received from the three communities with which they must interact: white Amerasians, black Americans, and Japanese. As one black Amerasian explained it: "*Moo yada*, I hate when White people and *Nihonjin* [Japanese] think I can only dance and sing or my dad is a *jyanguru no dojin* [native of the jungle]."[179]

According to some, Amerasians are not singled out by the Japanese but instead face the general prejudice against anyone who is different. In this racially monolithic nation there are more than three million outcasts, called *eta*, who until recently were legally second-class citizens. Most still live in certain areas of Hiroshima and Kyushu. *Eta* refers to being unclean and indicates that in times past these people worked at occupations considered dirty, such as slaughtering animals. Now referred to as *Shin-heimin*, or new citizens, they cannot legally be discriminated against, but they still encounter much bias, especially in employment and marriage. It is little wonder that many Japanese reject the children of interracial couples, with part-black children often considered the bottom of the heap.[180]

Despite the dominant beliefs about Amerasians, recent research suggests that while many, if not most, live very hard lives, such a picture is too simplistic when describing all Amerasians. It has been found that they vary in family background, socioeconomic status, level of education, and the amount of discrimination encountered; most of their mothers are not prostitutes.[181] The ideas persist, however, that they are all downtrodden and dispossessed, in part because it is popular to believe that since racial prejudice is endemic to Asian and American societies, their mixed status is synonymous to being mixed-up, torn by the internal conflict implicit in their very being. This view is common in research on multiethnic people generally.[182]

The United States has used various policies to deal with the situation faced by Amerasians. Before 1982, no special provisions were made for them; they were inadequately covered under U.S. law, which directed that the American father overseas must establish the paternity of the child born out of wedlock *and* marry the alien mother in order for the child to be granted U.S. citizenship. All this must have happened before the child was twenty-one. Furthermore, under U.S. law, the father had to live in the United States for ten years before the child's birth, a period that included at least five years after the father's fourteenth birthday, a provision in the law that automatically denied citizenship to the offspring born to servicemen and women age eighteen or nineteen.[183]

The first official policy drafted specifically for Amerasians came in 1982. The Amerasian Immigration Act gave top priority for immigration to the United States to children fathered by Americans in Korea, Laos, Vietnam, Cambodia, and Thailand. It granted immigration only to Amerasians, which led to many mothers of minors signing a release for their children to immigrate.[184] This act was followed by several others, all of which were problematic.[185] The 1987 Amerasian Homecoming Act improved on previous legislation but remained insufficient. With this law, Amerasians could enter with one immediate family member (which forced them to choose one parent), including an unmarried sibling, spouse, or child. The legislation failed to consider that many Amerasians were by then eighteen years of age or older and might have started their own families.[186] As a result of this provision in the act, many Amerasians chose a parent or relative, assuming that later it would be easier to sponsor a spouse. Given the policy, Amerasians became valuable commodities for Vietnamese seeking to immigrate to the United States. Some bought Amerasians to obtain entry. Historically, Amerasians had been known as "dust of life"; since the 1987 act, they are also called "gold children."[187]

In 1992, a class-action suit was filed to obtain medical and educational benefits for underaged Amerasians. These primarily Vietnamese Amerasian refugees in the Philippines sued the United States for breach of contract embedded in its plan to cut aid to Amerasians and their families on 30 June 1997.[188] This move by the U.S. government came a little more than twenty-two years after the withdrawal from Vietnam.

Conclusion

Africans are in Asia primarily because a workforce was necessary to further the interests of powerful people and countries. Whether to attain a measure of social status by showing off one's blacks, as in the Philippines and China, as a means of making great wealth for Arabs and Portuguese, or to act as the hammer of U.S. foreign policy in Japan and Vietnam, people of African ancestry have long played a role in the Asian landscape. They were so well known in Asia as work horses that local prejudices linked with stereotypes to create an ideology that justified black enslavement. Their positions of subordination were seen as reflecting inferiority in African people, a view often promulgated by those who oppressed them in the first place. The significant numbers of Asians of African descent represent one element in a larger global pattern. The peculiarities of their situations are a function of the particular culture in which they live, but they also are part of the global dynamic of racial dominance and unequal social relations. That dynamic continues with the abandonment of Amerasians by the United States in the late twentieth century and is reflected in the inattention to African and African American concerns, whether domestically or internationally.

NOTES

1. F. Lenormant, *Histoire Ancienne des Pheniciens* (Paris: Levy, 1890), 429; see also Bernard Lewis, "The African Diaspora and the Civilization of Islam," in *The African Diaspora: Interpretive Essays*, ed. M. Kilson and R. Rotberg (Cambridge, Mass.: Harvard University Press, 1976), 40–41.
2. Cheikh Diop, *The African Origin of Civilization: Myth or Reality* (New York: Anchor Books, 1969),

127, 128. See also J. A. Rogers, *Sex and Race: Negro-Caucasian Mixing in All Ages and Lands*, Volume 1: *The Old World* (New York: Helga M. Rogers, 1967), 95.

3. His name is alternately spelled Antarah or Antar. The Arabs, proud of their pure descent, call some blacks of antiquity, descended from an African mother and an Arab father, "the Ravens of the Arabs" (aghriat-al'arab) because of their dark complexions.

4. Ignance Goldziher, *A Short History of Classical Arabic Literature*, rev., trans. J. Desomogri (Hildesheim: Olms, 1966); Graham Irwin, *Africans Abroad: A Documentary History of the Black Diaspora in Asia, Latin America, and the Caribbean during the Age of Slavery* (New York: Columbia University Press, 1977), 40–41; and Lewis, "African Diaspora," 39–40.

5. Lenormant, *Histoire*, 429.

6. J. A. Rogers, *World's Great Men of Color* (New York: MacMillan, 1972), 1:539–40.

7. Ibid., 143–47; and Lewis, "African Diaspora," 41.

8. Rogers, *Sex and Race*, 59.

9. Diop, *African Origin*, 127.

10. Ibid., 72. See also Martin Bernal, *Black Athena: The Afroasiatic Roots of Classical Civilization*, vol. 1 (New Brunswick, N.J.: Rutgers University Press, 1987) and Ali Mazrui, *The Africans: A Triple Heritage* (Boston: Little, Brown and Co., 1986), for similar claims.

11. No one has yet explained how one branch of Noah's family suddenly changed from white to black because of a curse, but if the people of the area were originally black, then the curse would change them to white. But was being black the curse? As Joel Rogers relates, African American folklore has risen to answer the question: The brothers Shem, Ham, and Japheth were all three black, but while traveling in Africa, Japheth woke one morning to see a great white pool of water, ran to it, jumped in, and was immediately turned white. Anxious to make his brothers white, too, he ran to awaken them. Shem arose, but Ham did not want to be bothered and went back to sleep. Shem raced for the water, but nearly all of it had disappeared, and he got only enough to turn brown. Both called to Ham, who finally got up but took his time, and there was just enough water to wet his palms and the soles of his feet (see Rogers, *Sex and Race*, 60–61).

12. Diop, *African Origin*, 107.

13. Mohammad Kamiar, "Slavery in the Middle East: A Selected Research Bibliography" (unpublished), 10–11.

14. J. Leroy, "Les Ethiopiens de Persepolis," *Annales d' Ethiopia* 5 (1963): 293–97.

15. Rogers, *Sex and Race*, 61.

16. J. Comhaire, "Some Notes on Africans in Muslim History," *The Muslim World* 46 (1956): 336–44.

17. Bernard Lewis, *Race and Slavery in the Middle East: An Historical Enquiry* (New York: Oxford University Press, 1990).

18. P. Hitti, *History of the Arabs* (London: Macmillan 1971), 467, cited in R. W. Beachey, *A Collection of Documents on the Slave Trade of East Africa* (New York: Barnes and Noble, 1976), 4.

19. Edward Alpers, "The African Diaspora in the Northwestern Indian Ocean: Reconsideration of an Old Problem, New Directions for Research," *Comparative Studies of South Asia, Africa and the Middle East* 17 (1997): 63–81.

20. C. Diehl, *Byzantine Portraits*, trans. H. Bell (New York: A. Knopf, 1927), 215.

21. Rogers, *Sex and Race*, 286. In response to an inquiry by the author, a Turkish government official categorically denied there was ever any black presence in the country.

22. George Saintsbury, *East India Slavery*, 2nd ed. (London: Charles Tilt, 1829), 14.

23. Basil Davidson, *A History of East Africa and Central Africa to the Late Nineteenth Century* (Garden City, N.Y.: Anchor Books, 1967), 145; and Dionisius Agius, "A Selfish Pursuit in a Slave Uprising of Third/Ninth Century Iraq," *Slavery and Abolition* 4 (May 1983): 3–18.

24. D. Sourdel, "The Abbasid Caliphaate," in *The Cambridge History of Islam*, ed. Peter Hold, Ann Lambton, and Bernard Lewis (Cambridge: Cambridge University Press, 1970), 1:129.

25. Jere Bacharach, "African Military Slaves in the Medieval Middle East: The Cases of Iraq (869–955) and Egypt (868–1171)," *International Journal of Middle East Studies* 13 (1981): 471–95.

26. Akbar Muhammad, "The Images of Africans in Arabic Literature: Some Unpublished Manuscripts," in *Slaves and Slavery in Muslim Africa*, ed. John Willis, Volume 1: *Islam and the Ideology of Enslavement* (Totowa, N.J.: Frank Cass and Company, 1985), 47–74.

27. Constance Hilliard, "Zuhur al-Basatin and Ta'rikh al-Turubbe: Some Legal and Ethical Aspects of Slavery in the Sudan as Seen in the Works of Shaykh Musa Kamara," in *Slaves and Slavery in Muslim Africa*, ed. John Willis, Volume 1: *Islam and the Ideology of Enslavement* (Totowa, N.J.: Frank Cass and Company, 1985), 167.

28. Ibn Butlan and Risala fi Shira al-Raqiq, eds., *'Abd al-Salam Harun* (Ciro, 1954), 374–75, cited in Lewis, *Race and Slavery*, 92.

29. Cited in J. Hunwick, "Black Africans in the Islamic World: An Under-Studied Dimension of the Black Diaspora," *Tarikh* 5 (1978): 20–40; see Lewis, "African Diaspora," 50–51, for other examples of Arab views of black Africans.

30. Charles Doughty, *Travels in the Arabia Desert*, abridged by E. Garnett (Gloucester, Mass.: Peter Smith, 1968), 37.

31. Goldziher, *A Short History*.

32. Hunwick, "Black Africans," 22, 23; William Ochsenwald, "Muslim-European Conflict in the Hijaz: The Slave Trade Controversy, 1840–1895," *Middle Eastern Studies* 1 (January 1980): 115–26; see also Lewis, "African Diaspora."

33. Bernard Lewis, *Race and Color in Islam* (New York: Harper and Row, 1971), 18–29, 64–78.

34. Lewis, "African Diaspora," 42–43.

35. Ann Pescatello, "The African Presence in Portuguese India," *Journal of Asian History* 11 (1977): 27.

36. Hunwick, "Black Africans," 32.

37. Richard Pankhurst, "The History of Ethiopia's Relations with India prior to the Nineteenth Century," paper presented at the Fourth Conference of Ethiopian Studies, Rome, Italy (November 1972), 55.

38. Joseph Harris, *African Presence in Asia: Consequences of the East African Slave Trade* (Evanston, Ill.: Northwestern University Press, 1971) 35.

39. Pescatello, "The African Presence in Portuguese India."

40. V. Rao, "The Habshis: India's Unknown Africans," *African Report* 5 (September–October 1973): 37; and Harris, *African Presence*, 91.

41. Ibid., 103.

42. Philip Colomb, *Slave Catching in the Indian Ocean* (New York: Longman, Green and Co., 1873), 96–97.

43. Geoffrey Barraclough, ed., *Times Atlas of World History* (Maplewood, N.J.: Hammond, 1979), 198–99.

44. Ibid., 199.

45. Beachey, *Slave Trade*, 48.

46. See N. Bennett, "Christian and Negro Slavery in Eighteenth Century North Africa," *Journal of African History* 1 (1960): 68–82.

47. Harris, *African Presence*; and H. Russell, *Human Cargoes; A Short History of the African Slave Trade* (New York: Longman, Green and Co., 1948), 48.

48. Alpers, "The African Diaspora in the Northwestern Indian Ocean."

49. Joseph Harris, "The Black Peoples of Asia," in *World Encyclopedia of Black Peoples* (St. Clair Shores, Mich.: Scholarly Press, 1975), 266; Hunwick, "Black Africans," 25; and Russell, *Human Cargoes*, 68.

50. Russell, *Human Cargoes*, 68.

51. J. E. Inikori, "The Origin of the Diaspora: The Slave Trade from Africa," *Tarikh* 5, no. 4 (1978): 1–19.

52. S. Arasaratnam, "Slave Trade in the Indian Ocean in the Seventeenth Century," in *Mariners*,

     Merchants and Oceans: Studies in Maritime History, ed. K. S. Mathew (New Delhi: Manohar, 1995), 195–208.

53. Kamiar, "Slavery in the Middle East," 13.

54. Harris, *African Presence*, 77.

55. Beachey, *Slave Trade*, 179.

56. Kamiar, "Slavery in the Middle East," 14–15.

57. Ronald Jennings, "Black Slaves and Free Blacks in Ottoman Cyrpus, 1590–1640," *Journal of the Economic and Social History of the Orient* 30 (1987): 286–302; Ehud Toledano, "The Imperial Eunuchs of Istanbul: From Africa to the Heart of Islam," *Middle Eastern Studies* 20 (July 1984): 379–90.

58. George MacMunin, *Slavery through the Ages* (London: Nicholson and Watson, 1938), 58. See Rogers, *Sex and Race*, 61, for a picture of a Kizlar Agasi.

59. About court eunuchs see H. Gibb and Harold Bowen, *Islamic Society and the West*, Volume 1: *Islamic Society in the Eighteenth Century*, pt. 1–2 (London: Oxford University Press, 1950), 76f.

60. Beachey, *Slave Trade*, 4, 171. Many eunuchs rose to power because they did not threaten the dynastic order, since they could not father heirs.

61. Hunwick, "Black Africans," 30.

62. Gabriel Baer, *Studies in the Social History of Modern Egypt* (Chicago: University of Chicago Press, 1969), 164, cited in Lewis, *Race and Slavery*, 76.

63. Beachey, *Slave Trade*, 171.

64. Bernard Lewis, "Slade on the Turkish Navy," *Journal of Turkish Studies* 2 (1967), 10, cited in Lewis, *Race and Slavery*, 70.

65. Lewis, "African Diaspora," 46.

66. Hunwick, "Black Africans," 33.

67. A. M. H. Sheriff, "The Slave Mode of Production Along the East African Coast, 1810–1873," in *Slaves and Slavery in Muslim Africa*, ed. J. R. Willis (London: Frank Cass, 1985), 2:161–68.

68. I. B. Kake, "The Slave Trade and the Population Drain from Africa to North Africa and the Middle East," in *The African Slave Trade from the Fifteenth to the Nineteenth Century* (Paris: UNESCO, 1979), 164–74.

69. Jan Linschoten, *Voyage, I–II* (London: Hakluyt Series 1, 1885), 1:70–71, 264–65, cited in Pescatello, "The African Presence in Portuguese India," 30.

70. Ibid.

71. See A. Rubin, *Black Nanban: Africans in Japan during the Sixteenth Century* (Bloomington: Indiana University Press, 1974) for an informative account of this black contribution.

72. Charles Boxer, *The Portuguese Seaborne Empire* (New York: Alfred Knopf, 1969), 302.

73. Pescatello, "The African Presence in Portuguese India," 47–48.

74. Ibid., 31–32.

75. W. Wriggins, *Ceylon: Dilemma of a New Nation* (Princeton, N.J.: Princeton University Press, 1960), 13; and Moses Nwuila, *Britain and Slavery in East Africa* (Washington, D.C.: Three Continent Press, 1975), 2.

76. Roger Pineau, ed., *The Japan Expedition 1852–1854: The Personal Journal of Commodore Perry* (Washington, D.C.: Smithsonian Institution Press, 1968), 38.

77. H. Ray, ed., *History of Ceylon* (Colombo: Ceylon University Press, 1959), 1:32; and W. Harris and Judith Levy, eds., "Ceylon," in *The New Columbia Encyclopedia* (New York: Columbia University Press, 1975), 794.

78. Ray, *History of Ceylon*, 32; T. B. Nayar, *The Problems of Dravidian Origins: A Linguistic, Anthropological and Archaeological Approach* (Madras: University of Madras, 1977), 8; Philip Gove, ed., *Webster's Third New International Dictionary* (Springfield, Mass: Merriam, 1971), 686; and N. Singh, *The Andaman Story* (New Delhi: Vikas, 1978), 57.

79. Rao, "The Habshis," 35–38; see also Harris, *African Presence,* for a much more elaborate account.

80. R. R. Chauhan, *Africans in India: From Slavery to Royalty* (New Delhi: Asian Publication Services, 1995), 2–3.

81. Dady Banaji, *Slavery in British India* (Bombay: Taraporevaba Sons, 1933), 245.

82. Beachey, *Slave Trade,* 50.

83. Jonathan Derrick, *Africa's Slaves Today* (New York: Schocken Books, 1975); see also Lord Shackleton, "The Slave Trade Today," in *Slavery: A Comparative Perspective,* ed. Robin Winks (New York: New York University Press, 1972), 190–91, for a discussion of slavery until the early 1960s.

84. Derrick, *Africa's Slaves,* 37.

85. Cited in Hunwick, "Black Africans," 37.

86. Derrick, *Africa's Slaves,* 138.

87. Cited in Harris, "Black Peoples," 268.

88. J. Laffin, *The Arabs as Master Slavers* (Englewood, N.J.: SBS, 1982), 71; C. W. W. Greenridge, "Slavery in the Middle East," *Middle Eastern Affairs* 7, no. 12 (1956): 435–40.

89. Laffin, *Arabs as Master Slavers;* A. G. B. Fisher and H. J. Fisher, *Slavery and Muslim Society in Africa: The Institution in Saharan and Sudanic Africa and the Trans-Saharan Trade.* (London: C. Hurst and Company, 1970); Lewis, *Race and Color in Islam.*

90. District Gazeteer, "Makran," *Bombay Times,* 1907, 69.

91. Government of Pakistan, *Census of Pakistan,* 1951.

92. Sayed Habib, District Gazeteer, "Kharan," *Bombay Times,* 1907, 34.

93. Harris, "Black Peoples," and Rao, "Siddis."

94. G. Freeman-Grenville, "The Sidi and Swahili," *Bulletin of the British Association of Orientalists* 6 (1971): 3–18.

95. Chauhan, *Africans in India,* 1.

96. Rao, "The Habshis," 79.

97. Harris, *African Presence.*

98. T. Palakshappa, *The Siddhis of North Kanara* (New Delhi: Sterling Publishers, 1976), 104.

99. T. Naik and Gaurish Pandya, *The Sidis of Gujarat (A Socio-Economic Study and a Developmental Plan)* (Ahmedabad, India: Jitendra Thakorebhai Desai, 1993), 12.

100. Harris, "Black Peoples," 272.

101. Chou Yi-Lang, "Early Contacts Between China and Africa," *Ghana Notes and Queries* 12 (June 1972): 1–3.

102. Martin Wilbur, *Slavery in China during the Former Han Dynasty 206 B.C.–A.D. 25* (New York: Russell and Russell, 1943), 93; also see Chang Hsing-lang, "The Importation of Negro Slaves to China under the T'ang Dynasty (AD 618–977)," in *Catholic University of Peking Bulletin* 7 (December 1930): 37–60; Bethwell Ogot, "Population Movement between East Africa, the Horn of Africa and Neighboring Countries," in *The African Slave Trade from the Fifteenth to the Nineteenth Century* (Paris: UNESCO, 1979), 176; and Jan Duyvendack, *China's Discovery of Africa* (London: Arthur Probsthain, 1949), 7 and passim.

103. Duyvendack, *China's Discovery of Africa,* 23; also see Chang, "Slaves to China," 37, 41.

104. Luther C. Goodrich, "Negroes in China," *Catholic University of Peking Bulletin* 8 (December 1931): 137–39; also see Chang, "Slaves to China," 44.

105. Duyvendack, *China's Discovery of Africa,* 23; see also Graham Irwin, *Africans Abroad: A Documentary History of the Black Diaspora in Asia, Latin America, and the Caribbean during the Age of Slavery* (Ithaca, N.Y.: Cornell University Press, 1977), 169.

106. Chang, "Slaves to China," 44.

107. Irwin, *Africans Abroad,* 169; and Kuwabara Kitsuzo, "On P'u Shoukeng," *Memoirs of the Research Department of the Toyo Bunko* 2 (1928): 63.

108. Chou, "Early Contacts," 1. Irwin describes the blacks who appear in these fables as resourceful, cun-

ning, and brave; they are strikingly larger than life *(Africans Abroad,* 172–76).

109. Chou, "Early Contacts," 3.

110. Duyvendack, *China's Discovery of Africa,* 18.

111. Charles Boxer, *The Portuguese Seaborn Empire 1415–1825* (New York: Alfred Knopf, 1969), 52, 53.

112. There is also mention of a trading company in Singapore that owned 3,292 black slaves or seamen. See P. Loh Fook Seng, *The Malay States 1877–1895: Political Change and Social Policy* (London: Oxford University Press, 1969), 186.

113. Rubin, *Black Nanban,* 10.

114. Boxer, *Seaborn Empire,* 57.

115. Rubin, *Black Nanban,* 10.

116. Charles Boxer, *Fidalgos in the Far East 1550–1770,* 2nd rev. ed. (London: Oxford University Press, 1968), 231.

117. Boxer, *Fidalgos,* 231. Boxer suggests that the violent Japanese civil war in the seventeenth century drove many people to sell themselves or family members into bondage. A flourishing traffic in human flesh grew up in such ports as Kyushu, and most of the victims were unwanted females, Chinese, Koreans, or malefactors. Many Japanese women from Shimabara Island, near Nagasaki, became prostitutes in brothels of China and Malaya from the Meiji era onward. Slavery was repugnant to many Japanese, and they especially resented the purchase of their countrymen (if not their country-women) by black slaves in the service of the Portuguese, which was considered the depths of degradation.

118. Philip Snow, *The Star Raft: China's Encounter with Africa* (Ithaca, N.Y.: Cornell University Press, 1988), 38–39.

119. Ibid., 39.

120. Charles Boxer, *The Christian Century in Japan* (Berkeley: University of California Press, 1951), 35.

121. Boxer, *Fidalgos,* 21; see also Michael Cooper, ed., *The Southern Barbarians: The First Europeans in Japan* (Tokyo: Kondansha International, 1971), 176.

122. Cooper, *Barbarians,* 201.

123. Rubin, *Black Nanban,* 10.

124. Ibid., 6.

125. Ibid.; Boxer, *Fidalgos,* 67.

126. Charles Boxer, *The Tragic History of the Sea 1589–1622* (Cambridge: Cambridge University Press, 1959), 11, 41.

127. Boxer, *Christian Century,* 152; see also Y. Okamoto, *The Nanban Art of Japan* (New York: Weatherhill/Heibonshai, 1972), 71.

128. Boxer, *Christian Century,* 355; Rubin, *Black Nanban,* 8.

129. Camara Manoel, *Missoes dos Jesuitas no Oriente nos Seculos XVI e XVII* (Lisbon: 1894), 119, cited in Michael Cooper, *They Came to Japan* (Berkeley: University of California Press, 1965), 71.

130. Hiroshi Wagatsuma, "The Social Perception of Skin Color in Japan," *Daedalus* 96 (1967): 408–13.

131. Morishima Churyo, in *Komo Zatsuwa* [Chitchat with the Dutch], ed. R. Ono (Tokyo: 1943), 545. Wagatsuma suggests that also at this time in Japanese history, prior to much contact with the West, the Japanese valued "white" skin as beautiful and deprecated black skin as ugly. The Japanese considered themselves white before contact with Europeans. "White" skin had been considered an essential quality of feminine beauty since the eleventh century. By the late eighteenth century the Japanese found objectionable such features as a large face, the lack of any tufts of hair under the temple, a large flat nose, thick lips, black skin, a too plump body, and brownish wavy hair. Along with influencing their views about Africans, the Western world also taught the Japanese something about a color hierarchy. See Wagatsuma, "Social Perception."

132. "Testimonio de los autos que siguio el Real fisco con el Cabildo secular de la Ciudad de Manila . . . 1 Deciembre 1681–8 Octubre 1682," *Archivo General de Indias: Filipinas* 67-6-13, cited in William

Scott, *Slavery in the Spanish Philippines* (Manila: De La Salle University Press, 1991), 7.

133. The King to Governor Hurtado de Corcuera, 2 September 1638, cited in Scott, *Slavery*, 28.

134. There is some evidence that blacks also appear in the South Pacific at this time. See Hazel McFerson, "'Part-Black Americans' in the South Pacific," *Phylon* 43, no. 2 (1982): 177–80. They probably went there as participants during the heyday of the whaling industry. It was the practice of Fijian chiefs to adopt visiting foreigners for their knowledge of Western ways and skills with munitions. They soon came to rely on them in their households, especially black Americans: "Negroes, who were sometimes landed from American ships, were even more prized than white men." See R. Derick, *A History of Fiji* (1946; Suva: Government Press, 1974), 27, cited in McFerson, "Part-Black Americans," 178 n. 2.

135. Arthur Davis, *A Black Diamond in the Queen's Tiara* (New York: A. Davis, 1974), 8.

136. Masayoshi Matsumura, "Nihon ni Kita sai Hatsu no Amerikia Kokujin" [The first black American to come to Japan], *Gaiko-Jihon* 1185 (summer 1981): 18–26.

137. Sidney Wallach, ed., *Narrative of the Expedition of an American Squadron to the China Sea and Japan* (New York: Coward McCann, 1952), 60, 78, 82.

138. George Sansom, *The Western World and Japan* (New York: Vintage Books, 1973), 279–80; and Bradley Smith, *Japan—A History in Art* (Garden City, N.Y.: Gemini-Smith, 1964), 230–31.

139. Masao Miyoshi, *As We Saw Them* (Berkeley: University of California Press, 1979), 61.

140. Ibid., 62.

141. See Michael Thornton, "Collective Representations and Japanese Views of African-Descent Populations," *International Journal of Sociology and Social Policy* 6, no. 1 (1986): 90–101, for a discussion of the role the West played in Asian views of people of African descent.

142. Wagatsuma, "Social Perception," 433.

143. Hiroshi Wagatsuma, "Mixed-Blood Children in Japan: An Exploratory Study," *Journal of Asian Affairs* 1 (spring 1977): 10.

144. F. Basabe, "Attitudes of Japanese Students toward Foreign Countries," *Monumenta Nipponica* 21, no. 1/2 (1966): 61–87.

145. See Thornton, "Collective Representations."

146. See Neil Henry, "An African in Peking," *The Crisis* (December 1976): 339ff; and J. Killens, "Report on a Journey: Black Man in the New China," *Black World* (November 1975): 28–42.

147. Cited in Killens, "Journey," 40. The Chinese influence in the United States is also reflected in the Black Panther Party, which drew a great deal of its philosophical inspiration and techniques from the teachings of Chairman Mao; see E. Smith, "Red Chinese Influence on the Politics of the Black Panther Party, " *Black World* (July 1971): 75–78.

148. Snow, *Star Raft*, 199; and E. Hevi, *An African Student in China* (New York: Frederick Praeger, 1962).

149. Snow, *Star Raft*, 16, 19–21. See also Michael Sullivan, "The 1988–89 Nanjing Anti-African Protests: Racial Nationalism or National Racism?" *China Quarterly* 138 (1994): 438–57.

150. Snow, *Star Raft*, 16–7, 19; Sullivan, "Anti-African Protests."

151. The following account is based on Jack Chen, *Inside the Cultural Revolution* (New York: Macmillan, 1975), 5; see Percy Chen, *China Called Me* (Boston: Little Brown, 1979) for pictures of the family; see also H. Boorman, ed., *Biographical Dictionary of Republican China* (New York: Columbia University Press, 1967), 1:180; and Rogers, *World's Great Men of Color*, 2:183–84.

152. Boorman claims Chen left Trinidad because others were so jealous of his success, which is the interpretation given by his son Jack.

153. J. Chen, *Inside;* and P. Chen, *China Called Me.*

154. Marie Seton, *Paul Robeson* (London: Dennis Dobson, 1958), 87.

155. J. Chen, *Inside.*

156. Cited in Rogers, *World's Great Men of Color*, 2:183–84.

157. John Shade, "Caring for the Amerasians: A Difficult Task," unpublished paper, 1978, 2, 8, 14; and

"Asian Children of American Servicemen Still Search for Their Roots," *New York Times*, 19 October 1980, 18.

158. *Konketsuji* is the Japanese term for mixed bloods. More derogatory terms are *ai-no-ko* ("child of mixture"), *hafu* (the Japanese pronunciation of the English "half"), or the more derogatory *kuronbo* ("blackone"). Of 13 regiments occupying Japan, one was all black; black troops made up about 12 percent of the Far East Command. See Morris MacGregor and Bernard Nalty, *Blacks in the United States Armed Forces: Basic Documents*, vol. 8, *Segregation under Seige* (Wilmington, Del.: Scholarly Resources, 1977), 114.

159. "War Babies of Japan," *Ebony*, September 1951, 15–22.

160. Wagatsuma, "Mixed-Blood Children."

161. Roberta Levenbach, "Biracial Children in Okinawa," *Christian Century*, 15 November 1972, 1156–60.

162. W. M. Hurh, "Marginal Children of War: An Exploratory Study of American-Korean Children," *International Journal of Sociology and the Family* 1, no. 1 (1972): 13.

163. Al Keane, personal correspondence with the author, February 1980.

164. Stuart Loory, *Defeated: Inside America's Military Machine* (New York: Random House, 1973), 225.

165. Committee on Foreign Relations, "Vietnam Children's Care Agency," hearings before U.S. Senate (Washington, D.C.: U.S. Government Printing Office, 1972), 58.

166. John Shade, personal correspondence, March 1980; and Era Thompson, "The Plight of Black Babies in South Vietnam," *Ebony*, December 1972, 106.

167. See D. Luce, "Amer-Asian Children in Vietnam," *Christian Century*, 25 August 1971, 996–97; J. Shade, personal correspondence, March 1980; Thompson, "Plight of Black Babies," 106; and B. Kurtis, "The Plight of Children Abandoned in Vietnam," *New York Times Magazine*, 2 March 1980, 18ff.

168. Luce, "Amer-Asian Children."

169. D. Renard and D. Gilzow, *The Amerasians* (Washington, D.C.: Refugee Service Center, Center for Applied Linguistics, 1989).

170. J. Felsman, F. Leong, and M. Johnson, "Estimates of Psychological Distress among Vietnamese Refugees: Adolescents, Unaccompanied Minors and Young Adults," *Social Science and Medicine* 31, no. 11 (1990): 1251–56; Kieu-Linh Valverde, "From Dust to Gold: The Vietnamese Amerasian Experience," in *Racially Mixed People in America*, ed. Maria Root (Newbury Park, Calif.; Sage, 1992), 144–61; and Fred Bemak and Rita Chung, "Vietnamese Amerasians: Psychological Adjustment and Psychotherapy," *Journal of Multicultural Counseling and Development* 25 (January 1997): 79–89.

171. "And Now a Domestic Baby Life," *Ebony*, June 1975, 134; and Thompson, "Plight of Black Babies."

172. Levenbach, "Biracial Children," 1156.

173. A. Keith, *Before the Blossoms Fall: Life and Death in Japan* (Boston: Atlantic Monthly Press, 1975), 67.

174. See George DeVos, "Achievement Orientation, Social Self-Identity and Japanese Economic Growth," *Asian Survey* 5 (December 1965): 575–89; and Ruth Benedict, *The Chrysanthemum and the Sword* (Cleveland: Meridian Books, 1946).

175. "Sailor to Movie Star," *Ebony*, August 1953, 46–51.

176. That there was a problem in Japan and other places in Asia can also be attributed to white soldiers who socialized Asians to the proper racial hierarchy. For example, during the Vietnam War, Anne Darling noted: "The Thai women have apparently learned about racial discrimination from the Americans. Several bar girls admitted that they were afraid of "dam-dam," the Thai word for black, and would refuse to sleep with them. So most brothers on R and R find their way to Jack's All American State Bar, a hangout for in-country Blacks to meet women." Cited in Loory, *Defeated*, 228.

177. Robert McKelvey, Alice Mao, and John Webb, "A Risk Profile Predicting Psychological Distress in Vietnamese Amerasian Youth," *Journal of the American Academy of Child and Adolescent Psychiatry*

31 (September 1992): 911–15; Felsman, Leong, and Johnson, "Estimates"; D. Gilzow and D. Renard, *The Amerasians: A 1990 Update* (Washington, D.C.: Refugees Service Center, Center for Applied Linguistics, 1990); Valverde, "From Dust to Gold"; and David Gonzalez, "For Afro-Amerasians, Tangled Emotions," *New York Times,* 16 November 1992, B1.

178. Gonzalez, "Tangled Emotions."

179. Teresa Williams, "Prism Lives: Identity of Binational Amerasians," in *Racially Mixed People in America,* ed. Maria Root (Newbury Park, Calif.: Sage, 1992), 300.

180. Era Thompson, "Japan's Rejected," *Ebony,* September 1967, 49; and Wagatsuma, "Mixed-Blood Children," 13.

181. Felsman, Leong, and Johnson, "Estimates," 1251–56; Gilzow and Renard, *The Amerasians;* Robert McKelvey, John Webb, and Roddy Strobel, "The Prevalence of Psychiatric Disorders among Vietnamese Amerasians: A Pilot Study," *American Journal of Orthopsychiatry* 66 (1996): 409–15; Robert McKelvey and John Webb, "Premigratory Expectations and Postmigratory Mental Health Symptoms in Vietnamese Amerasians," *Journal of the American Academy of Child and Adolescent Psychiatry* 35 (February 1996): 240–45; and F. Leong and M. Johnson, "Vietnamese Amerasian Mothers: Psychological Distress and High Risk Factors," Department of Health and Human Services, Administration for Children and Families, Office of Refugee Resettlement (April 1992).

182. See Michael Thornton and Harold Gates, "Black, Japanese and American: An Asian American Identity Yesterday and Today," in *The Sum of Our Parts: Mixed-Heritage Asian Americans,* ed. Teresa Williams-León and Cynthia L. Nakashima (Philadelphia: Temple University Press, 2001), 93–105, for a discussion of stereotypes of mixed racial people; see Nathan Strong, "Patterns of Social Interaction and Psychological Accommodations among Japan's Konketsuji Population," Ph.D. diss., University of California, Berkeley, 1978, for a discussion of nontraumatized Amerasians from middle-class families.

183. At the time, children born overseas out of wedlock acquired U.S. citizenship through their mother if the mother had the nationality of the United States at the time of such person's birth, and if the mother had previously been physically present in the United States or one of its outlying possessions for a continuous period of one year. See Roger Shoemaker, "Children Born Overseas: What Are Their Rights?" *Army Times,* 5 May 1980, 39.

184. Robert Mrazek, Analysis of the Vietnamese Amerasian Situation and the Need for Congressional Action Report (Washington, D.C.: U.S. Government Printing Office, 1987).

185. Valverde, "From Dust to Gold."

186. M. Brenden, *Amerasian Update* (Washington, D.C.: Office of Refugee Resettlement, 1990).

187. Valverde, "From Dust to Gold."

188. "Refugees Stranded in Philippines," *National Catholic Reporter,* August 1, 1997, 11–13; Emeka Nwadiora and Harriette McAdoo, "Acculturative Stress among Amerasian Refugees: Gender and Racial Differences," *Adolescence* 31 (Summer 1996): 477–87; and Belinda Rhodes, "Sins of the Fathers: Filipinos Sue U.S. Over Plight of Amerasian Children," *Far Eastern Economic Review* 156 (17 June 1993): 40–41.

Portrait of the Past: Black Servicemen in Asia, 1899–1952

Michael C. Thornton

A FRICANS HAVE A LONG HISTORY IN THE ASIAN LANDSCAPE, BUT SIGNIFICANT African American involvement began at the turn of the twentieth century. As part of the initial troop deployment to fight insurgency, black Americans went to the Philippines in fall 1899. Many of them had been involved in Cuba a short time before, and they stayed in the Philippines until 1902, when they were sent home supposedly because they had become too attached to the local population. Willard Gatewood shows that while this was an exaggeration, there was a special bond between Filipinos and black soldiers.[1] Letters from these troops to black newspapers in the United States spoke of a bond based on skin color and similar treatment by whites, such as referring to them both as "niggers."

Because these black Americans often felt more at home in this distant land than in their homeland, their desertion rate often was high. One black serviceman who deserted took a commission in the insurgent army and fought the U.S. military for two years.[2] Others took more traditional avenues to show their affinity to this society; they married Filipino women, opened businesses, and accepted appointments to minor posts in civil government. By 1903 the black colony numbered between 500 and 1,000.[3] Most blacks remained ambivalent about their involvement in the war: They often sided with their colored brethren but also wanted to prove that they were good Americans, worthy of full citizenship. This dilemma has dogged most blacks throughout their service in America's armed forces.

One of the most extensive accounts of the black military presence in the South Pacific, commissioned by the U.S. Department of the Army, was concerned only about troop performance during World War II and said little of how black troops felt about their experiences.[4] The all-black 93rd Division was stationed in the Solomons, the Moluccas, the Admiralty Islands, the Philippines, and Australia; the 368th Regiment was in the Russell Islands; the 369th Regiment was in New Georgia; and the 25th Regiment was in Guadalcanal, Bougainville, and the Green Islands.[5] There were also marine detachments stationed in the South Pacific during the war. The 52nd Marine Defense Battalion went to Guam and the Marshall Islands, and the 51st Marine Defense Battalion was stationed on Ellice Island and then with the Samoan Defense Group in Nanomea, Funafuti, and Nukefetau.[6] While many were trained for infantry service, most black soldiers and marines were used on mop-up operations or as stevedores.

In his study, Ulysses Lee notes the problem the army had in finding countries willing to accept black troops. Black troops were dispatched only when no other troops were available for service or where no other troops would go. On occasion, they were used where it was felt their color would be more "suitable."[7] They were commonly sent to tropical areas in Asia, such as the New Hebrides, Iwo Jima, New Caledonia, New Guinea, Burma, India, the Persian Gulf, Guadalcanal, and Fiji. As of December 1942, there were 193 black Americans on Christmas Island, 2,360 in the New Hebrides, 1,397 on New Caldonia, 8,025 in Australia and New Guinea, 2,523 in the China-Burma-India (CBI) area, and 253 in the Persian Gulf.[8]

Black journalists who covered the Iran and CBI theaters during World War II reported substantial black involvement in opening and maintaining supply routes. In Iran, "about 10 per cent of the American troops were blacks who performed the nastiest, hottest jobs of all." In the CBI, "before the [Ledo Road] was completed, some 15,000 Americans had strained their muscles on it, and 60 percent of them were black." At least fourteen black units were stationed near Tehran, Iran, and there was much American activity around Khorramshahr. All port battalions were black. The Trans-Iranian Railroad was maintained and manned by black troops, and at Camp Stalingrad, in the mountains of northeastern Iran, they made up about 10 percent of the Americans.[9]

Black troops who hacked the Ledo Road out of the world's densest jungles and drove convoys across it to China were there because of the stereotypes others had of them:

The military, with its mystical belief in the special adaptability of blacks to jungle climates, turned to black laborers, as the army had turned to them for garrison duty in yellow fever-infested Puerto Rico in 1898. The black troops had shown themselves no more immune than whites a half-century before, but that lesson was conveniently forgotten. Most of the black troops were from the South, but they never had tried to build roads in an area with 150 inches of rain a year, where torrents could raise rivers 11 feet in a day, where roads became yellow soup, and the jungle reclaimed sections faster than they could be cleared.[10]

While their presence in Asia was often due to prejudice, black troops also encountered prejudice in countries they were fighting to defend. Chiang Kai-shek initially decreed that no blacks were to enter China, claiming that their sudden appearance in remote parts of the country would upset the inhabitants, but he later relented. It is alleged that Mme. Chiang Kai-shek was the real culprit, for she "wanted to avoid any race mixing and was herself deeply racist."[11] Concern about the Chinese people was misplaced, however, for "in some villages, the Chinese gawked at the blacks, embarrassing and angering some of the drivers. Through a translator . . . [it was] learned that they were not hostile, but only amazed that men of so many pigmentations all spoke the same language."[12]

Until the end of World War II, blacks served in segregated units, but after this war the U.S. military began to experiment with mixed racial units. In 1948, President Truman issued an executive order ending discrimination and segregated units in the military. The all-black 24th Regiment, however, remained intact at the start of the Korean War. The last remnant of the famous Buffalo soldiers, it had been created shortly after the Civil War in honor of the sacrifices of the 250,000 blacks who fought for the Union. The unit had fought Indians and Texas outlaws, honored itself at San Juan Hill in Cuba during the Spanish-American War, and served in the Philippines and with General John J. Pershing in Mexico in pursuit of Pancho Villa.[13]

When entire companies of the 24th disappeared during the first panicky days of the Korean War, according to official Army history, their disappearance was attributed to the black soldier's supposed tendency to panic under pressure. Conventional wisdom, even after one hundred years of contrary experience, depicted black soldiers as lazy, afraid of the dark, distrustful, and not willing to stand and fight. This performance provided the rationale for the unit to be disbanded in 1951. Forty-five years later, the army reexamined the record, which highlighted the role of racism in the unit's actions. In the reassessment of what happened to the 24th in Korea, it was concluded that stereotypes kept the best black officers from rising to positions of authority, and the best white officers did not want to serve with all-black units in part because they believed the stereotypes about black troops. No single reason was found for what happened; inadequate equipment, inexperience, leadership failures, and a lack of bonding all played a part.[14] The belief that they are inadequate soldiers has been a legacy blacks have had to endure for as long as they have served in the U.S. armed forces.

NOTES

1. Willard Gatewood, *"Smoked Yankees" and the Struggle for Empire: Letters from Negro Soldiers, 1898–1902* (Urbana: University of Illinois Press, 1971), 237–316. See also George Marks, "Opposition of Negro Newspapers to American Philippine Policy, 1899–1900," *Midwest Journal* 3 (summer 1951): 1–25, for black views on the war.

2. Michael Robinson and Frank Schubert, "David Fagen: An Afro-American Rebel in the Philippines, 1899–1901," *Pacific Historical Review* 44 (February 1975): 68–83.

3. See Era Bell Thompson, "Veterans Who Never Came Home," *Ebony* 27 (October 1972): 104–15; and Gatewood, *"Smoked Yankees,"* 16.

4. Ulysses Lee, *The Employment of Negro Troops* (Washington, D.C.: U.S. Government Printing Office, 1965).

5. Mary Motley, ed., *The Invisible Soldier: The Experience of the Black Soldier, World War II* (Detroit: Wayne State University, 1975), 73–135.

6. Henry Shaw and Ralph Donnelly, *Blacks in the Marine Corps* (Washington, D.C.: History and Museum Division, Headquarters, U.S. Marine Corps, 1975). Hazel McFerson claims to have met descendants of black American servicemen on South Pacific islands in the 1970s, all of whom were aware and proud of their African ancestry; see McFerson, "'Part-Black Americans' in the South Pacific," *Phylon* 43 (June 1982): 177–80.

7. Lee, *Employment*, 597–610; and John Stevens, "From the Back of the Foxhole: Black Correspondents in World War II," in *Journalism Monographs* (Lexington, Ky.: Association for Education in Journalism, 1973).

8. Lee, *Employment*, 433.

9. Stevens, "Back of the Foxhole," 396–98.

10. Ibid., 400.

11. Ibid., 402.

12. Ibid., 403.

13. Joseph Galloway, "The Last of the Buffalo Soldiers," *U.S. News and World Report* 120 (May 6, 1996): 45. See Morris MacGregor and Bernard Nalty, eds., *Blacks in the United States Armed Forces: Basic Documents*, Volume 8: *Segregation Under Siege* (Wilmington, Del.: Scholarly Resources, 1977), regarding policy aimed at ensuring equal representation of black troops in different theaters of operation, which in part explains why the 24th was in Korea. For a personal account of black experiences in Korea, see Curtis Morrow, *What's a Commie Ever Done to Black People?* (Jefferson, N.C.: McFarland and Company, 1997).

14. William Bowers, William Hammond, and George MacGarrigle, *Black Soldiers, White Army: The 24th Infantry Regiment in Korea* (Washington, D.C.: Center for Military History, U.S. Army, 1996).

Two Courtiers of African Descent in the Kingdom of Judah: Yehudi and Ebedmelech

John T. Greene

I T HAS BEEN CONVINCINGLY ARGUED THAT THE DEUTERONOMISTIC HISTORY WAS written in two installments. D1 was intended to demonstrate that King Josiah was the greatest, most loyal to Yahweh, and therefore most successful Judean monarch since David. Completed while the king was still alive, it served as propaganda to undergird his reforms. D2 is an addendum designed to show that his successors ruined his achievements and prepared the way for neo-Babylonian overlordship.[1] D2 spotlights the activities of kings Jehoiakim and Zedekiah (Mattaniah), during whose reigns black courtiers played a role. One of them attempted to save either the writings or the life of the priest/prophet Jeremiah.

For some time it has been accepted that Ebedmelech, who served at the court of King Zedekiah, was a black man, but little is known about Yehudi, who served King Jehoiakim.[2] A number of studies of the last turbulent years of the Kingdom of Judah have been written,[3] but these historians acknowledge that many details are still missing. This research offers plausible reasons for the presence of two blacks at the Judean court during the final two decades before the Exile and then explains why they occupied such high and influential positions. Moreover, it is important to understand why Jeremiah calls attention to their race. Through the activities of these two courtiers, more may be learned about the sixth century B.C.E. kingdom on the eve of its destruction.

Africans in Judah

After the death of King Josiah at Megiddo, Judah became a vassal state of Egypt and then neo-Babylonia. The victorious Neco removed Jehoahaz, the people's choice as Josiah's successor, after three months of ruling.[4] In the Egyptian army there were numerous units of black African troops, especially bowmen,[5] who were noted for their fierceness and accuracy. Thus, after 609 B.C.E. there would have been numerous African soldiers among the occupying forces, and a substantial number may have chosen to remain after their period of service ended.

Black Africans had been commonplace in Judah long before this time, such as the Cushite soldier who served King David during the revolt of Absalom.[6] After the prince's death, it was this soldier who took the news to David, in whose personal army he was a mercenary. It is probable that the courtiers Yehudi and Ebedmelech were the offspring of such men. There is some evidence of this in the genealogical framework in which Yehudi is presented,[7] although Ebedmelech is merely referred to as an Ethiopian.[8]

The name Yehudi means simply a person residing in Judah, or a Judean. (We would not write Jew at this point for technical reasons.[9]) The name signals the fact that some African people distinguished themselves as indigenous to Judah. Yehudi was a court scribe, which is more a title than a function. Ebedmelech is comprised of *ebed* (servant [of]) and *melech* (king).[10] Below I shall argue that it should be understood as an official title at court rather than as a personal name.[11]

The Scribal Profession in Judah

It is well known that the administration of King David's court resembled that of his predecessor (the Jebus/Jerusalem tradition) and of the Egyptian pharaoh.[12] The position of *mazkir*, which is closest to what became the *sofer* or scribe,[13] refers to one who informs, the counselor.[14] The word *sofer* was in use before the Exile,[15] but it is difficult to determine its exact meaning then, due to superimpositions by post-Exile editors. In general, however, scribes wrote down oral material or copied existing literature, and they could be found at any ancient Near Eastern court.

One of scribes' most important responsibilities was the court chronicle, such as those in 1 and 2 Kings, and they were indispensable to the administration of a kingdom. Several specialized subgroups emerged: those who recorded business transactions; those who accompanied armies to chronicle events and list booty captured or keep a body count; those who functioned much like librarians; and those who handled diplomatic correspondence. Some taught the profession to others, and some arrived with occupying armies to establish procedure in the vassal state.

YEHUDI THE SCRIBE

Yehudi makes cameo appearances in Jeremiah 3:14, 21a and b, and 23, in narrative material that mentions Jeremiah in the third person. That is, he appears in material written *about*, not by, Jeremiah. (The author has been identified as either Jeremiah or Baruch, the son of Neriah, to whom Jeremiah dictated the contents.[16]) Jeremiah has been identified as the motivating force behind the production of the Deuteronomistic history, whose purpose was to praise the administration of King Josiah and to demonstrate that as high priest of the kingdom he had no peers. It was written from the perspective of the Shiloh priesthood, to counter any claims made by its archrivals, the Aaronids. Jeremiah is said to have been a priest in Anathoth,[17] a small town within walking distance of Jerusalem, and his book must be read in the context of the political/sacerdotal skirmishes that took place at court.

Yehudi served King Jehoiakim (609–598 B.C.E.), who was a vassal of Egypt until Pharaoh Neco's defeat at the battle of Carchemish in 598. Jehoiakim also was a vassal of the Babylonian king, Nebuchadnezzar II, for three years (2 Kings 24:1). Despite these calamities, and although he does evil in the sight of the Lord (2 Kings 23:37), he is judged less harshly by the author of 1 and 2 Kings than many other kings, perhaps because he is Josiah's son; most of the blame for accepting and worshiping foreign gods is attributed to his predecessor, Manasseh.

In 605–4 B.C.E. (implied by Jer. 36:1) Jeremiah is said to have dictated his book, which filled a scroll, to the scribe Baruch, who also was given the task of reading it "on a fast day" (36:6) before an assembly at the Jerusalem Temple. Jeremiah could not do this himself because he was "debarred from going to the house of the Lord" (36:5). He was a priest who had worn out his welcome in the holy precincts. Let us look briefly at Baruch, who was both a scribe and a priest, since he had access to the Temple courts and could participate formally in a fast day observance. Because Jeremiah had chosen him as his proxy, Baruch must have also subscribed to the Shiloh line.

The fast day apparently did not present itself until the following year (36:9), and a slight embellishment of the text (36:10) clarifies the meaning:

Then, in the hearing of all people, Baruch read the words of Jeremiah from the scroll, in the [priestly precincts] of the house of the Lord, in the chamber of Gemariah the son of Shaphan the secretary [*mazkir*], which was in the upper court, at the entry of the New Gate of the Lord's house.

Baruch discharged his duty before a highly selective group; "all people" simply means everyone present in the room. The audience was in the chamber (office) of Gemariah, whose father was a *mazkir,* and whose son, Michaiah, was also there, along with (1) Elishama, another secretary; (2) Delaiah, son of Shemaiah; (3) Elnathan, son of Achbor; (4) Zedekiah, son of Hannaniah; and (5) several more princes of (evidently) lesser light. Then Yehudi appeared, and was chosen to be sent as an agent from this princely body, and his pedigree is given:

Father	Cushi (= the Cushite, a black person)
Son	Shelemiah (see 37:3, where it is this man's son, Jehucal, and Zephaniah the priest, the son of Maaseiah, who are sent by Jeremiah)
Grandson	Nethaniah
Great Grandson	Yehudi

When Baruch has read to them, they do not like what they have heard and want to confirm the source: "Tell us, how did you write all these words? Was it at his dictation?" (36:17). Jeremiah's name had not yet been mentioned, but presumably that is the antecedent for "his." Baruch replied that "he dictated all these words to me," whereupon the scroll was confiscated, and the king was informed.

Jehoiakim sent (the enforcer) Yehudi (36:21) to retrieve the scroll and read it before the king and the princes who were with him. As Yehudi finished each three or four columns, Jehoiakim cut them off the scroll and threw them into a fire. "Yet neither the king, nor any of his servants, who heard all these words, was afraid, nor did they rend their garments" (36:24). What were the dire predictions they ignored?

The king of Babylon will certainly come and destroy this land, and will cut off from it man and beast (Jer. 36:29).

Jehoiakim shall have none to sit upon the throne of David, and his dead body shall be cast out to the heat by day and the frost by night. And I will punish him and his offspring and his servants for their iniquity; I will bring upon them, and upon the inhabitants of Jerusalem, and upon the men of Judah, all the evil that I have pronounced against them, but they would not hear (Jer. 36:3031).

It was Jeremiah's practice to deliver his oracles publicly, but here we see a totally new situation: oracle by proxy. Since the words were read aloud by Baruch and Yehudi, they became prophets by default. This was indeed unusual in the history of the Israelite prophetic movement,[18] and it had occurred only once before in the Deuteronomistic history. Concerning Josiah, 2 Kings 22 reads:

> And Hilkiah the high priest said to Shaphan the secretary, "I have found the book of the law in the house of the Lord" (v. 8).
> Then Shaphan the secretary told the king, "Hilkiah the priest has given me a book." And Shaphan read it before the king (v. 10).
> And when the king heard the words of the book of the law, he rent his clothes (v. 11).

A common thread in both cases is Shaphan the secretary, who reads before Josiah and who is the father of Gemariah, in whose office Baruch reads the Jeremiah scroll. Yet, some important differences between these two blocks of material point to a significant issue.

The book read before Josiah is said to be contained in Deuteronomy 12–26,[19] that is, statutes purportedly spoken by Moses and connected by some narrative. In contrast, Baruch's scroll contains the oracular "I," which signals a *dbr-yhwh*, the word of God. It is important to know when a given prophet is speaking and when the prophet is supposed to be speaking the word(s) of Yahweh if "messenger speech" is to be singled out. To complicate matters, however, there are portions of prophetic literature that do not refer to Yahweh at all, so it is often difficult to determine whether the speaker is Yahweh or the prophet.[20]

In Jehoiakim's court, one group (A) believes Baruch's scroll is the word of God, but the king and his group (B) do not—hence there is no rending of garments. At the heart of the matter is a hermeneutical duel between scribes. Group B (and the king) appears to reject the position that a *dbr-yhwh* can be delivered in any form other than by a *nabi*, a prophet. To them, Baruch is a servant of Jeremiah and a professional colleague who merely reads words that he claims Jeremiah dictated. The dictated words of a prophet cannot equal a *dbr-yhwh*. Otherwise, a scribe reading aloud words in the first person ("I") then becomes the conduit for God's word and, thus, a prophet. It then follows that anyone who picks up the scroll and reads aloud also would have to be considered a prophet. Moreover, a scribe could produce his own scroll, claim that it was dictated by a prophet, present it publicly as a legitimate *dbr-yhwh*, and thereby influence public policy.

It is not without import, therefore, that the original group of scribes who heard Baruch's reading referred the matter to the king. Given the political/religious implications, the king had to render the official decision. Yehudi evidently was a trusted and reliable scribe, for he was sent to retrieve the scroll and read it before the king. Jehoiakim ruled (in essence) that the contents did not constitute a *dbr-yhwh*, and he was not opposed in this judgment by the scribes of group B.

The scribes of group A did not have such a rigid view of how the word of God could be transmitted. Baruch was not claiming to be anything other than a priest/scribe, since he pointed to the source of the words. For group A the source was Jeremiah the prophet, so the words had legitimacy as a *dbr-yhwh*. Thus, Elnathan, Delaiah, and Gemariah "urged the king not to burn the scroll" (Jer. 36:25).

The presence of so many scribes in the Jeremiah 36 account is significant. These scribes are of high status (princes), both priests and counselors to the king, at the very heart of the government. They are well educated and have a stake in the destiny of their country. There are other scribes who are not so highly placed but who are acknowledged as professionals by those in the inner circle. Baruch falls within the latter category; whatever his other duties, he exercises the simplest of scribal functions: he takes dictation. His colleagues in the inner circle apparently had, as one of their duties, to review all documents destined for the king and determine which would be sent on to him. Yehudi also must have had high status, since he was the official reader before the king.

Although numerous prophecies ascribed to Amos, Hosea, Micah, and others were grouped into collections, we have no record that any of these written oracles were presented orally by anyone other than the prophet to whom they are attributed. Baruch, then, must be viewed as the progenitor of a scribal type whose job it was to collect such writings. Eventually, the scribe would become mediator, and God's word to Israel would be contained in books. There would no longer be a question of whether the *dbr-yhwh* was legitimate and efficacious when written down by a scribe, regardless of how closely associated he was with a prophet.[21]

Ebedmelech and the Zedekian Administration

Two important features of the D2 story should be noted. First, Jeremiah is concerned with providing details about the influential leadership that helped destroy the kingdom. To that end, genealogies are often rendered to the third generation. Such minute detail normally reveals a priest at work, and the intent is to establish clearly the identity of the culpable as well as the "innocent," or those faithful to Yahweh and the covenant.

Second, the names can be divided into two major categories for purposes of analysis: theophoric and nontheophoric. There are more people with Yahweh as part of their name than one finds in many other biblical texts. It is used ironically to imply that those bearing the name of God did not know God. (The theophoric name Jeremiah is presented positively, however.) Names must be understood, then, as a polemical device in D2.

Two names of interest are Hammelech and Ebedmelech, which may tell us something that previous research into this period has overlooked. In the Hebrew text, Malchiah, the son of Hammelech, is mentioned in connection with other princes and as the son of the king. Many English translations of Jeremiah 38:6 render Hammelech as a proper noun instead of a title. Was Malchiah Josiah's grandson? I think not, for there is a more plausible explanation. Egyptian influence on Judah's administration included the position of viceroy. A picture of that function is gained from a text describing Tutmose III's vizier as a most important man in the pharaoh's court, who relied heavily upon messengers to maintain law and order in the far-flung empire, who ordered the gates of the king's house opened and closed each day, who heard complaints and adjudicated legal cases, and who sealed edicts. The official Egyptian title for this person was "king's son."[22] Thus, when the king's son took Jeremiah from King Zedekiah, this was not an act of rebellion against a father but a demonstration of power by the viceroy over the king. This helps clarify why the king addressed Jeremiah in secret and beseeched him to "inquire of Yahweh" on his behalf.

Having come to understand that *ben* Hammelech (king's son) can have more than one meaning, prudence suggests that we regard the name Ebedmelech more carefully than heretofore. Emphasis has been placed on the fact that he was a eunuch,[23] based on the assumption that his name was a proper noun. Let us focus on the activities of the man bearing the name. The nouns *'abd* and *mlk* form an expression meaning king's servant. Hebrew construction suggests that this is quite different in meaning from being merely a servant of the king. This court officer would be opposed to the viceroy-led, pro-Egyptian, anti-Jeremiah coalition at court. On the other side of the court-intrigue equation, then, was the *bn hmlk* (the king's son) Malchiah.

Let us follow *'abd-mlk's* (Ebedmelech's) activities. (1) He approaches Zedekiah on Jeremiah's behalf to save him. The impetus comes from him, not the king, and signals to the latter that he has an ally in him. His appearance suggests to the king that a certain balance of power exists at court (38:7). (2) The king then commands *'abd-mlk* to take thirty men (unquestionably loyal to *'abd-mlk* and now also loyal to the king's coalition) and part of the royal bodyguard, and remove Jeremiah from his place of detention (38:10). (3) The writer stresses that *'abd-mlk* is an Ethiopian, to emphasize not his skin color but the fact that he is a foreigner, not a Judean. It appears that the royal practice of not trusting personal safety to indigenous Judeans was still in force during the final decade of the kingdom. It is likely that the thirty men were foreign mercenaries. (4) Thus, 'abd-mlk was the strong arm on which the king leaned during this period of power struggle. He led the security force within the royal precincts to free Jeremiah. He was unopposed in this action by other armed men at court (38:13). (5) Although liberated from the palace detention center below the treasury, Jeremiah was not set totally free. Until the day that Jerusalem was taken by the Babylonians (38:28), he was kept in the court of the prison where the king constantly sought his advice secretively (38:1428). (6) Jeremiah remembered being rescued by the actions of 'abd-mlk and his troops and assured him that he (who lived by the sword) would not fall by the sword when the Babylonians executed the Judean leaders that had opposed them (39:18).

The term 'abd-mlk can be translated as "king's servant" (2 Kings 18:234) but is more often interpreted as "king's messenger."[24] In Egyptian literature one finds:

> Shortly before the Queen Hatshepsut's ninth year as queen, she made an expedition to the land of Punt. . . . One of the members of this expedition was the "king's-messenger," of whom it is written: "The arrival of the king's-messenger in God's Land, together with the army, which is behind him, before the chiefs of Punt . . . for the sake of life . . . and health of her majesty."[25]

These and many more examples point to the fact that the "king's messenger" refers to a commanding officer, since he regularly appears at the head of an army.

Given what we know about royal bodyguards from the time of David onward, and reading the account of Jeremiah's incarceration in light of the politico-military situation prevailing in Judah during the time of Zedekiah, it is reasonable to suggest that Ebedmelech the Ethiopian was a foreigner who served as a high officer of the royal bodyguard. He was depicted by the hypercritical chronicler (Jeremiah/Baruch) as performing his function unswervingly and as having the loyalty of (at least thirty) men under his command. Through his agency, Zedekiah kept open the lines of communication with Yahweh through the prophet, the mediator of the deity's word.

Conclusion

The well-educated Yehudi and the loyal 'abd-mlk remind us that, more often than one would expect, the Bible "speaks" through a chorus of opposing views about the word of God and what it meant to those attempting to solve the problem of how God communicates with our world. The story of Yehudi and *'abd-mlk* suggests how that problem was approached. It also offers additional insights in terms of understanding the structural location and identities of Africans in Judah. In the case of Yehudi we get a sense of African presence and lineage over generations in ancient Near Eastern states and kingdoms.

It is instructive that Yehudi means a person residing in Judah, a Judean. In present-day terminology this implies a national or citizen. Africans were long recruited as military men, trained and skilled in the art of warfare; they were "foreigners" entrusted with the protection of rulers and the defense of kingdoms. Yehudi and Ebedmelech provide insights into how Africans came to occupy important and trusted positions in military and political arenas because they were "inside-outsiders." They attained positions as trustworthy soldiers, courtiers, messengers, and scribes in an environment in which rulers were often apprehensive about remanding their personal safety and "secrets of states" to "insiders." In this instance, African or Ethiopian "strangerness" was an asset, defining in part who they were within the context of this ancient time-space. Thus, their "inbetweenness" could be an avenue of social mobility in a social-political milieu where insiders were viewed with suspicion in the contested arenas of the day.

NOTES

1. Richard Elliot Friedman, *Who Wrote the Bible?* (Englewood Cliffs, N.J.: Prentice-Hall, 1987), 123, 125–27; and Brian Peckham, *The Composition of the Deuteronomistic History* (Atlanta, Ga.: Scholars Press, 1985).

2. Bishop Alfred G. Dunston Jr., *The Black Man in the Old Testament and Its World* (Philadelphia: Dorrance and Company, 1974); F. S. Rhoades, *Black Characters and References of the Holy Bible* (New York: Vantage Press, 1980); and Charles B. Copher, "The Black Man in the Biblical World," *Journal of the Interdenominational Theological Center* 1, no. 2 (1974): 716.

3. Martin Noth, *The History of Israel*, 2d ed. (New York: Harper and Row, 1960); John Bright, *A History of Israel*, 2d ed. (Philadelphia, Pa.: Westminster Press 1976); and Harry Orlinski, *Ancient Israel* (Ithaca, N.Y.: Cornell University Press, 1960).

4. Kings 23:31.

5. See Dunston, *The Black Man*, 101–19, which discusses black warriors.

6. Sam. 18:19–33.

7. Jer. 36:14.

8. Jer. 38:7ff.

9. See H. Keith Beebe, *The Old Testament* (Belmont, Calif.: Dickenson, 1970), 303 n. 1; and James King West, *Introduction to the Old Testament*, 2d ed. (New York: Macmillan, 1981), 378 n. 7, for discussions concerning the term *Jew*.

10. See John T. Greene, *The Role of the Messenger and Message in the Ancient Near East,* Brown Judaic Studies (Atlanta, Ga.: Scholars Press, 1989), 113 and 234.

11. See the figure of the Rabshakeh in 2 Kings 18:13–24.

12. See Beebe, *The Old Testament;* Joachim Begrich, "Sofer und Mazkir," *Zeitschrift für die Altestamentliche Wissenschaft* 58 (1940): 1–29; 2 Sam. 6:12–22 (esp. verse 14b); and 1 Kings 8:22, concerning Solomon.

13. Neh. 8.

14. Begrich, "Sofer und Mazkir"; 2 Kings 18:18, 37; 2 Sam. 8:15–18; 20:23–26; and Greene, *Role of the Messenger,* 6, 14, 127, 128, 135, and 225.

15. Begrich, "Sofer und Mazkir."

16. Friedman, *Who Wrote the Bible?* 125–27.

17. See the superscription to Jeremiah.

18. This differs radically from the thesis contained in the study of Simon J. Devries, *Prophet Against Prophet: The Role of the Michaiah Narrative (1 Kings 22) in the Development of Early Prophetic Tradition* (Grand Rapids, Mich.: Eerdmans, 1978).

19. Friedman, *Who Wrote the Bible?*

20. Greene, *Role of the Messenger,* 192.

21. The issue continued to be significant in post-Exile Judah, however, when the Sadducees and Pharisees brought the hermeneutic debate to a fever pitch.

22. Greene, *Role of the Messenger,* 28–30; and James H. Breasted, ed., *Ancient Records of Egypt: Historical Documents from the Earliest Times to the Persian Conquests* (Chicago: University of Chicago Press, 1906–7), 2: 206.

23. Compare and contrast Nehemiah the eunuch, a court officer during the Persian period. The Hebrew word *saris* does not always imply an emasculated male. Sometimes, a better translation is chamberlain or simply officer.

24. Greene, *Role of the Messenger,* 29–94. Examples include 1 Kings 20:6; 1 Sam. 25:39d–42; 2 Kings 18:23–24; 2 Kings 5:6b.

25. Greene, *Role of the Messenger,* 29–94.

Portrait of the Past: African Moslems in Yugoslavia

Michael C. Thornton

THE TOWNS OF ULCINJ AND BAR, LOCATED ON THE SOUTHERN COAST OF THE Montenegro Republic in Yugoslavia, have had Africans in their midst for more than one hundred years. They were originally brought by Ulcinj seamen who had enticed them with promises of high wages, or they had been purchased in Benghazi, Algiers, Tripoli, Tunis, and other North African ports. Most of these Africans originated from the Sudan, especially the Bagirmi country, near Lake Chad. Many Ulcinj seamen brought home black children ranging in age from two to sixteen years; all of the Ulcinj blacks came as children to their new home. This correlates with the fact that most Yugoslavians preferred to buy young slaves in Sudan who were between seven and ten years of age. The more slaves a family possessed, the greater their reputation. Those serving as slaves served for a specific number of years and were then freed by their masters, often given a house and land by their ex-owners. All served as seamen, as house servants, or in the fields and were never allowed to engage in crafts.

During Turkish rule, about 100 black families lived in Ulcinj. In 1877 there were only about 50 families, totaling almost 150 members. Later, only about thirty families lived in Ulcinj, nearby Shtoj, Bar (Antivari), and Scutari in Albania. Since 1958 most have lived as Moslems and generally marry within the black community. Eventually they were accepted into the wider community. For a more detailed account see Alexander Lopashich's, "A Negro Community in Yugoslavia."[1]

N O T E

1. Alexander Lopashich, "A Negro Community in Yugoslavia," *Man* 58 (1958): 169–73.

The World Is All of One Piece: The African Diaspora and Transportation to Australia

Cassandra Pybus

TRANSNATIONAL HISTORICAL CONSCIOUSNESS AND A CAPACITY TO ENCOM-pass experience in disparate time and space are great strengths of African diaspora studies. In so far as there is a weakness, it is that the Atlantic world remains the locus of discussion. While some attention has begun to drift toward the Indian Ocean, less scholarship has been directed toward the distant Pacific. Yet the antipodean penal colonies established in the late eighteenth century (modern-day Australia) were necessarily implicated in the same economic and social processes that drove the slave trade. In this essay I explore some of the unexpected points of connection to the Atlantic world, drawing on the records of African convicts transported to the Australian penal colonies in the early decades of settlement.[1] My point is not that this cohort of convicts is especially significant to the history of Australia—though it certainly challenges the conventional reading of colonial experience—but to examine what it can tell us about the wider world. In the detailed penal transportation records we can find information about the African diaspora at the end of the eighteenth century that is very hard to come by elsewhere and that points in directions in which historians may not otherwise look.

The antipodean penal experiment began at Portsmouth, England, in 1787, with a fleet of eleven ships loaded with 759 British felons sentenced to "transportation beyond the Seas" and a few hundred marines to guard them. A decade earlier they would have been shipped to the American colonies but since the defection of the Americans, the home secretary, Viscount Sydney, had been desperate to find a new dumping ground for his unwanted felons. He had considered several proposals for convict settlements on the west coast of Africa—near the slave factory of Cape Coast Castle; on the coast of Sierra Leone; on an island miles up the Gambia river—before he chose an impossibly distant and utterly unfamiliar place on the east coast of New Holland that the explorer James Cook had named New South Wales.[2]

Provisioned at Treasury expense by the very same firm were two ships destined for Sierra Leone on the West Coast of Africa. The fleet for New South Wales and the fleet for Sierra Leone sailed within days of each other. Australian historians have drawn attention to the connection between these two bizarre colonial projects, yet interest in the ill-fated expedition to Sierra Leone ends with departure from England.[3] I have found the connection between the two projects more complex, multifaceted, and far-reaching.

Few historians have noticed that aboard the first fleet were a dozen African convicts. Who were they and where did they come from? The most notorious was John Caesar, six feet tall, reputed to be the strongest man in the settlement at Sydney Cove, and described by the judge advocate David Collins as "incorrigibly stubborn."[4] "Black Caesar," as he was known, has a claim to being a historical figure of major importance: he was Australia's first bushranger.[5] The name Caesar suggests that this man was originally a slave, and he was believed to have come from Madagascar, which presents a problem since slaves from Madagascar were not sold in Britain or the West Indies in the eighteenth century.[6] On the other hand, in the American colony of Virginia, Malagasy slaves were highly prized, and in the early eighteenth century several shipments came to Virginia all the way from the Indian Ocean. Nevertheless, if Caesar had been a slave in a tidewater plantation, how did he end up, aged about twenty-two, at the Maidstone court in 1786, being sentenced to seven years' transportation for theft?[7] One possibility is that he was brought to England as a slave by a loyalist refugee after the Revolution, but this is unlikely since the Mansfield Judgment of 1772 made it impossible to hold slaves in England. And even if this doubtful explanation were made to fit Caesar, how would it account for his fellow African first fleeters, many of whom also appear to have come from the American colonies?

The first clue about who these African Americans could be and how they could end up in London, indigent and threadbare, living by their wits and what they could steal, came from another convict who arrived in Sydney Cove on a later transport ship. William Blue, the black ferryman and smuggler, became an institution in the fledgling colony and a famous Sydney landmark bears his name.[8] Blue is a fascinating character, but what is of interest in this case is a petition for land in which he claimed to have fought for the British and to have been a spy for Cornwallis at

Yorktown.[9] So far my rudimentary search of the revolutionary muster roles have not specifically found William Blue, but I have found very many other Africans in the British services in every possible department of the army. I found others of the same name: Blew, Blaw or Blue, all from New York or New Jersey. There was even an African regiment, the Black Pioneers, and its commander at the time of British withdrawal from New York was Stephen Bluecke, a runaway slave whose name, like Blue's, is probably a derivative of the Dutch word for black. Memorials sent to the Loyalist Claims Commission held in the Public Records Office include quite a few from African Americans who fought for the loyalist cause, and they include supporting documents from General Cornwallis, as well as Generals Clinton and Carelton.[10] Many of these African Americans worked as spies and guides for the British army, while others were part of the British navy.

Tens of thousands of slaves flocked to the British lines when they were promised their freedom in exchange for supporting the King.[11] The enormity of the defection was such that it could be considered the biggest single act of slave rebellion in modern history.[12] George Washington's voluminous papers contain revealing insights into how this great and just father of the American republic reacted to this economic catastrophe, which included quite a few of his own slaves. Following the British capitulation Washington was besieged with complaints from slaveholders that during the evacuation of Charleston and Savannah tens of thousands of slaves were taken away in contravention of the treaty negotiated in Paris. Washington was furious and demanded of the British commander-in-chief, Sir Guy Carleton, that there would be no removal of slaves. At the same time he wrote to his commissioner in New York asking to catch his own runaway slaves among the African Americans in the British lines.[13]

At tense meetings between Washington and Carleton, the victorious Washington reiterated the Treaty of Paris stipulation that slave property was not to be carried off. The defeated Carleton explained that several thousand black refugees had already departed and that the national honor of the British would be kept with regard to "people of any complexion." His government did not intend to violate their faith to the men who came into the British lines under the protection of a British proclamation, he told Washington, and he would construe any suggestion that the King would agree to such "a notorious breach of public faith" as an unfriendly act and a slur on British honor. For his part, Washington insisted that Carleton's conduct violated both the letter and the spirit of the Treaty of Paris. "There is no honour in this, sir," he is reported to have shouted before he stormed out.[14] The next day Washington received a pointed snub from Carleton, who merely sent a letter to say that when he came to New York he found the Negroes were free and therefore he had no right to keep them from going anywhere in the world they wished.[15] He instructed the British generals to issue certificates of freedom to anyone who could demonstrate that they had been with the British for over a year, and a record was to be kept of the status of all departing Negroes. This admirable act was Carleton's own initiative. I have seen nothing to suggest this was in fact the position of the Crown at the time.

There is no way of saying with certainty just how many Black Loyalists got to Britain, but it is known that the population of blacks in London had blown out to around 10,000 by 1786 and that British philanthropists and the British government believed the growth to be largely due to the arrival of refugees from America. By no means did all who went to Nova Scotia settle there. I know that John Moseley, once the property of John Cunningham of Virginia, was recorded as leaving for Nova Scotia with the Wagon-Master-General's Department in 1783, but in 1784 he was arrested in Portsmouth for impersonating a seaman in order to get his wages.[16] Jahel Gordon, formerly of Charleston, left New York for Nova Scotia, but was arrested near Portsmouth two years later in possession of stolen clothing.[17] Then there were the numerous Black Loyalists recruited into various British Army regiments, as well as Hessian regiments returning to Germany.[18] Many of these may have made their way to England. John Randall, originally from New London, Connecticut, was almost certainly from a disbanded British regiment when he was sentenced for stealing a watch in Manchester in 1785.[19]

What is clear is that they did not find any means of support in England. They had no pensions, and their claims to the Loyalist Claims Commission were always rejected, either because they had no proof of a loss of property or more commonly because having gained liberty in the rebellion were deemed "not entitled to ask or expect anything from the government."[20] It is not surprising that a good many ended up in the prison hulks charged with minor felonies, such as stealing food or clothing. So great was the concern for this indigent black community that the Committee for the Black Poor was founded to help them. They secured Treasury support to pay a small bounty given out every fortnight at certain key points in London. The Treasury papers and the newspapers of the day indicate that it was believed that these were loyalist refugees, to whom the government owed a debt that prompted the bounty.[21] In return, the government asked the beneficiaries to sign on for the expedition to establish a free black community in Sierra Leone. In 1786 John Caesar was among the first to sign on for the bounty.[22] Unfortunately, he was charged with theft at the Maidstone court around the same time. The names of two other African men, subsequently transported on the first fleet, Thomas Orford and James Williams, also appear on this list, and they too were in prison. My supposition is that their family and friends collected the bounty in their name, and possibly on their behalf, in the hope they would be allowed to swap prison for exile in Sierra Leone. This idea probably had currency because Orford had originally been sentenced to transportation to Africa, as had about 25 percent of those who were on the first fleet to New South Wales.[23]

At Sydney Cove, the founding settlement in New South Wales, Caesar managed to profoundly irritate the judge-advocate, David Collins, who penned an appraisal of this recalcitrant convict that suggests he shared much of the mindset of slaveholders. Noting that "in his intellect he did not differ widely from a brute," Collins concluded Caesar was forced to steal to feed his brutish appetite and extended his seven-year sentence to life.[24] On 13 May 1789, Caesar headed into the bush armed with a musket and cooking pot, having decided, I guess, that the terrors of the unknown hinterland were less fearsome than a penal system arbitrated by David Collins. No matter how many times he was caught and brutally punished, Caesar always absconded back to the bush, encouraging half a dozen other absconders and raiding outlying settlements. Australia's first bushranger was eventually shot by convict bounty hunters in 1795. In a brief, dismissive obituary to the man who had consistently given him more trouble than any other in the settlement, Collins wrote: "Thus ended a man, who certainly, in life could never have been estimated at more than one remove above the brute."[25] Caesar's legacy did live on, however. He had a daughter born in Australia.

However harsh the penal settlement at Sydney, most of Caesar's compatriots achieved their freedom and got land grants within a few years. Among the first-generation settlers in Australia were at least four with African fathers: Lydia Randall, born 1791; Mary Anne Poore, born 1792; Mary Randall, born 1793; and John Randall Jr., born 1797. Moreover, in 1812 Mary Randall married another African first fleeter, John Martin. The Martin-Randall marriage produced 13 children and 52 grandchildren. Descendants of that union are now said to number 25,000.

In 1803, a second penal colony was established in Van Diemen's Land (modern-day Tasmania). In the records of Van Diemen's Land I have found several hundred men from the African diaspora listed in the indents of convict transport ships. Since convicts who came through the Van Diemen's Land system had their bodies minutely described, I was able to locate some by descriptors such as "complexion: black, hair: black woolly, eyes: black, lips: thick, nose: broad." Six of these men were military offenders from the West India army regiments, court-martialled for desertion or mutiny, and had English or Irish names: John Patterson, tried in Nassau in 1833; Alexander Duff, tried in Barbados in 1833; John Warrow, tried in Trinidad in 1834; William Davis, tried in Trinidad in 1836; Henry Terrence, tried in Trinidad in 1837; and William Fegan, tried in the Bahamas in 1838.[26] There is nothing in these commonplace names to distinguish these men from the great mass of English and Irish convicts, many of whom had been sentenced by military courts martial, arriving in the antipodean penal colonies. What distinguishes these men is that they identified Africa as native land, and their ritual scar patterns indicated that they had lived in Africa until at least adolescence. Differences in scar patterns suggest they came from various locations in Africa.

Since the American Revolution, the British impressed slaves into the British military regiments.[27] As Roger Buckley has pointed out, the African soldier became indispensable in the defense of the British West Indian slave plantations, and the British Army became the largest individual buyer of slaves. No single British estate purchased slaves in the numbers bought by the government. Buckley says that at least 19,000 slaves were bought on the public account for the military in the West Indies.[28] In 1808, on the very same day that the act to abolish slavery came into force, the British government moved to establish Sierra Leone as a Crown colony. There they set up a vice-admiralty court to which all illegally transported slaves captured by Royal Navy ships were to be taken. Hence, Sierra Leone functioned as a receiving depot for liberated Africans and condemned slave ships, as well as a site for trying British slave traders and foreigners running slaving operations on British soil.[29] An Order-in-Council of 16 March 1808 directed that all fit Africans taken from captured slavers be turned over to military and naval authorities for enlistment into Britain's land and sea forces. In the Colonial Office files for Sierra Leone, a dispatch from Governor McCarthy states that between 1808 and 1825, 2,738 liberated Africans entered the services. Some of these went into the Royal Africa corps, and some into the navy, but most went into the West Indian regiments.[30] Since Liberated Africans continued to be received at Sierra Leone until the late 1840s, my cohort of six black soldiers were most likely to have been recruited through the vice admiralty courts there, especially since two of the six report their native place as Sierra Leone. According to Johnson Asiegbu, the numbers of Africans in the West India regiment by 1840 must have risen to 12,000 or more.[31] A survey of the files from the Colonial Office on Sierra Leone bear out the supposition that these were probably liberated Africans impressed into the army, and they almost certainly include my cohort.[32]

In 1833, the year before Alexander Duff and John Warrow arrived, James Brown landed in Van Diemen's Land, having been convicted for seven years for stealing shoes in London. To the clerk taking down his conviction he gave this mini-autobiography by way of an explanation for his thieving: "I was taken when a child as a Slave from the Congo River and sold to a Spanish Slaver. [The slave ship was] Captured by a British King's Ship & liberated at Sierra Leone. [I was] Brought away from thence as servant to Mr McCormack." Fantastic though this tale may have seemed to the convict clerk, Brown spoke the truth.

In addition to providing a recruitment station, Sierra Leone also served the purpose of providing settlement for many slaves liberated from captured ships. By 1820 the largest proportion of the Sierra Leone population was made up of these recaptives, who were initially "apprenticed" to settlers such as John McCormack, an Irish trader who settled in Sierra Leone in 1816. By 1830 McCormack was living in London, where he must have taken his "apprentice." However, in 1831 McCormack was back in Sierra Leone, without his man Brown, who remained in London with his own wife and two children. McCormack's departure suggests that Brown's decline into vagrancy and theft might have been triggered by his inability to find adequate subsequent employment to support himself and his family.[33]

While it is rare to find such a direct statement of a slave past as that of James Brown, for the majority of the 800 or so black convicts transported to Australia, their formative experience was of slavery: as runaways from North America, recaptives from slave ships, or chattel slaves and "apprentices" transported directly from Mauritius and the Caribbean. While it is fascinating to discover this distant antipodean link in the chain of African diaspora, these penal records flag something even more intriguing. Even at this raw stage of analysis it is possible to see an interconnection between various regimes of coerced labor that were in operation simultaneously—indenture, chattel slavery, penal labor, military impressment—feeding off each other in order to sustain a massive colonial enterprise and dynamic capitalist expansion. The world is all of one piece.

NOTES

1. This paper has been strongly influenced by pathbreaking research on black convicts by my colleague at the International Centre for Convict Studies, Dr. Ian Duffield of Edinburgh University.
2. Public Records Office T1/369.
3. See especially Alan Atkinson, *The Europeans in Australia*, vol. 1 (Melbourne, Vic.: Oxford University Press, 1997).
4. David Collins, *An Account of the English Colony in New South Wales: With remarks on the Dispositions, Customs, Manners, etc. of the Native Inhabitants of that Country*, ed. Brian Fletcher (Sydney: A. H. and A. W. Reed, 1975), 57.
5. The bushranger is Australia's outlaw hero. The most famous bushranger, Ned Kelly, is seen by many as the iconic Australia figure, celebrated most recently in Peter Carey's *The True History of the Kelly Gang* (New York: Knopf, 2000).
6. This point is made by Duffield in "Constructing and Reconstructing Black Caesar," in *Romanticism in Wild Places: Essays in Honour of Paul Edwards*, ed. Paul Hullah (Edinburgh: Edinburgh University Press, 1998) 57–93.
7. Public Records Office Assizes 35/226, 38.

8. Blue has been the subject of some interest, notably Meg Swords, *Billie Blue the Old Commodore* (North Sydney: North Sydney Historical Society, 1979) and Ian Duffield "Billie Blue: Power, Popular Culture and Mimicry in Early Sydney," *Journal of Popular Culture* 33, no. 1 (summer 1999), 2–7.

9. NSW Archives Petition Of William Blue: Reel 6056 4/1764, 215.

10. Loyalist Claims Commission, Public Records Office AO 12/99; AO 13/27; AO 13/29; AO 13/70; AO 13/114; AO 13/130.

11. For a fuller discussion see Benjamin Quarles, *The Negro in the American Revolution* (Chapel Hill: University of North Carolina Press, 1961); Sylvia Frey, *Water from the Rock: Black Resistance in the Revolutionary Age* (Princeton, N.J.: Princeton University Press, 1991).

12. There is a difference of opinion on this subject. Alan Kulikoff says the figures quoted at the time—maybe as many as 100,000—were highly inflated, and he estimates only 5 percent of all blacks in the southern colonies defected to the British; see "Uprooted People: Black Migrants in the Age of Revolution" in *Slavery and Freedom in the Age of American Revolution*, ed. Ira Berlin and Ron Hoffman (Charlottesville: University Press of Virginia, 1983), 144.

13. Washington to Harrison, 30 April 1873; Washington to Parker, 28 April 1783, in *The Writings of Washington From the Original Manuscripts*, ed. John C. Fitzparick (Washington, D.C.: U.S. Government Printing Office, 1931–44), 26:364–70.

14. "The Substance of the Conference between General Washington and Sir Guy Carleton at an interview at Orangetown, May 6 1783," in *The Writings of Washington*, ed. Fitzparick, 26:402–6.

15. Carleton to Washington, 12 May 1783, Public Records Office 30/55, 313.

16. Old Bailey Session papers, 1783–84, 555.

17. Winchester Quarter Session Records, 5 April 1875, Hampshire Record Office.

18. Public Records Office 30/55.

19. Manchester Quarter Session Records, 14 April 1875, Lancaster Record Office.

20. Public Records Office AO 12; AO 13

21. See the London papers *Public Advertiser* and the *Morning Chronicle* throughout 1786–87; Proceedings of the Committee for the Relief of the Black Poor, Public Records Office T1/631; T1/632.

22. Caesar appears on two lists written by different hands: Thomas Ceasor, Public Records Office T1/638, 227–228, and John J Casar, Public Records Office T1/638, 249. I have little doubt that these represent the same man, although he may not have appeared in person to claim the bounty.

23. Stephen Braidwood points out in *Black Poor and White Philanthropists: London's Blacks and the Foundation of Sierra Leone, 1786–1791* (Liverpool: Liverpool University Press, 1994) that the expedition was delayed by attempts to get men signed up for the expedition out of jail.

24. Collins, *An Account of the English Colony in New South Wales*, 57.

25. Ibid., 381.

26. Archives Office of Tasmania, CON 18/15.

27. Roger Buckley, *Slaves in Redcoats: The British West India Regiments, 1795–1815* (New Haven, Conn.: Yale University Press, 1979). Though it was true that African troops fared better than white soldiers, their mortality from disease was also very high.

28. Roger Buckley, *The British Army in the West Indies: Society and the Military in the Age of Revolution* (Gainesville: University of Florida Press, 1998), 136–38. Buckley admits his figures are an estimate as the returns are far from comprehensive. He suggests that if statistics were available for slaves serving in South Asia and the Navy the figure would be much higher.

29. One British slaver, Robert Bostock, was found guilty of slave-trading in Sierra Leone and transported to New South Wales. He appealed his sentence and won. He then sued the chief justice of Sierra Leone. He went on to become an important landowner in Van Diemen's Land.

30. Public Record Office CO 267/153/328.

31. Johnson Asiegbu, *Slavery and the Politics of Liberation, 1787–1861: A Study of Liberated African*

Immigration and British Anti-Slavery Policy (London: Longmans, 1969).

32. Public Record Office CO 267/153/328.

33. Brown's story is explored in Ian Duffield, "'Stated This Offence': High-Density Convict Micro-Narratives," in *Chain Letters: Narrating Convict Lives,* ed. Lucy Frost and Hamish Maxwell-Stewart (Carleton South, Vic.: Melbourne University Press, 2001).

A Little-Known Chapter in African American and Russian Cooperation

Joy Gleason Carew

A FRICAN AMERICANS SERVED AS TECHNICAL EXPERTS IN AGRICULTURAL, INDUS-trial, and artistic fields in the former Soviet Union. Some were attracted by the promise of an alternative to the oppressive political and socioeconomic systems under which they struggled in the United States; the majority, however, were drawn by the promise of economic and professional opportunities. Racism and bigotry prevented them from using their talents fully in the United States, but they were welcomed by the new Soviet society. Many African American immigrants originally signed one- or two-year contracts in the 1930s and then chose to renew them or to settle in the Soviet Union permanently. Subsequently, cold war tensions virtually prevented contact with the West, and for many of those who chose to remain, it was not until the dissolution of the Soviet Union that they were able to renew ties with relatives in the United States and elsewhere. The children and grandchildren of these African American fathers and Russian mothers are now providing us with invaluable insight into their lives and those of other African Americans and Afro-Russians who became willing or unwilling players in the superpower game.

Current research focuses on the relationships between black Americans and the Russian people and government, looking in particular at those who went to the Soviet Union between the two world wars. Through the prism of their lives we can learn about both the wider black experience and the geopolitical stratagems that underlaid relations between black people and the powers that be in the United States and the Soviet Union.

This work comes at a time when the United States has a keen interest in establishing cordial relations with Russia and the former Soviet Asian republics, regions where large groups of African Americans settled. Indeed, this research can provide key insight into economic development and cultural and race relations in the former republics of Uzbekistan, Tajikistan, and Kazakhstan, which were virtual colonies whose natural resources and strategic location were ruthlessly exploited by the central government for its own military and economic purposes. The arrival of the African American specialists was a matter of great importance, as they would prove to be catalysts in the modernization of Soviet Asia and other regions of the USSR. They helped develop one of the major cotton enterprises in the former USSR, and their inventions and improvements dramatically increased the efficiency of the Soviets' industrial and technical plant. Furthermore, as non-Communists for the most part, they were able to form a unique partnership with people who, themselves, were dark-skinned and had struggled with their own forms of discrimination.

Today, many of these nascent countries are threatened by an upsurge in Islamic fundamentalism from neighboring states. At the same time, they feel keen pressures to bring themselves up to economic par with the rest of the industrialized world. It may well turn out that the African American pioneers in the 1930s and their descendants will play significant roles in the development of these newly independent states and in helping to establish cordial relations with the United States.

The story of the African American pioneers of the 1920s and 1930s is not found in history books but largely exists in the anecdotal accounts of their descendants,[1] in private papers, and in the few biographies and autobiographies that have surfaced in recent years.[2] At the same time, an understanding of their relationships with the Soviet government is not complete without taking into consideration the larger geopolitical context. Fortunately, we can now benefit from the appearance of several thoughtful histories and from the new access to Russian and U.S. archives.

Recruiting the Specialists

In 1930, Premier Joseph Stalin contacted Dr. George Washington Carver of the famed Tuskegee Institute and asked him to serve as a senior technical advisor to the Soviet Ministry of Agriculture and to help organize a group of Negro specialists for a project there.[3] At the time, Carver not only was a renowned research scientist but also was profoundly interested in improving race relations, both in the United States and abroad. Stalin wanted him to oversee the revamping of the Soviet cotton industry,[4] and the Ministry of Agriculture was well aware of the prestige that Carver's support would bring to the regime. Foreign specialists commonly were contacted through a local intermediary, in this case Oliver Golden, a former student of Carver's. After several years in the Soviet Union, Golden was back in the United States to encourage industrial and agricultural specialists across the country to go to the USSR to work.[5] Membership in the Communist Party was not a prerequisite, and those who took up the offer during the Great Depression jumped at the opportunity, not only because the money was good but also because Soviet leaders praised rather than denigrated workers.

When Golden wrote to Carver, he couched his appeal in a way that he knew would have the greatest effect: "Fifty of America's largest industrial concerns have sent 2,000 of their representatives to Soviet Russia to help develop the Russian industry. Yet so far we have not on record any Negro specialists in Russia."[6] Golden also must have known of Carver's frustration at not being able to provide truly meaningful jobs for his highly talented students. Carver declined for himself, citing poor health and advanced age, but he agreed to alert Tuskegee graduates of the offer.[7] For example, he wrote to John Sutton:

> At times you have expressed a desire to go abroad. The Soviet Russian government has asked me to select 25 to 30 colored specialists in cotton growing to go over there and stay two years to help develop the cotton industry in their new territory. I have told them that I am not sure that I can go myself. He [Golden] says he is coming down from New York for a conference with me to complete further arrangements. I do not know, of course, all the details with reference to remuneration, etc., but provided the remuneration is sufficient I am wondering if such a trip would interest you.[8]

Golden wrote again on 18 April 1931, and clarified the proposal. The Soviets were offering remarkable inducements: round-trip transportation, all-expense-paid vacations on the Black Sea, full health benefits, and housing, not only for the specialists but also for their families. Most important, the Soviet Union officially outlawed racial inequality and promised to put them to work immediately.

> Instead of 25 or 30 cotton specialists, we want specialists of all branches of agriculture. Such as cotton, live stock, gardeners, poultry, rice raisers, etc., numbering 50 or more if possible. This does not mean only men, women specialists are accepted on the same basis as men.
>
> As I stated in my previous letter, the passage to and from the U.S.S.R., for the men and their families, will be paid by our office. The minimum salary will be between three

Dr. George Washington Carver

Carver was frequently called upon to lecture or to advise on specific projects. His acclaim was such that he was elected a fellow of the Royal Society of London, and in 1925 there was sentiment in the professional community that Carver should be nominated for the Nobel Prize.

At home, his work with the Commission on Inter-racial Cooperation and the YMCA (Young Men's Christian Association) often brought him into contact with the larger American society. As he wrote to one of his colleagues, "I am being invited to places to speak where we thought, a few years ago, that never would open to colored people." More and more articles were written about him and his work, and people frequently responded to these articles by contacting him about new projects. Carver regularly corresponded with a number of prominent business people and officials who shared both his research interests and his concern about improving interracial relations. Among these were Henry Ford and two U.S. secretaries of agriculture—James Wilson and Henry A. Wallace. In fact, Carver's contacts with the latter were such that Wallace accepted an invitation to visit Tuskegee in 1933 and they continued to correspond into the time when Wallace accepted the vice presidency in 1941.

and four hundred rubles a month. (Equivalent to one hundred fifty to two hundred dollars.) This is the minimum. The maximum will be much more, but this will be determined according to your recommendation and their ability. But no one will receive less than the above figure.[9]

Golden saw Carver and the Tuskegee Institute as pivotal in shaping the future for blacks in America. He argued that the project would enhance the reputation of all concerned.

Russia is inviting you to see her country, the largest agricultural country in the world, and to get your views.

It would be a pleasure, we think, for you [Dr. Carver] to accompany your men into a new field of work.

Tuskegee is national and somewhat internationally known, but your going to the U.S.S.R. and the success of these men will give Tuskegee [an] international character. . . . You owe it to your race. Russia is the only country in the world today, that gives equall chances to black and white alike. . . . It is necessary to get these men stationed in leading positions, so when other groups come, whether white or black, they will work under the supervision of these specialists.[10]

The message was not lost on Carver, but he had to tread carefully. Tuskegee depended on philanthropic support, and too-close ties with Soviet Russia might be costly. Word had gotten out that he had been approached by the USSR, and a Bahamian newspaper reported:

> Prof. George Washington Carver, one of the foremost agricultural scientists in the world, has been offered a position by Soviet Russia, to aid in developing the country's agricultural programme, it is rumoured here.
>
> Prof. Carver is in great demand in the United States. We understand some years ago, the Carnegie Institute offered him a position with a large salary in their laboratory.[11]

Immediately, letters arrived cautioning Carver about the dangers. For example:

> Somewhere I saw where the Soviet government of Russia had tendered you an offer. . . . I meant to write and remind you not to "trust" any people who spit in the face of Almighty God. . . . Recently a man returning from Russia said they [young Russian engineers who were sent into the Bessemer, Alabama, region to observe the industries there] failed in some way to please Stalin and he lined everyone of them up and had them shot. If they were that treacherous to their own—what would they be toward you?[12]

Of course, life in the United States was not much healthier for blacks. In 1930 alone, about twenty African Americans were lynched,[13] and atrocities were all too common.[14] This opportunity to go abroad gave Tuskegee graduates and other young "Negro specialists" the chance to work and live in a country that officially stood for equality among all, no matter their color or class. Despite Carver's support, however, the fifty people requested did not come forward. In fall 1931, together with Golden and his wife, a group of fourteen people left the United States for Soviet Russia.[15]

LIFE IN SOVIET ASIA

Oliver Golden took his role as an agent for the Soviets quite seriously. Upon his return to the United States in 1927, he actively sought out African Americans who could serve as specialists in the Soviet Union. An African American from Memphis, Tennessee, Golden had entered Tuskegee in 1912, but he did not graduate and was reportedly expelled following a brawl with a white man in the town. Nevertheless, he maintained contact with former classmates and Carver.

In 1925 Golden and four other African Americans were the first Americans to attend the Soviet University of the Toilers of the East (KUTVA). Also called the Far East University, it had been established to train students from the new eastern additions to the Soviet Union as well as foreigners.[16] According to Harry Haywood, a member of that early group:

> Its student body represented more than seventy nationalities and ethnic groups. It was founded by the Bolsheviks for the special purpose of training cadres from the many national and ethnic groups within the Soviet Union—the former colonial dependencies of the czarist empire—and also to train cadres from colonies and subject nations outside the Soviet Union.[17]

In 1936, following the death of his first wife, who had accompanied him to the Soviet Union, Golden returned to the United States to recruit experts to work in the USSR.

Both Golden and Carver recognized the importance of opening doors to college-educated blacks, most of whom could not find work in their chosen field in the United States. As Golden's granddaughter has noted in her book, *Soul to Soul: A Black Russian American Family, 1865–1992,* "for several of the men sailing on the *Deutschland,* the Soviet offer meant their first, and only, chance to work as professionals rather than waiters."[18] Joe Roane, who was part of the original group, stated:

> I hardly knew where the Soviet Union was when Golden came to my college to speak. No one called me a Communist for going, because no one in my circle knew exactly what a Communist was. . . . I signed on for two reasons. In the first place, Amtorg [the official Soviet agency that hired foreign workers] was offering better pay for a month than a lot of people would make in a year in the Depression. Secondly, I was young and I wanted to see the world. I thought this might be the only chance I'd ever get.[19]

The specialists who accompanied Golden and his second wife on what was to be a four-week journey arrived in November 1931. After various delays and a six-day train ride to Uzbekistan, they finally settled in Yangiyul, a village about forty miles from Tashkent. There they worked at an agricultural experiment station responsible for cotton, sugar beets, peanuts, and other crops.[20]

None of these specialists was really prepared for the living conditions on a Soviet collective, despite Golden's detailed briefings. Only Golden's second wife, Bertha, seemed to be aware that the Russians did not have the kind of material comforts that even black Americans under Jim Crow in the South and de facto segregation in the North enjoyed. She took her sewing machine and her typewriter but ultimately let the former go, retaining the typewriter because of her duties in handling correspondence.[21]

Life on the collective was more arduous than anticipated. When Harlem Renaissance writer Langston Hughes visited Tashkent and Yangiyul a year later, he found a group forced to depend largely upon itself for social amusement. Nevertheless, Hughes wrote,

> Christmas Day was wonderful. We even had pumpkin pie for dessert, and the tables were loaded down with all the American style dishes that those clever Negro wives could concoct away over there in Uzbekistan.[22]

As much as the group complained about the living conditions, it was clear that special dispensations had been made for them. The Soviet government had provided them with a large house divided into apartments, and they had access to foodstuffs and other materials that the local people did not. "This was important, because forced collectivization of the land created famines in Uzbekistan and many other areas during the thirties."[23] In addition, none of the wives were required to work outside the home, and all had maids to help with the housework.[24]

As Hughes described them, the group was made up of college graduates and "simple" cotton farmers, but he failed to recognize their skills, which would produce a new strain of cotton within three years. When he arrived they were still trying to adjust.

> Conditions on the Soviet collective, while a great change for the better for the Uzbeks, were for Negroes from America more primitive than most of them had known at home, especially for the younger college people. . . . I could understand why, though well paid, they were not happy. In the first place, the trip there was physically worse than any Jim Crow train trip I ever made in the United States. And, due to the almost continual snows that autumn, I found the whole collective farm a vast swamp of Asiatic mud in which a man sank almost to his ankles. The houses were comfortable, but there were no fireplaces, no gas stoves, no radio programs, and no jukeboxes or movies anywhere in driving distance.[25]

Yet, most of the group signed on again at the end of their two-year contract period and continued to do so throughout the decade. By the end of the 1930s, however, when faced with the choice of becoming Soviet citizens and giving up their U.S. passports or leaving the country when their contracts expired, only George Tynes and Oliver Golden and his wife chose to remain. Notably, after a visit to the United States in 1936, Tynes was more than happy to return to the USSR, and in 1939 he opted for Russian citizenship.[26]

This group of pioneers, along with their Uzbek and Russian coworkers, helped to develop one of the largest cotton industries in the world, and many of their innovations dramatically improved production. The wives of the specialists did much to encourage the local women to be more liberated.[27] Ironically, though victims of discrimination in their homeland, they were able to provide models of liberation for others.

BUILDING THE INDUSTRIAL PLANT

The Soviets also sought specialists who could help with their industrial needs.[28] There were two competing development philosophies. One held that agriculture was of primary importance, and the other maintained that the industrial base must be shored up before turning attention to other sectors. The former view was espoused by Nicholai Ivanovich Bukharin, a close confidant of Lenin and a key policy maker, but the latter approach was favored by Iosif Vissarionovich Djugashvili (otherwise known as Joseph Stalin).

Bukharin was a powerful figure whose writings shaped much of the party line from 1925 through 1927, but by early 1929 his influence was waning. Bukharin contended that by helping the peasants, the whole country would benefit. He did not oppose rapid industrialization, but he adamantly believed it would fail without a strong agricultural sector.[29] Stalin's approach, on the other hand, was to have the industrial sector take the lead:

> In the period from 1928 to 1933 alone, 1,500 big enterprises were built and the foundations were laid for branches of industry that had not existed in tsarist Russia: machine-tool production, automobile and tractor manufacturing, chemical works, airplane factories, the production of powerful turbines and generators, of high-grade steel, of ferrous alloys, of synthetic rubber, artificial fibers, nitrogen, and so on. . . . Stalin put considerable effort into the huge task of building a modern industry in the Soviet Union.[30]

Both policies required foreign specialists.

In April 1930, representatives of the Soviet government visited the Ford Motor plant in Detroit, Michigan, in an effort to attract workers to one-year contracts. About 270,000 people worked around the clock in three shifts at Ford. The machine tool division, of particular interest to the Russians, had 700 men, all but one of them white. This one black man was Robert Robinson, who was a naturalized American originally from Jamaica. Robertson found the Soviet's invitation attractive as well and decided to join the initial group of recruits.[31] This machine gauge grinder recognized that he would have more opportunity in the USSR than in the United States. Like the agricultural contracts, the terms being offered were incredible for the times. After three years at Ford, Robinson was making $140 month, a very good salary in 1930, but the Russians would provide $250 a month, free living quarters, paid vacation, and round-trip passage. They even agreed to deposit $150 per month of Robinson's wages in an American bank during his stay in the USSR. According to Robinson the fact

> that whites were competing for the same job made it easier for me to sign the contract. To get something they wanted was appealing; it also helped to ease my doubts about actually going to the Soviet Union, because I was aware of media accounts criticizing the Soviet system. But to think about the obstacles I was facing, trying to advance within the institutionalized racism in America—and recalling that a cousin of mine had just been lynched three months earlier—I made up my mind on the spot.[32]

Robinson had found that everything from deliberate misinformation to sabotage was used to prevent him from getting ahead. Through perseverance, he managed to rise from floor sweeper to trained machinist, and it was his meticulousness in the latter that made him attractive to the Soviets. He and forty-four others made the long journey, but during the four-day layover in London, Robinson was the only one not allowed to stay in the same hotel as the rest of the group. Upon arrival in Leningrad, he learned that, even there, the three white Americans assigned to share a room with him had refused, but there were no other rooms available. Robinson wryly noted that they still found a way to shut him out: "They did not say a word to me. Even though they could not get another room, and had to stay with me, they were going to make the best of it by acting as if I was not there."[33] While this behavior was not unexpected, Robinson was totally unprepared for other examples of the difference between Soviet Russia and the United States that were to come.

When Robinson reached the Stalingrad tractor factory to which he was assigned, he expected to have to prove himself but was amazed by his welcome. Yet, the tensions with his white American coworkers remained, and ten days later he was beaten by two of them. Much to his astonishment, the Russians listened sympathetically to his story, and there were repeated public expressions of indignation and solidarity.

> The Stalingrad newspaper ran an editorial denouncing the American racial prejudice and warned the Americans not to export their "social poison" to Russia. . . . For three days I was the center of attention, with everyone in the complex engrossed in how I was being treated by my fellow countrymen. On the fourth day after the incident there was a massive rally in the square in front of the administrative building . . . thousands of people gathered to hear twelve passionate speeches on the evils of racism.[34]

A week later, the two men were tried; one was sent home, and the other was allowed to finish out his one-year contract with no possibility of renewal. The quick and forthright response underscored the official position against racial discrimination. When Robinson returned to the Stalingrad plant, the Soviet workers celebrated his courage, and the white Americans were intimidated into repressing any further signs of racism. The Soviets later arranged for Robinson to further his technical training, and he became a senior engineer at the First State Ball Bearing Plant near Moscow. In 1934 he was elected to the Moscow Soviet (city council), and in 1937 he was recognized for at least twenty-seven industrial inventions.[35] Many years later, Robinson became disenchanted with what he saw as the hypocrisy and dictatorial nature of the Soviet bureaucracy. He doggedly petitioned for permission to leave the USSR, which finally was granted in the mid-1970s, when he left for Uganda. He was finally able to return to the United States in the 1980s. Although Robinson, in his book *Black on Red: My Forty-Four Years Inside the Soviet Union*, appears to downplay his role there, it is clear that both he and his Soviet hosts benefited from his presence. The recognition of his innovations and inventions, the fact that they paid for his education at the university, and the fact that as an elected member of the Moscow Soviet he was the sole person in charge of all quality assessments for all of the machine tool plants in the Moscow region speak volumes to the kind of opportunities that he was given that few African Americans would have had in that same period in the United States.[36]

ARTISTS, INTELLECTUALS, AND OTHERS

A third group of African Americans were attracted to the Soviet Union by the promise of no racial discrimination. Among them were Langston Hughes; the former postal clerk and journalist Homer Smith; and Paul Robeson and his brothers-in-law, Frank and John Goode.

When the Soviets invited Hughes to work on a film project in the early 1930s, he jumped at the chance.

> This . . . seemed to open a new door to me. . . . Many young white writers whom I knew had well-paid Hollywood writing jobs, but . . . Hollywood was still a closed shop—with the Negroes closed out.[37]

Hughes and twenty-two other African American men and women, under the auspices of the Meschrabpom Film Corporation, were to spend four months in the USSR fleshing out the screenplay for and acting in *Black and White,* intended as a true depiction of life for blacks in the United States.

When he got the word, Hughes was visiting Noel Sullivan, a wealthy patron of the arts and liberal causes, who lived in San Francisco. Their nascent friendship would survive the period Hughes spent in the Soviet Union, even though Sullivan was a severe critic of communism. Sullivan sent a stipend to Hughes's mother while he was away, helped him with subsequent medical expenses, and provided him with a cottage where he could write during the year after his return to the United States.[38]

Like Carver, Hughes was deluged with warnings from colleagues and friends. He describes the response of Lincoln Steffens, whom he had met in California:

> In light of his experiences there [he proceeded] to give me some "good advice." It consisted mostly in warning me to be prepared not to like anything in the Soviet Union—except what he called "its potential." Steffens informed me that the physical facts of life in the U.S.S.R. might well appall an American like myself accustomed to at least having in sight—if not in possession—all the heart desires, from groceries selling caviar to drugstores filled with mousetraps and waterproof watches. . . . As I left him on the steps of his home . . . he wished me well.
>
> "I'm glad you're going to Russia. . . . It's time Negroes were getting around in the world. Can you tell me why in the hell they stay home so much?"[39]

Indeed, it could not have been clearer to Hughes why going to a country without racial discrimination would be so appealing. That same weekend, as he continued up the West Coast for one last engagement, he and his traveling companion could not find hotel accommodations for Negroes in Oregon. They ended up relying on the police to help them find a place to stay.[40]

It took Hughes several weeks to get back to New York and assemble what he needed for his journey. Once he embarked on the *Bremen*, he got to know his traveling companions and was amazed to learn that only two of them had any previous experience with films or acting. Nonetheless, they saw this as a unique opportunity, even though they had to pay their own passage and had not yet seen a formal contract from the Russians.

> These two professionals [Wayland Rudd and Estelle Winwood] were also the only real mature people in our group, everyone else being well under thirty and some hardly out of their teens. . . . Among these . . . were an art student just out of Hampton, a teacher, a girl elocutionist from Seattle, three would-be writers other than myself, a very pretty divorcee who traveled on alimony, a female swimming instructor, and various clerks and stenographers . . . very few professional theatre people were willing to pay their own fares to travel all the way to Russia to sign contracts they had never seen. Only a band of eager, adventurous young [people] were willing to do that.[41]

In Germany, the group boarded a Swedish ship to Helsinki and then made the final leg of the journey by train across Finland. In Moscow, they were comfortably lodged in one of the better hotels, but work on the film was delayed. After three months of uncertainty, script changes, and adjustments, the project fell through. Hughes was not happy with the original script: "I went through the scenario with the studio heads page by page, scene by scene, pointing out the minor nuances that were off tangent here, the major errors of factual possibility there, and in some spots the unintentional portrayal of what amounted to complete fantasy."[42]

Many in the group began to complain about the accommodations, the uncertainty, and their boredom. Most left the USSR some months later, but four opted to remain: the actor/singer Wayland Rudd, the artist Lloyd Patterson, Homer Smith, and Hughes. The first three eventually married Russian women and two of them started families. Rudd and Patterson never went back to the United States for any length of time, but Smith did return just after World War II. Although he had gone as part of the film group, Smith had worked in the U.S. Postal Service to put himself through school and, as a result, when the film project folded he "got a contract with the Russian postal service and introduced the first special delivery to Moscow."[43] Smith had also studied journalism at the University of Minnesota, and he became the only African American foreign correspondent behind the lines in the Soviet Union during World War II. His dispatches sent to the Negro Press and Associated Press provided a unique inside picture.[44]

The film project was never realized, many now contend, because the Soviets wanted diplomatic relations with the United States. George Padmore writes:

> The Soviet cinema industry had planned to make a film depicting lynchings and racial oppression in the Southern States [U.S.] and a cast of coloured American actors had been engaged and taken to Moscow for the purpose. Before work on the film was started, the news leaked out and Colonel Hugh L. Cooper and other white Southern American engineers directing the construction of the Dnieperstroi hydroelectric project protested to Stalin, who ordered the film to be abandoned. . . . Shortly after their return to the United States in 1933, President Roosevelt extended diplomatic recognition to the Soviet Union. It was only then that the full story about the suppression of the Negro film was revealed in the press by Mr. Henry Lee Moon and Mr. Ted Poston, both distinguished coloured journalists who had been engaged as script writers.[45]

Such geopolitical juggling between the United States and the USSR became the norm in the Stalinist era and continued through World War II and into the cold war period. Still, ordinary Russians continued to receive blacks warmly, regarding them as representatives of a people who had endured extreme difficulties. The Scottsboro case inspired Hughes to write one of his more direct protest poems, "Justice is a blind goddess / To this we blacks are wise / Her bandage hides two festering sores / That once perhaps were eyes."[46] This was a cause célèbre in Soviet Russia. Along with the International Labor Defense and the Communist Party, the Soviet government joined an international campaign to have the young men exonerated. The case was so famous that virtually every Russian encountered by African Americans in the early 1930s knew about it. The Russians also sincerely appreciated the fact that these foreign specialists were willing to put their talents to work alongside them as they worked to build the Soviet society. Thus, while profiting from the skills that African Americans brought to the USSR, the Soviet government also made use of them as sources of information about the deplorable condition of blacks in the United States, and as political weapons in the superpower struggle.

As for the film group, in the midst of the uncertainty of whether the project would continue or not, they did enjoy what Robert Robinson called "the red carpet treatment," replete with tours that highlighted the successes of the Soviet people since the revolution.[47] Though disappointed at not having been able to accomplish their dream of being in the movie, the majority took up the Soviets' face-saving offer of an all-expense-paid tour of Europe prior to continuing back to the United States. In fact, the Soviets offered the group one of two options: an extended tour of Europe, or a tour of the Soviet Union. Half of the group decided to stay on for the tour of the USSR, while the others chose to leave for Europe. Eventually, though, only four stayed on: Rudd, Patterson, Smith, and Hughes.

In Hughes's case, the interest was not in remaining indefinitely, but, rather to explore areas where darker-skinned peoples lived.

> [A]bout half accepted the travel invitation before applying for exit visas. It did not take us long to agree among ourselves that the portions of the Soviet Union we would most like to see were those regions where the majority of the colored citizens lived, namely Turkmenistan in Soviet Central Asia. This gave our trade-union hosts pause because, at that time, this part of the Soviet Union was forbidden territory to foreigners.[48]

It was during this extended journey that Hughes came across a young engineering graduate from Howard University, Bernard Powers, and the group of agricultural specialists. Both Powers, who was working in Tashkent, and Hughes were invited to spend Christmas with the African American group at their Soviet collective farm some forty miles outside of the city, and it was this visit that Hughes immortalized as the "Dixie Christmas USSR" in his autobiography, *I Wonder as I Wander*.

Many others also went to the Soviet Union in search of a more hospitable place in which to live and work. A case in point is Paul Robeson, who was fascinated by the USSR and over a number of years read everything he could about the evolving Soviet society. He viewed it as a place where the race question "seems to work to my advantage. . . . Soviet theory is that all races are equal—really equal, socially equal, too, as well as economically and politically."[49] According to his biographer, Robeson

> has deliberately and for a long time been laying plans and preparing to move to the U.S.S.R. as the most suitable center for the important work of artistic innovation which he has in mind, and because he has decided on the basis of much evidence that it is a place where a man may do such work with the greatest freedom and facility.[50]

When Robeson went for his first visit at the end of 1934, his brothers-in-law, Frank and John Goode, decided to go as well. Frank was particularly close to his sister, Eslanda Goode Robeson, and wanted to make sure this was the right choice for her.[51] The Goode brothers arrived in the USSR in December 1934, almost a month before the Robesons.

The brothers were quite different, which may explain why Frank stayed on and John returned to the United States after three years. John wanted to be a mechanical engineer but could not afford to study in the United States, so he hoped to take advantage of the free education in the Soviet Union. Frank had no particular plan, and his flexibility may have made his adaptation to life in the USSR easier. He eventually became a professional wrestler. According to Eslanda Goode Robeson,

> John had gotten work as a bus driver at the Foreign Workers' Club garages, and Frank, more recently arrived had—as a towering, powerfully built man—the prospect of being billed as a "Black Samson" in a wrestling troup tour of circuses and carnivals. He "is already acclimated," Essie wrote her mother, but she didn't like the looks of John—"cold, and worn and old."[52]

Several years into his stay, Frank married a Russian woman and had a daughter he named Eslanda. John, however, had a difficult time trying to learn Russian while working full time, and he finally gave up his plans. Harry Haywood had a similar experience ten years earlier, when preparing to attend the Soviet University of the Toilers:

> I was having my own problems with the Russian language. On first hearing it, the language had sounded most strange to me. I could hardly understand a word and wondered if I would ever be able to master it. As the youngest Black American, I applied myself seriously to its study. The first hurdle was the Cyrillic alphabet—its uniquely different characters intimidated me.[53]

Ultimately, Haywood took a crash course at the university and set up a systematic program of self-study, but for many who went to the Soviet Union this was not possible.

Paul Robeson's decision to move to the USSR was never realized, although he and his wife visited there frequently. At one point, they established an apartment there for their son, Pauli, and his grandmother Eslanda Cardozo Goode while Pauli attended school in Moscow from 1936 to 1938. Robeson explained this choice in a *New York Times* interview: "I want the boy to be brought up in an atmosphere like the Soviet's, if possible . . . that is, brought up as a free human being. I don't see why he should have to bear the burdens of racial prejudice—the world is too big for that today."[54] The young man and his grandmother left when the threat of impending war became too great. The Robesons then settled in England, where young Paul attended the Russian Embassy school.

THE CHILDREN AND OTHER LEGACIES

A number of African Americans who settled in the Soviet Union had children there. When these children grew up, some married Russians and raised another generation. Relatively little is known about their lives, although some information is more accessible with the dismantling of the Soviet Union.

For many, their understanding of African American cultural traditions has been limited to infrequent letters and other contacts with the West. With glasnost, several took the opportunity to establish ties with their extended family. According to Yelena Khanga, the granddaughter of Oliver Golden: "My favorite song was We Shall Overcome, which I learned in English as a small child. Those black American voices, resonant with a world of sorrow and joy, came to us on records, gifts from a steady stream of black American visitors who passed through our home."[55] Many yearned to visit the United States but were disappointed to discover the stultifying effects of American racism and U.S. chauvinism. Suddenly forced into the black-white box of a worldview that frequently shapes relationships in the United States, they found they did not fit. They were Russians, not Americans or African Americans. As Khanga writes:

> In spite of the many strands in my heritage, I am also Russian to the core. Russian was my first language, though my mother and grandmother often spoke English at home. My schooling was Soviet, beginning with the kindergarten where I was taught to love *Dedushka* (grandpa) Lenin. My mind and soul have been shaped by the compassionate irony of Chekhov, the poetry of Pushkin, the romantic music of Tchaikovsky.[56]

These difficult adjustments are matched by the experiences of specialists who returned to the United States after spending years abroad. Robinson visited the United States in 1970 and was even more convinced that his choice to stay in the USSR had been the right one.

> Manhattan was different than I had imagined, and I was especially saddened to see how much Harlem had deteriorated. I had expected it to be better than it had been in 1933 [the last time he had visited], not worse. We walked down 125th Street, and Seventh Avenue, which used to be full of well-dressed high rollers. But now it was a dump, and when I saw the condition of the people, I asked my brother when it had started happening. I had been told that blacks were politically, economically, and socially better off in the United States, so I had expected something much better.[57]

The research into these early African American pioneers continues. It is anticipated that their descendants, both here and in Russia, will play a key role in providing information about these and other African Americans and about the nature of
this early cooperation. Learning about these early contacts will enable us to interpret
both pre– and post–cold war relationships between the Russian people and their government and the various peoples of the African diaspora.

NOTES

1. I first became interested in black Americans in the USSR when I learned about Lily Golden, the
   daughter of Oliver Golden, a black man who moved to Russia in the 1930s with a group of agricultural specialists. Some years ago, I happened to share a conference panel with Lily Golden's
   daughter, Yelena Khanga. Later, I met Eslanda Goode, who is a niece of Paul Robeson and whose
   father moved to the USSR in 1934.

   I have always been intrigued by Alexander Pushkin, whose grandfather came from Africa.
   Considered the father of Russian literature, Pushkin helped the Russian people develop a love for
   their own language. He chose it, the language of his nanny, over the French typical of the privileged
   class of his time. The great Russian author Dostoevsky said that "no Russian writer was ever so inti-
   mately at one with the Russian people as Pushkin" (Norris Houghton, ed., *Great Russian Short
   Stories* [New York: Dell, 1960], 8).

   Also, I was fascinated by my parents' stories of their travels to the USSR, first with a group of
   educators in 1957, and of the warmth and generosity the Russians showed them. What struck them
   most profoundly was that they were treated with far greater civility than they had ever been in the
   United States. Furthermore, I have been very warmly received there, both as a student in the late
   1960s and on other trips.
2. William Davis, "How Negroes Live in Russia," *Ebony*, 1 January 1996, 65–78. William Davis, a former Foreign Service officer and an African American, discovered a colony of these expatriates when
   he went to the Soviet Union in the late 1950s. Ultimately, he would play a key role in bringing attention to them in the 1960s and in helping many of them renew ties with their American families in
   subsequent years.
3. Oliver Golden to G. W. Carver, 18 April 1932, George Washington Carver Papers at Tuskegee
   Institute (The National Historical Publications and Records Commission), reel 12 (Jan. 1930–Aug.
   1931), #974; and Yelena Khanga, *Soul to Soul: A Black Russian American Family, 1865–1992* (New
   York: W. W. Norton, 1992), 74.
4. Carver's first overseas technical assistance project, in 1899, was to upgrade cotton production in
   the German colony of Togoland (Khanga, *Soul to Soul*, 50–51).
5. Ibid.
6. Golden to Carver, 12 December 1930, Carver Papers, reel 11.
7. Carver to Golden, 7 May 1931, Carver Papers, #1000.
8. Carver to John Sutton, 26 January 1931, Carver Papers, #731.
9. Golden to Carver, 18 April 1931, Carver Papers, #973, 974.
10. Ibid.
11. "Russia Seeks Carver," Carver Papers, reel 12 (1931), #797.

12. Linda Robertson to Carver, 28 May 1931, Carver Papers, reel 12, #1084.
13. Allison Blakely, *Russia and the Negro: Blacks in Russian History and Thought* (Washington, D.C.: Howard University Press, 1986), 99.
14. Forrest Brown to Carver, 3 November 1930, Carver Papers, reel 12.
15. Khanga, *Soul to Soul*, 72.
16. George Padmore, *Pan-Africanism or Communism* (Garden City, N.Y.: Doubleday, 1971), 296–97.
17. Harry Haywood, *Black Bolshevik: An Autobiography of an Afro-American Communist* (Chicago: Liberator Press, 1978), 155.
18. Khanga, *Soul to Soul*, 76.
19. Ibid., 77.
20. Blakely, *Russia and the Negro*, 97.
21. Khanga, *Soul to Soul*, 75.
22. Langston Hughes, *I Wonder as I Wander* (New York: Thunder's Mouth Press, 1989), 180.
23. Khanga, *Soul to Soul*, 83.
24. Blakely, *Russia and the Negro*, 98.
25. Hughes, *I Wonder as I Wander*, 176–77.
26. Blakely, *Russia and the Negro*, 97.
27. Khanga, *Soul to Soul*, photo caption between pages 128 and 129.
28. Roy Medvedev, *Let History Judge: The Origins and Consequences of Stalinism* (New York: Columbia University Press, 1989), 436.
29. Ibid., 202.
30. Ibid., 248.
31. Robert Robinson, *Black on Red: My Forty-Four Years Inside the Soviet Union* (Washington, D.C.: Acropolis Books, 1988), 26.
32. Ibid., 29.
33. Ibid., 26.
34. Ibid., 68.
35. Blakely, *Russia and the Negro*, 101.
36. Robinson, *Black on Red*, 430.
37. Hughes, *I Wonder as I Wander*, 65.
38. Arnold Rampersad, ed., *The Collected Poems of Langston Hughes* (New York: Vintage Classics, 1994), 10.
39. Hughes, *I Wonder as I Wander*, 65–66.
40. Ibid., 66.
41. Ibid., 70.
42. Ibid., 77.
43. Haywood, *Black Bolshevik*, 385.
44. Homer Smith, *Black Man in Red Russia* (Chicago: Johnson, 1964), 172.
45. Padmore, *Pan-Africanism*, 286.
46. Hughes, *I Wonder as I Wander*, 58.
47. Robinson, *Black on Red*, 320.
48. Hughes, *I Wonder as I Wander*, 102.
49. Paul Robeson, *Paul Robeson Speaks: Writings, Speeches, Interviews, 1918–1974*, ed. Philip S. Foner (Larchmont, N.Y.: Brunner/Mazel, 1978), 94.
50. Ibid., 96.
51. Interview with Eslanda Goode, Frank Goode's daughter, 1996.
52. Martin Duberman, *Paul Robeson: A Biography* (New York: New Press, 1989), 185.
53. Haywood, *Black Bolshevik*, 160.

54. Robeson, *Paul Robeson Speaks*, 104.
55. Khanga, *Soul to Soul*, 21.
56. Ibid.
57. Robinson, *Black on Red*, 413.

A Perspective on African Diaspora: Cultural Workers and Communities in Russia

Michael C. Thornton

THE PRESENCE OF AFRICANS IN MANY PARTS OF THE GLOBE IS MOST DIRECTLY related to the worldwide slave trade. While some of the first Africans to go to Russia were slaves (almost all of whom quickly left or were released from slavery), most blacks who migrated there were not. The African presence in the Soviet Union is made up of three types: long-time residents in Georgia, servants and other workers, and expatriates and exiles looking for the promised land. The question of whether Russia is and has been the savior of third world people, blacks in particular, has always been part of the debate about the black presence there. Suffice it to say that from 1900 to 1970 most people of African ancestry in Russia had greater control of at least their professional lives than they did in places like the United States.

AFRICAN RUSSIANS OF LONG-STANDING

About the time of World War I, five hundred blacks were officially discovered in the Crimea, Azerbaijan, Georgia, and near the port city of Sukhumi, in the Soviet Union.[1] They were mostly assimilated into the local population; they spoke the local language, wore the local dress. Most also lived in poverty.[2] There is uncertainty about where they came from and how long they have been in that part of the Soviet Union; some claim their ancestors settled there thousands of years ago, others say that their people have been there since the slave trade of the fifteenth century.[3] In any case, they are the only extant black population that appears to be indigenous to the country.

Servants and Other Workers in Imperial Russia

Peter the Great was the primary influence in getting Africans and other blacks to come to Russia. Their arrival began as a fad among the nobility—it was all the rage in Europe—but continued on a larger scale with increasing contact with the outside world through ever-widening trade relations.

Blacks in Russia were called *arapy, efiopy,* or *negry* (blackamoors, Ethiopians, or Negroes).[4] Until the nineteenth century, many were acquired as slaves via Turkey, North Africa, or Amsterdam, but many also came from America. Although they arrived in Russia as slaves, many quickly secured freedom in exchange for a lifetime service obligation.

Throughout the nineteenth century blacks were a highly valued group of servants to the czar. The very first black American *valet de pied* appears to be a man named Nelson, a manservant who accompanied John Quincy Adams and members of his family when they visited St. Petersburg in 1809. Adams wrote about Nelson:

> Nelson left us about four months ago to enter the service of his Imperial Majesty, who has about a dozen menial attendants of that color. I had not been there very long before Nelson found out that it would be possible for him to obtain that situation. I gave him his discharge.[5]

Adams also helped Claud Gabriel, a native of Martinique, obtain a position at court. He was so welcome there that the czar offered both to indemnify the owners of the ship that brought him and to pay the expenses of transporting Claud's wife and children to Saint Petersburg.[6]

The royal court had a small permanent staff of servants, about ten to twenty. Nancy Prince, a black woman who traveled to Russia in the mid-nineteenth century and who was married to one of the servants at court, described life for blacks there at that time:

> The number of colored men that filled this station was twenty; when one dies, the number is immediately made up. Mr. Prince filled the place of one that had died. They serve in turns, four at a time, except on some great occasions, when all are employed. Provision is made for the families within or without the palace. Those without go to court at 8

o'clock in the morning; after breakfasting, they take their station in the halls, for the purpose of opening the doors, at signal given, when the Emperor and Empress pass.[7]

She also described her feelings when she was presented to the emperor:

As we passed through the beautiful hall, a door was opened by two colored men in official dress. The Emperor Alexander, stood in his throne. . . . [A]s I entered, the Emperor stepped forward with great politeness and condescension, and welcomed me, and asked several questions. . . . They [the Emperor and Empress] presented me with a watch, &c. It was customary in those days, when any one married, belonging to the court, to present them with gifts. . . . [T]here was no prejudice against color; there were all casts, and the people of all nations. . . .[8]

That there were black Americans in Russia during the nineteenth century seemed to come as a surprise to many, including the American ambassador, Andrew White. Upon leaving a ceremony in the White Palace, White encountered a guard, "an enormous creature, very black, very glossy." He believed him to be a "Nubian," brought specially from Central Africa. He was greatly surprised when the guard was one of "my own compatriots."[9]

With their involvement in world trade, ships from a number of countries would dock in Russian ports. Among the crew of many of these ships were black seamen, including Matthew Henson, who would later be the first black man to reach the North Pole.[10] International ties would also bring students from Ethiopia by the end of the nineteenth century. Some would stay to become educators.[11]

Because black Americans appeared so often in Russia in the nineteenth century, many Russians believed that the color of a genuine American was black. Mina Curtiss recounts a story told by John Maxwell, secretary to the American Minister in Moscow, who met

several old gentlemen who manifested much curiosity in all that related to the United States. We were regarded as objects of rare interest, and asked all kinds of questions. . . . Doubts were even entertained as to whether we were the genuine article, because our tongue was English and because, forsooth, all former Americans who had passed the vision of some of these Muscovites, were as black as the ace of spades.[12]

Still convinced that the men were English, one Russian insisted on taking Maxwell and his companions to a musical, where he claimed it would be proven that they were not Americans. What he wanted to show them was "a well-dressed negro whose hair looked as if it had been frosted. He was tuning up his fiddle. . . . [H]is body swung so lazily back and forth as to convince us at once that he was bred among the minstrels somewhere south of Mason's and Dixon's line."[13]

By the twentieth century some blacks had achieved notable measures of success in Russian history. Three such cases are illustrative. Two are from the same family tree, Abrahm Hannibal and his great-grandson, Alexander Pushkin. The other, Ira Aldridge, achieved fame on stage at a time when he was not allowed to perform in many venues in his homeland, America.

Abrahm Hannibal, "Le Negre du Czar"

The most prominent of this group was Abrahm Hannibal. He began life as a slave, but by the time of his death he had become a general and a man of great wealth, leaving a legacy of ancestors who were to be prominent in Russian literature and politics.[14]

Hannibal entered the czars' service in 1705 and apparently was one of the czar's favorites, for by 1707 he was baptized into the Russian Orthodox Church, with the czar as his godfather. In 1716, at the age of nineteen, he went to study in France where he became known as Le Negre du Czar, "the Negro of the Czar." He stayed there until 1723, whereupon he returned to St. Petersburg.

When his benefactor Peter the Great died in 1725, he was succeeded by his wife, Catherine the Great. But soon after there came to the throne someone to whom Hannibal was considered a threat. Hannibal was therefore exiled to Siberia in 1727. Eleven years later the daughter of Peter the Great acceded to the throne, restoring his favor. Hannibal was made major general, and given command of the city of Revel (now Tallinn) in Estonia and ten villages with several thousand white slaves. In 1762 he retired with the rank of general-in-chief. He died in 1782, at the age of 85, survived by several children. Ivan, his eldest son, gained fame as a military leader. Another son, Peter, was also in the military, as was another brother, Ossip (Joseph), who was a naval officer. Ossip's daughter, Nadezhda, married into a well-established Russian family named Pushkin. A daughter was born in 1797; in 1799 a son named Alexander was born.

Alexander Pushkin

While all his works could be bound together in one volume, thousands of books have been written about Alexander Pushkin and what he created.[15] Numerous monuments have been erected in his honor throughout Russia, and special magazines are dedicated to his life. In the paintings done of him, one can see his black curls, olive skin, and thick lips, which speak to you of his ancestry. He was proud of his lineage, speaking of his great-grandfather in many verses. In fact, he was writing about this man when he died, and a book entitled *Arab Petra Velikogo* (The Negro of Peter the Great) was published posthumously. But like the great Dumas family of French society (*The Three Musketeers*), the Pushkin family's African heritage goes unheralded outside of their country of residence. Pushkin died a magnanimous death in a duel at the early age of thirty-eight. However, his legacy lasted well past his death: a son commanded the Russian troops in Poland in 1890; a grandson, Georgori Pushkin, was also a military commander. Homer Smith, the only black journalist stationed in Russia during World War II, gives an account of his meeting Georgori and Catherine Pushkin (a great-granddaughter of Alexander) in his book *Black Man in Red Russia*. Smith quotes Catherine Pushkin as saying, "Alexander Sergeevich was dark-complexioned. . . . I am so sorry that my color is so light."[16] It is an interesting sidelight that, after the revolution in the Soviet Union and the communist takeover, the Pushkins, being landed gentry, lost their positions and status.

Ira Aldridge

Before Paul Robeson stole the hearts of the Russian people in the twentieth century, Ira Aldridge did much the same in the nineteenth. Much of Aldridge's success can be attributed to his being in the right place at the right time. Just previous to his arrival in Russia, the serfs were liberated, and *Uncle Tom's Cabin* had been released in translation for the first time in 1858. Upon his arrival, he became the symbol of his oppressed people. And though Aldridge's success is partially attributable to timing, much of it was due also to his ability in performing Shakespeare, which, before his arrival, had not been presented in the Soviet Union because there were no Russian translations available there. A French critic of the time, who had expected to find Aldridge's acting barbaric and savage, described Aldridge's performance and his effect on the Russian population in the following terms: "He was the lion of Saint Petersburg and seats for the theatre had to be taken days before. At first he played Othello. . . . His own skin was right for the role. . . . It was Othello himself as Shakespeare created him."[17]

Many liberal and radical leaders who had encouraged and befriended Aldridge were arrested or exiled during the revolutionary movement that followed the freeing of the serfs. With that shift in the political and professional atmosphere, Aldridge's career changed. The prevailing climate of reaction and terror in the 1860s also infected the theater, causing better actors to avoid the risk of appearing with the "Negro Symbol of Freedom." So what initially made Aldridge so successful later led to his demise. He soon left for Poland, where he died in 1867. Despite not being allowed to perform in Russia during the season prior to his death, his career as a Russian actor was successful. As a black man, Aldridge was never allowed to perform on stage in the United States, and specifically in New York. It was not until 1880, thirteen years after his death, that the first black actor participated in a Shakespearean performance on a New York stage.

Notes on Expatriates, Exiles, Enlightened Socialism, and the Twentieth Century's Promised Land

Many of African ancestry came to settle in Russia for other reasons. The most notable for monetary gain obtained after moving to Russia was probably Jimmy Winkfield, who won two Kentucky Derbys before moving to Russia to ride for wealthy noblemen. With the 1919 Russian Civil War, however, he was said to have lost some $50,000 and 4,000 shares of Russian railroad stock.[18] George Thomas arrived in St. Petersburg in the late nineteenth century as a valet. He subsequently accumulated a fortune and by World War I owned a large amusement park complex in Moscow. However, when the Bolsheviks seized power in 1917, he was forced to flee because his wealth caused him to be considered an enemy of the state.[19]

The belief in a humane socialist society brought many black people to the "Promised Land," especially in the early years of the twentieth century. In 1932, for example, a plan was proposed to make a movie, *Black and White*, about American racial injustice. The cast, which would be all black, would be paid by the Comintern (Communist International) to film the movie in Moscow. Many blacks had high expectations for this project because the Communist International Congress had long shown support for black American issues, beginning with support for the abolition of slavery in 1863, to Lenin's publicizing the grim conditions of southern blacks at the turn of the century, to the 1928 Comintern doctrine proclaiming that southern blacks deserved the right to self-determination. When the American communists extended efforts to boost black membership to black industrial workers in the 1930s, the Comintern offered to underwrite production of *Black and White*. It would serve as proof of the manner in which capitalism discriminated against oppressed colored citizens.[20] Among those who would participate in this project were some of the era's most influential black literary figures, for example, Langston Hughes and Dorothy

West (a noted contributor to the Harlem literary renaissance). While they were to represent black workers in the movie, most of the participants had achieved white-collar status.

On their way to Moscow, they met others of the diaspora, including a black waiter in a Turkish coffeehouse. But they were especially impressed with their treatment in Russia, where Jim Crow did not exist. One participant felt that "Unconsciously I have lost that depressing subconsciousness of being a Negro, [and] the ever-present thought that my dark skin must circumscribe my activities at all times. I was a bit surprised how absolutely normal my moving about the Russian people has become." And while most had a good experience, racial prejudice was still to be found in some circles. One of the Russian officials involved in the movie project thought all blacks were pitch black. That the black performers varied in color greatly disturbed him: "We needed genuine Negroes," he protested.[21]

Paul Robeson, Kwame Nkrumah, W. E. B. DuBois, and George Padmore are just a few others who saw socialist nations, especially the former USSR, as having greater potential for a more humane understanding of the world and African people in particular.[22] Paul Robeson believed this "gathering around the Communist banner" was a means of blacks attaining full human dignity. Robeson's abiding friendship with the Soviet Union was formed in 1934 when he visited Germany and was to witness the worst forms of degradation because of his color; but in Russia he was met with open arms. Robeson saw socialist society as an advance to a higher stage of life, a form of society that was economically, socially, and culturally superior to a system based upon production for private profit. He was especially impressed by the strides toward universal egalitarianism that the Soviet Union had ostensibly taken. It appealed to his deep sense of the equality of men. He witnessed that the Soviet Union accepted black Americans and nonwhites from its own population as their equals, a policy not found elsewhere in the world.[23]

It may be coincidental, but at the time of his first visit to Russia in the 1930s he was developing and advocating African literature and anti-imperialism, both ostensibly advocated by the Soviet Union. Robeson linked the liberation struggle of blacks in America with the same struggle of peoples of Mother Africa. The international significance of the USSR was its emergence as an anticolonialist and antifascist system, with the potential to use its military-political power to aid the national liberation movements against colonialism in Africa and America. This Pan-Africanist approach was advocated by Robeson as well as other important black figures such as Nkrumah and Padmore.

Smith, the lone black reporter stationed in the Soviet Union during World War II, mentions in his book several others who came to live in Russia in the 1920s and

1930s because of its image of assisting oppressed people: Loft Forte-Whitman, an organizer of the American Negro Labor Congress; William Burroughs, an announcer for broadcasts of Radio Moscow beamed to the United States; and Coretta Arli-Titz, a popular singer in Moscow. Smith also mentions a black woman named Emma (a mother figure to all Americans in Moscow) who was well-to-do before the revolution but was at the time of his visit "declass bourgeoisie." Smith met an uncle of soprano Margaret Tynes in Moscow, and Paul Robeson's brother-in-law near Moscow.[24]

Not all blacks would see Russia as the promised land. Other expatriates would write of their experiences in Russia during the early years of the twentieth century, and would suggest that it is much more complicated than those above would have us believe: while an improvement on capitalist countries it still was far from perfect for blacks. One of the first blacks to defect to the USSR was Robert Robinson, who describes his life there as being a little different from that he left in Detroit, at least in one regard: he could work at a profession not open to him in the United States at the time he left for Russia in the 1930s. About his experience in the Soviet Union Robinson wrote: "I can say . . . that in some respects I benefited from my stay in Moscow. In the United States of the 1930s," my race would have kept me from becoming a mechanical engineer. But, "I was never really accepted as an equal," and "I could never, ever get used to the racism in the Soviet Union." By the time he defected back to the United States in the 1970s he felt used by the Soviets, who he thought had exploited his color for propaganda.[25]

Others would become disillusioned after participating in Comintern schools. While blacks could enroll at Stalin Communist University in the mid-1920s, it was only after coming under Comintern jurisdiction in 1923 that the school began recruiting black Americans and Africans. Ostensibly giving its students a rigorous education, its other goal was to provide training in communist doctrine. One of the first to attend the school was Bankole Awoonor-Renner, an Ashanti who came from the Gold Coast in 1925. Treated as honored guests, these students received preferential treatment on all fronts, and this set them apart from the average Soviet citizen. While they experienced little direct discrimination while attending the Comintern schools, they did encounter it at the hands of foreign whites—usually Americans, Canadians, and Britons.

Although discrimination from Russians was minimal, it still existed. Institutional discrimination was well evident, especially in the Russian understanding of Africa, black Americans, and the image of blacks in Soviet society. Additionally, because these schools were more intent on teaching their colored brethren about socialism, black and African students found that the officials in charge often would give mere lip service to inherent problems encountered by students in the program. Because they were so convinced of the idea of the racial promised land, when students encountered even this kind of discrimination they were surprised and became disillusioned because it blatantly contradicted official policy. After examining the experience of black and African students in Comintern schools from 1925 to 1934, Woodford McClellan concluded: "The episodes and attitudes enumerated here reveal a more antagonistic situation with regard to race relations than either Soviet reports or most black memoirs and other accounts have indicated."[26] Nonetheless, the atmosphere in the schools was perhaps still the best blacks could have gotten anywhere in the world, and it offered them opportunities not forthcoming in Europe or the United States.

More recently, there are other signs supporting this notion of a less-than-perfect promised land for blacks in Russia. In the late 1980s, Yelena Khanga drew media attention. Khanga's paternal grandparents left the United States to go to the USSR in the twenties after they found that their interracial marriage would not be accepted; Khanga is the married name of their daughter, Yelena's mother, who married a Zanzibarian. On the jacket of her book Yelena is described as "two Yelenas—a Russian filled with the poetry of Pushkin and the music of Tchaikovsky, and a black, with American accents, who loved the rhythms of Billie Holliday and Duke Ellington." The dichotomy between being African and Russian suggests something about the quality of black life in Russia.

And indeed, she has been one of the few black commentators on Soviet television. Because she has led a privileged life, she never felt like a stranger in her black skin and was never made to feel less than others. However, in her travels she encountered black Russians who felt differently about blacks, one of whom noted that she hated being in Russia in part because people discriminate against her and call her a monkey. Khanga's mother tells of how she decided to write a book about the isolated and impoverished black population in Soviet Georgia that she discovered in the sixties. Russian officials did not want the impoverished living conditions of these black Russians advertised. Before the book was published, the information on black poverty was removed.[27]

Much of the information about the current circumstances of blacks in Russia is troubling, as well. While some headlines ostensibly refer to the idea of a promised land for African students, the articles that follow them often recount how the promise is unfulfilled; some Africans were forced to work for the KGB, while others were beaten or killed.[28] African and Asian students and a black U.S. marine have been assaulted by Russian skinheads,[29] and black students have suffered threats and discrimination at Moscow's People's Friendship University.[30]

Despite the long tradition of Africans in Russia, and there are about 12,000 Africans there today, many Russians are unused to relating with them except in caricature. As one report suggests, where Africans are in numbers, such as in Moscow, they are "liked." One Russian said that he liked blacks because he loves Michael Jordan.[31]

The assessment that Russians are uneasy with blacks was reinforced on a trip Gwendolyn Brooks took to the Soviet Union in 1982. She traveled with some American writers (including Susan Sontag, Studs Terkel, and Arthur Schlesinger Jr.) to the Soviet-American Writers' Conference. After reading her poem "The Life of Lincoln West," about the traumas of a little black boy who is constantly told that his color and black features are ugly, but who finally starts to discover his identity, the Russian representative at the reading began describing the boy as darling, with "nice white teeth and nice rough hair." The representative also said that he did not pay any attention to the fact that Lincoln was black. Brooks observed that all participants, American and Russian, seemed to support this interpretation and thus "were pleased with me." Upset with the response to her subject, Brooks angrily bemoaned how isolating it was to be black in Russia and that Russians did not understand blackness:

> During my three weeks away, entire, I am to see not one other Black woman, although I've been told by Russia-traveling friends that there is an "ample" contingent of Black women living in Russia. No Russian wants to talk about this, however. I'm looked at strangely, when I'm inclined to mention it, am abruptly left alone in the middle of the floor! No one feels any reason to cite blackness because on the Soviet side there is very little association with Blacks. Soviets see very few. And on the American side there is as little association with Blacks as can comfortably be managed, although there is great opportunity in the United States of America."[32]

The final assault on her senses came when Brooks visited "St. Cyril's Church, Kiev: Plastered with religious paintings. One of them in particular seizes me: a thin, coal black devil, with protruding teeth (you just know the artist considered this blackness the essence of evil 'incarnate')."[33]

Russia's history with Africans has been helped by its reputation as a bastion of support for the oppressed; since the nineteenth century, until very recently, Russia was described as *the* place for blacks and Africans to go for racial liberalism.[34] This reputation continued for much of the twentieth century, in part because those who went there were treated specially; they could live a life better than their compatriots in Africa or America. Some say this suggests something intrinsic about the Soviet system. Others see it as a reflection of political machinations, in which the black/African presence could be used as proof of the superiority of communism over capitalism. But perhaps what brought most people of African descent to Russia were the ideas communism exposed about community—ideas that seemed to work in a way democracy had not for them in the United States. But a truism in life is that ideas and ideologies rarely match up to reality—for reality is much more complex and harder to comprehend. The idea of Russia as the promised land would hold for some, but for most Africans, Russia has held a reality that is tinged with good and bad.

NOTES

1. Sula Benet, *Abkhasians, The Long-Living People of the Caucasus* (New York: Holt, Rinehart and Winston, 1974), 1–8.
2. L. Golden Hanga, "Africans in Russia," in *Russia and Africa* (Moscow: Nauka Publishing House, 1966), 25. See also Allison Blakely, *Russia and the Negro: Blacks in Russian History and Thought* (Washington, D.C.: Howard University Press, 1986), 5–12. Much of the following description of the black presence in Russia is taken from this award-winning book.
3. Patrick English, "Cushites, Colchians and Khazars," *Journal of Near Eastern Studies* 18 (1959): 49–53; also Frank Snowden Jr., *Blacks in Antiquity* (Cambridge: Harvard University Press, 1970), 270.
4. Blakely, *Russia and the Negro*, 13.
5. Quoted in Mina Curtiss, "Some American Negroes in Russia in the Nineteenth Century," *Massachusetts Review* 9 (1968): 270.
6. Curtiss, "Some American Negroes," 270–71.
7. Nancy Prince, *A Black Woman's Odyssey Through Russia and Jamaica: The Narrative of Nancy Prince* (New York: Markus Wiener, 1990), 18. This memoir is one of the few surviving autobiographical accounts by a free black woman in the pre–Civil War North. Prince was in Russia during the St. Petersburg flood of 1824, the succession crisis, and the Decembrist Revolt of 1825.
8. Ibid., 17–18.
9. Curtiss, "Some American Negroes," 279.
10. Blakely, *Russia and the Negro*, 17.
11. Hanga, "Africans in Russia," 30, 31. These international ties may also explain the possibility that blacks may have been in Alaska prior to the United States buying it from Russia in 1867. See Pamela Johnson and Valerie Vaz, "Alaska's Black Heritage," *Essence* 25 (October 1994): 112.
12. Curtiss, "Some American Negroes," 279–80.
13. Ibid., 280.
14. This brief biography, as well as Pushkin's, is abstracted from Blakely, *Russia and the Negro*.
15. Dorothy Trench-Bonett, "Alexander Pushkin—Black Russian Poet," *The Black Scholar* 20 (1989): 2–9; "Alexander Pushkin: Father of Russian Literature," *Ebony* (October 1988): 76–80.
16. Homer Smith, *Black Man in Red Russia: A Memoir by Homer Smith* (Chicago: Johnson, 1964), 46.
17. Curtiss, "Some American Negroes," 282.
18. "The Saga of Jimmy Winkfield," *Ebony* (June 1974): 64–70.
19. R. Bruce Lockhart, *British Agent* (New York: G. P. Putnam and Sons, 1933), 71.
20. J. El-Hai, "Black and White and Red," *American Heritage* 42 (May/June 1991): 84.
21. Ibid.
22. See also Harry Haywood, *Black Bolshevik: Autobiography of an Afro-American Communist* (Chicago:

Liberator Press, 1978). Many blacks would attain high positions with the Communists over the years, including Claude McKay, George Padmore, and Carlton Goodlet. See "New York Times Ignores Black Publisher's Red Record," *Human Events* 53 (11 April 1997): 13–16.

23. Blakely, *Russia and the Negro*, 147–55.

24. Smith, *Black Man in Red Russia*, 25, 36, 46, 64.

25. Robert Robinson, *Black on Red: My 44 Years Inside the Soviet Union* (Washington, D.C.: Acropolis Books, 1988), 14–15.

26. Woodford McClellan, "African and Black Americans in the Comintern Schools, 1925–1934," *International Journal of African Historical Studies* 26 (1993): 371–90.

27. Yelena Khanga, *Soul to Soul: The Story of a Black Russian American Family, 1865–1992* (New York: Norton, 1992) 139, 227.

28. "Death in the Ukraine," *Newsweek*, 16 September 1985, 49–51.

29. Michael Gordon, "Black U.S. Marine Assaulted in Wave of Racism in Moscow," *New York Times*, 5 May 1998, A5.

30. Byron MacWilliams, "Black Students Face Racism in Moscow," *Chronicle of Higher Education* 43 (23 May 1997): A55.

31. Steven Shabad, "'Chocolate Colored'?" *World Press Review* 40 (1993): 36.

32. Gwendolyn Brooks, "Black Woman in Russia," *Humanities* 15 (May/June 1994): 24.

33. Ibid.

34. I wonder if Russia's liberalism toward blacks may have been an influence in why a black woman became director of Soviet and Eastern European Affairs. See L. Randolph, "Black Women in the White House," *Ebony* (October 1990): 76–81.

Passages and Portraits of African Descent People in Germany: From Ancient Times to the 1960s

Ruth Simms Hamilton

I N CONTRAST TO THE AMERICAS, GERMANY DID NOT HAVE A SIGNIFICANT NUMBER of black residents until the mid-twentieth century, although there has been a small presence since early times. Contours and portraits of some of these individuals are presented here, depicted both in the context of their own time and in comparison to one another. Their paths and life histories are in many ways representative of the geosocial movements and encounters, conflicts and changes, and spiritual and emotional passages of people of the African diaspora.

This chapter is divided into two parts. The first covers the period up to Germany's unification and emergence as a nation-state in 1871. A number of exceptional individuals, whose origins and passages were diverse, contributed to the social fabric of this time. Their voices are silent, but their persistence is quite remarkable. The second part focuses on the period between the 1850s and the 1960s, when situational and social conditions resulted in the presence of African diaspora cultural workers in Germany. Their professional and personal involvements included the performing and visual arts, political activism, scientific research, and other intellectual pursuits. They represented the cultural productions, views, attitudes, and aspirations of people of African descent and their communities in specific and general terms. Most significantly, their voices provide a clear indication of how they acted as subjects of their own history, not as the objects presented in other people's history. They show us how cultural leaders contribute to the formation of African diaspora identity and communities of consciousness as well as to the historical dissemination of the numerous cultural products of African people worldwide.

EARLY TIMES

The area now known as Germany was once part of the Greco-Roman empire.

> The West included parts of Africa as well as of Europe, and Europe as we know it was divided by the Rhine-Danube frontier, south and west of which lay the civilized provinces of the Empire, and north and east the "barbarians" of whom the civilized world knew almost nothing. To the Romans "Africa" meant Tunisia–Algeria, "Asia" meant the Asia Minor peninsula; and the word "Europe," since it meant little, was scarcely used by them at all. It was in the half-millennium from the fifth to the tenth centuries that Europe as such for the first time emerged with its peoples brought together in a life of their own, clearly set-off from that of Asia or Africa.[1]

A Neanderthal skull of the Old Stone Age found at Dusseldorf in the mid-nineteenth century was identified as "Negroid,"[2] and there is even more archaeological evidence of Africans among skulls found in Cologne. "Julius Caesar undoubtedly took Negroes in his legions to Germany."[3] Mauritius, a Catholic saint also known as Maurice, may have been one such soldier. The Roman Empire, which ruled much of the world until the fifth century, often waged war with "Ethiopia," a term that was used for the region from northeastern Africa to the Horn.[4] In these wars, soldiers and civilians were captured. At least some of these captives may have become Roman soldiers, and one of them may have been Saint Maurice.

Although the legend of Saint Maurice may combine fact and myth, to some extent it reflects circumstances and relationships between Africans and Romans.[5] During the third century, Maurice and his men were slaughtered by one of their commanders for refusing to engage in pagan sacrifices practiced by the Romans. One Roman emperor during the third century was Diocletian (284–305), who was well known for his persecutions of Christians around 303.[6] During that time, Germania Romana included much of southwestern Germany as well as parts of Switzerland and northeastern France.[7] It may have been in a community in that area that Maurice and his soldiers refused to engage in the sacrifice. His name is thought to derive from the word Maur or Moor, which indicates his place of origin as the Thebaid in Egypt.[8]

During the Greco-Roman period there was considerable mixing of people.

Moreover, there may have been considerable spread of Egyptian influence, as suggested by "relics of the worship of Isis . . . found in the Moselle region."[9]

> One of the very earliest manifestations of the Black Goddess syndrome was the Venus of
> Willendorf (15,000–10,000 B.C.) found near Vienna, Austria. It was carved by the Blacks
> of the Grimaldi race living in Europe, and is the oldest known representation of the
> human body. It is now in the Vienna Museum. We find this theme of the Black Goddess,
> the Black Venus carried from century to century in Europe right down to the years of the
> slave trade and slavery.[10]

Furthermore,

> there can be no denying that the African woman in Europe was viewed in different lights,
> the dominant one being that of a desirable physical object, either as a sex goddess or
> courtesan, a wife, a concubine or a prostitute, or all these molded into one beautiful
> black body. At the other extreme, she was likened to a Madonna, the mother of Jesus. It
> was the opposite of the same coin. Hence the cult of the Black Madonna and child that
> has dominated the Catholic world, particularly Europe.[11]

During the Middle Ages, African people began to enter Europe in increasing numbers. Many arrived through slave trafficking associated with the Almoravid conquest of Spain, but others came as merchants in connection with the rise of Islam and long-distance trading. The increasing visibility of Africans in Europe can be gleaned from their representation in literature and the visual arts. From the twelfth century there is strong evidence of growing European artistic awareness of people from distant lands. The epic *Parzival,* written by Wolfram von Eschenbach between 1198 and 1210, presents the first images of Africans in Germany. By the early Renaissance (1300–1510), more Africans appeared in paintings, only to increase as West African trade with Europe developed after 1440.[12]

> In the age of the Crusades, Europe began to develop consciousness as a geopolitical entity
> and at the same time to be dimly conversant of Africans as a separate race in the human
> community. Early contacts (1000–1450) through Spain were made with Africans as
> "humble slaves and wild warriors." In the Middle Ages, although the world of Islam was
> wedged in between Christendom and the land of Africa, contact between the two conti-
> nents was made on three spots: in Spain from Morocco to Sudan; from and in Italy
> through Sicily, Tunis and Cyrenaica; and through Jerusalem from the lands of the Nile
> (Egypt, Ethiopia and Sudan). It is out of these countries that emerged Europeans'

St. Maurice

St. Maurice or Mauritius was an African officer in the legions of Rome under Emperor Diocletian (284–305). It is said that Maurice was ordered to command his men to participate in a sacrifice to the Roman gods. When Maurice refused, some of his men were executed. Again Maurice was ordered to participate in the sacrifice, and again he refused. This time the executions included Maurice himself. Iconographic representations of St. Maurice are most common in central Europe. These statues in the cathedral of Magdeburg in the former German Democratic Republic (for which Maurice is the patron saint) are historically significant because they are the first (c. 1260) to depict him realistically as an African.

A statue of St. Maurice in the garden. This image of St. Maurice is near the altar in the cathedral of Magdeburg.

medieval image of the African. In Spain there were African soldiers and officers as well as servants among the Moslem conquerors ever since Tarik invaded the Iberian peninsula in 711 A.D.[13]

Aside from geopolitical conditions, the close proximity of Europe to Africa helps account for the ongoing movement of African people toward the north. For example, the Visigoths, a Germanic people, invaded Spain during the 400s and ruled there until displaced in 711 by the Moor general, Tarik-bin-Ziad, whose army consisted of

6,700 native Africans and 300 Arabs.[14] Different Moorish dynasties ruled Spain, including the Almoravids (people of the ribat, in Senegal), who were succeeded by the fourth and last Moorish dynasty—the Almohade. When the Moors were banished around 1230, they dispersed throughout Europe and Africa. Spain, ruled for eight centuries by Africans and before them by the Visigoths, was a locus for the mixing of Germans and Moors. Consequently, new people were created culturally and biologically, and they traversed Europe, including Germany, where thousands settled in Hamburg alone.[15] The presence of these miscegenated peoples in Germany belies the later ideological arguments regarding Aryan "purity."

DISPLACEMENT AND LINKS TO
TRANSNATIONAL FORMATIONS

Around the fifteenth century the presence of African people in Germany can be linked to the European colonization of the New World and the attendant slave trade. Commerce among Africa, Europe, and the Americas took on qualitatively different dimensions. The competition for land and resources, the nature of monetary exchanges, and the quest for political and economic power changed not only the relationships among the competitors but also the way they defined and engaged in social relationships with Africans. For example, "trade between Portugal and the Netherlands brought a considerable number of Africans to Antwerp."[16]

As Africans increasingly became human cargo, it is no surprise that their global physical presence grew. Although the demand for field slaves was not a factor in Europe, many came as house servants. In 1521, the famous German painter Albrecht Dürer (1471–1528) sketched a portrait of twenty-year-old Catherine, the servant of a Portuguese trader. This is one of the earliest depictions of an African in Europe.[17] There also is a portrait of Angelo Soliman (Mmadi Make), born in Africa around 1721, and it is speculated that the name of Soliman may indicate origins in the northern Cameroon or northeastern Nigeria, which at the time was ruled by a king named Mmadi Make. Sold as a child into slavery, Angelo worked in Morocco as a camel herdsman, and there is a record of him in Messina, Sicily, in 1732–34. His owner sent him as a present to a family, who passed him on to another family. "Although officially a footman, he . . . spoke Italian, German, French, English, Czech and Latin. For some time he was chairman of the Freemasons' Lodge in Vienna. He died in 1796."[18] Although many Africans were domestic servants and artisans, some were soldiers, seamen, and performing artists. They tended to concentrate in ports such as

Antwerp. A few were part of the royal courts: Queen Charlotte Sophia, the German-born consort of England's King George III (1760–1820), was identified as "Negroid."[19]

There were Africans who were showpieces at court, especially little children, who were treated as pets ("blackamoors"). Others were objects of curiosity and "scientific" experimentation. Signs of social status for noble families were black pages, youngsters who lived in their homes, enjoyed a position of privilege, and often married into white families.[20] One example in the eighteenth century was Nzima Amo of Ghana, who was a gift to the duke of Brunswick-Wolfenbuttel and who became a scholar. Others were Francis Williams of Jamaica, who studied at Cambridge in the early 1700s, and Juan Latino, born in 1516 in Guinea and brought to Spain at age twelve, who later earned university degrees and became a distinguished literary scholar. Also in this august group was Jacobus Eliza Johannes Capitein, born in Ghana in 1725 and purchased as a slave. He later wrote a dissertation that in part "upheld the propriety of the African slave-trade" and earned a Ph.D. in theology.[21] In the late 1840s, Aquasi Boachi, an Ashanti prince, was sent to Germany "as security for a contract" and later matriculated at the Mining Academy of Freiberg, the first African to do so.[22] These young people took advantage of opportunities afforded them by their sponsors, performed at the highest level of their respective professions, and pursued distinguished careers in Europe.

The achievements of these exceptional individuals did little to change the mind of adherents of Aryanism or Teutonic superiority, but their presence is integral to understanding the "enlightened" discussions among Europeans of the period. Did African children have the same "natural" capacity to learn and excel as Europeans? What was the capacity of African children to learn in a European milieu? They sought to answer such questions by experimenting with the lives of these people, which is another instance of not only the workings of European wealth at the time but also the arrogant appropriation of individual lives. Both Amo and Capitein were taken from home at an early age and raised as "Europeans" by their wealthy sponsors, but when this financial support was no longer available, both went back to Ghana. Capitein worked "as chaplin to the colonists and started a small school for Blacks and Mulattos at Elmina in 1742,"[23] and Amo returned to live with his family.

While the achievements of blacks such as these two men were data used by the scientific community, including J. F. Blumenbach (1752–1840), who attributed racial difference to climate and believed in the superiority of white people, what do we know about their reactions to being experiments in a white world?[24] Where is their voice? What of their personal lives? What did it mean to be isolated from their family and roots? How did they define their sense of self and personal identity? We have only secondary interpretations by those who owned or studied them. A classic case of a voiceless person is Machbuba, a "womanchild" born in what is today Ethiopia, who was purchased as a slave by a German prince and eventually became his paramour.

MACHBUBA: AFRICAN WOMANCHILD IN NINETEENTH-CENTURY GERMANY

In his diary, the German prince Hermann von Puckler-Muskau wrote of his Ethiopian slave, paramour, and companion, who traveled with him in the Middle East and Europe, and who died in his home in Bad Muskau, Germany.[25]

> I was able to bring up this sweet foster child for myself and myself alone as a painter draws his ideal picture according to his fancy, and I could write a romantic novel of several volumes if I wished to develop in the form of a story the highly interesting details of this education and the wonderful relationship which developed from it. I became everything for her and she everything for me. Not only in feeling and thinking, but also in the most material aspect of life, and if I was in this even without wishing it a hundred times more the receiver than the giver, she always the servant, I always the master, it had to be thus and could not be otherwise. And yet with this irresistible power she was again my master. Everything between us was in common. She kept my house and looked after my purse without control, and I have never lived better, more comfortably, yet more cheaply.[26]

Machbuba (also Mahbuba) was captured by slave traders at around ten years of age, taken to Khartoum, and offered at a slave market in Cairo in 1837, when she was around age thirteen. She was part of the thriving Islamic/Arabic slave trade in East Africa, where more than 25,000 persons per year were exported to the Sudan, Egypt, India, Arabia, and other points East.[27]

Machbuba was purchased by Prince Puckler, who was deeply impressed with her beauty. They left immediately on a boat trip up the Nile and then journeyed to Palestine, Lebanon, Syria, and Istanbul. Initially, the prince kept her under lock and key as a harem wife, but this relationship changed as he fell in love with her.[28] Early in their travels, he took her to social meetings with English royals in Lebanon, where she sat with him "veiled from head to foot in the Egyptian manner."[29] This was not well received by his hosts. The prince began to teach her Italian, which Machbuba comprehended quickly. During these travels, Prince Puckler wrote a series of letters to his wife about the slave-girl but concealed the nature and intensity of his feelings

Anton Wilhelm Amo from Axim in Guinea-Africa (Nzima Amo)

The remarkable Nzima Amo was born in Ghana around 1703.[a] Brought to Amsterdam in 1707, he was given that year as a present[b] to Duke Anton Ulrich Brunswick-Wolfenbuttel of Saxony for his son August-Wilhelm.[c] The duke, who had marital ties to Czar Peter I of Russia, shared the ideals of the Enlightenment,[d] which encouraged experiments to determine the humanity and educability of Africans.[e] He took Nzima to the castle chapel to be baptized on July 29, 1708, with the name Anton Wilhelm, but uncharacteristically for the time, Amo maintained his original last name.[f] In the same chapel in 1721, Amo was confirmed with the name Anton Wilhelm Rudolph Mohre.[g] In 1727, Amo registered at the University of Halle under the name Anton Wilhelm Amo ab Aximo in Guinea-Africana (Anton Wilhelm Amo from Axim in Guinea-Africa).[h] In 1729 he graduated with a degree in law, based on his dissertation "De Jure Maurorum in Europa" (The legal rights of blacks in Europe). This dissertation shows Amo's "awareness of his position as an African and his preoccupation with the problem of slavery and the social condition of Blacks in Europe."[i]

In 1730, Amo entered the University of Wittenberg, where he obtained a master's degree in philosophy and liberal arts. Two years later he was registered as a student of medicine and philosophy at the same university, and it was here in 1734 that he successfully defended his second dissertation, "De humanae mentis apatheia" (On human apathy). Amo was the first black to attain this highest German degree.[j] He lectured at the university from 1734 to 1736, at which point he returned to the University of Halle, where he had applied for and been granted faculty status.[k] Between 1737 and 1739 Amo directed students in their dissertations while he himself wrote and published a collection of lectures, *Tractus de Arts Sobrie et Accurate Philosophandi*. It was

and their relationship. In one instance he wrote about her beauty and deep loyalty to him: "She has grown very elegant and is also pretty in the face *for a black woman* [emphasis added] and is moreover good and honest like a few European women, I am firmly convinced that after a short stay with you, supported bodily and spiritually by you, she will become the most original *dame de compagnie*."[30]

In 1839 Puckler and Machbuba returned to Europe and stopped in Austria, where they had to occupy separate lodgings. Machbuba lived in a boarding house during this time that the Prussian government appointed him Geheim-Rat (state counsellor) of Berlin.[l]

An application for a teaching position and the announcement of lectures at the University of Thuringia place Amo in Jena in 1739.[m] This is confirmed by an autograph he signed there in 1740.[n] What Amo did until 1747 is unclear, although he probably taught at Jena. At least one biographer has suggested that he "became the victim of racist intrigue and left Germany."[o] In any case, Amo was in Ghana in 1753, where he was met by David H. Gallaudet, a Swiss physician traveling as a ship's doctor.[p] He describes Amo as living with his sister and father. Amo's brother had long since been sold as a slave to Suriname.[q] Shortly after this meeting, Amo died.[r]

a. Pauline J. Hountondji, *African Philosophy* (London: Hutchinson and Co., 1983), 114.
b. Burchard Brentjes, *Anton Wilhelm Amo: Der Schwarze Philosoph in Halle* (Leipzig: Koehler and Amelang, 1976), 29.
c. Fikes, "Intellectual Capacity," 127.
d. Burchard Brentjes, "Anton Wilhelm Amo, First African Philosopher in European Universities," *Cultural Anthropology* 16 (September 1975): 443.
e. Fikes, "Intellectual Capacity," 120.
f. Brentjes, *Amo,* 30.
g. Hountondji, *African Philosophy,* 115.
h. Ibid.
i. Ibid.
j. Ibid., 116.
k. Fikes, "Intellectual Capacity," 128.
l. Brentjes, Amo," 444.
m. Alexander Francis Chamberlain, "The Contribution of the Negro to Human Civilization," *Journal of Race Development* 1 (April 1911): 497.
n. Brentje, "Amo," 444.
o. Hountondji, *African Philosophy,* 118.
p. Brentjes, "Amo," 444.
q. Chamberlain, "Contribution," 129.
r. Brentjes, "Amo," 444.

and in a Salesianerinnen, a school for noble girls. She continued to accompany the prince on visits to other royals and prominent people, and she even attended several balls with him. Machbuba was suffering from consumption, so Puckler took her to a health resort in Marienbad and, upon her release, to his home at Muskau. His wife was in Berlin and also ill, and the prince left Machbuba in the care of his physician, who looked after her until her death on October 27, 1840.

Dr. Freund busied himself with Machbuba's funeral. He arranged for a portrait of the Ethiopian girl to be drawn by the local artist Sarau, and for a plaster cast of her head, hand, and foot to be made, while the prince, anxious to perpetuate the memory of his beloved, gave instructions for her heart to be preserved. The slave-girl was then dressed in the oriental costume her prince had so adored, and was buried in the Muskau church on October 29. The church register, which is still extant, states that she was then but sixteen years old. Her grave, which can still be seen, is simple, decorated with a snake in relief, and bears the single word, MACHBUBA. Though her mask, which was copied in bronze in 1921, disappeared . . . when Muskau castle was burned down in 1945; a bust made from it by the Berlin sculptor Menzmer is preserved in the Muskau museum. [In a letter written on November 18 to Countess Thurn, Puckler declared] What I have suffered by it I cannot express, and although man must be able to pull himself together about that which he cannot bring back, the loss will never cease to wound, 'for Mahbuba,' . . . the being I loved most of all in the world.[31]

The story has all the makings of an opera—intrigue, romance, and tragedy. From one perspective, the life of Machbuba is like that of other black women enslaved during this time. She was purchased for personal use and won the heart of her master, not unlike the similar story of Sally Hemmings and Thomas Jefferson. These relationships may have been loving, but both women were owned, which was demeaning. We have the interpretations and voices of the "masters," but there is a deafening silence from these "objects" in other people's history. It seems safe to say, however, that Machbuba had a will to survive and took advantage of opportunity. Her family was "mercilessly killed" when she and her sister were captured, separated, and sold into slavery. Yet, "she was very eager and intelligent and learnt a lot; she had an aptitude for languages and spoke fluent Italian after a short while."[32]

What does Machbuba's story tell us about the conditions under which people connect and the implications at a personal level? What does it tell us about the dynamics of the African diaspora? For example, it is believed that Machbuba was an Oromo from Ethiopia. At this time there were Oromos (a Galla people) from Ethiopia assisting the German scholar Karl Tutscheck in producing the first Galla dictionary and grammar.[33] While at Muskau, Machbuba "came in contact with a young compatriot of hers, Otshu Aga, who was then in Germany, and through him with the German scholar Tuscheck, then studying the Oromo language in Munich. The association was useful for . . . she taught Otshu 'many' songs, some of which the scholar wrote down, and . . . preserved."[34]

Machbuba is today a locus of identity for Afro-German women, ideologically and in practice, who call themselves "Machbuba's Sisters" to convey "Black German identity and self-assertion in a period of new racist attacks in Germany."[35] Afro-Germans, especially women, often feel isolated because a German national identity rests on whiteness as a precondition for "insider status."[36] Thus, at least for some, identity as Machbuba's sister recognizes a historically conditioned psychosocial situation and the activism and persistent struggle involved in being of African heritage in a "culture of white domination," politically and demographically.

Part Two: Passages of Diaspora Cultural Workers to Germany: 1850s–1960s

In December 1849, sixteen years before abolition in the United States and two decades before the modern German nation-state appeared, James W. C. Pennington, a former slave and free man living in Long Island, New York, received an honorary doctoral degree from the University of Heidelberg. Significantly, Pennington requested the degree in recognition of his intention to establish a school to educate and proselytize "my people." He had completed work at Yale's School of Divinity and in 1841 wrote *A Text Book of the Origin and History of the Colored People.*[37]

The first famous black American Shakespearean actor on the European stage, Ira Aldridge (1807–1867), also was recognized in Germany. Born in either Maryland or New York of free black parents, Aldridge was a student at the African Free School of Manhattan and performed with other blacks at the African Grove Theater on Bleecker Street, where "white hoodlums stoned [the theater, which] was forced to close its doors."[38] In his teens, his parents sent him to study at the University of Glasgow, but by age twenty Aldridge was playing Othello at major theaters in London. The King of Prussia, Frederick William, was a major sponsor of Aldridge and presented him with the Order of Chevalier. "He gave Aldridge one of the only four medals for distinction in the arts and sciences he ever conferred on anyone—the other three being Liszt, Humboldt, and Spontini. The Duke of Saxony knighted Aldridge, while other German rulers gave him command performances."[39]

Before slavery ended in Cuba (1886), there were at least six Afro-Cuban musicians playing professionally in the European genre, that is, the works of Bach, Beethoven, Mozart, and so on. They were "violinists Joseph White (1836–1918); Claudio Brindis de Salas (1800–1872), called 'El rey de las octavas'; Joseph R. Brindis (fl. ca. 1880), known as the 'Colored Remenyi'; and the Jimenez family, violinist Jose Julian (1833–1890 or thereafter), and his sons, *violoncellist* Nicasio (d. 1891) and pianist Jose Manuel Jimenez-Berroa (1855–1917)."[40] One author notes that the king of

Germany "had a coal-black Negro at his court, the celebrated musician, Brindis de Sala [sic], whom he made a baron. Brindis de Sala, who was court violinist, had previously scored resounding triumphs in Paris, Milan, and other cities."[41]

The Jimenez family lived and worked throughout Germany as a trio, billed as "Das Negertrio" (Negro Trio). The father, Jose Julian, who was born in Trinidad de Cuba, received early training from his father and studied violin at the Leipzig Conservatory from 1849–1852, after which he returned home. His two sons were later sent to the same conservatory to further their musical studies, Nicasio in 1868 and Jose Manuel around 1869.[42] The father returned to Germany in 1868, seeking refuge from Cuba's Ten Years' War against Spain.[43]

Between 1868 and 1876, the three Jimenez performed professionally both as individuals and as a trio beginning in 1871. They gave more than forty-seven concerts during this period in Poland, Czechoslovakia, and the German states of Bavaria, Hessen, Sachsen, Anhalt, Saxony, Wurttemberg, Thuringia, and the Rhineland. They played at such German resorts as Bad Kissingen, Ems, and Elster and in Hamburg and Bohemia.[44] In 1876, the trio played its final concert in Paris and disbanded. Nicasio moved to Tours, France, and became professor of violoncello at the conservatory there. Jose Manuel entered the Conservatory of Paris for further piano study. Three years later he and his father returned to Cuba, where Jose Manuel gave performances and taught piano in Cinefuego for about ten years beginning in 1881. Around 1891 he returned to Germany to take up residence in Hamburg, where he composed, performed, and taught piano at the city's Conservatory of Music until his death in 1917.[45]

After the Franco-Prussian War of 1870, the southern German states agreed to join the North German Confederation under Prussian control. On January 18, 1871, Wilhelm I of Prussia was crowned the first kaiser (emperor) of the united German Empire. This period coincided with Reconstruction (1863–1877) in the United States and preceded European colonization of Africa by about a decade. Black minstrelsy had already made its appearance in the emerging nation.[46] The Georgia Minstrels, founded in Macon in 1865, was one of the early black troupes to circulate New World diaspora cultural productions worldwide. Under the management of black American Charles Barney Hicks, the group performed in Germany in 1870.[47]

During the same year as German unification, the Jubilee Singers of Fisk University in Nashville, Tennessee, were organized and traveled nationally and internationally to raise money for the school. These four young men and six women were pilgrims for a cause, and they sang in 1872 for "Queen Victoria and the royal family, the Russian czarina, and members of the British Parliament. . . . On a second European trip that lasted from May 1875 to July 1878, they traveled on the Continent, singing for the king and queen of the Netherlands, Kaiser Wilhelm and Crown Prince Frederick of Germany, and the duke and duchess of Saxony."[48]

Ella Sheppard, one of the original Jubilee Singers, provides some insight into their experiences at the first concert in Germany, where critics were on the front row.

> We trembled. One of our basses was absent, which left only one bass to balance nine voices. We grouped as usual, leaned heads toward each other, and paused for oneness of effort. Then everything else forgotten, in a musical whisper, 'Steal Away' floated out so perfectly that one could not tell when it began. The astonishment upon the fixed, upturned faces of the critics told us that we had won; we were again at ease and did our best to maintain the good impression. Our concert was received with great enthusiasm. The audience, representing the greatest and best of the city, was in evening dress. We had never seen such an array of sparkling jewels as were worn that night. After the concert many came up and congratulated us. One [newspaper] article was filled with such expressions as these: "What wealth of shading! Such a pianissimo, such a crescendo and decrescendo as those at the close of 'Steal Away' might raise envy in the soul of any choir master. Something may be learned from these Negro singers."[49]

Generally, reactions to blacks were not positive. Individuals such as Aldridge and the Jimenez family challenged pervasive ideologies and stereotypes of African peoples. In the early nineteenth century, the German philosopher Hegel viewed the African, "whether in his native land or transported into slavery," as infantile and unreflective, incapable of attaining higher values and fixing them in abstractions, unable to achieve education on his own, and lacking in individuality. For Hegel, blacks were outside history.[50] Not all Europeans held that view. Black musicians, like most performers of the time, needed and received sponsorship from wealthy patrons, who were almost exclusively white. Nonetheless, many significant accomplishments by diaspora blacks were acknowledged ungenerously and permeated by racialist imagination. Two press reports in the *Musikalisches Wochenblatt* regarding the Jimenez trio are illustrative.

> At first glance, it may appear peculiar, almost comic, to hear interpretation of works . . . of German masters skillfully performed by Negroes—though we must confess that the Herren, not educated in vain at the Leipzig Conservatory, acquitted themselves perfectly of their respectable task. . . . Pianist Manuel . . . did not succeed the entire evening on the piano . . . his black fingers hopping up and down, looked sufficiently grotesque (correspondent in Bohemia, July 1873).

The Jimenez opened the performance with Raff's Trio, Op. 102. From a cultural-historical standpoint, it is certainly advanced for us to think that the conquest of German music has already been made by the Ethiopian race. That perspective was thereby offered in a lively fantasy: Symphony No 9 . . . performed by court musicians of the Sultan of Wadai [in the Sudan], and so forth. Of course, whoever contemplated with cool intellect the appearance of the Negro Trio as a purely musical event would not have been edified entirely by the masses (correspondent from Saxony, February 1874).[51]

Seeking Spaces of Creativity and Self-Actualization

The concept of "cultural workmen," developed by C. Wright Mills, refers to "all the organizations and milieux in which artistic, intellectual and scientific work goes on, and the means by which such work is made available to circles, publics and masses."[52] Similarly, African diaspora cultural workers are the various individuals or groups who represent and spread the historical experiences, memories, and aspirations of people of African descent. This may be a deliberate process or may result from serendipitous situations and social relations. Some workers create black cultural products and practices; others primarily convey them; some do both. Black music, traditions, styles, and varying art forms were "circulated" to the world beyond the black communities long before the age of mass communication. Those earlier generations helped establish judgments about value and canons of taste and beauty as they pertain to diaspora culture.

The Jimenez family, the Fisk Jubilee Singers, and others were seeking opportunities to enhance life chances for themselves and their family. They symbolized the more universal diaspora quest, of New World blacks in particular, for humanity, freedom, decency, and self-actualization. They wanted to control their own destiny. Ira Aldridge, for example, was sent by his parents to Europe to escape the racism and thuggery of white working-class immigrants in northern U.S. cities in the early decades of the nineteenth century. White mobs often attacked institutions and observances in black communities, including churches, temperance halls, performances, and events. "They demanded in essence that African-Americans remain in their places as 'anticitizens' at the separate, undisciplined bottom of urban society, as a touchstone against which a wide variety of ill-disciplined popular white behavior could be justified both to the respectable and to the rowdy fretting about respectability."[53]

Cultural workers who went to Germany and other parts of Europe were seeking zones of freedom to learn and practice their artistic talents. They also sought escape from slave societies and especially the racism that excluded them from opportunity and denied them decency. Certainly, Europe and Germany were not Utopia; more important, however, was the process of taking action for themselves, of seeking a better life. A stream of black artists, entertainers, intellectuals, political figures, scientists, teachers, preachers, and others visited Germany from the late nineteenth century to the last half of the twentieth century. Two of the most prominent were W. E. B. DuBois and Angela Davis.

IN SEARCH OF KNOWLEDGE: W. E . B. DuBois AND ANGELA DAVIS

One of the most eminent social scientists and intellectuals of the twentieth century, William Edward Burghardt DuBois was born in 1868 in Great Barrington, Massachusetts, and died in Accra, Ghana, on August 27, 1963, the day before the famous civil rights march on Washington. A brilliant scholar and prolific writer, DuBois is without peer among black intellectuals up to the present.[54] He was a founder of the National Association for the Advancement of Colored People (NAACP); an advocate for Africa and the recognition of its contributions to world history; a supporter of former colonial peoples of the colored and socialist worlds; and a leader of early Pan-African movements and congresses, for which reason some call him the "soul" of Pan-Africanism.[55]

DuBois was born three years after abolition in the United States, on February 23, 1868. He attended Fisk University, one of the institutions founded by the American Missionary Society to educate black students after the Civil War. Entering the sophomore class at age seventeen, he received a B.A. degree in 1888. He then went to Harvard, where he received a second B.A. in philosophy in 1890 and an M.A. in 1892. At this point DuBois decided he needed further training in Europe, the center of the social sciences emerging at the dawn of the twentieth century. In his view,

> the German universities were at the top of their reputation. Any American scholar who wanted preferment went to Germany for study. The faculties of Johns Hopkins and the new University of Chicago were beginning to be filled with German Ph.D's, and even Harvard had imported Munsterberg for the new experimental psychology, and Kuno Frank had long taught there. British universities did not recognize American degrees and

French universities made no special effort to encourage American graduates. I wanted then to study in Germany. I was determined that any failure on my part to become a recognized American scholar must not be based on any lack of modern training.[56]

Already a serious and ambitious scholar, DuBois, like his peers and teachers of the time, wanted to be at the center of the action during a period of profound global change. It was an era marked by the Second Industrial Revolution and global colonialism.[57] This was the beginning of mass production, the systematic application of science to industry, and the displacement of independent firms by large cartels, which ushered in monopoly capitalism. Science played a strong role in the Second Industrial Revolution. "The laboratories of industrial research equipped with expensive apparatus and staffed by trained scientists who carried on systematic research on designated problems supplanted the garrets or workshops of lone inventors."[58] Germany led the world in the scientific arena, as did the United States in the transformation to mass production.

In the social arena, scholars focused on how the technological and scientific changes affected workers, class relations, families, and social structures; the organization and efficacy of emerging state systems; and the meaning of nations and nationalism. Others were interested in how the increasing scale of production and the spectacular generation of profits among Western countries related to the upsurge in empire-building, as colonial possessions became "mechanisms for redistributing wealth within the metropolitan centers."[59] These were some of the factors transforming how knowledge was defined and studied, that is, redefining the epistemological bases of the new social sciences.

Granted a John F. Slater scholarship, DuBois went to Germany and "began to understand the real meaning of scientific research and the . . . methods of employing its technique and its results."[60] He studied and traveled there from 1892 to 1894. At the Friedrich-Wilhelm III Universitat in Berlin, his courses, seminars, and tutorials covered various topics in history, political economy, historical economics, economics, and sociology. His intellectual mentors were two professors of political economy, Gustav von Schmoller and Adolf Wagner, who envisioned an elitist and well-trained core of state bureaucrats to guide "the guardian state scientifically as it intervened between the citizen and the market place. Believing that capitalism was too serious a system to be managed solely by capitalists, they exhorted the state to ride herd on the great cartels." Moreover, "Schmoller and Wagner [modernized] social science in their time. In stressing the primacy of observed phenomena over theory or ideal constructs, they were a force against the system-building [grand theories] dominant in the social sciences at the end of the nineteenth century."[61]

Much has been written on how the scholarly production and social activism of DuBois were influenced by his studies at the University of Berlin, as well as by his exposure to European socialism during this period. His notion of the "talented tenth" and the souls of *blackvolk* have intellectual roots in Germany. Adolf Reed presents a forceful argument that DuBois exemplified the scientific approach to social inquiry and the interventionist orientation characteristic of social science in the late nineteenth century. DuBois' seminal study, *The Philadelphia Negro* (1899), and his notions of elitism, expertise as a legitimate social force, the role of the state, and the significance of technology are cited by Reed as indicators of his social thought.[62]

How did this twenty-four-year-old black man, racialized and marginalized in the United States, view his "pilgrimage"? Similar to a religious pilgrim, DuBois journeyed to a distant place to seek "higher scientific knowledge and power" and in the process underwent personal transformation in his behaviors and perceptions of himself, the larger world, and the future of "his people." Several examples in his own words illustrate.

On mountain and valley, in home and school, I met men and women as I had never met them before. Slowly they became, not white folks, but folks. The unity beneath all life clutched me. I was not less fanatically a Negro, but 'Negro' meant a greater, broader sense of humanity and world fellowship. I felt myself standing, not against the world, but simply against American narrowness and color prejudice, with the greater, finer world at my back.

In Germany in 1892, I found myself on the outside of the American world, looking in. With me were white folk—students, acquaintances, teachers—who viewed the scene with me. They did not always pause to regard me as a curiosity, or something subhuman; I was just a man of somewhat privileged student rank, with whom they were glad to meet and talk over the world; particularly the part of the world whence I came.[63]

Of greatest importance was the opportunity which my *Wanderjahre* in Europe gave of looking at the world as a man and not simply from a narrow racial and provincial outlook.[64]

DuBois began to develop an understanding of how other people in the world viewed U.S. social practices and realities; he also began to see people in a world context.

I found to my gratification that [Europeans], with me, did not regard America as the last word in civilization. Indeed, I derived a certain satisfaction in learning that the University of Berlin did not recognize a degree even from Harvard University, no more than Harvard did from Fisk. Even I was a little startled to realize how much that I had regarded as white American, was white European and not American at all: America's music is German, the

Germans said; the Americans have no art, said the Italians; and their literature, remarked the English, is mainly English.[65]

I began to see the race problem in America, the problem of the peoples of Africa and Asia, and the political development of Europe as one.[66]

As for the intersection of racial and national identities, DuBois began to form his heuristic conceptualization of "double-consciousness."

The pageantry and patriotism of Germany in 1892 astonished me. In New England our patriotism was cool and intellectual. Ours was a great nation and it was our duty to preserve it. We "loved" it but with reason not passion. In the South, Negroes simply did not speak or think of patriotism for the nation which held their fathers in slavery for 250 years. . . . When I heard my German companions sing "Deutschland, Deutschland uber Alles, uber Alles in der Welt" I realized that they felt something I never felt and perhaps never would. The march of soldiers, the saluting of magnificent uniforms, the martial music and rhythm of movement stirred my senses.

If I, a stranger, was thus influenced, what about the youth of Germany? I began to feel that dichotomy which all my life has characterized my thought: how far can love for my oppressed race accord with love for the oppressing country? And when these loyalties diverge, where shall my soul find refuge?[67]

DuBois represents one aspect of the experiences of diaspora cultural workers at the turn of the nineteenth century. Alain Locke would follow his path, registering as a Rhodes Scholar at the University of Berlin in 1910. A philosopher and Harvard graduate, Locke later taught at Howard University and is associated with the Harlem Renaissance.[68] His travels also can be compared to a pilgrimage. Many other cultural workers found such experiences transforming.

Almost a century after DuBois returned from his studies in Germany, Angela Davis arrived to begin hers. Born in Birmingham, Alabama, in 1944, she attended public schools there and later in New York, where she graduated from high school. At Brandeis University in Waltham, Massachusetts, Davis majored in French literature and spent her junior year in France, 1963 to 1964. During her senior year in college she studied with the philosopher Herbert Marcuse, who fled Germany shortly after the Nazis seized power. In June 1965, Davis, a member of Phi Beta Kappa, graduated magna cum laude.[69]

In fall 1965, Davis sailed for Germany. She places the discussion of her German experiences under the heading "Waters," accompanied by a quotation from Federico Garcia Lorca: "I go into Genesis' landscape of rumblings, collisions, and waters."[70]

Davis pursued a Ph.D. in philosophy at the University of Frankfurt, "the best place to study Kant, Hegel, and Marx." "Frankfurt was a very intensive learning experience. Stimulating lectures and seminars conducted by Theodor Adorno, Jurgen Habermas, Professor Haag, Alfred Schmidt, Oscar Negt. Tackling formidable works, such as all three of Kant's *Critiques* and works of Hegel and Marx."[71]

During her two years in Frankfurt, Davis witnessed a great deal of upheaval and conflict, not only in Germany but also worldwide. This included the Vietnam War, the assassination of President Kennedy, urban insurrections in major U.S. cities, and the formation of the Black Panther Party for Self-Defense in Oakland, California. In West Germany there were major student and worker rallies against U.S. aggression in Vietnam and demonstrations directed toward other German and international issues. Davis spent time in the German Democratic Republic, mainly in East Berlin, where she developed some friendships, interacted with other African Americans, and came into contact with Cubans who shared with her the "way in which they were developing the old Yoruba dances, which before the revolution had been restricted to the remote areas of the country where Black people still retained African customs."[72]

Toward the end of her stay, Davis felt the pull to "return home."

The more the struggles at home accelerated, the more frustrated I felt at being forced to experience it all vicariously. I was advancing my studies, deepening my understanding of philosophy, but I felt more and more isolated. I was so far away from the terrain of the fight that I could not even analyze the episodes of the struggle. . . . it was increasingly hard to feel a part of the collective coming to consciousness of my people.

I am certain that what I was feeling was a variation and reflection of the same feelings that were overwhelming larger and larger numbers of Black people abroad. Many others of us must have felt pained, when reading about some new crisis in the struggle at home, to be hearing about it secondhand.

I had thought mine was the perfect dilemma: the struggle at home versus the need to remain in Frankfurt until the completion of my doctorate, for I was certain that Frankfurt was far more conductive to philosophical studies than any other place. But each day it was becoming clearer to me that my ability to accomplish anything was directly dependent on my ability to contribute something concrete to the struggle.

The struggle was a life-nerve; our only hope for survival. I made up my mind. The journey was on.[73]

To this day, the brilliance and activism of Angela Davis are revered by black women and men throughout the Americas. It is not uncommon to see large posters of her on the walls of black cultural centers in Brazil, Colombia, and other locations in which diaspora people are struggling for political and economic rights and are striving to reclaim their African heritage and identity.

The journeys of DuBois and Davis to Germany were pilgrimages to obtain knowledge. Like a religious pilgrimage, it was voluntary and personal; it created within them a heightened awareness of the profound changes in the larger world order.[74] A pilgrimage requires leaving home and traveling a great distance to obtain a blessing, to worship, to engage in something "sacred," the likely result of which is major personal transformation. Attention has been called to the "temporal structure of the pilgrimage process, beginning in a Familiar Place, going to a Far Place, and returning to a Familiar Place, theoretically changed. The mere fact of spatial separation from the familiar and habitual . . . may . . . have punitive, purificatory, expiatory, cognitive, instructional, therapeutic, transformative, and many other facets, aspects, and functions."[75]

Even more important is the experience of dwelling between the far place and the familiar place, which can heighten seeing, knowing, experiencing, contemplating, confronting, and examining. For DuBois and Davis, it appears that Germany represented "a threshold, a place and moment 'in and out of time,'" that resulted in personal transformation.[76] In essence during what Turner calls an "intervening laminal period,"[77] one is neither here nor there, an outsider or stranger, temporarily set apart from both the far and the familiar.

These pilgrimages also intensified for DuBois and Davis their sense of identity with "home" and the ongoing struggle of their people as well as the need to be part of it, to contribute to it. Both became high-profile intellectuals and activist cultural workers. They experienced a "transition rite, which accompanies every change of state or social position."[78] As outsiders looking in, dwelling in-between, they could assess realities at many levels. Their transition rites resulted in new passages, in the crossing of new "waters."

In Search of a Better Life

As early as 1896 it was estimated that more than 100 African Americans were performing in Germany.[79] Following World War I, many went to Europe to earn a living and find an environment less hostile and racist than the United States. Among them were musicians, such as Herb Fleming and Sam Wooding; playwrights and producers; and actors, including Louis Douglas, who played "Negro" roles in German films.

Dancers and singers performed in black revues, such as "Chocolate Kiddies" and "La Revue Negre." Paul Robeson starred in Eugene O'Neill's *The Emperor Jones* at Max Reinhardt's Deutsches Kunstlertheater in Berlin. Roland Hayes gave concerts, as did Robeson, who sang in Dresden and Dusseldorf. Josephine Baker appeared in the revue "Bitte einsteigen" (All Aboard) at Berlin's *Theater des Westens* in 1928.[80]

After World War I from 1920 to 1930, the rhythm of the era was jazz. Although Paris was a magnet city for African-American artists, Berlin was not left out. Not only did the most famous African Americans perform in Berlin (Louis Armstrong and Sidney Bechet) but also lesser-known orchestras. Sam Wooding's "[Neger] Jazz Band" became the mentor of many German jazz bands. Most African-American jazz bands could be heard at the Scala Casino, the Mercedes Palast, or the Heinroth Palast. In 1924 the queen of the New Year's Eve festivities was undoubtedly Josephine Baker, who was christened the "black goddess" by much of the press. Some of the African guests of Emperor Wilhelm II (by then German citizens) joined African-American orchestras. Half a decade later, African-American jazz bands were banned from Germany. Jazz was perceived by the Nazis as an overly sensuous rhythm that evoked chaos and moral abandon and was dangerously interpreted by individuals of an inferior race.[81]

Germany had a lower cost of living than the United States, and many earned three or four times more than they could at home. "Black entertainers also found better working conditions and less racial discrimination in Europe. Besides all-black casts, many international groups were formed in Germany in the 1920s. Therefore, African Americans performing in Germany had greater control choosing whom to work with than in the United States. This was especially true for musicians in bands and orchestras."[82]

Thus, aside from economic motives, escape from stifling racism was another reason blacks left the United States. Yet another is illustrated by the biologist Ernest Everett Just (1883–1941).[83]

ERNEST JUST: THE SEARCH FOR PROFESSIONAL RECOGNITION

In January 1929, at age 46, Ernest Just and his sixteen-year-old daughter, Margaret, boarded the *Dresden* in New York. After a stopover in Paris they arrived in Naples, Italy, where Margaret enrolled in school for four months while her father engaged in scientific research at the Stazione Zoologica. He was warmly received by the laboratory director, Reinhard Dohrn, son of Anton Dohrn, an eminent nineteenth-century German zoologist and founder of the Stazione.

> Things got off to a good start. Dohrn . . . had arranged to place Margaret in a special school for foreign students, and on the first day he even escorted her to class. At the Stazione itself, arrangements for laboratory space and equipment and introductions to the staff were ably handled by Dohrn's secretary, Margaret Boveri. Almost immediately, Just was working away on *Nereis dumerilii* . . . bending over his microscopes and slides for hours on end; writing up reams of notes on ideas and experiments.[84]
>
> [For Just, it was a major relief to be away] from the crowd of students and young investigators that had plagued him at the MBL, forever asking elementary questions and generally making nuisances of themselves. . . . At the Stazione it was all research and not teaching, and scientists could work there year-round.
>
> Just was happy. The pressure and anxieties of life in Washington and Woods Hole seemed . . . a thing of the distant past. In Naples everyone was kind and his research went like clockwork. . . . He began to strike up some close friendships. . . . A relationship of special intimacy developed between Just and Margaret Boveri.
>
> Just was careful not to allow distractions, romantic or otherwise, to sway him from his main purpose: getting some serious work done and establishing some solid contacts in the European scientific community. By mid-April he had done . . . more than he was able to do in several summers at Woods Hole.[85]

The path to the Stazione was long, tortuous, and circuitous for Ernest Just. Born in Charleston, South Carolina, into a family that struggled economically, he was fortunate enough to have a mother for whom the success of her children was a major priority. He attended public schools until age 12 and then completed a three-year course at the Colored Normal, Industrial, Agricultural and Mechanical College (South Carolina State College) in Orangeburg. In 1899 he received a license that qualified him to teach in the state's black public schools. To complete the equivalent of a high school education, he attended Kimball Union Academy in Meriden, New Hampshire, as a scholarship student.

Just began undergraduate study at Dartmouth College in fall 1903 and graduated magna cum laude on June 26, 1907. According to Manning, who has written a well-researched and meticulous biography of Just, during his years at Dartmouth he "won everything." He was named the Rufus Choate Scholar for superior grades and won the Grimes Prize for the most satisfactory progress during his college career. He was elected to Phi Beta Kappa; was recognized at commencement "for averaging above 85 percent in his course work for four years"; received honors in botany, history, and sociology; and was awarded special honors in zoology. "He alone graduated magna cum laude. Three classmates received the lower rank of *cum laude,* none the higher honor of *summa cum laude.*"[86]

Professional opportunities in 1907 were limited to the "Black World," and Just accepted a teaching position at Howard University in Washington, D.C. It was an undergraduate institution at that time, and research facilities were almost nil. Beginning in 1912, Just spent every summer working with Dr. Frank R. Lillie at the Marine Biological Laboratories (MBL) in Woods Hole, Massachusetts. Lillie was also head of the department of zoology at the University of Chicago. Also in 1912 Just married Ethel Highwarden, a black instructor of German and English at Howard.

Just became an authority on the embryology of sandworms and sea urchins. Between 1912 and 1915 he published six exceptional papers on his work at MBL and in 1915 was awarded the NAACP Springarn Medal, presented annually to the black person who performed the foremost service to his or her race.[87] "In June 1915 Lillie decided that Just had completed the research requirements for the Ph.D., and he agreed to accept previously published articles as a doctoral thesis."[88] The other requirement was an additional year of residency at the University of Chicago, where Just received the Ph.D. in 1916 at age 33.

> Before [World War I] his field in general and his own work in particular had been "going big" among European workers. . . . Citations of his work had been more frequent in European journals than in American ones; workers in France and Germany had expressed interest in his work on the embryology of invertebrates. . . . Then came the war. Mobilization took precedence over research.[89]

In contrast, Just had a relatively obscure reputation in the United States. He made persistent requests of senior colleagues at MBL to recommend him for membership in scientific societies, which they took their time in doing. Eventually he was accepted into the Society of Physiologists, the American Society of Zoologists, and the American Society of Naturalists. He challenged the work of the eminent biologist Jacques Loeb of the Rockefeller Institute for Medical Research and proved his theory wrong. This gave him a higher profile professionally, but Loeb was in a position to veto the research grants Just sought from the National Research Council and the Julius Rosenwald Fund.[90]

Just developed a small circle of close friends at Woods Hole, but this did not shield him from the racism of the time. He spent summers there alone, while his wife and three children remained in Washington. The one summer he convinced his wife

Ethel to accompany him, she was received with indifference or insults. Moreover, he was excluded from enough social activities because of his color to create within him a "bitterness of spirit."[91]

Despite his scientific achievements, it was always difficult for Just to receive public funds or foundation grants. He was given little or no support, and in some instances there was deliberate obstruction by white scholars upon whom the foundations relied for professional evaluation. One such was E. A. Davenport, a well-known eugenicist who believed in the inferiority of black people, who on at least one occasion was referee for a grant application by Just. Just did receive support from his mentor, Lillie, and was awarded small grants from the Rosenwald Fund.[92]

In the meantime, new horizons were opening up for Just on the international scene, and he was eager to meet colleagues in Europe, where his work was read with interest and was considered "'far-reaching.' . . . He had been elected to honorary societies in France, appointed to the editorial boards of German journals. . . . In 1927 he had a chance to speak at international zoologists' meetings in Berlin, Budapest, and Rome. But he could not attend—there was no money."[93] Through persistence and a determination to take advantage of any degrees of freedom available to him, Just finally received, in 1929, a substantial award from the Rosenwald Fund for the Department of Biology at Howard and for his "personal leadership."

This overview of Just's struggles provides only a glimpse of how he finally arrived at the Stazione in Naples in 1929. The next year Just went to the Kaiser-Wilhelm-Institut in Berlin as a guest professor.

> German scientific and educational institutions had been isolated from the rest of the world as a result of the First World War, and the effects of that isolation were still noticeable at the Kaiser-Wilhelm-Institut. . . . The only foreign scientists invited to the Institut were those who were thought to have something special to share with and gain from their German counterparts. . . . [Just] was admired in Germany. Other American scientists had come to the Institut, but they had not been given the same privileges and they were obliged to pay large fees.
>
> Just was proud of the position of honor he had been accorded by the Germans. Never before had he felt so respected by his peers, so confident in his work. He was rather amused that the other Americans at the Institut seemed jealous of his position.[94]

Manning suggests that Just was impressed with the sense of community at the institute, which atypically employed Jewish scientists despite widespread anti-Semitism in Germany, a sentiment held by Kaiser Wilhelm, for whom the facility was named. In contrast to Woods Hole and the overall situation of blacks in the United

States, Just viewed the situation at the Berlin institute as one in which everyone worked in harmony and helped one another. The "harmony" may have been a facade, however. A few weeks after Just arrived in Berlin, he was invited by Adolf von Harnack, an eminent theologian and a founder of the institute, to live at Harnack House, an honor and an opportunity to enhance contacts with other scientists.

> What [Just] did not know was that there was a reason behind the invitation. Scientists at the Institut had been talking about him and Boveri [with whom he had developed a relationship in Naples], and were upset [by their living together.] They did not want to see the Boveri name tainted. The memory of Theodor Boveri, one of Germany's top biologists and the original choice as director of the Institut, was sacred, and it was simply too scandalous for his daughter to live openly with a married man, a black one at that. . . . How could a separation be finessed? Hartmann [Just's sponsor at the Institute] spoke to Harnack and came up with the idea of inviting Just to move out of Berlin and into the Dahlem neighborhood. This diplomatic solution did not break up the lovers' relationship altogether, but it at least helped make the affair a little less visible.[95]

After 1931, Just continued a peripatetic existence between Howard University, MBL, and Europe. His work was going well in Germany, but his family relationships deteriorated, and his professional relations at Howard and MBL were discordant. In the meantime, he developed a relationship with another German, Hedwig Schnetzler, whom he married two years before his death. In 1938 he went into self-imposed exile in Europe and had little in the way of economic resources. The advance of Nazism in Germany eventually led him to the Station Biologique in Roscoff, France, near the English Channel. When the Nazis took Paris in early June 1940, Just was trying to book passage to the United States, but Hedwig did not have immigration papers. "In early August the Nazis interned Just in a camp, probably Chateaulin. When Hedwig's father found out he mobilized his Nazi contacts on the board of the Brown, Boveri Company, and an official was dispatched to France to obtain Just's release."[96] In September, Just returned to the United States, and on October 27, 1941, he died of cancer at age 58.

The life of Ernest Everett Just mirrors many of the experiences of black Americans and diaspora peoples in general. Persisting against so many odds, Just was intent on making a way for himself. As accomplished as he was, no white institution of higher education in the United States would hire him in the early decades of this century. His personal goals were restricted, and his need to achieve was constantly blocked, which made his life a tortuous struggle. According to his mentor, Lillie, "an element of tragedy ran through all Just's scientific career due to the limitations

George Padmore (Malcolm Nurse):
Pursuing the Political Kingdom[a]

Malcom Ivan Meredith Nurse, better known as George Padmore, Pan-Africanist cultural worker, was born in the Arouca district, Tacarigua, Trinidad, in 1902. He attended Tranquility School and St. Mary's College of the Immaculate Conception. In 1925 he came to the United States, entered Fisk University, and transferred to New York University Law School in September 1927. Later he enrolled at Howard University Law School in Washington, D.C.[b]

While in New York, Padmore joined the Communist Party, which he saw as a serious instrument for putting an end to racial discrimination. It was during this time that he changed his name. In the Communist Party, Padmore quickly ascended through the ranks because of his devotion to the party and because of its desire to attract more black members. In 1928, with Roger Moore, an organizer of the American Negro Labor Congress, Padmore edited the *Negro Champion*.[c] Padmore's rise in the party eventually led him to Frankfurt, Germany, where he attended a World Congress of the Comintern. He became secretary of the Red International of Labor Unions of Negro Workers (RILU-NW), which was a salaried job.

In 1930 Padmore organized the first International Conference of the Negro Workers in pre-Hitler Hamburg. Seventeen delegates attended, most from Africa. Germany was unwilling to let many of the delegates into the country, which presaged problems Padmore faced later.[d] During the same year, Padmore became editor-in-chief of the *Negro Worker*, the official organ of the International Trade Union Committee of Negro Workers (ITUC-NW).[e] Germany was becoming more and more hostile to communism, and the printing presses of the *Negro Worker* were concealed in a house that was converted to a seamen's club in Hamburg. The club also provided a convenient way for the journal to maintain contact with its main readers in Germany, black seamen.[f] Hamburg was

imposed by being a Negro in America, to which he could make no lasting psychological adjustment in spite of earnest efforts on his part. The numerous grants for research did not compensate for failure to receive an appointment in one of the large universities or research institutes. He felt this as a social stigma, and hence unjust to a scientist of his recognized station."[97]

Then as now, this is the story of African diaspora cultural workers worldwide, the site of the 1932 conference of dockers and seamen that Padmore organized.

In 1933 Padmore was interned by the Nazis for three to six months. There is some dispute as to whether he was held in Copenhagen or Germany; he was later released to the British government.[g] Around 1935, Padmore left the Communist Party. It is asserted that he was dismissed for "arguing that the Emperor of Japan was the legitimate protector of the world's darker races."[h] He also lashed out at the Soviet Union, contending that it was willing to sacrifice Ethiopia to Mussolini if it served Soviet interests, which was evident from the USSR's desertion of colonial peoples since the rise of the Third Reich.[i] Padmore returned to Germany in 1938 as a reporter for the *Chicago Defender* to cover the riots at the University of Berlin.[j] He later became active in Pan-Africanist activities and was closely associated with Kwame Nkrumah and the new Republic of Ghana in 1958. He died in London in September 1959. The "ashes were flown to Ghana at the Prime Minister's request. There they were interred at the Christiansborg Castle on October 4."[k]

a. This material was prepared by Darren McCants, an undergraduate research intern with the African Diaspora Research Project during summer 1991. He received the B.A. degree with a major in telecommunications in 1993 from Michigan State University and is currently working on a second degree with a major in English.

b. The major source on George Padmore is James R. Hooker, *Black Revolutionary: George Padmore's Path from Communism to Pan-Africanism* (London and New York: Fredrick A. Praeger, 1967); also see Russell Warren Howe, "George Padmore," *Encounter* 23 (December 1959): 52–55.

c. Hooker, *Black Revolutionary*, 8.

d. Ibid., 17.

e. Wilson Record, *The Negro and the Communist Party* (New York: Atheneum, 1971), 84.

f. Hooker, *Black Revolutionary*, 18.

g. Ibid., 30. Hooker states that Padmore was imprisoned by the Nazis in Copenhagen, Denmark, but an article in a Ghanaian newspaper places his imprisonment in Germany. See Kwame Nkrumah, "His Memory Will Endure Forever," *Ghana Evening News*, September 23, 1964, 7.

h. Record, *The Negro*, 85.

i. George Padmore, "Ethiopia and World Politics," *Crisis* 42 (May 1935): 6.

j. Hooker, *Black Revolutionary*, 54.

k. Ibid., 139.

whether in the former European colonies or in the United States. It is also the story of "everyday people." They, like Just and others, migrated within their countries or across borders to seek a better life, "the higher ground." For Just, Germany and Europe were places of refuge. The younger Just, more diplomatic and conciliatory, gave way at mid-life to a man on the "outside looking in" and standing up "for his rights as a scientist, an oppressed black man, a human being."[98] For him, movement to and from Europe and the United States provided a transitory space for living in his search for personal and professional satisfaction and affirmation of his humanity.

EXILIC PASSAGES: OLIVER WENDELL HARRINGTON

"Ollie" Harrington, called "America's greatest black cartoonist" by Langston Hughes, died on November 2, 1995, at his home in Berlin at age 84. He had lived in the former East Berlin since 1961. Harrington's route to Germany was a gradual transition.[99] Born on February 14, 1912, in Valhalla, New York, he was the son of Herbert Harrington, an African American from North Carolina, and Eugenia Harrington, of Jewish descent from Budapest, Hungary. The family moved to the South Bronx, where Harrington attended public schools. He graduated from high school in 1929, as the Great Depression began, and moved to Harlem to strike out on his own. With the help of senior cultural workers seasoned by the Harlem Renaissance, he was able to find odd jobs and pursue work as a freelance artist. He started classes at the National Academy of Design in New York City while working for various black newspapers and publications, for which he drew cartoons and pursued other assignments. Harrington did work for the *Amsterdam News* in New York, the *Afro-American* in Baltimore, the *Courier* in Pittsburgh, and the *Defender* in Chicago. His famous cartoon, "Bootsie," appeared in 1935 under the panel *Dark Laughter* in the *Amsterdam News*.[100]

Harrington enrolled in the Yale University School of Painting and Architecture in 1934 and graduated in 1939 with a B.F.A. His work toward an M.F.A. was interrupted by the outbreak of World War II, during which he went to North Africa and Europe as a war correspondent for the *Courier*. After the war, Harrington was hired by Walter White to create a public relations department for the NAACP, and he was very outspoken on the racism and violence directed toward black Americans.

At the opening session of the New York *Herald Tribune*'s forum on "The Struggle for Justice as a World Force" on 28 October 1946, Harrington challenged then U.S. Attorney General Tom Clark, who had announced a massive federal investigation of the lynching of four men at Monroe, Georgia, but still had no convictions, by declaring, "For the crime of race hate and lynching there has never been a conviction in the history of the United States."

Harrington would remain convinced that this debate was what led Clark later to label him a Communist.[101]

Because of its advocacy for civil rights, the NAACP and those connected with it became objects of investigation by Senator Joseph McCarthy and the House Un-American Activities Committee. Harrington, warned by a friend of an impending investigation of him, left the country for Paris and permanent exile in 1951.[102] He became part of a larger group of black American cultural workers living there, including authors Chester Himes and Richard Wright, the latter of whom became a very close friend of Harrington.[103] Ollie lived in Paris for a decade and contributed much to the vitality of the expatriate community. He continued to draw and publish cartoons, mailing them to the *Courier* and the *Defender*. Wright died in 1960, and a year later Harrington moved to Berlin, where he accepted "an offer from the Aufbau Publishers to illustrate a series of American literary classics being translated into German."[104]

Harrington said he found himself on the wrong side of the border when the Berlin Wall went up, and he was stuck because of visa problems. "I heard a very sinister sound . . . looked out my tiny hotel window and down below there was a stream of tanks. . . . They were Soviet tanks. . . . I had had enough of wars and I didn't want to be in the middle of any war after that. . . . I found that I couldn't leave because I didn't have the proper visas. . . . I was a virtual prisoner. . . . I lost my French apartment, I lost everything."[105]

After a frustrating attempt to work as an illustrator for the East German publishing company, Harrington became a writer and announcer for a local radio station, which he directed and produced for the American blacks stationed in West Germany.

Jazz was absolutely forbidden in the GDR, absolutely forbidden. It was called negermusik. . . . I told them a program such as mine didn't have a chance in the world with Black troops especially, if it didn't have some of the "negermusik."[Gradually they got some jazz.] I had a lot of influence . . . got the program going with the best Black music there was. . . . A lot of it I had to buy myself. . . . Naturally this created other problems because young people here in the GDR were taping that stuff so they had "negermusick" all over the place. Then I began doing drawings for magazines here . . . in particular *Eulenspiegel*. I did this for years and enjoyed it very much.

I built up a department [at the radio station] with four Black Americans in it. One of them was a guy I'd known in New York whom I called Professor Lobo. . . . He was one of the best jazz critics and jazz historians I've ever known. . . . I had a difficult time getting him here because he was hanging around Paris at the time. . . . I wrote Black sketches for the program almost every night; it was a swinging program, fantastically popular.[106]

During the early years in East Berlin, Harrington met Helma Richter, a Ph.D. in economics, whom he eventually married. Out of their marriage came a son, Oliver Jr. In the late 1960s Harrington's cartoons again appeared in the United States, in the New York *Daily World* (formerly *The Worker*). Inge contends that these attained a new level of acerbic criticism of U.S. policies and practices, ranging from the Vietnam War to the invasion of Grenada. In 1972 a portfolio of Harrington's cartoons, *Soul Shots*, was exhibited in recognition of his sixtieth birthday.[107]

Harrington was also critical of racism in the GDR. In 1991 he stated:

Propaganda told an entirely different story about socialist relationships with Blacks. . . . The racism that has broken out here now is not new, it's just been discovered, it's always been undercover. . . . It's simply that racism has come out in the open. The reason for that I think is because the government that existed here for the last forty years required and insisted on quiet, peace. . . . And so racism, open racism was openly discouraged. But everybody knew it was there. And nothing was done to wipe it out. . . . So it flourished undercover. A Black person living here for twenty-nine years is really living in an intellectual desert. There are no normal relationships with other people. They don't exist. Even in the US, where racism has been a main problem for a long time, even in the US there is a kind of reciprocal movement always between Blacks and whites because both sides know what racism is. Here they don't know what racism is. And I've found that to be true in other socialist countries that I've visited. . . . And so in twenty-nine years of living here I would say I am insulted on the streets on an average of about five times a day. Well if you multiply that you . . . can see what the situation is.[108]

At Michigan State University in January 1994, Harrington expressed alarm at the growth of neo-Nazism in Germany. "I've been attacked twice in public. . . . Once it was a verbal harassment. The other time I was hit in the head with a baseball bat. . . . What shocked me is that the area was filled with people and they were all laughing at me. I've been very, very careful since then."[109]

Harrington is considered "one of the all-time top five editorial cartoonists in U.S. history."[110] Despite exile, Harrington always considered himself an American. Like others of his generation, he served in the armed forces and was deeply embittered by the treatment of black Americans, who have historically been among the most loyal of U.S. citizens. Many among the intelligentsia were convinced they would never realize their creative and personal goals in the United States. Harrington sought refuge from the McCarthy witchhunts and the rampant racism of the time, and in the process he sought new opportunities.

The mounting cold war of this period led many White Americans to consider protests against racism as somehow linked to Communism, partly because both represented vague threats to the status quo, partly because Communists abroad delighted in fiercely attacking America's racial injustices. Of the major exiled writers, only Richard Wright had any formal ties (long since renounced) to the Communist Party, yet their forthright antiracist declarations and activities, combined with their involvement in progressive (and interracial) milieus . . . easily fostered suspicions of anti-Americanism.[111]

Harrington lived in East Germany for almost a quarter of his life. In Berlin he did not have the comfort of a community of exiled cultural workers that he had in Paris. He had to create economic and political-cultural spaces through his creative work as a cartoonist and radio announcer. He drew upon a black cultural heritage of humor and jazz. Although he married and created a family, the larger system of social relations in Germany in the late twnetieth century was a constant reminder, emotionally and physically, of the difficulty of escaping racism and the racialization process. A year before his death, Harrington made it clear that he had never joined the Communist Party, although he was sympathetic to its cause, and he was equally emphatic that he had never given up his citizenship and would have liked to return to the United States permanently.

CONCLUSION

These selected portraits focus on the reasons for the African diaspora presence in Germany over a long period. From earliest times through most of the eighteenth century, we learn about them mainly as objects in "other people's history." Their voices are not heard. As we move closer to the twentieth century, these people have a voice and are better understood as "subjects of their own history," acting in their own interests. All of them are framed within the parameters of time and space, structural inequalities, racism, and the extent to which they use opportunities to affirm themselves.

African diaspora cultural workers of the last century have made important contributions to universal civilization through their artistic and intellectual creativity and political actions. They have been instrumental in organizing, creating, transmitting, disseminating, and speaking to historically constructed black diaspora cultural identities at national or global levels. Significantly, George Padmore and W. E. B.

DuBois were both associated with Pan-Africanism in the early part of this century and contributed to the making of a community of consciousness for African peoples worldwide. Both lived in and actively served the emerging state of Ghana in the late 1950s and 1960s, and they were close associates of Kwame Nkrumah, the first president of that country. Today, one can visit the W. E. B. DuBois Conference Center and the George Padmore Library in Accra. DuBois was invited by Nkrumah to "pass the evening of his life" there, and he was given a state funeral and entombed at Osu Castle in Accra.

Germany is important as the place where these cultural actors lived at critical points in their lives. It has been a locus for various passages, whether as refugees, exiles, or sojourners on the way to other places. All these individuals who lived, worked, and studied in Germany were witnesses to, and participants in, some of the most profound social, political, economic, and scientific transformations of the late nineteeenth and twentieth centuries. Some were there to expand their intellectual horizons and develop scientific skills; some were there to earn a livelihood by conveying such black traditions as music; others were engaged in the political dramas of the times. Diaspora people from the United States sought a space to live and work, far from Jim Crowism and other forms of racial oppression that obstructed opportunities and decreased life chances. Those from the Caribbean also sought opportunities and an escape from racism, colonial subjugation, and imperialism in their homeland. Germany, as did other nation-states and localities, functioned as a place where diaspora people could engage in "transition rites" for numerous reasons. Whatever the cause of their geosocial mobility, they came to that Far Place and often were transformed.

NOTES

1. R. R. Palmer and Joel Colton, *A History of the Modern World* (New York: Alfred A. Knopf, 1965), 13.
2. Edward Scobie, "The Black in Western Europe," in *African Presence in Early Europe*, ed. Ivan Van Sertima, (New Brunswick, N.J.: Transaction, 1990), 197; J. A. Rogers, *Sex and Race: Negro-Caucasian Mixing in All Ages and All Lands*, Volume 1: *The Old World* (New York: Helga M. Rogers, 1967), 176.
3. Rogers, *Sex and Race.*
4. Frank Snowden Jr., *Blacks in Antiquity: Ethiopians in the Greco-Roman Experience* (Cambridge, Mass.: Belknap, 1970), 110, 135.
5. Gude Suckale-Redlefsen, *Mauritius: Der Heilige Mohr* (Munchen: Verlag Schnell and Steiner, 1987), 28, 125.
6. Snowden, *Blacks in Antiquity,* 136.
7. Donald S. Detwiler, *Germany: A Short History* (Carbondale: Southern Illinois University Press,

1989), 5–6.

8. Wayne B. Chandler, "The Moor: Light of Europe's Dark Age," in Van Sertima, ed., *African Presence*, 146–47.

9. Rogers, *Sex and Race*, 176.

10. Scobie, "The Black in Western Europe," 206.

11. Ibid.

12. Edward Scobie, "African Women in Early Europe," in *Black Women in Antiquity*, ed. Evan Van Sertima, special issue of *Journal of African Civilizations* 6, no. 1 (1988): 135.

13. Chandler, "The Moor," 154. Also see Stanley Lane-Pools, *The Moors in Spain* (London: T. Fisher Unpin, 1887); and W. E. B. DuBois, *The World and Africa* (New York: International Publishers, 1972).

14. Scobie, "African Women in Early Europe," 205.

15. Carol Aisha Blackshire-Belay, "Historical Revelations: The International Scope of African Germans Today and Beyond," in *The African-German Experience: Critical Essays*, ed. Carol Aisha Blackshire-Belay (Westport, Conn.: Praeger, 1996), 89–123.

16. Hans W. Debrunner, "Africa, Europe, and America: The Modern Roots from a European Perspective," in *Crosscurrents: African Americans, Africa, and Germany in the Modern World*, ed. David McBride, Leroy Hopkins, and C. Aisha Blackshire-Belay (Columbia, S.C.: Camden House, 1997), 8.

17. Ibid.

18. Charlotte von Graffenried, "Bauer, Wilhelm A. 1993. Angelo Soliman, der hochfürstliche Mohr. Herausgegeben und eingeleitet von Monika Firla-Forkl. Berlin: Edition Ost, Cognoscere," *Mga-Tchad*, nos. 1 and 2 (1998): 28.

19. Scobie, "African Women in Early Europe," 204–5.

20. Scobie, "The Black in Western Europe," 197.

21. Robert Fikes, "Confirming Intellectual Capacity: Black Scholars in Europe during the Renaissance and the Enlightenment," *Presence Africaine*, no. 114 (1980): 120–31.

22. Ibid., 27.

23. May Opitz, "Precolonial Images of Africa, Colonialism, and Fascism," in *Showing Our Colors: Afro-German Women Speak Out*, ed. May Opitz, Katharina Oguntoye, and Dagmar Schultz, trans. Anne V. Adams (Amherst: University of Massachusetts Press, 1992), 4.

24. For information on Blumenbach, the "father" of physical anthropology, consult Stephen Jay Gould, *The Mismeasure of Man* (New York: W. W. Norton, 1981). Also see Ivan Hannaford, *Race: The History of an Idea in the West* (Washington, D.C.: The Woodrow Wilson Center Press, 1996); and Fikes, "Intellectual Capacity," 127.

25. For details see Richard Pankhurst, "Mahbuba, the Beloved: The Life and Romance of an Ethiopian Slave-Girl in Early Nineteenth-Century Europe," *Journal of African Studies* 6 (Spring 1979): 47–55; Kathrin Schmitt, "Machbuba–An Oromo Slave-Girl who won the heart of a German Prince," *Oromo Commentary* 4, no. 2 (1994): 32–34; and Eliza M. Butler, *The Tempestuous Prince (Hermann Puckler-Muskau)* (London: Longman Green, 1929).

26. Pankhurst, "Mahbuba," 51.

27. Ibid., 47.

28. Schmitt, "Machbuba," 32.

29. Pankhurst, "Mahbuba," 49.

30. Ibid., 51.

31. Ibid.

32. Schmitt, "Machbuba," 33.

33. Pankhurst, "Mahbuba," 47.

34. Ibid., 53.

35. Schmitt, "Machbuba," 34.

36. See Opitz, Oguntoye, and Schultz, *Showing Our Colors.*

37. Leroy Hopkins, "'Black Prussians': Germany and African American Education from James W. C. Pennington to Angela Davis," ed. McBride, Hopkins, and Blackshire-Belay, in *Crosscurrents,* 67–68.

38. Langston Hughes and Milton Meltzer, *A Pictorial History of the Negro in America,* 3d rev. ed. (New York: Crown, 1968), 74.

39. Rogers, *Sex and Race,* 178.

40. Josephine Wright, "*Das Negertrio* Jimenez in Europe," *Black Perspective in Music* 9 (Fall 1981): 161. Claudio Brindis de Salas formed an orchestra in Cuba, La Concha de Oro. As a free black he was imprisoned and tortured under Cuban Governor O'Donnel for possible involvement in a plot to foment a slave rebellion in the 1840s. See Robin D. Moore, *Nationalizing Blackness: Afrocubanismo and Artistic Revolution in Havana, 1920–1940* (Pittsburgh, Penn.: University of Pittsburgh Press, 1997), 18–20.

41. Rogers, *Sex and Race,* 178.

42. Wright, "*Das Negertrio,*" 162.

43. The war began when a revolutionary group demanded independence and the abolition of slavery, which was rejected by Spain. The conflict ended in 1878, with the Pact of Zanjon, which provided for gradual abolition and political reforms.

44. Wright, "*Das Negertrio,*" 162, 164–65.

45. Ibid., 168.

46. As popularly expressed in the United States, minstrelsy was the "white imitation of a black contented slave," a white imitation of black culture. Staged performances of dance, song, and dialogue were given by white male performers with a blackened face and broad white lips, one of the most famous of whom was Al Jolson. Minstrelsy appeared around the 1820s among the northern white working class, and black troupes emerged toward the latter part of the nineteenth century. See Jan Nederveen Pieterse, *White on Black: Images of Africa and Blacks in Western Popular Culture* (New Haven: Yale University Press, 1992); David R. Roediger, *The Wages of Whiteness: Race and the Making of the American Working Class,* rev. ed. (New York: Verso, 1991); and Michael Rogin, *Blackface, White Noise: Jewish Immigrants in the Hollywood Melting Pot* (Berkeley: University of California Press, 1996).

47. Richard Waterhouse, *From Minstrel Show to Vaudeville: The Australian Popular Stage 1788–1914* (Kensington, Australia: New South Wales University Press, 1990), 49–52.

48. Dorothy Sterling, ed., *We Are Your Sisters: Black Women in the Nineteenth Century* (New York: W. W. Norton, 1997 [1984]), 386.

49. Ibid., 387.

50. Louis Horowitz, ed., *Power, Politics and People: The Collected Essays of C. Wright Mills* (London: Oxford University Press, 1967), 406.

51. Sander L. Gilman, *On Blackness without Blacks: Essays on the Image of the Black in Germany* (Boston, Mass.: G. K. Hall, 1982), 93–100.

52. Wright, "*Das Negertrio,*" 166–67.

53. Roediger, *Wages of Whiteness,* 108.

54. DuBois wrote almost 25 books, including *The Philadelphia Negro: A Social Study* (1899), *The Souls of Black Folk: Essays and Sketches* (1903), *Darkwater: Voices from within the Veil* (1921), *Africa—Its Place in Modern History* (1930), *Black Reconstruction in America: An Essay toward a History of the Part Which Black Folk Played in the Attempt to Reconstruct Democracy in America, 1860–1880* (1935), *Dusk of Dawn: An Essay toward an Autobiography of a Race Concept* (1940), and *The Autobiography of W. E. B. DuBois: A Soliloquy on Viewing My Life from the Last Decade of Its First Century* (1968).

55. The following provide critical analyses of the many contributions of DuBois: James Blackwell and Morris Djinnis, ed., *Black Sociologists: Historical and Contemporary Perspectives* (Chicago: University of Chicago Press, 1974); Francis Broderick, *W. E. B. DuBois: Negro Leader in Time of Crisis* (Stanford,

Calif.: Stanford University Press, 1959); Shirley Graham-DuBois, *His Day is Marching On: A Memoir of W. E. B. DuBois* (Philadelphia: J. B. Lippincott, 1971); Gerald Horne, *Black and Red: W. E. B. DuBois and the Afro-American Response to the Cold War, 1944–1963* (Albany: State University of New York Press, 1986); David Levering Lewis, *W. E. B. DuBois: Biography of a Race 1868–1919* (New York: Henry Holt, 1993); Arnold Rampersad, *The Art and Imagination of W. E. B. DuBois* (New York: Schocken Books, 1990); and Alolph Reed Jr., *W. E. B. DuBois and American Political Thought: Fabianism and the Color Line* (Cambridge, Mass.: Oxford University Press, 1997).

56. DuBois, *Autobiography*, 150.

57. L. S. Stavrianos, *Global Rift: The Third World Comes of Age* (New York: William Morrow, 1981), chapter 13.

58. Ibid., 257.

59. Ibid., 261.

60. DuBois, *Autobiography*, 160.

61. Lewis, *DuBois*, 142.

62. Reed, *DuBois;* also see Blackwell and Djinnis, *Black Sociologists*, 73; Lewis, *DuBois;* and Rampersad, *DuBois.*

63. DuBois, *Autobiography*, 157.

64. Ibid., 159.

65. Ibid., 157.

66. Ibid., 162.

67. Ibid., 168–69.

68. "Alain Leroy Locke," *American National Biography*, vol.13, eds. John A Garraty and Mark C. Carnes (New York: Oxford University Press, 1999); Leonard Harris, *The Philosophy of Alain Locke: Harlem Renaissance and Beyond* (Philadelphia: Temple University Press, 1989); and Russell J. Linnemann, *Alain Locke: Reflections on a Modern Renaissance Man* (Baton Rouge: Louisiana State University Press, 1982).

69. Angela Davis, *Angela Davis: An Autobiography* (New York: Random House, 1974).

70. Ibid., 115.

71. Ibid., 142.

72. Ibid., 140–41.

73. Ibid., 144–45.

74. For more general discussions of the pilgrimage process see Victor Turner, *Dramas, Fields, and Metaphors: Symbolic Action in Human Society* (Ithaca, N.Y.: Cornell University Press, 1974); B. Lewis, "Hadj," in *Encyclopedia of Islam* (Leiden: Brill, 1966); May Opitz, Katharina Oguntoye, and Dagmar Schultz, ed., *Muslim Travelers: Pilgrimage, Migration and the Religious Imagination* (Berkeley: University of California Press, 1990); and James Clifford, *Routes: Travel and Translation in the Late Twentieth Century* (Cambridge, Mass.: Harvard University Press, 1997).

75. Turner, *Dramas*, 195–96.

76. Ibid., 197.

77. Ibid., 232.

78. Ibid., 231, drawing from the work of Arnold van Gennep, *The Rites of Passage* (London: Routledge and Kegan Paul, 1960 [1908]).

79. Christine Naumann, "African American Performers and Culture in Weimar Germany," in *Crosscurrents*, ed. McBride, Hopkins, and Blackshire-Belay, 96.

80. Ibid., 99, 102, 104.

81. Marilyn Sephocle, "Black Germans and Their Compatriots," in Carol Aisha Blacksire-Belay, ed., *The African-German Experience: Critical Essays* (Westport, Conn.: Praeger, 1996), 25.

82. Naumann, "African American Performers," 96.

83. Kenneth R. Manning, *Black Apollo of Science: The Life of Ernest Everett Just* (New York: Oxford

University Press, 1983; and Herman A. Young and Barbara H. Young, *Scientists in the Black Perspective* (Louisville, Ky.: Herman A. Young and Barbara H. Young, 1974).

84. Manning, *Black Apollo*, 171.

85. Ibid., 172–73.

86. Ibid., 35.

87. Young and Young, *Scientists*, 88. See Manning, *Black Apollo*, 52–55, for a discussion of the politics of award selection.

88. Manning, *Black Apollo*, 56.

89. Ibid., 77.

90. Ibid., 88–89.

91. Ibid., 103–10.

92. For a more complete picture, see Manning, *Black Apollo*, chapter 4.

93. Ibid., 155.

94. Ibid., 188–89.

95. Ibid., 190.

96. Ibid., 324.

97. Ibid., 329.

98. Ibid., 206.

99. See M. Thomas Inge, ed., *The Satiric Art of Oliver W. Harrington* (Jackson: University of Mississippi Press, 1993); Lester Sloan, "The World According to Ollie," *Emerge* (November 1992): 71–72; and Tom Greenwood, "Cartoonist Drawn Back Home: Oliver Harrington Accepts Temporary Post at MSU after Years in Europe," *Detroit News*, January 17, 1994, B1–2. Inge presents a good list of sources by and about Harrington.

100. Inge, *Satiric Art*, xx–xxii.

101. Ibid., xxxiv.

102. Ibid.

103. Tyler Stovall, *Paris Noir: African Americans in the City of Light* (New York: Houghton Mifflin, 1996), 147–48.

104. Inge, *Satiric Art*, xxxvii.

105. Ibid.

106. "Interview with Oliver Harrington," *VISA. Journal of the Immigrantenpolitische Forum* (Berlin) Heft 1 (May 1991). The text was translated by Maria Pease, research assistant, African Diaspora Research Project.

107. Inge, *Satiric Art*, xxxviii.

108. "Interview with Oliver Harrington."

109. Greenwood, "*Cartoonist*," B2.

110. Stovall, *Paris Noir*, 147.

111. Ibid., 185.

African Resistance to German Colonialism and Its Legacies, 1884-1913

Ruth Simms Hamilton with Getahun Benti

AFRICANS EXPERIENCED THEIR SHARE OF GERMAN COLONIALISM, JUST AS THEY experienced Portuguese, Spanish, Dutch, British, French, Belgian, and Italian colonialism. As in most other cases, German colonization was preceded by a long presence of missionaries and commercial interests in the prospective colonies. Although the period of German colonialism was relatively brief, it was no less costly and destructive than other colonial regimes. In the nineteenth century Europeans stepped up trade in Africa, especially after the demise of the slave traffic. The technological and scientific advances resulting from the Industrial Revolution, such as improved ammunition and better transportation and communications systems, allowed greater penetration of the African continent.

This chapter provides a snapshot of the different yet similar African experiences with German colonialism in the West African trading economies and the labor reserves in eastern and southern Africa. The places of direct concern, as shown in Figure 1, are Togoland (Togo), the Cameroons (Cameroon), South-West Africa (Namibia), and East Africa (Tanzania). The emphasis is on how Africans defined and acted upon the loss of their freedom, racialization, and the forced appropriation of their labor, land, and resources. Their story is one of resistance and persistent efforts to find avenues of freedom as they continuously redefined themselves. The colonial experience on the mother continent, as in other parts of the African diaspora, provided a context for the emergence of new social identities and legacies that still have relevance today.

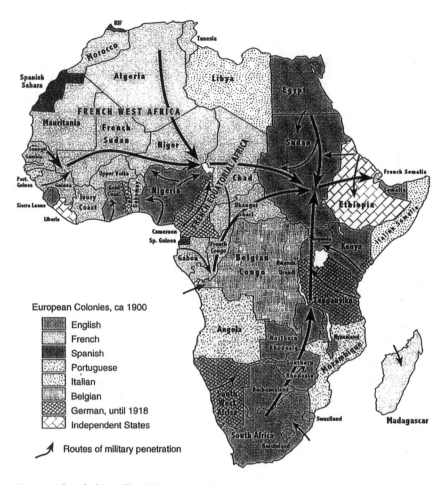

Figure 1. Colonial Africa. Ellen White, cartographer, geography department, Michigan State University.

GERMANY IN THE AFRICAN LAND GRAB

In West Africa, German merchants had established commercial ventures in Togoland and the Cameroons by the mid-nineteenth century. By 1884, about fifteen German firms were operating in the coastal areas, controlling about sixty factories and carrying on a lucrative trade with the interior through the intermediary of local tribes. These early ventures also extended to regions of present-day Liberia, Gabon, and Angola, but the most significant German interests were in the Cameroons. There, unlike Togoland, they did not face strong competition from the British and French.[1]

During the same period, the Germans were exploring East Africa, and trade with Zanzibar and the coastal areas was flourishing. Commercial interests, missionaries, and explorers wanted their government to declare a protectorate over Zanzibar.[2] In response to this increasing pressure for colonial expansion, a group called the Exploration of Equatorial Africa was founded in Germany in 1873.[3]

Germany and other European powers were in search of raw materials and agricultural products to reduce the cost of production at home. They established agricultural settlements in Africa, displacing traditional farming as they acquired land and cheap labor. Although some African leaders benefited, the masses did not. A power struggle emerged because of the resistance of the village communities to "their dispossession in favor of European planters" and to being transformed into "proletarians on the plantations."[4] African traders used a range of tactics to protect their interests. They bypassed the European companies and sold directly to Europe, withheld supplies to keep prices high, or destroyed the bases that companies established inland so they could buy commodities more cheaply from the producers. Consequently, "European firms called on their governments to use force to beat down what they considered to be unreasonable obstructionism by native growers and merchants."[5]

In various parts of the continent, Europeans claimed territory and often competed with one another for natural resources and land, which ultimately led to the partitioning of Africa. The process was facilitated by explorers and others who laid the ground for the claims of the respective European powers they represented. For instance, Henry Stanley explored the Congo Basin in 1879–80 for King Leopold of Belgium; Count de Brazza, for whom Brazzaville was named, served France; in East Africa, Karl Peters claimed territory for Germany. The "scramble for Africa" was settled at the Berlin Conference of 1884–85, which sought a peaceful partition of Africa among European powers. They agreed to inform each other of their intentions and to settle any disputes over land grabbing by arbitration. Effective occupation of African lands legitimated ownership. Excepting Ethiopia and Liberia, the entire African continent was partitioned and colonized by 1914.[6]

The Anglo-German Agreement of 1886 repeated these rules of land apportionment for East Africa. The northern hinterlands there went to Britain, and the southern area passed to Germany. The Germans had wide designs for East Africa and formed various companies and colonization societies to achieve these ends. In fact, the German East Africa Company signed a questionable treaty with the king of Buganda, which the British disputed. Another treaty was signed in 1890 to resolve their differences.[7]

The Germans established their African colonies between July 1884 and May 1885. Togoland and the Cameroons were occupied in July 1884,[8] and South West

Africa was taken in August. The occupation of German East Africa began in May 1885, but frontiers were not completed until 1890.[9] Germany occupied the third largest share of African lands (910,150 square meters); France had 4,086,950 square meters, and Britain had 3,701,411 square meters.[10] Although the Germans negotiated with the British to divide Portuguese colonies, the design did not materialize.[11]

With the establishment of full-fledged colonial rule came the era of European brutalization and exploitation of Africans. Samir Amin categorizes the various regions of Africa that were exploited and shaped by the colonial powers in their quest for cheap exports as the colonial economies of trade or *economies de traite* (West Africa), the labor reserves (eastern and southern Africa), and the concessionary companies (Congo Basin).[12] The areas of German occupation fall within the first two categories.

RESISTANCE TO GERMAN COLONIALISM IN THE ECONOMIES DE TRAITE

Germany and other colonial powers operating in West Africa shaped a complex social structure to serve large-scale production of cash crops, such as palm kernels, groundnuts, cotton, sugarcane, cocoa, and tobacco. The process included the organization of a trade monopoly via import-export houses; taxation of peasants in money, which forced them to produce the designated products or become laborers on white-owned plantations in order to earn the cash needed to pay their taxes; alliances with chiefs and other privileged classes that allowed them access to political and economic resources in exchange for their support of the appropriation and development of plantations; and importation of labor foreign to the local ethnic group, which not only depleted labor reserves elsewhere but also deprived local people of employment opportunities. Coercion and forced labor were alternatives when these other procedures were ineffective. In Togoland and the Cameroons this process had varying effects, although in both cases the policies were instituted as methods of political domination and social control.

Togoland

The occupation of Togoland was preceded by German missionary and commercial activities on the West African coast that dated from 1856.[13] After a series of maneuvers in competition with the British and French,[14] as well as treaty agreements with local chiefs that were "designed to play the Africans off against each other,"[15] the Germans hoisted their flag at Bagida on 5 July 1884, and on the next day at Lome. They established protectorates over different chieftaincies, which eventually led to the creation of a German colony in Togoland.[16]

Because "business opportunities were limited to trading," the economic prospects of Togoland were uncertain, and it failed to attract much interest in colonial and business circles.[17] To facilitate trade, the Germans built railway lines to connect major coastal and inland centers. This not only opened up the interior for exploitation but also brought a number of German firms into the country.[18] Some firms developed plantations, to produce mainly palm oil but also coconut, cacao, and rubber for export, as well as food for local consumption.[19] The focus was on the production of raw materials for the home market, so the Germans did not make significant contributions to the industrialization of Togoland, with the exception of a very few small-scale factories. By 1914 there were ten cotton ginneries, four refineries (three for palm oil and one for sisal products), one soap factory, and one lime kiln in the colony.[20]

Although Germany did grant limited autonomy to local chiefs, German policies strongly reflected the goals of the colonial power complex—full control of every aspect of African life. For example, by preventing access to educational opportunities, the emergence of an African intelligentsia was suppressed; and by controlling customs and market regulations, African traders were marginalized or forced out of business. In the thirty years of German colonialism, various forms of oppression from genocide to other forms of structural and physical violence (often expressed in the flogging of individuals) were imposed on the colonized Africans—all expressions of "great power" domination, racism, and chauvinism.[21]

A little known dimension of the Togoland colonial experience was the presence of black American graduates of Tuskegee Institute (now Tuskegee University). The first group arrived on 1 January 1900, and consisted of three graduates and one staff member. Over ten years, nine Tuskegee graduates were employed "to help develop cotton culture under the aegis of a German colonial development company" in Togoland. The "Tuskegee pioneers" demonstrated to Booker T. Washington and German colonial officials that agricultural education and industrial schemes developed at their campus in Alabama could be used in school systems at home and abroad.[22] Allegedly, the Germans, after observing the industrial training methods taught by the Tuskegee group, decided to introduce these into other schools in the colony. Togoland was one of several locations in Africa where Tuskegee influenced educational policy.[23]

The Cameroons

After intense competition with the British over the Cameroons, the Germans finally raised the flag there on 14 July 1884, just nine days after the occupation of Togoland. They subsequently declared a protectorate,[24] and here, too, they developed rubber, rice, coffee, cocoa, tobacco, palm oil, and cotton plantations.[25] This region was attractive to German planters because the mountains and rich agricultural lands provided raw materials to German industries, and the close proximity to the coast facilitated easy access for shipping abroad.[26]

Because of the economic costs and internal political conflicts in the Reichstag, Otto von Bismarck, chancellor of the German Empire, did not want the responsibility of governing the colony. Thus, German commercial firms operated as de facto colonial administrators. Until the early 1890s, their activity was limited to the coastal areas; they wanted to penetrate into the interior, but the government did not provide them with a force to implement this objective. The companies bought 370 slaves from Dahomey (today Benin), with whom they created a police force of their own and moved inland via a series of bloody encounters with the local people.[27]

Most members of the police force were not paid or given sufficient food. Moreover, the acting governor, Karl Theodor Heinrich Leist, forced the wives of these policemen to work without pay for colonial authorities (defiance was punished by flogging) and to engage in nonconsensual sex. On 15 December 1893, Leist ordered the lashing of twenty to twenty-five of the women in front of their husbands. The men revolted. They attempted to kill Leist, who escaped, and they drove out the colonial officials, who took refuge in ships anchored offshore. The revolt lasted a week; Wilhelm II dispatched a company of marines and brought the situation under control. "With the exception of 15 insurgents, who remained at large until May 1894, all captured members of the police force were summarily executed."[28]

The absence of strong ethnic unity and lack of cohesion among the various groups in the Cameroons prevented organized resistance to colonial rule. Yet, there was brave but isolated resistance that delayed further extension of German rule.[29] In at least one case, however, there was a degree of interethnic cooperation.

> An uprising in the northwest began in January 1904 with a successful attack by the Anyang on a military expedition headed by the station chief of Ossidinge and designed to open up new districts to the trading activities of the Gesellschaft Nordwest-Kamerun. The death of the station chief [Graf von Puckler-Limburg] and the rout of the few surviving mercenaries set off a general uprising. Within 18 days all trading posts of the

company and the administrative station in the Cross area had been destroyed, and all German and African employees and troops killed or driven away. Tribes speaking different languages (Anyang, Keaka, Banjang, Boki) united for a systematic struggle with the aim of expelling the Germans once and for all and ending years of colonial rule in the region. It took the greater part of the "protective force" almost six months to "pacify" the Cross area although the mercenaries were equipped with modern weapons and the insurgents were armed only with muzzle-loaders. The campaign ended with execution of the leaders of the uprising. Some of those who had taken part were hanged as late as 1910.[30]

According to Chilver, blame for the Anyang uprising was placed on Calabar traders, angered that their "middleman monopoly" had been broken. The early success of the uprising brought some unity among most of the ethnicities in the Cameroons. The Bali, long co-opted by the Germans, did not participate. Resentment of these collaborators was an important factor in the uprising, and the Bali took part in the punitive expeditions to crush the rebellion.[31]

Although the Germans quashed the Anyang revolt, weakened resistance continued until the end of their rule following World War I.[32] As in South West Africa, abuses of authority by colonial officials, the inequities of judicial decisions based on race, harsh penalties and floggings, and unpaid and forced labor were among the sources of discontent. Protests, including petitions to the German government to replace abusive officials and judges, were continuous.[33]

The Labor Reserves

In eastern and southern Africa colonial powers needed a large labor force to exploit the great mineral wealth (copper in Northern Rhodesia, gold and diamonds in South Africa) and to work in agriculture (Kenya, Tanganyika, Southern Rhodesia, and South Africa). To obtain this proletariat, the colonizers dispossessed the Africans by violence, and they deliberately drove them into poor regions for farming. In order to survive, they became temporary or permanent migrant laborers in the mines, on European farms, and later in the manufacturing industries. Amin maintains that one cannot apply the term "traditional" to society in the labor reserves, because the migrant proletariat that was created had nothing to do with "tradition."[34]

East Africa (Republic of Tanzania)

The German Business Society was actively exploring East Africa by the mid-1800s, and trade with Zanzibar and the coastal areas was flourishing. As noted earlier, commercial interests, missionaries, and explorers wanted the government to declare a protectorate over Zanzibar.[35] Perhaps in response, the Exploration of Equatorial Africa was founded in Germany in 1873, and in 1884 the German Colonization Society was formed.[36]

So-called treaties of eternal friendship were signed with chiefs, which brought almost 60,000 square meters under German control, and territory increased when the German East Africa Company developed out of the Colonization Society.[37] The company was instrumental in facilitating settlement and in developing plantations, most of which were privately owned and heavily subsidized by the German state.

In 1885, the German government agreed to grant protection to the ventures in Zanzibar and adjacent areas. Through a series of agreements and commercial concessions in some cases, through intervention in conflicts between various local chiefs in others,[38] the Germans colonized Zanzibar, nearby islands, and Tanganyika, which became German East Africa.[39] (Zanzibar and Tanganyika formed the Republic of Tanzania in 1964.)

To exploit their East African colony effectively, the Germans constructed railway lines from Dar es Salaam, the capital of Tanganyika, into the interior to compete with the British-built Ugandan railway.[40] This enhanced trade and growth of the colony, especially by facilitating transport of plantation products.[41] The latter included coffee, rubber, cotton, and sisal hemp. "Actual to semi-slave labour" was used on these plantations.[42] Although the return was not as high as in southwestern Africa, gold mining also was established in German East Africa.[43]

The Maji-Maji uprising of 1905–6 was triggered by German policy that forced cash cropping (cotton) and money taxation on the peasants. The rebellion began in July 1905, when the Kitaba people refused to take part in forced labor on government-owned cotton plantations, and by August it had spread throughout the colony.[44] People from almost all the ethnicities participated,[45] although most of the leaders were Pogoro. The uprising was put down quickly, but not before rebels attacked foreigners and their institutions, ranging from colonial offices to missionary centers. The claim that the use of "magic water (Maji-Maji) that 'turns rifle bullets into water'" would protect the insurgents rallied a large number of followers to sack one town after another. By August the capital was in serious danger.[46]

Although accounts of the movement have elements of myth, the major events are well documented. With reinforcements and superior arms, the Germans cruelly suppressed their African antagonists; they ruthlessly destroyed crops, appropriated cattle, and robbed, killed, and enslaved the inhabitants. One result was a severe famine in which 120,000 Africans died.[47] In the war alone, 75,000 were reportedly killed.[48] Conditions were worse for the Africans after the rebellion: The Germans obtained laborers under circumstances similar to slave hunts.[49]

Southwestern Africa (Namibia)

German missionaries were in southwestern Africa as early as 1824, and the first German station was set up at Windhoek (capital of Namibia) in 1834.[50] German commercial interests were active in the region and competing with similar firms from other countries from the mid-nineteenth century. Both of these circumstances paved the way for colonization.[51] Indeed, individual Germans were long involved in the conflicts among the different ethnic groups in the area and sought the intervention of their government. Germany stood aloof for a long time, however.[52] The German flag was hoisted in August 1884 at Angra Peguna, which marked the beginning of official colonization.[53]

The economy underwent major changes from 1907 to 1914 due to significant developments in transportation, mainly railway construction. The building of a 2,104-kilometer line, the most extensive in any German colony, facilitated the settlement of German farmers. The period also saw the concentration of land in the hands of white farmers and developers as the white population increased dramatically, from 3,701 in 1903 to 14,840 by 1913.[54] The authorities also encouraged raising sheep for the German wool industry, as well as the establishment of ostrich farms. The discovery of diamonds in May 1908 led to a "white rush," and mining assumed considerable importance in the last years of German administration. Earnings from exports of diamonds and copper soon became quite significant.[55]

The Germans wanted to contain African resistance by diplomacy, in the form of "treaties of protection," but ethnic leaders, first the Hottentots and later the Hereros, saw this as surrendering their sovereignty.[56]

> From the outset, even before any economic conflict had arisen, the South West African tribes refused to accept the legitimacy of German rule and opposed every move to institutionalize sovereign power. Either they openly refused to make "treaties of protection," as was the case with a number of the Hottentot tribes, or they disregarded the inferences derived from them, as was the case with the Hereros.[57]

The Herero Rebellion was the bloodiest of all uprisings against German rule in Africa, and the response was a brutal war of extermination. The main cause was appropriation of Herero land and continuous white encroachments.

With the exception of the Ovambos, the African tribes were stripped of their political power and driven from their land. Their tribal structure was destroyed. They were integrated into the European economic system as laborers. They had no political rights and were accorded inferior social standing. The decisive confrontations were the Herero rising of 1905–07 and the Hottentot rising of 1904–07. These rebellions, which took the colonial authorities and settlers, even the missionaries, completely by surprise, started with a successful rampage of killing and plunder by the Hereros.[58]

The Germans considered the indigenous economy inefficient and wanted to replace it with "a modern agrarian economy, organized according to European principles."[59] Vast areas of the region were arid, and only the lands already occupied by Africans were suitable for farming. For the Hereros, to cede their lands and be laborers for white men was unacceptable. By 1903, there were 813 concessionaires, and more than half of the Herero herds had passed into German hands.[60] Even when dispossessed, the Hereros refused to become laborers and roved from place to place, crossing borders. This angered the Germans, who made a series of border adjustments between the Hereros and their neighbors, usually at the expense of the former, in order to cultivate an alliance with the latter.[61] The German authorities declared that Africans must put themselves at their disposal or go into the reserves set apart for them.[62] Moreover, the government threatened the power of the chiefs by attempting to enforce "a modern 'well-organized system of government,'" in which private citizens were "permitted to develop as they pleased within the legal framework."[63]

In the war that lasted for two years, the Herero resisted fiercely and at times inflicted heavy casualties on the Germans, but ultimately they were "practically exterminated or driven into the vastness of the Kalahari Desert, there to eke out a miserable existence until many finally succumbed to hunger and thirst."[64] Lothar von Trotha, the German general who waged the war, issued the Herero an ultimatum to leave the country or face extermination.[65] He was unequivocal about his intentions of applying "force by unmitigated terrorism" and cruelty in order to "destroy the rebellious tribes by shedding rivers of blood."[66] Bounties were placed on the heads of Hereros, dead or alive; men, women, and children were shot or hanged.[67] "Within the germa borders [of Namibia] every Herero with or without a gun, with or without cattle, will be shot. I will no longer accept women and children, I will drive them back to their people or I will let them be shot at. These are my words to the Herero people."[68] The Herero, both warriors and civilians, were pushed northward to Waterberg, where they were attacked by Von Trotha and his force of 10,000. "When the two sides met at the Battle of Waterberg, Von Trotha deliberately left very light forces to the south-east so that the defeated Herreros, including the women and children, could escape,"[69] but the only exit was toward the Omaheke Desert, which was then sealed off for a year. Von Trotha, "the butcher," constructed guard posts along a 150-mile line and bayoneted those who tried to escape. The remaining Hereros were rounded up and placed in labor reservations.[70]

Under German rule, the native population decreased from about 300,000 in 1898 to roughly 100,000 in 1912.[71] Three-fourths of the Hereros died either in combat or from starvation. In essence, the Germans opened the twentieth century with written orders to eliminate the Hereros, who numbered around 80,000 in 1904 and about 15,000 by 1910.[72] The "survivors had lost everything: a united tribe of rich cattle-raisers had become a mass of fugitives obliged to live by keeping the herds of others on the land they themselves had once owned."[73]

The crushing of the Hereros was followed by even harsher colonial rule. The governor issued orders in 1907 that Africans were barred from owning land and raising cattle.[74] Freedom of movement was curtailed through pass laws, which were extended to Africans who had not participated in the war. Their lands taken and their mobility controlled, they became laborers on farms, at construction sites, or in mines.[75]

Most of these people became unfit to work because of the hardships to which they were exposed. Scurvy was rampant, and many contracted venereal diseases, which affected their reproductive capacity, and it was not unusual for women to terminate pregnancies rather than bring unhealthy children into the world. As the population continued a dramatic decline, the Germans sought additional migrant labor. When this was insufficient they adopted a policy of capturing Africans within the colony who had escaped to inaccessible areas during the war.[76]

It is clear that Africans were not passive onlookers to German colonial conquest; they engaged in persistent struggles and wars of liberation. Even the incorporation of myth into their narrative, the use of "magic water" against bullets, is a vital part of their collective identity. From the perspective of the subjugated Maji-Maji, the logic of magic and myth was a rational contestation of the values and technologies of their German oppressors, a rejection of an alienating and repressive social system. To survive against such odds demanded a reinterpretation of life forces and a "reservoir of meanings" to take to the battlefield and to daily struggles.[77] As one scholar puts it,

> Magical beliefs are revelatory and fascinating not because they are ill-conceived instruments of utility but because they are poetic echoes of the cadences that guide the innermost

course of the world. Magic takes language, symbols, and intelligibility to their outermost limits, to explore life and thereby to change its destination. . . . [Moreover] magical rites stimulate the vision and sustain the morale upon which that struggle depends.[78]

When the persistence of a group is at stake, a "fantasy that binds" may provide a redefinition of individual and group identity. In this context, the process is no different from those of Christians, Jews, and Muslims who have historically invoked prayers and elicited blessings in preparation for battle, and who have used religious beliefs to rationalize wars and to subjugate others. Myths are often used to provide a sense of identity within a larger system of beliefs and meanings, as well as to enhance and revitalize the energy and spirit of a people.[79]

African traders and plantation workers, ordinary men and women, waged war, protested, established underground economies, and in general resisted German occupation. In many instances they were sold out by their leaders and others who collaborated with the German colonial state and commercial interests. The whites had overwhelming technological and military advantages, but Africans never lost their desire for freedom, which cost far too many of them their lives.

MAINTAINING GERMAN RACIAL AND CULTURAL "PURITY" IN AFRICA

In many ways, German colonialism in Africa resembles that of other European nations in the Americas. Underlying the political and economic dominance, use of violence, and plunder of indigenous people was the ideology of German superiority. At the onset, German colonial attitudes toward Africans were characterized by "denigration and contempt for the indigenous peoples as 'culturally inferior,' 'morally depraved,' 'lazy and hopeless.' . . . The German refusal to admit that the interests, let alone the rights of the African peoples were of any relevance for the theory or practice of colonial rule found support from the mid-1890s onwards in the ideas of Social Darwinism and in the pseudo-scientific doctrine of the biological, virtually immutable inferiority of all 'coloured' peoples, particularly 'Negroes,' compared with white men."[80] Also like the European colonies in the Americas, in German colonies there were few white women among the early settlers. German men came as merchants and traders, farmers and plantation workers, miners, missionaries, and colonial administrators. They developed sexual liaisons with African women and girls, which resulted in few marriages but a significant number of mixed offspring. By 1905 there were at least 1,500 *mischlingskinder* (mixed or "hybrid" children), who were considered inferior to "pure" Africans and Germans. They were believed to embody the negative characteristics of both parents as well as "laziness, slovenliness, dirtiness, alcoholism, promiscuity, dishonesty and a growing threat to spread venereal diseases."[81]

These children, marriages (*Misch Ehen*), and liaisons did not complement notions of German racial superiority and had implications for the future of the German people. There was fear that within a short time "the mixed household would cause the transplanted German institutions such as the bureaucracy, the school curriculum, legal and penal systems to lose meaning and effect. The productive citizenry of South-West Africa would become ethnically different from the Germans in the 'homeland' and Germany would eventually forfeit the colony and its people."[82] Again, like the Spaniards in Costa Rica and Venezuela and the Portuguese in Brazil, the authorities decided that one solution was to encourage white immigration.[83] In the case of South West Africa, the focus was on German women. As early as 1898 the German Colonial Society recruited single women, many of whom came to the colony to work as servants for the settlers. By 1914, 953 women had arrived.[84] The Women's Association of the German Colonial Society, founded in 1907, was instrumental in this process. Among the women were "nurses, domestic workers, and teachers. Many traveled to the colonies to work in the mission schools and stations there, to take jobs in already established households, or to get married."[85]

Another important strategy to preserve racial purity and German civilization was government legislation and policies of racial separation. Africans were considered a "barrier to progress," and racists maintained that there should be "a deliberate erection of a social barrier between the two races in order to ensure the continued supremacy of the Europeans, and the German bureaucracy adopted just this approach. The principle of strict racial separation was put into practice by the expulsion of the Duala in Cameroon from their home town."[86]

In 1905 the governor of South West Africa banned marriages between whites and Africans; the law was amended in 1907 to make all such marriages before 1905 null and void. Moreover, men who remained married were deprived of German citizenship rights and disenfranchised. A special decree of 1912 required that the birth of all "semi-white" children be registered and added: "If the cohabitation of a non-native man with a native woman becomes a source of public annoyance, the police may require the parties to separate and, if this does not happen within a specified time, may compel such a separation."[87] Although there were only forty-two mixed marriages as of 1908, these rulings stripped the African wives and the children of any privileges of German citizenship.[88] For example, the children of these unions had attended German government schools, but under the new policy they were defined as Africans and henceforth subject to native laws and restrictions.

The pejoratively-called *Rehobothers* represented a slightly different pattern as

> Afrikaan-speaking descendants of Boer farmers and Nama women who trekked up from the Cape in the latter half of the eighteenth century [formed] an independent, half-caste—or—"Bastard" territory, the Rehoboth Gebiet. They acquired their land in what is now South West Africa through negotiations with a Nama chief, later approved in 1870 at a meeting of Herero and Nama at Okahandja. When the Germans landed, the Rehobothers concluded a treaty with them that granted German protection to a sovereign Rehoboth community and left them their own criminal and civil law.[89]

European colonialists were primarily driven by their desire to acquire economic profit and political supremacy within and outside their empire. To accomplish these ends, they used violent means to dominate subject peoples. They also were concerned with maintaining their "civilization" and their power and privileges. These socioracial and cultural attitudes could be flexible when profits were at stake. For example, just as Spaniards in the Americas sanctioned marriage with the offspring of indigenous chiefs in order to acquire property, German officials saw merit in permitting marriage between German men and African women who could bring wealth in land and cattle. Some missionaries even married indigenous women whom they hoped to convert to their faith.[90] These were the exceptions and not the rule, however; ideology and practice were aimed at protecting and preserving Germanness—biologically, culturally, and politically.

The German state did not encourage colonial officers to bring home African servants (and mistresses).[91] "In 1913 a government spokesman in the Reichstag stated that the theoretical possibility of allowing a 'native' to take German nationality had only been adopted in the case of a few half-castes, since 'pure natives' did not possess 'the necessary educational, economic and moral standard' to justify an equalization with Germans."[92] But actions were not always congruent with policy. To accomplish economic and political goals, there were always trade-offs. For example, Emperor Wilhelm II signed agreements with rulers in the Cameroons and Togoland.

> These agreements stipulated that the African kings had to send a number of their compatriots to Germany in order to educate them the German way so that they could serve the German empire more efficiently upon their return to Africa. Thus hundreds of West Africans found themselves scattered all over Germany at the turn of the century. Things

did not go according to the emperor's plan, and some Africans remained on German soil where they married and fathered children.[93]

The official policy did not stem the birthrate of mixed children in German colonies anymore than it did in Europe's American colonies.[94] In general, the "coloured class" that emerged assumed an interstitial or buffer position between whites at the top and blacks at the bottom. Mulatto entitlements, privileges, and social positions were defined by the colonial power complex (state, church, and commercial and civil society), which delineated physical and social boundaries, including living spaces, access to opportunities, patterns of dress, marriage, and family relations.

Thus, whether in colonial Africa or the Americas, the "coloureds" developed within a complex of historical structures and social relations that resulted in their specific sociocultural identities. Furthermore, specific times and places gave rise to similar yet qualitatively and quantitatively different social patterns and relations. For example, in the Americas, where the slave trade and colonialism occurred over centuries, larger populations were involved, and socioracial patterning and structures were deeply embedded. The "coloureds" of South Africa are much closer to the American model than are those of the former German colonies, where German occupation was relatively brief (although other European masters followed).

African Legacies and Memories

When the Germans were defeated in World War I, their colonies became League of Nations mandate territories and were distributed among the victors. German East Africa was divided between Britain (Zanzibar and Tanganyika) and Belgium (Burundi and Rwanda). South West Africa was placed under the mandate of South Africa. Togo and Cameroon went to France. Germany's colonial administration in Africa lasted a little more than three decades. Its colonies were taken over by other Europeans, who then imposed their own "ways," adding more layers to the colonial legacy. Yet, consequences of German occupation remain. The Hereros of Namibia are seeking recognition from Germany of the damage that was done, including possible reparations, or what one Herero leader has called a "mini-Marshall Plan." They want the German government to admit publicly to the violence and extermination policy against their ancestors. Germany continues to have economic and political links with Namibia, and German political leaders have made visits to the country. During a 1995 visit, Chancellor Kohl refused an invitation to meet with Herero leaders and organizations. When President Herzog visited Namibia in March 1998, he also declined to meet but referred to the massacre of the Hereros as "a dark chapter in our bilateral relations" and indicated that German colonial administrators "acted incorrectly . . . a burden on the conscience of every German."[95]

Herero leaders compare their historical subjugation to the Japanese abuse of Korean "comfort women," the genocide of Jews in Germany, and the internment of Japanese in the United States during World War II. In recent years, government leaders in Japan, Germany, and the United States have acknowledged these past injustices with reparations, formal apologies, memorials, monuments, and so on. Hereros want similar gestures. After the Ovambo, the Hereros are still one of the largest ethnic groups in Namibia. A portion of the group did flee to Bostwana after or during the Herero-Nama-German War of 1904–7. After their defeat they were banned by law from raising cattle in order to make them available as manpower for the European farms and mines. Yet, the cattle-raising tradition survived among the Herero, who have little economic and political power.[96] Their collective identity is rooted in their history, which today is taking on new meanings and directions through the actions of subsequent generations. It will continue to change as the Hereros pursue their goals as an actively mobilized community of consciousness at the beginning of the twenty-first century.

In all the former German colonies, many people still speak the language and give German names to their children. The descendants of the *mischlingskinder* have distinctive identities in Togo, Cameroon, Namibia, and Tanzania, although there has been little or no contact with Germany since the end of empire. Many of mixed African-German descent "have retained a form of the German language and some aspects of German culture," which has affected their "integration into the majority societies of these four African countries," although patterns differ from one nation to another. In Lome, Togo, for instance, there is the *Klub der Deutschen Mischlinge* (Club of Mixed Germans). Most of the founders are deceased or at least are octogenarians, and membership in the early 1990s was around twenty-five. "At the beginning they met on a regular basis but now they meet only a few times a year, generally for the funeral of one of the club members."[97] In Namibia, the Rehobothers are about 2 percent of today's population. Another group of South African colored also migrated to Namibia and hold skilled and nonskilled jobs, comprising around 2.5 percent of the total population. During a period of active political organizing beginning in the late 1950s, the Rehoboth people formed the Rehoboth Burgers' Association, often referred to as the Bastersraad.[98]

Figure 2. Hereros in German period dress. John Grobler, NYT Pictures.

Perhaps one of the most fascinating cultural "interpolations" is the wearing of German period dress and military uniforms by Hereros at ethnic and national commemorative events. "Herero women habitually wear hoop skirts. They adapted their high-waisted dresses and hats that jut out like cattle horns from the wives of Victorian-era missionaries." On holidays such as Red Flag Day and Heroes Day, "they wear versions of the dress in red and black, the colors of Herero nationalism—and the nineteenth-century German Empire. Their men wear the German volunteers' uniform."[99] Moreover, German diplomats are invited to such observances and are often asked to give keynote speeches. Ritualized practices are part of the continuing struggle of a people for social justice and identity; they are for remembering the past and for recognizing and reinforcing the dynamics of politicocultural and institutional life. Yet, it may be that the Hereros still tend to see themselves as objects in

German history and not fully as subjects of their own history, for which reason they perpetuate aspects of the German colonial social formation.[100] At the same time, some combination of idealization and hatred constitute actions and fantasies of the dominated toward their oppressors. By culturally incorporating the dress and clothing style of Germans who annihilated their people, Herero "behavioral expression—whether with manipulative intent or not—of idealization would be ingratiation. Idealization might also take the form of emulation . . . and other attempts of distance oneself from the oppressors' stereotype of blacks."[101] In this sense, dress symbolizes affirmative identity with the colonial past in public space. This does not mean that hatred—insolence and rejection—are absent from the consciousness and behavioral expressions of Hereros. Rather, they may be backstage or part of a "hidden transcript."[102]

From another perspective, Frantz Fanon points out that in the colonial world, "the Negro enslaved by his inferiority, the white man enslaved by his superiority alike behave in accordance with a neurotic orientation. . . . In the man of color there is a constant effort to run away from his own individuality, to annihilate his own presence."[103] The perspective offered by Fanon is that the paradoxical behavior of the Hereros—perpetuating the culture and dress of those who massacred them—is due to inferiority arising from being colonized and robbed of self-worth, thus resulting in a collective identity in step with their oppressors.

It is obvious that collective identity is full of contradictions and conflicting tendencies. The "collective self" is a composite of many forces and multiple perceptions of those forces. It encompasses a concept of the past that is remembered and acted upon in the present (e.g., the political economy of Namibia and local, national, and international contexts). It is always interpretive, reflective, dynamic, and full of paradoxes.

NOTES

1. Evans Lewin, *The Germans in Africa* (London: Cassell, 1939), 152–53.
2. Ibid., 181, 192.
3. S. N. Varma et al., *Tanganyika: A Background Study* (New Delhi: Africa Publications, 1961), 14.
4. Samir Amin, "Underdevelopment and Dependence in Black Africa: Historical Origin," *Journal of Peace Research* 9, no. 2 (1972): 113.
5. L. S. Stavrianos, *Global Rift: The Third World Comes of Age* (New York: William Morrow, 1981), 279.
6. Ibid., 281–82.
7. Sylvia M. Jacobs, *The African Nexus: Black American Perspectives on the European Partitioning of Africa, 1880–1920* (Westport, Conn.: Greenwood Press, 1981), 118–19.

8. The Cameroons was the name given to an area that was later under the British and the French, who divided it between themselves after German defeat in World War I. The British took the northern part and added it to their Nigerian colony; the French took the rest. Both powers governed their "booty" under a League of Nations mandate and, after World War II, as United Nations trustee-ships. In 1961, the people of British Cameroun voted during a UN-monitored referendum to become part of the Cameroon Republic.

The experience of Togoland is similar. The British and French divided it, and in a 1956 refer-endum in British Togoland people of that western area voted for integration with Ghana. French Togoland became independent Togo in 1960.

Thanks go to Dr. Ezekiel Walker, assistant professor of African history, University of Central Florida at Orlando, for helpful information.

9. Other German colonies included New Guinea, occupied in December 1884; Kiaochow, occupied in 1898; and Samoa, occupied in 1899. A. J. Taylor, "Germany's First Bid for African Colonies," in *Problems in the History of Colonial Africa, 1860–1960,* ed. Robert O. Collins (Englewood Cliffs, N.J.: Prentice-Hall, 1970), 23.

10. Stavrianos, *Global Rift,* 182.

11. Horst Drechsler, "Germany and South Angola: 1898–1903," *Presence Africaine: Cultural Review of the Negro World* 14/15 (1962): 51–52.

12. Amin, "Underdevelopment," 114–18.

13. Peter Sebald, "Togo 1884–1900," in *German Imperialism in Africa: From the Beginnings until the Second World War,* ed. Helmuth Stocker (Atlantic Highlands, N.J.: Humanities Press International, 1986), 83; and Robert Cornevin, "The Germans in Africa before 1918," in *Colonialism in Africa, 1870–1960,* vol. 1, *The History and Politics of Colonialism, 1870–1914,* eds. L. H. Gann and Peter Duigan (Cambridge: Cambridge University Press, 1969), 390. For details on missionary activities and stations in Togo before official colonization, see Gann and Duignan, *Colonialism in Africa,* 390–91.

14. Cornevin, "Germans," 391–93.

15. Sebald, "Togo 1884–1900," 84.

16. Lewin, *Germans,* 158–59.

17. Sebald, "Togo 1884–1900," 85–86.

18. Peter Sebald, "Togo 1900–1914," in *German Imperialism in Africa: From the Beginnings until the Second World War,* ed. Helmuth Stoecker (Atlantic Highlands, N.J.: Humanities Press International, 1986), 176–77.

19. Albert Frederick Calvert, *Togoland* (London: T. W. Laurie, 1918), 54–59.

20. Sebald, "Togo 1900–1914," 181.

21. Sebald, "Togo 1884–1900," 88.

22. Kenneth James King, *Pan-Africanism and Education: A Study of Race Philanthropy and Education in the Southern States of America and East Africa* (Oxford: Clarendon Press, 1971), 14.

23. For more details see King, *Pan-Africanism,* 14, 99–109, and Jorge Silva Castillo, "The Diaspora in Indo-Afro-Ibero-America," in this book.

24. Lewin, *Germans,* 160–63.

25. For details on the expansion of the plantation economy in the colony, see Albert Frederick Calvert, *The Cameroons* (London: T. W. Laurie, 1917), 24–55.

26. Calvert, *Cameroons,* 24; Mark W. DeLancey, *Cameroon: Dependence and Independence* (Boulder: Westview Press, 1989), 9–11.

27. Helmuth Stoecker, "Cameroon, 1885–1906," in *German Imperialism in Africa: From the Beginnings until the Second World War,* ed. Helmuth Stoecker (Atlantic Highlands, N.J.: Humanities Press International, 1986), 63–64.

28. Ibid., 64–65.

29. Ibid., 80.

30. Ibid., 80–81.

31. Elizabeth M. Chilver, "The Paramountcy and Protection in the Cameroons: The Bali and the Germans, 1889–1913," in *Britain and Germany in Africa: Imperial Rivalry and Colonial Rule,* ed. Prosser Gifford, W. Roger Louis, and Allison Smith (New Haven: Yale University Press, 1967), 498.

32. DeLancey, *Cameroon,* 9, 13–14.

33. Stoecker, "Cameroon, 1885–1906," 81–82.

34. Amin, "Underdevelopment," 114–15.

35. Lewin, *Germans,* 181, 192.

36. Varma, *Tanganyika,* 14.

37. Jacobs, *African Nexus,* 118.

38. For details see G. C. K. Gwassa, "The German Intervention and African Resistance in Tanzania," in *A History of Tanzania,* ed. I. N. Kimbambo and A. J. Temu (Evanston, Ill.: Northwestern University Press, 1969), 85–122; and Lewin, *Germans,* chap. 12.

39. For details, see Varma, *Tanganyika,* 14–16; and Lewin, *Germans,* 201–3.

40. Lewin, *Germans,* 300–301.

41. Albert Frederick Calvert, *German East Africa* (New York: Negro University Press, 1970), 104–12.

42. Gordon Le Sueur, *Germany's Vanishing Colonies* (New York: McBride, Nast, 1915), 101, 102. For details, see Calvert, *German East Africa,* 40–77.

43. Calvert, *German East Africa,* 84–86.

44. John Iliffe, "The Effects of the Maji Maji Rebellion of 1905–1906 on German Occupation Policy in East Africa," in *Britain and Germany in Africa: Imperial Rivalry and Colonial Rule,* ed. Prosser Gifford, W. Roger Louis, and Allison Smith (New Haven: Yale University Press 1967), 560.

45. Varma, *Tanganyika,* 16–17.

46. Cornevin, "Germans," 412–13.

47. Varma, *Tanganyika,* 17.

48. Iliffe, "Maji Maji," 561.

49. Varma, *Tanganyika,* 17. Varma notes: "The German rule in East Africa has been condemned as cruel and tyrannical. And it is often claimed that the Allied conquest during the First World War came as a deliverance to Africans" (19).

50. Cornevin, "Germans," 385.

51. Lewin, *Germans,* 75–76, 84.

52. Cornevin, "Germans," 386.

53. Richard A. Voeltz, *German Colonialism and the South West Africa Company, 1884–1914,* Monographs in International Studies, Africa Series Number 50 (Athens: Ohio University Center for International Studies, 1988), 1.

54. Horst Drechsler, "South West Africa 1907–1914," in *German Imperialism in Africa: From the Beginnings until the Second World War,* ed. Helmuth Stoecker (Atlantic Highlands, N.J.: Humanities Press 1986), 143, 144.

55. Albert Frederick Calvert, *South-West Africa during the German Occupation, 1884–1914* (London: T. W. Laurie, 1916), 67–105. For more data on export earnings up to 1913, see Drechsler, "South West Africa," 146–47.

56. Helmut Bley, "Social Discord in South West Africa, 1894–1904," in *Britain and Germany in Africa: Imperial Rivalry and Colonial Rule,* ed. Prosser Gifford, W. Roger Louis, and Allison Smith (New Haven: Yale University Press, 1967), 616–18, 622.

57. Ibid., 616–17.

58. Ibid., 609–10.

59. Ibid., 614–15.

60. Cornevin, "Germans," 387.

61. Voeltz, *German Colonialism*, 45; for details on the uprising, see 45–54.
62. Lewin, *Germans*, 135.
63. Bley, "Social Discord," 616.
64. Lewin, *Germans*, 137.
65. Jan-Bart Gewald, *Herero Heroes: A Socio-Political History of the Herero of Namibia, 1890–1923* (Athens: Ohio University Press, 1999), 172–73.
66. Clive Ponting, *The Twentieth Century: A World History* (New York: Henry Holt, 1998), 503.
67. Lewin, *Germans*, 137–40.
68. Gewald, *Herero Heroes*, 172–73.
69. Ponting, *Twentieth Century*, 503.
70. Donald G. McNeil Jr., "Its Past on Its Sleeve, Tribe Seeks Bonn's Apology," *New York Times*, 31 May 1998, 3.
71. Lewin, *Germans*, 127–28.
72. Ponting, *Twentieth Century*, 503.
73. Cornevin, "Germans," 388.
74. Drechsler, "South West Africa," 136.
75. Bley, "Social Discord," 610.
76. Lewin, *Germans*, 136–39.
77. The term "reservoir of meaning" is used by Paul Connerton in his book *How Societies Remember* (New York: Cambridge University Press, 1989), 56.
78. Michael T. Taussig, *The Devil and Commodity Fetishism in South America*. (Chapel Hill: University of North Carolina Press, 1980), 230, 231.
79. For a discussion of the significance of myths in building the identity of peoples and nations, see Anthony D. Smith, *The Ethnic Origins of Nations* (Oxford: Blackwell, 1986), 61–68.
80. Helmuth Stoecker, "The German Empire in Africa Before 1914: General Questions," in *German Imperialism in Africa: From the Beginnings until the Second World War*, ed. Helmuth Stoecker (London: C. Hurst, 1986), 209–10.
81. Kathleen J. Reich, "Racially Mixed Marriages in Colonial Namibia," in *Crosscurrents: African Americans, Africa, and Germany in the Modern World*, ed. David McBride, Leroy Hopkins, and C. Aisha Blackshire-Belay, (Columbia, S.C.: Camden House, 1998), 159–60.
82. Ibid., 160.
83. Mary Kritz, "The Impact of Inter-National Migration on Venezuelan Demographic and Social Structure," *International Migration Review* 9 (winter 1975): 517–19; Vera Lucia Benedito, "West Indian Migration to Brazil," M.A. thesis, Michigan State University, 1990; Thomas Skidmore, "Racial Ideas and Social Policy in Brazil 1870–1940," in *The Idea of Race in Latin America, 1870–1940*, ed. Richard Graham (Austin: University of Texas Press, 1990), 7–36; and Ruth Hamilton and Lorein Powell-Benard, *The African Diaspora in Colonial Costa Rica: A Case Study* (East Lansing: Michigan State University Press, forthcoming).
84. Stoecker, "German Empire," 211.
85. Opitz et al., *Showing Our Colors*, 27.
86. Stoecker, "German Empire," 211–12.
87. Ibid., 211.
88. Reich, "Mixed Marriages," 159–60; and Stoecker, "German Empire," 211.
89. Richard Gibson, *African Liberation Movements: Contemporary Struggles against White Minority Rule* (London: Oxford University Press, 1972), 111.
90. Reich, "Mixed Marriages," 162.
91. Hans Werner Debrunner, *Presence and Prestige: Africans in Europe, A History of Africans in Europe before 1918* (Basel, Switzerland: Basler Afrika Bibiliographen, 1979), 351.
92. Stoecker, "German Empire," 210–11.

93. Marilyn Sephocle, "Black Germans and Their Compatriots," in *The African-German Experience: Critical Essays*, ed. Carol Aisha Blackshire-Belay (Westport, Conn.: Praeger Publishers, 1996), 24. Also see Opitz et al., *Showing Our Colors*, 52, 57, 113.

94. See H. Hoetink, *Slavery and Race Relations in the Americas: An Inquiry into Their Nature and Nexus* (New York: Harper Torchbooks, 1973).

95. McNeil, "Past on Its Sleeve," 3.

96. Gibson, *African Liberation Movements*, 110–11.

97. Carol Aisha Blackshire-Belay, "Historical Revelations: The International Scope of African Germans Today and Beyond," in *The African-German Experience: Critical Essays*, ed. Carol Aisha Blackshire-Belay (Westport, Conn.: Praeger Publishers, 1996), 106, 107.

98. Gibson, *African Liberation Movements*, 111, 120.

99. McNeil, "Past on Its Sleeve," 3.

100. See Leo Spitzer, *Lives in Between: Assimilation and Marginality in Austria, Brazil, and West Africa 1780–1945* (London: Cambridge University Press, 1989), 132–34. Spitzer draws from Althusser's view of ideological "interpellation." Louis Althusser, "Ideology and Ideological State Apparatuses (Notes towards an Investigation)," in *Lenin and Philosophy and Other Essays*, trans. Ben Brewster (New York: Monthly Review Press, 1971).

101. James Scott, *Domination and the Arts of Resistance: Hidden Transcripts* (New Haven: Yale University Press, 1990), 39–40.

102. Ibid., 40.

103. Frantz Fanon, *Black Skin, White Masks: The Experiences of a Black Man in a White World* (New York: Grove Press, 1967), 60; also see 92–100.

Reassessing Diaspora Connections and Consciousness: Global Africa and World War I

Ruth Simms Hamilton

AT THE OUTBREAK OF WORLD WAR I MOST AFRICAN PEOPLE WERE COLONIZED subjects of Western European states, mainly Belgium, Britain, France, and Germany. Although Caribbean colonialism was long established, the partition of Africa by European powers occurred relatively late, between 1880 and 1920, rationalized by the ideology of the White Man's Burden. The United States, already the leading industrial power in the world, advanced its own ideology of Manifest Destiny and annexed Puerto Rico, pacified the Philippines, and occupied Cuba. Political disenfranchisement, separate and unequal legal segregation and Jim Crowism, lynchings, and impoverishment were the burdens of the black "internal colony" of the United States. Almost parallel with the Great War was a major watershed for African Americans: the great migration from the rural South to urban areas in the North and South. Following the Anglo-Boer War, 1899–1902, South Africa became part of the British empire; and within the Union of South Africa, disenfranchised Africans were confronted with the passing of the 1913 Native Lands Act, prohibiting them from acquiring land, except in the native reserves, which were about 10 percent of the country.[1]

These examples indicate the oppression and subordination of Africa and the diaspora in the world ordering system in the early twentieth century. Empire and domain were directly tied to a culture of violence, exploitation, and racist ideologies and practices. For Africa and its diaspora as well as non-European peoples, economic exploitation and racial exclusion became localized realities that affected not only collective identities but also emergent forms of struggle, rooted both in the past and in unfolding communities of consciousness.

The increase in European nationalism in the nineteenth century, accompanied by shifting military alliances, the competition for colonies, and the drive for political and economic supremacy, was a factor in the outbreak of World War I. By late 1914 Austria-Hungary, Germany, and the Ottoman Empire were at war with Belgium, France, Great Britain, Russia, and Serbia. The United States and other nations joined later. Although the battles were centered in Europe, other fronts included North (Egypt), East, and South-West Africa (Namibia); Mesopotamia (Iraq) and Palestine; and Asia. The fighting ended with an armistice in November 1918, and a settlement was reached at Versailles in 1919. The Europeans had been willing to pay a high price for ruling the world, using racism and colonial subjugation to facilitate their goals. This conflict had major implications for how global Africa viewed and acted in its relationship to the empires at war and the colonial state-military complex. Most important, changing views of humanity and strategies of liberation emerged. The twenty-first century begins with numerous legacies and fading memories emanating from this past.

This chapter explores some of the contours of black African and diaspora military and civil experiences in relationship to World War I. There are seven major divisions of the paper. The first two provide background discussions of the early involvement of Africa and its diaspora in facilitating military and imperial conquests of their European colonizers and oppressors. The underlying question is how and why did oppressed people protect and defend a social order that oppressed them? How was African and diaspora labor militarized and made integral to all sides of the war? In what ways did this war and its outcomes generate global collective actions by diaspora peoples? Part three takes a general look at the contributions and "blood price" of global African troops and laborers in the African and European Theaters of World War I.

For comparative purposes, three case studies demonstrate the general and specific ways men of Africa and the diaspora were drawn into this global war and used by the Allied powers to serve their interests. The shared and interconnected nature of their broader experiences, however, raises a question regarding the ways this war and its outcomes generated global collective actions by diaspora peoples. Within the limits of freedom and opportunities available, how did the oppressed act in their interests and develop new layers of consciousness, becoming subjects of their own history? In other words, if the victims of imperialism and colonialism were its defenders, why did they at the same time develop new levels of consciousness and understanding, experience new visions of freedom, and act in ways to make their image of a decent society a reality? The South African Native Labor Contingent (SANLC), the British West Indies Regiment (BWIR), and the Ninety-Second and Ninety-Third Black Divisions of the United States Expeditionary Forces are discussed in parts four, five, and six, respectively. The final discussion summarizes and draws comparisons, while raising the larger questions of the significance of a global African consciousness for diaspora studies.

BACKGROUND: GLOBAL AFRICA AND THE SHAPING OF EUROPEAN IMPERIAL QUESTS

The use of colonial military forces to facilitate European conquest did not begin with World War I. The West India Regiments, formed in the eighteenth century (1795), were deployed by the British in various wars and in the defense of British colonial territories in the Caribbean and Africa, including the Ashanti War of 1823. Several West India battalions fought in the early stages of World War I against the Germans in Kamerun (Cameroon) and in East Africa.[2] The First Regiment of the Tirailleurs Sénégalais (Senegalese Riflemen) was constituted in 1857 and, with further expansion, was the key to French conquest of the West African interior. "As the French empire extended to other parts of Africa and Asia as well, units of the Senegalese Rifles were dispatched to far-off places. They served . . . in Madagascar, Morocco, . . . Algeria, Syria, Lebanon, Indochina, and . . . China, indeed anywhere the Third Republic determined that the Tricolor should be raised." They also served in the Crimean War (1853–56) and Franco-Prussian War (1870–71).[3]

Africans from other French colonies enlisted in the Senegalese Rifles. Although the Senegalese were dominant, there were substantial numbers of enlistees from Dahomey (Benin), French Sudan (Mali), and Upper Volta (Burkina Faso). Les Tirailleurs Soudanais (the Sudanese Riflemen) were formed in the 1890s but later became a regiment of the Tirailleurs Sènègalais (the Senegalese Riflemen). After this merger, Senegalese Riflemen (Senegalese Rifles) became the generic term for black African soldiers in the French colonial army.[4]

Established by the British between 1897 and 1898, the West African Frontier Forces (WAFF) were comprised of regiments, battalions, and artillery and engineering units located in Nigeria, the Gambia, the Gold Coast (Ghana), and Sierra Leone. The East Africa Rifles, formed in 1895, included Sudanese, Swahili, Punjabis, and members of other ethnic groups, and the Central African Rifles were organized with newly recruited Africans and a cadre of Indian army volunteers in 1896. Two years later, this force was reorganized as the Central African Regiment (CAR). In the early twentieth century, the armed forces of the British protectorates in East Africa were reorganized and incorporated into a new regiment, the King's African Rifles (KAR), with battalions in Nyasaland (Malawi), the East African Protectorate (Kenya), Uganda, and Somaliland.[5]

Much has been written of blacks in the U.S. military before World War I.[6] Most scholars tend to agree that the first American to die in the Revolutionary War was a black man, Crispus Attucks, although it has been argued that he was an American Indian. King George III and the British actively recruited enslaved African people, many of whom joined with the expectation of freedom and land grants in return. More than five thousand former slaves, who became known as Black Loyalists, fled with the defeated British to parts of the empire, including Nova Scotia, Canada; the Bahamas, Trinidad, and other parts of the West Indies; and England. Many were eventually incorporated into the Krios ethnic group in Sierra Leone.[7]

African Americans continued to play a part in conflicts. During the War of 1812 they were still unwelcome in the U.S. armed forces, although there were strategically located black militia units and battalions, and "one-sixth of the sailors were blacks."[8] In the early years of the Civil War, blacks were impressed by the Confederacy as laborers on fortifications, as teamsters, and in a range of service jobs to support the troops.[9] It is estimated that around 186,000 black troops fought on the Union side, and another 25,000–30,000 served in the navy. All were under the command of white officers.[10]

At the end of the Civil War, the War Department incorporated "two black infantry regiments [the 24th and 25th] and two black cavalry regiments [the 9th and 10th] into the twenty-five regiments of the regular army. . . . These black units saw extensive service in the Indian wars of the post-bellum generation."[11] Eventually these regiments became known as the Buffalo Soldiers, a label allegedly bestowed by American Indians because of the color of their skin or the resemblance of their hair texture to the tuft between the buffalo's horns. Another view is that the designation is based on the buffalo-hide coats they wore.[12] These regiments later fought in the Spanish-American War, and the 24th and 25th were deployed to the Philippines.

At the beginning of the twentieth century, colonial troops of global Africa were deployed across vast geosocial spaces of empires. These far-reaching movements brought them into contact with one another and with other people, which arguably helped reshape their own histories and social identities. This circulation of global Africa within the framework of colonialism, racism, and imperialism created intersecting forces and processes that are integral to understanding the connectedness of diaspora peoples on a world scale.

RECRUITMENT AND MILITARIZATION
OF AFRICAN LABOR POWER

By the end of 1914, four months after the outbreak of the Great War, 300,000 Frenchmen had been killed, 600,000 wounded, out of a male population of twenty million, perhaps ten million of military age. By the end of the war, nearly two million Frenchmen were dead, the majority from the infantry, . . . which had lost 22 per cent of those enlisted.

. . . Losses in September [1914], killed, wounded, missing and prisoners, exceeded 200,000, in October 80,000 and in November 70,000; the August losses, never officially revealed, may have exceeded 160,000.

Appalling loss of life was the result of the first day of the Somme [offensive, July 1, 1916]. . . . When, in the days that followed, the 200 British battalions that had attacked began to count the gaps in their ranks, the realization came that, of the 100,000 men who had entered no man's land, 20,000 had not returned; another 40,000 . . . were wounded. In summary, a fifth of the attacking force was dead.

By 19 November 1916 . . . the Germans may have lost over 600,000 killed and wounded in their effort to keep their Somme positions. The Allies had certainly lost over 600,000, the French casualty figure being 194,451, the British 419,654. The holocaust of the Somme was subsumed for the French in that of Verdun. To the British, it was and would remain their greatest military tragedy of the twentieth century.[13]

The need for global Africa's labor power was directly related to the enormous death toll for Europeans in the early period of the Great War and certainly within the first two years (1914–1916). Aside from the colossal loss of life on the Western Front, there were other sites of battle, especially in areas of German colonization in West Africa: Kamerun (Cameroon), Togoland (Togo); South-West Africa (Namibia); and German East Africa (Tanzania).

Such military units as the WAFF, the KAR, and the Senegalese Rifles were ordered into combat against African *askaris* (soldiers) in the service of Germany. The European nations also looked to their respective reservoirs of colonized manpower for military laborers to serve in a support capacity, which released Europeans for active military service.

The British and French used multiple strategies to secure African laborers, who were largely unwilling to enter a distant war for those who took their land, and who were already making labor demands within the colony. A cursory review of the recruitment process provides some understanding of how global African identities were redefined within the colonial power complex of state ("center" governments in

Europe and their apparatuses and agents in the colonies), commerce (including industrial sectors), church (religious and missionary groups), and civil sectors (other voluntary institutions outside the state).

France initiated conscription in West Africa in 1912. "Service was for three years, and often involved combat in colonial brush fire wars or garrison duty in remote and uncomfortable outposts of empire. The pay, food, and perquisites were considerably lower than for French citizens; few if any skills or trades beyond those of the infantry-man were taught; only a tiny handful of conscripts moved up in time to a career as a native officer, and even in these cases the maximum grade obtainable was that of captain." These new recruits were incorporated into the Senegalese Rifles, which was transformed into a conscript army.[14]

Conscription by the French and "voluntary" recruitment by the British shared certain features and also varied with place and time over the five years of the war and beyond. A colony's socio-cultural history, people, political and economic organization, and physical location were germane to the recruitment process. Persuading men to leave their daily lives and go to war was extremely difficult. Therefore, state agents in the colonial periphery used a range of strategies that included impressment, hostage-taking, and monetary rewards. Some of these approaches are discussed below.

Advertisements, Seduction, and Propaganda

In 1916, through colonial representatives and agents, Britain issued calls for volunteers to serve in non-artillery military labor regiments. Posters were put up, circulars distributed in villages and towns, and ads placed in newspapers. Appeals were made to patriotism as well as loyalty to the empire and King George. Africans of different ethnicities who were on active duty or returning from service were sent to their home areas to meet with young men and encourage them to enlist. Some wrote testimonial letters urging them to join.[15] In Nyasaland (Malawi) the colonial state sent the KAR marching band to different areas, hoping to seduce enlistees. "Some expected to learn to play the instruments; others merely wanted to acquire the smart uniforms. . . . There was frequent bitterness, however, when men found that they were expected to fight and received few if any of the perquisites they had expected."[16] Such strategies did yield recruits who sought travel and new adventures or who viewed the military as an employment opportunity; a few may have been attracted to the brave warrior role to defend the land.

Using the Classes to Attract the Masses

The plea for loyalty and patriotism was more successful among educated elites. Associations such as the South African Native National Congress (SANNC), predecessor of the African National Congress (ANC), offered to assist the state with recruitment. SANNC took the position that it was their right to fight as British subjects of South Africa and that their involvement in the war would demonstrate their loyalty and identity with the empire, which they hoped would result in political payoffs and enfranchisement.[17]

It is interesting that these views are somewhat similar to the admonishment to black Americans by W. E. B. DuBois during the same war: Show loyalty, put your country first and your rights later; close ranks with whites and fight for democracy.[18] The more advantaged Africans of the period were expected by the colonizers to prove . their loyalty, "yet their very attempt to prove it was held against them as the evidence of their duplicity and, in all probability, also of subversive intentions. The circle was bound to remain vicious, for the simple reason that the values to which [African and diaspora peoples] were told to surrender in order to earn acceptance were the very values which rendered acceptance impossible."[19]

At the time, most African elites were educated in religious and mission-run schools. Europeanization and Christianization were integral to the education process, which sought to convert "heathens" to civilized ways and taught thought and behavior associated with the "superior" culture. Some Africans were psychologically and socially distant from their people, for whom penury was the norm. The latter were not interested in becoming military laborers; the work was across the sea and not very different from their current toil and the wretchedness of everyday life. In contrast, as an aspiring class, many educated Africans

> had integrated the values of a Christian-British education with their own, African consciousness. They shared a common ideological outlook and at the time of the First World War the effects of their socialization were discernible in their support of the British empire—a symbolic embodiment of "justice and fairness"—and the perception that their own future was linked to that of the Empire.[20]

Nevertheless, some educated individuals and organizations took a more critical view of the significance of empire and subject loyalty. For instance, two young scholars in Ghana encouraged men not to sign up, and a teacher at the Basel Mission School in Accra persuaded more than a hundred new recruits from Eastern Krobo not to sign the attestation for enlistment and led them to desert.[21]

The "twoness" phenomenon DuBois considered a structural factor in the identity conflict of African Americans has particular relevance in this context. What kind of insights and conceptual understandings are likely to emerge when local communities, a country, or a nation are analyzed within the context of the larger global or world system? Empire as "center," for example, can be a space of imagined identity formation, including the oppressive processes and hierarchical structures of power and place that are vital to its construction. Colonized people and places exist in relation to that center, both in practice and in ideology. Since identity (re)formation is always relational, an empire can be an imagined community for those on the bottom looking up as well as for those on the top looking down.

Class, gender, nationality, place, and race are structures of inequality that account for differences that matter in identity formation. Some African elites, for instance, sided with the colonial state and assisted with recruitment. Do their actions reflect a perception of themselves as occupying a social space between the colonial periphery and the center? Are they not both internal and external to that center? Even within an oppressive system, class position is directly related to how marginal actors view the present self in relationship to the anticipated future self, as well as the implications for social mobility and access to opportunities.

Hail to the Chiefs

Some African chiefs actively supported recruitment, which they viewed as an opportunity to exercise greater control over their domains, to ingratiate themselves with state authorities, and to prove loyalty or to reap monetary rewards. In the Gold Coast (Ghana) and Nyasaland (Malawi), some of these leaders impressed men into service; others cajoled their subjects by offering money to enlist. Reactions were mixed: Some headmen were confronted by their subjects, others were threatened with death, and the house of at least one headman was burned down.[22]

Certain chiefs refused to assist the colonial state. A few were outright defiant, and others pretended to cooperate but never delivered; a few crossed into other colonial areas. Several examples from the Northern Territory of the Gold Coast are insightful. Chief Lo Wiili moved into French territory with his cattle and personal belongings to avoid cooperating with the British. Another, who detested the "high-handedness" of British officials, declared he would not play the role of "sergeant-major" and force men into the military. In March 1917 what became known as the Bole riots erupted in Gonja and required a detachment of British troops to subdue.[23]

Chimtunga Jere, an Ngoni chief in northern Nyasaland,

at first simply refused to respond and later was openly defiant . . . expressing general dissatisfaction with the demands for carriers [laborers]. The government, however, as well as local missionaries, saw the affair as the boisterous, verbal excess of an incompetent (and frequently inebriated) chief. He was therefore removed from office by the governor and exiled to the far south of the protectorate. Ironically, his protest inspired his people to greater co-operation, since many considered that Chimtunga's release and restoration might be secured through their own sacrifice in government . . . service."[24]

Relationships of reciprocity and exchange between chiefs and their people were greatly compromised, and this contributed to the gradual decline of chieftaincy as an institution. Their forceful imposition of military service against the will of those they represented fostered distrust, suspicion, and resentment. This kind of repression and its divisive consequences also furthered the interests of the colonial state.

The use of chiefs and others of the educated elite as recruiting agents was not very successful in attracting volunteers, although thousands did enlist. Stronger measures were needed.

From General Mobilization to Abduction, Duplicity, and Extortion

One legal venue available to British governors was a general mobilization order, which required anyone within the area to perform services necessary for its safety or defense. In South-West Africa, an order was issued at the beginning of the war, followed by specific ordinances, such as the 1916 British Protectorates (Defence) Order of Council. The latter provided the basis for enlisting men into military labor contingents but not into the KAR. Using fear as the weapon, British officials painted themselves as the "good colonists" in contrast to the Germans, who would take more land and enslave and kill Africans. In other words, help the benevolent British or your suffering will increase.

Men still found ways to avoid service or simply fled across borders. They did not want to carry "heavy loads through tsetse- and mosquito-ridden swamps and over sun-baked savannah in humid tropical weather . . . one of the toughest, most grueling assignments of the war."[25] Victimization and violence were used. The police and the courts were ordered to procure men by such means as arresting tax defaulters and putting them into service as carriers. Government trackers ambushed unsuspecting children and farmers. A district commissioner reported that "young men were rounded up during the night" to fulfill labor requisitions.[26] Duplicitous measures, such as spreading rumors to mobilize ethnic groups or calling for volunteers to put down a disturbance, were not unusual. Men who responded realized too late that they were put in service to fight the Germans. In Nyasaland, the benevolent British held wives hostage so their husbands would sign up.[27] And yet the men, their families, and communities still resisted.

Resisting That Thangata Thing

"Any WW I conscript was a man who had been induced not to run away."[28] In Chichewa, a language of Nyasaland (Malawi), the word thangata

> literally means "help" and originally referred to a system of "narrowly structured exchanges of services between chiefs and their dependents prior to British colonization." In the colonial situation, however, the term was applied to the demands, usually from new European landlords, for labour in exchange for "rent" and taxes. Thangata . . . gradually came to signify not "help" but unwarranted demands by Europeans for African service. "Work which was done without real benefit."
>
> Inevitably, the entire war became associated with the unpopular demands for military labour; it was the "war of thangata."[29]

Men who worked in industries, such as mining and shipping, and some in agriculture, such as cocoa farmers in Ghana, simply ignored the call to recruitment. There were many reasons for their lack of interest, but in particular their wages were higher than the going rate for military laborers.[30] Many who refused to serve engaged in avoidance or evasive resistance, such as flight and refuge, migration, and desertion. Men fled to Liberia and areas under British rule from French territories of West Africa. As many as eighteen thousand may have fled from the French into the Western Province of the Gold Coast: "A large part of the road labor force in 1917 was from French territory, as were many of the mine workers in 1921–22."[31] Maroonage, widely practiced throughout the Americas during slavery, was another option, and men throughout Africa took refuge in remote areas. Workers in the Abusai gold mines in the Gold Coast ran away to elude impressment by government agents. Sotho men of Basutoland (Lesotho) fled across the border to the Orange Free State in South Africa to escape recruiters, and many took jobs with white farmers.[32]

The desertion rate for new recruits was very high. Thousands of them crossed into Portuguese Guinea, Liberia, and Sierra Leone from French Guinea. At one location in Guinea, Fouta Djallon, desertion was as high as 23 percent in 1918, and that was considered a good year. "Entire cantons decamped, and the population of others suddenly halved" to avoid conscription.[33] The desertion rate in the Gold Coast was one-fourth to one-third of all new recruits. In South Africa, desertions during train journeys to recruitment centers were very high, especially among men whom head-men compelled to enlist. The state reacted with stricter supervision and hasty deployment; in the Gold Coast troops were sent to Sierra Leone and East Africa without full training. Seeking refuge in a rival empire usually did not result in deportation because both the British and French welcomed the added manpower. Interestingly, German *askari* prisoners of the British in Nyasaland were recruited to join the KAR in exchange for freedom, which many accepted.[34]

Some segments of the colonial power complex were on the side of the Africans because it served economic interests. In the commercial-industrial sector, which depended on cheap labor, there was a concern about the loss of workers through flight and forced recruitment. In the Gold Coast, colonial agents looked to gold and manganese mines for enlistees, and workers often fled to the bush to escape impressment. In South Africa, business owners and managers feared that African military laborers might become more class conscious if exposed to ideas of socialism prevalent in Europe at the time. Labor-dependent white South African farmers often used intimidation to undermine recruitment and even threatened to evict the families of men who enlisted.[35]

Most whites had major reservations about the militarization of Africans, who might use their training and weapons against Europeans. Furthermore, some believed that Europeans and non-Europeans "fighting with and against each other on equal terms . . . was likely to seriously undermine the future maintenance of the existing state of . . . relationships by devaluing the concept of race as an effective means of forestalling the emergence of class as an alternative, overt, basis for the organization of social and political relations."[36] A white newspaper editor in South Africa expressed the view clearly: "The empire must uphold the principle that a coloured man must not raise his hand against a white man if there is to be any law or order in either India, Africa, or any part of the Empire where the white man rules over a large concourse of coloured people. In South Africa it will mean that Natives will secure pictures of whites chased by coloured men, and who knows what harm such pictures may do?"[37]

In the end, the desperate need for manpower superceded ideology. Government and military leaders at the center of the empire and their agents in the periphery may have shared the goal of preserving empire and racial superiority, but manpower needs on the battlefield took precedence. All available strategies would be used to keep the flow of labor abundant, despite the social, political, and economic costs in the short and long term.

Carrots Along with the Stick

British and French authorities eventually offered enlistment bonuses and pay higher than that of the most lucrative sectors of civilian employment. In Nyasaland, *askari* earned three times more than most prevailing wages, and the pay scale for carriers was increased considerably. The call for fifty thousand men from French West and Equatorial Africa in 1917 granted special privileges.

> Their exemption from prestations—labour duties—rendered them immune from chiefly authority in one of its most important manifestations. . . . the vast majority of conscripts from the Forest, the Fouta Djallon and Upper Guinea had in fact—though not in law—been slaves up to the moment of their enlistment. . . . they no longer had to answer the call to build roads or produce agricultural surplus.[38]

The French state also appointed Senegal's first African deputy, Blaise Diagne, commissioner general of recruitment (of troops in French West and Equatorial Africa), a rank equivalent to governor-general. He also had a contingent of several African officers with the rank of lieutenant or captain. Diagne brought in an astonishing 60,000 or more men after securing a number of concessions from the government. Two of these were quite significant to African conscripts: living allowances for their families and exemption from the *indigenat*, a system of administrative justice whereby penalties could be imposed on Africans without judicial reference. Penalties covered "a large number of loosely defined acts of insubordination or disrespect towards the French or any of their agents."[39]

State officials also worked out compromises with business owners and managers, their competitors for African labor. In March 1917 the Ashanti Goldfields Corporation of the Gold Coast convinced authorities not to recruit from the labor force at key mining locations, in return for which AGC would suspend recruiting in April. This paved the way to enlist more men from the Northern Territories, where most of the mine workers originated. In South Africa, the Chamber of Mines agreed that "African labourers recruited from Mozambique to work on the goldfields would be employed for the first three months of their annual contract on railway construction in South-West Africa. The approval of the Portuguese governor-general was obtained. . . . In addition, a considerable number of Africans engaged by the railway administration in the Union were summarily transferred to South-West Africa, for similar service in that territory."[40]

Enlarging Spaces of African Resistance

The war took its toll on African family life and livelihood, especially because many food essentials were heavily taxed or simply not available. The export trade of African farming and commercial interests was eroded by the war. Yet, with so many whites leaving for military duty, job opportunities opened up for Africans, including school teaching and ministerial work previously controlled by missionaries. Nevertheless, civil disturbances increased throughout the colonies as Africans focused on the *thangata* thing: harsh recruitment measures, high taxes, and assorted ill-treatment and demands by colonial authorities. Women actively encouraged men not to go to war. Between 1914 and 1918 there were numerous strikes among dock workers and miners from West Africa to southern Africa. African soldiers mutinied at camps, attacking white officers and in some instances killing local whites. In the Gold Coast, there were major riots in the Northern Territories and in the Central Province.[41]

Districts of East Griqualand in South Africa's northern Transkei were the site of disturbances: Several thousand peasants destroyed cattle-dipping tanks and burned and looted stores, which sent white farm families fleeing to town for safety. This uprising took place from 12 to 19 November 1914, when many of the white males, especially policemen, were in service with the South African Defense Forces. Seeing the vulnerability of whites, Africans seized the moment, although they were eventually overpowered by the superior arms of the so-called Citizen Force.[42]

In French territory there also was increased activity by Africans.

From 1915 on, resistance to military service intensified, as the wounded and mutilated began to return and as it became obvious that no adequate provision was made for the families of absent soldiers. There was a major rising in Soudan [Mali], which spread to Upper Volta (Burkina Faso). The Tuareg rose in a war against French authority and in 1916 there was a rising in Borgu and in other parts of Dahomey. Whole villages hid in the bush to avoid conscription and thousands of young men crossed the border into British colonies. Some even mutilated themselves.[43]

One of the most infamous acts of resistance against the colonial order was the Chilembwe Revolt, also referred to as the Nyasaland Native Uprising. John Chilembwe, born in the late 1860s or early 1870s, was reared in Nyasaland, where he received primary and secondary education. A little before the turn of the century, he traveled extensively in the United States and studied for a couple of years at Virginia Theological Seminary and College at Lynchburg. He was sponsored by the Reverend

William W. Brown of the High Street Baptist Church of Roanoke, Virginia, who was later "minister of the important Negro Metropolitan Baptist Church of New York."[44]

In 1900 Chilembwe returned to Nyasaland and established his Providence Industrial Mission with the assistance of the National Baptist Convention and black American missionaries, including Thomas Branch, Rev. L. N. Cheek, and Ms. Emma B. DeLany.[45] He was the visionary leader of a rebellion directed against the growing control and regulation of the colonial state, especially the increase in rate of the hut taxes and the abuses of African laborers by white-dominated commercial centers and farming estates. The uprising began on 23 January 1915 and lasted almost two months; Chilembwe was killed on 3 February. He was able to build "battalions" of men by capitalizing on their resentment of demands for military laborers, mistreatment by the whites for whom they worked, and white racism, arrogance and disrespect for them and their kin, as well as their general unwillingness to accept repression.

From the perspective of the diaspora, Chilembwe and African Americans shared relationships in both the United States and Nyasaland. Numerous African American cultural workers—particularly in religious, educational, and news organizations and diplomatic circles—had worked in and visited areas of Africa since the early nineteenth century. The religious groups, however, tended to support Europe's "civilizing mission" in Africa, although World War I demanded a re-evaluation of that position. Whatever the influence of African Americans and the large National Baptist Convention on Chilembwe, it is likely that the realities of his life and the lives of his countrymen most mediated his activity in 1915.[46]

Well-known sectarian and millenarian movements also proliferated and were directly tied to anti-European and anti-war sentiments. *Nyau* secret religious groups in Nyasaland were strong opponents of forced recruitment.

> *Nyau* members would flee from their villages and hide in graveyards or special caves in the hills where the societies' dance masks were stored; others donned the masks and hid in small holes, or *machemba*, which they had dug in the earth. The caves, graveyards, and masks were all sacred and could thus offer sanctuary to the fugitive. Since many of the African recruiters were themselves members of the societies, the extraordinary social position of the *nyau* and its sacred precincts successfully shielded some men from the demands for military labor. This success, more than any other factor, may have accounted for the rising popularity of the societies during and after World War I.[47]

Some blacks in South Africa interpreted the war as a prefiguration of their return to control of their land; others saw the Germans as the instrument of annihilation of the whites. Various African prophets, such as Nkabindi in Pietermaritzburg, attracted a number of believers.[48] In southwestern Uganda, adherents of the *Nyabingi* sect believed access to supernatural power was through spirit possession, which was eventually used to secure access to secular power. Members also celebrated legendary heroes, one of whom was Muhumusa, a widow of one of their late leaders. "What is striking is that . . . the Nyabingi cult succeeded in immobilizing the administrative efforts of three colonial powers [Belgians, British, Germans] for nearly two decades, until its final suppression in 1928."[49]

A religious movement led by the Somali patriot Sayyid Muhammad Abdille Hassan immediately turned against colonialism in British Somaliland, and later expanded into Italian and Ethiopian Somalilands. In an act of solidarity, the young Ethiopian ruler Iyasu Michael provided military support to Sayyid. Germany and Turkey, at war with the British in East Africa and in the Middle East, viewed this situation favorably and increased their influence at the court of Iyasu. Seeing the danger in the Ethiopian-Somali alliance, Britain intervened in the power struggle at the Ethiopian court between Iyasu and his opponent Ras Tafari, the late Haile Sellassie. Tafari, grateful for Allied support, helped the British crush the revolt of Sayyid. This "local" act of Pan-African solidarity and resistance was integral to the globalized politics and policies of European Axis and Allied powers during the war. It also had long-term implications for Ethiopian and African political transformation within the global system. Ironically, the rise of Haile Sallassie provided important political and cultural legacies and meanings for communities of consciousness and identity throughout the African diaspora, especially Garveyism, Rastafarianism, and reggae music.[50]

The appropriation of land and its resources and access to an unlimited supply of labor were two major goals of colonialism. During World War I, the Allies needed this vast reserve of cheap labor to become victorious. Those who were tapped to supply the labor power, however, were largely unwilling and on a significant scale became "refuseniks." The examples cited are only a few of the actions initiated by Africans to address *thangata* and other aspects of their repression under colonialism. The longer the war lasted, the more contentious and violent acts of resistance and reactions by the colonial state became. The daily lives of families and communities were disrupted, and there was little interest in "crossing the waters" to fight the battles of the oppressors. The position articulated by John Chilembwe may be representative of how Africans viewed the war and "that *thangata* thing."

The Voice of the Natives in the Present War

We have been invited to shed our innocent blood in this world's war which is now in progress throughout the wide world. . . .

A number of our people have already shed their blood, while some are crippled for life. And an open declaration has been issued. A number of Police are marching in various villages persuading well built natives to join in the war. . . .

. . . For our part we have never allowed the Nyasaland flag to touch the ground, while honour and credit have often gone to others. We have unreservedly stepped to the firing line in every conflict and played a patriot's part with the Spirit of true gallantry.

But in time of peace the Government failed to help the underdog. In time of peace everything for Europeans only. But in time of war it has been found that we are needed to share hardships and shed our blood in equality. . . .

But regarding this world-wide war, we understand that this was not a royal war, nor a government war, nor a war of gain for any description; it is a war of free nations against a devilish system of imperial domination and national spoliation.

. . . Let the rich men, bankers, titled men, storekeepers, farmers, and landlords go to war and get shot. Instead poor Africans who have nothing to own in this present world, who in death, leave only a long line of widows and orphans in utter want and dire distress, are invited to die for a cause which is not theirs.

John Chilembwe,
In behalf of his countrymen

The full letter is reproduced in Shepperson and Price, *Independent African*, 234–35. The original letter was published in the *Nyasaland Times*, 26 November 1914, no. 48, 7, column 6.

CROSSING THE WATERS:
THE THEATERS OF WAR

Four days before Britain declared war against Germany (31 July 1914) the first military operation of World War I was launched from the Gold Coast (Ghana) against the German colony of Togoland. With the assistance of African troops under French command, the Gold Coast Regiment of WAFF occupied Togoland within one month. "More serious operations were needed to invade the Cameroons [Cameroon was another German colony], eventually involving twenty-six companies including elements of the West Africa and West India Regiments. French and Belgian troops were also involved, as well as the Indian 5 Light Infantry, which arrived shortly before the campaign was completed in February 1916."[51] From the very beginning of the war Pan-African and diaspora British and French colonial forces were at the forefront of the campaigns, crossing multiple imperial boundaries as well as socio-cultural spaces—ethnicity and race, language, and religion.

Combatants under the Tricolor

On 4 August 1914, there were 30,742 black African troops under arms for France, about 14,000 of which were in French West and Equatorial Africa, and the rest were in Morocco, Algeria, and Madagascar; there were no black troops in France. Algerian forces had two black battalions; Morocco had thirteen plus a squadron of Senegalese *spahis*, two groups of mixed colonial artillery, and four companies of Senegalese *conducteurs*; Madagascar had one Senegalese battalion.[52]

From 1914 to 1918, French Africa sent 450,000 troops and 135,000 military workers to Europe, the majority from North Africa.[53] In French West Africa, Senegal contributed the largest number—151,000. Madagascar contributed 46,000. French Guinea contributed close to 30,000 men. "The First World War exacted a heavy toll on West African soldiers. Over five years of combat, FWA furnished 170,891 men, . . . Casualties for black Africans ran at approximately 185 per thousand, or 30,000 killed in action."[54] Compared to the British, the number of Africans participating in the war effort from French colonies was much greater. This was due in no small part to the introduction of compulsory military service in the French colonies in 1912.[55] Totally, the French raised about 850,000 non-white colonials as laborers during World War I; many loaded and unloaded vessels and performed a variety of non-combat work.[56] Similar to their African and diaspora counterparts, Senegalese troops were in segregated units primarily under the leadership of white officers; they also had separate hospitals in France at Marseilles and at Menton. During the war, French African troops participated as combatants on all the major fronts.

> They served in France and Belgium in the autumn of 1914; they were with the French at the Dardanelles in 1915; they fought at Verdun and on the Somme in 1916; they were on the Asine in 1917. And "everywhere where the colonial troops and, in particular, the Negro troops attacked, on the Somme [and elsewhere], deeds of heroism were multiplied." Above all other places, it was at Verdun that they distinguished themselves the most. . . . [demonstrating] their gallantry in leaving the trenches and assailing the enemy in the open . . .[57]

The majority of the 34,000 conscripts who came to France from the French West Indies (Guadeloupe, Guiana, and Martinique) were of African descent. Some were combat soldiers but most were support laborers and factory workers. The exceptions were a few West Indian officers. "Captain Helidore C. Mortenol, a Negro naval officer from Guadeloupe, was reportedly in charge of the air defense of Paris throughout the war. . . . Another Negro officer, Lieutenant Colonel D'Alenson, was for a while chief of staff at Verdun."[58]

By January 1919 there were 133,000 black African colonial troops under arms: "60,000 in France, 10,000 in the near East, 15,000 in Algeria and Tunis, 11,000 in Morocco, 18,000 as the corps of occupation in French West Africa, 7,000 in French Equatorial Africa, 2,000 in the Cameroons, and 10,000 recruits of 1918 in French West Africa."[59]

The South-West Africa (Namibia) Front

The South-West Africa campaign started in August 1914 and was completed within six months. A few days after the start of World War I, Britain asked the Union of South Africa to invade this region and seize the harbor and radio stations as well as occupy Windhoek and strategic rail, road, and waterway positions from Swakopmund to Ludertizbucht. Approximately 67,000 South African expeditionary forces engaged in the campaign along with 35,000 Africans, including 1,326 from Bechuanaland (Botswana) and 58 from Basutoland (Lesotho). Most blacks served in a support capacity, including members of the Native Artillery Drivers in the South African Field Artillery.[60] Africans were dock and transport workers, especially on railways.

Approximately 500 blacks worked as stevedores in Walvis Bay where they assisted in unloading war supplies, while a considerable number were responsible for all the animal transport and served as drivers of ammunition and supply wagons. Most, however, were employed to repair rail links destroyed by the retreating Germans and particularly in the construction of new railways, linking the northern South African station, Prieska, to the southern station in the war zone, Kalkfontein (modern Karasburg).

The strategic importance of the railways to the South African war effort made their speedy completion imperative, and to this end relay teams of black workers toiled day and night.[61]

The "blood price" for these support workers was very high. Many were captured by the Germans and as war prisoners were subjected to castration, ear severing, and eye gouging. Large numbers died or fell seriously ill due to injuries and tropical diseases. Many were victims of the cruelty and injustice of white overseers and military personnel, in many ways not unlike the earlier experiences of enslaved Africans throughout the Americas. White South African "gang bosses," for example, flogged Africans for minor misbehavior or to coerce work, and they pocketed fines of one or two pounds that were levied arbitrarily against men who earned only three pounds a month. Resort to the system of justice, military or civilian, was not a viable alternative, as illustrated by the case of three Africans who refused to work on the docks after their contract expired. They informed their supervisors of this a month in advance but were arrested and tried before an assistant provost-marshal, who dismissed their case and sentenced them to be horsewhipped. Nonetheless, Africans were not without agency: In 1915, when about 365 workers demanded to be returned to South Africa and refused to work, officials "were forced to accede to their demand."[62]

Africans, most of whom were not "volunteers," experienced not only the rigors of war but also the rigors of race. The behavior of whites, on the battlefield or elsewhere, was rooted in their belief in their own superiority, which for them was evident in their success as conquerors and colonizers. These views were reinforced by the pseudoscientific biological rationalizations of eighteenth- and especially nineteenth-century thinkers. Among the major contributors were Johann Friedrich Blumenbach (a founder of physical anthropology and craniology, who originated the category Caucasian), Count Arthur de Gobineau (race is the result of degenerate biology), Charles Darwin (race is a matter of natural selection and a result of biological evolution), Herbert Spencer (only the fit survive, and arrangement of human societies depends on natural selection), and Houston Stewart Chamberlain (races are unequal; normal evolution leads to greater distinctiveness and purity of blood).[63]

The East African Front

Following the pacification of German West Africa, attention shifted eastward. At the beginning of the war, Britain and Germany were the dominant European powers in East Africa, and the area became a significant battleground. Initially, battalions of the KAR guarded their respective borders, but an offensive was needed to oust the enemy from German South-West Africa (Namibia) and German East Africa (Tanzania). With a force of Europeans and African *askaris*, the Germans inflicted heavy losses on British, South African, and other troops. The *askaris* came from these German colonies and were used almost exclusively in the East African theater. In addition, African troops from Kamerun (Cameroon) who earlier mutinied against the Germans were exiled to South-West Africa, where some of them were placed in the service of the Germany military as noncombatants. "The 'Rehoboth Basters,' . . . who had also served the Germans during the earlier uprisings in [Southwest Africa],"[64] were a racially mixed group of distinctive identity. They were Afrikaans-speaking descendants of Boer farmers and African women, mainly of Nama ethnicity, who migrated from the Cape in the eighteenth century.[65] Significantly, before South-West Africa fell to the Allied forces, the Rehoboth Basters "staged a rebellion against the Germans, which was crushed by German troops."[66]

Tropical diseases accounted for high death rates among Africans and Europeans in the first two years of the war. During January and February 1917, almost 2,000 (80%) of the men in areas heavily infested with malaria died. Among the eighteen thousand black South Africans who served, monthly mortality increased from 5.4 to 22.2 per thousand.[67] In addition to these losses, as the European units departed for the front, Britain needed large and continuous quantities of "fighting commodities," which they acquired from their vast reservoir of colonized peoples throughout the world.

To the East African Theater the British brought in troops from far and near, including India, South Africa, the West Indies, West Africa, and Central Southern Africa. For example, three battalions of the British West Indies Regiment were "transferred to the East African Expeditionary Force, Mombasa, to be attached to the 2nd West India Regiment, . . . to garrison the territories taken from the Germans."[68] By reforming old units and creating new ones, the KAR had expanded from five to twenty-two battalions by the time the Germans surrendered in 1918. As shown in table 1, 68 percent of the non-white fighting forces were East Africans in the KAR: "More than three in five troops were K.A.R., of whom over 34,000 were recruited; and toward the end of the war, their greatest strength was close to 31,000, almost half of whom came from Nyasaland."[69] Matabele and Mashone men were brought into serv-

Table 1. Estimates of African Troops Serving in East Africa, 1914–1918

PLACE OF ORIGIN	NUMBER
King's Africa Rifles (kar)	
Nyasaland (Malawi)	15,000
East African Protectorate (Kenya)	10,500
Uganda	10,000
German East Africa (Tanzania)	2,000
Zanzibar and Mafia	1,000
Subtotal	38,500
West African Frontier Forces (waff)	
Nigeria	6,216
Gold Coast (Ghana)	3,956
Gambia	380
Subtotal	10,552
Central and Southern African Forces	
Northern Rhodesia (Zambia)	3,437
Southern Rhodesia (Zimbabwe)	2,752
South Africa	1,500
Subtotal	7,689
Total	56,741

Source: Constructed from data in G. W. T. Hodges, "African Manpower Statistics for the British Forces in East Africa, 1914–1918," *Journal of African History* 19, no. 1 (1978), and Roger Perkins, *Regiments: Regiments and Corps of the British Empire and Commonwealth 1758–1993: A Critical Bibliography of Their Published Histories* (Chippenham, Wiltshire, U.K.: Antony Rowe, 1994). Later, Tanganyika and Zanzibar came together to form Tanzania.

ice when the Rhodesia Native Regiment was formed in May 1917, later expanded with troops from Basutoland (Lesotho) and Bechuanaland (Botswana).

Early in the East African campaign, the Union of South Africa formed a volunteer colored infantry corps for active combat duty. Under the Imperial War Council and paid by the British government, the corps was commanded by white South African officers and noncommissioned officers (ncos). In 1916, the first battalion of the Cape Corps, consisting of thirty-two white officers and 1,022 coloreds, was dispatched to East and Central Africa; a second battalion was formed later. Altogether, about eighteen thousand men served in the Cape Corps in East Africa, and members of the 2nd battalion served in Egypt and Palestine. The Cape Auxiliary Horse Transport (around 2,800 drivers) and the Cape Colored Labour Corps worked on the Western Front.[70]

When WAFF units joined the East Africa campaign in 1916, the majority of fighting forces there were "black African units—those raised locally and those from Nigeria, the Gold Coast, and The Gambia."[71] The Gold Coast Regiment (with a light battery) and the Nigeria Brigade (four battalions and a light battery) served in East Africa for the last two years of the war, along with a company from Gambia. Nigerians and Gambians were repatriated in February and March 1918, and the Gold Coast Regiment, with its newly formed mounted infantry, remained until the end of the war.[72]

The Carriers

The military demand for general laborers, "followers" and "carriers," was high priority. Followers included gun porters (front-line carriers of machine guns, ammunition, signal equipment, mortars, bombs, and shells). Carriers performed a number of roles (load bearers, general laborers, cooks, grooms, personal servants, sweepers, interpreters, armed scouts, canoeists, tailors, carpenters, and other casual laborers). They also served as police to prevent desertion, and as medical support workers.[73]

The largest number of Africans contributing to the defeat of the Germans were carriers. They provided the foot and muscle power needed to transport food and ammunition to the troops through semi-desert, bush, and swamp areas. The following description indicates the dependency of the British on the Carrier Corps.

> Nyasaland carriers fall into three main groups: front line men, line of communication men, and finally road labour, woodcarriers and food carriers, which included "some women and children." . . . The third group, and probably also many of the second, who presumably carried mainly from the head of the lake to the German border, were under civil control, locally based and on short contracts. The same most probably applied to the Uganda "job porters." Under such arrangements large numbers could have served several contracts, mainly during the dry season, which is from April to October in that part of Africa. . . .
>
> The situation in Northern Rhodesia [Zambia] was somewhat similar to that in Nyasaland: a six hundred mile line of communication from railhead to the German border, supplemented by a waterway. In Northern Rhodesia, there was a corps of canoe

Table 2. Estimates of African Followers/Carriers Serving in the British East African Campaign by Place of Origin and Type of Work, 1914–1918

	TYPE OF WORK				
PLACE OF ORIGIN	GUN PORTERS	MEDICAL STAFF	CARRIERS	CASUAL LABOR	TOTAL
German East Africa (Tanzania)	2,436	1,595	197,312	125,817	327,160
Nyasaland (Malawi)			195,652	1,262	196,914
East African Protectorate (Kenya)	9,237	7,374	162,578	10,961	190,150
Portuguese East Africa (Tanzania)	3	1	10,927	79,083	90,014
Uganda	449	540	55,074	1,243	57,306
Northern Rhodesia (Zambia)			56,000		56,000
Sierra Leone			5,005	9	5,014
Nigeria	812		3,987		4,799
Zanzibar and Mafia	4	107	3,404	27	3,542
Seychelles			776		776
Gold Coast (Ghana)	177		204		381
Southern Rhodesia (Zimbabwe)			300		300
South Africa			22	1	23
Urundi (Burundi)				8	8
Total	13,118	9,617	691,241	218,411	932,387

Source: These are estimates constructed from data in G. W. T. Hodges, "African Manpower Statistics for the British Forces in East Africa, 1914–1918," *Journal of African History* 19, no. 1 (1978). For some functions, the statistics are unknown or unavailable.

men, from the Bangweulu Swamps and adjacent rivers, of whom 12,000 were actually registered in 1916–17. This linked the Luapula and Chambeshi rivers in a four-hundred mile water route. As in Nyasaland, the work was seasonal and busiest in the dry season, though it must also have been kept going during the rains. Food supplies could be brought in anywhere en route, and only once did the whole line have to be fed from base. . . . About 50,000 men from the east and north-east of Northern Rhodesia served as carriers: the 12,000 canoe men, 30,000 other men on lines of communication, and 8,000 with the fighting forces. Another 6,000 came from the north-western part of Northern Rhodesia.[74]

From 1914–1918, the British recruited almost one million followers and carriers, approximately 35 percent from German East Africa (Tanzania). These people fled German territory or were recruited after the British pacified the area. As shown in table 2, Nyasaland and the East Africa Protectorate (Kenya) together provided another 40 percent. Carriers accounted for about 74 percent of all followers, and casual labor was the second largest function (23 percent).

The noncombatant members of the Carriers Corps paid a high "blood tax"—in excess of 100,000 men or an average of 10 percent. Deaths were most numerous among those with longer terms of service, especially from the East African Protectorate (Kenya). The death rate for African troops was even higher, at 20 percent; more than ten thousand died of disease or were killed in action.[75] Sharing a common frontier with German East Africa, Nyasaland bore the brunt of war casualties. More than 200,000 Nyasalanders served as troops and followers, and it is estimated that war-related deaths accounted for more than 2 percent of the total adult male population.[76]

In absolute terms, however, the heaviest burden was borne by German East Africa [Tanzania]. In the first place, it was, of course, the scene of almost all the fighting. . . . In the second place, its menfolk suffered conscription by both sides. In March 1916, when German forces were at the peak of their strength, they included 12,100 askari and 45,000 carriers and other followers. By the end of the war, 1,798 German askari had been killed, while 2,847 had deserted. . . . In the third place, by the end of the war the British had recruited more carriers from German East Africa than from any other territory, even though they were only free to do so from early 1916.[77]

The overall human cost of the East African campaign was extremely high. The East African campaign, like the one in West Africa, was successful mainly due to the labor power provided by Africans from different parts of the continent. The vast majority of the carriers and followers were not educated; they were common laborers and peasants with little exposure to the world outside their kinship networks and villages. The fact that they shared experiences with other Africans, many from great distances, almost certainly raised individual and collective awareness. Exposure to other languages, religions, and the like made it clear, at the very least, that African people are diverse in physical appearance and culture. New knowledge, imaginings, and communities of consciousness were made possible for people with little or no schooling and previous geosocial mobility.

The World War I mobilization of Africans was the second major forced displacement across waters and boundaries to do other people's bidding. It did not take place over centuries, as did the slave trade, but in a shorter time frame it was devastating both to those who were displaced and to those who stayed behind. African males were the targeted population, although women were involved as well, particularly as carriers and casual laborers. Once again, families and communities were deprived of fathers, husbands, and sons for long periods of time and in many cases forever. Both displacements plundered Africa of its manpower wealth, its future: the young, the robust, and those in their most economically productive years. What are the cumulative effects of these major diaspora movements for black Africa today?

Over time, enslavement and forced displacement of Africans to the New World gave rise to new peoples and their social identities, along with innovative road maps for living and dying and imaginative cultural production to advance the new peoples' development while contributing to world civilization. The second major displacement also gave rise to new identity formations and new visions of freedom and justice. World War I mobilization not only fed into movements of African nationalism, but also planted the seeds of Pan-African communities of consciousness among everyday people.

THE SOUTH AFRICAN NATIVE LABOR CONTINGENT

The great Franco-British offensive on the Somme began on 1 July 1916, with the loss of nearly 60,000 British troops on the first day for a negligible gain of ground. . . . The First South African Brigade, all white troops, played its role there two weeks later. They were ordered to capture and hold Delville Wood and in six days and five nights of fierce fighting they obeyed their orders. The Brigade numbered 3,153 when the attack commenced. Only 143 came out of what was left of the wood for the first roll call when they were relieved. The final muster on 21 July was 780.

While the Somme battle was still in progress and South Africa mourned its dead of Delville Wood, the British government asked the South African prime minister . . . to recruit ten thousand black troops to serve in labour battalions under British command in France.

On 7 September 1916 [Louis] Botha [the South African prime minister] agreed to the British request.[78]

The insatiable need for manpower led to the formation of the SANLC and another chapter in the use of Africans to meet the needs of their oppressors. The conditions of service and displacement bore likenesses to slavery, as did the racial division of labor and the culture of violence and control. The legacies remain.

It was agreed that all expenses related to SANLC would be covered by Britain, and the South African government made stipulations to which the needy British acceded: SANLC would be commanded by white South Africans and would be kept segregated from other military units and the civilian population in France. White South Africans were not enthusiastic about SANLC. Aside from the view that Africans should not be involved in Europe's "family" warfare, they were fearful that blacks might be contaminated by European social ideas and return with a heightened level of consciousness and desire for fundamental change. The ideological framework underlying the entire system of apartheid would be imperiled.

Raising the Contingent

The recruitment of black South Africans was not successful initially, and the government resorted to "compulsion through the agency of the chiefs."[79] White farmers and business interests, especially the Chamber of Mines, were not supportive out of concern for their own labor needs. It is significant that among the enlistees were a disproportionate number of well-educated Africans, such as teachers, interpreters, clergymen, and clerks, who apparently saw an opportunity for self-improvement, education, and future political rewards in recognition of their loyalty. "The majority, however, were young men who had grown up, with little opportunity for education, herding cattle in the tribal areas and working for money—very little money—in the mines, on white-owned farms, and as unskilled laborers in the towns."[80]

Britain initially requested ten thousand men but in January 1917 raised the number to forty thousand, a goal to which they never came close. Between September 1916 and January 1918, around twenty-five thousand blacks were enlisted to serve under the British Imperial War Council as noncombatant laborers in France. Roughly twenty-one thousand (84 percent) served overseas. The Cape Colored Labor Corps was also raised during this period.[81]

The men recruited for SANLC came not only from South Africa but also from the British protectorates of Basutoland, Bechuanaland, and Swaziland, presently referred to as BLS (Botswana, Lesotho, and Swaziland). A small number also came from Southern Rhodesia (Zimbabwe) and Nyasaland (Malawi).[82] As shown in table 3, Africans from the Transvaal comprised the largest number of enlistees, followed by men from the Cape area; and Swaziland provided the least. It is odd that the Transvaal, much less populous than the Transkei or the Eastern Cape, generated more than half the recruits. Perhaps economic conditions account for its disproportional representation. "At the time of the recruiting drive [the Transvaal] experienced

Table 3. SANLC Enlistees by Number and Origin, 1916–1918

ORIGIN	NUMBER	PERCENTAGE
Transvaal	13,500	54.00
Cape Province	7,000	28.00
Natal	1,500	6.00
Basutoland	1,500	6.00
Orange Free State	800	3.00
Bechuanaland	600	2.00
Swaziland	100	1.00
Total	25,000	100.00

Source: Constructed from data in Norman Clothier, *Black Valour: The South African Native Labour Contingent, 1916–1918, and the Sinking of the Mendi* (Pietermaritzburg: University of Natal Press, 1987), 150.

an intense drought . . . the worst . . . in 26 years [which] severely undermined the self-sufficiency of African peasants dependent on agriculture. Moreover, other avenues of employment were restricted. . . . Joining the SANLC meant that poverty stricken Africans were at least assured of an income, part of which could be remitted to their destitute families." In addition, peasants in the area were under tighter control of their chiefs, who were under greater control of the apartheid government. Hence, the pressure to enlist was greater than in some other regions.[83]

The recruits signed a twelve-month contract as general laborers at an entry rate of three pounds a month plus. They also received "rail fares and food to the Depot at Capetown, and rations, quarters and medical attendance until discharged at the Depot at Capetown on return there."[84]

Mapping the Racial Hierarchy for the Western Front

To maintain ideological order and segregation, the South African state developed a blueprint for racial structure on the front. Differences ranged from food, wages, and military dress, to codified restrictions enforced by white officers, NCOs, and other military personnel, many of whom "knew the ways of the natives" due to their former service in the South African Native Affairs Department.

INFERIOR DRESS—INFERIOR RANK

Social status is denoted in many ways, from job and income to education and lifestyle, and one indicator is quality and type of dress. Under slavery, especially in Latin America, for instance, European sumptuary laws were often applied by church and state to free mulatto and colored women; codes of dress, fabric, or even the type of veil to be worn at mass were meant to reinforce their inferiority to white women. The South African government conveyed its view of the low status of the men of the SANLC through the quality of their uniforms, which were badly made, shoddy looking, and of poor material. SANLC issues were variously described as "atrocious," "vile-smelling," "cotton velveteen," "brown corduroy," and "only fit for convicts."[85]

Rank and promotion were other areas of inequality. Africans could reach only the level of lance corporal. "Initially, blacks could be promoted to the rank of sergeant—called 'chief induna' so as not to embarrass white sergeants—but as these appointments were in terms of authority on par with those of their white counterparts, they soon ceased." Similarly, white chaplains held the rank of captain, whereas African chaplains held no military rank.[86]

THE RULES OF ENGAGEMENT

To limit contacts by Africans with the French and military laborers from other parts of the world, specific rules of segregation were established. The list that follows is only partial.[87]

1. The Contingent will be administered in accordance with military law under the Army Act by white South African officers appointed by the government of South Africa.
2. The most suitable work for the Contingent would be quarrying, road-making, forestry and the like because it would be easier to maintain segregation in such work.
3. Natives must not be employed in the fighting zones.
4. Natives must be segregated.
5. Natives will be housed in Nissen huts in compounds with barbed wire enclosures except in towns where corrugated-iron enclosures would suffice. Fences are to be six feet high with barbed wire running along the top.
6. Natives are not permitted outside the camps except when accompanied by an officer or NCO.
7. Natives are not permitted to enter premises where liquor is sold, and others are forbidden from purchasing intoxicating liquors on their behalf.

8. Natives are not permitted to enter or to be entertained in the houses of Europeans.

9. Natives are not to be trusted with white women. Any Native found wandering about without a pass and not under the escort of a white officer or NCO is to be returned to his unit under guard and/or handed over to the military police.

10. Care should be taken to prevent unauthorized persons from entering the Camp or conversing with Natives to prevent familiarity between Europeans and Natives, as this is subversive to discipline.

11. Disciplinary measurers will be dealt with within the Corps; a Native prison will be staffed with Native wardens.

12. Two Native hospitals will be provided, one at Dieppe, France, with 500 beds and a second at Boulogne with 200 beds. All personnel will be provided by South Africa.

13. Natives will be buried in the same cemeteries and in the same manner as British soldiers, but separate plots will be provided. Natives should be accorded a funeral, however, no European troops or firing parties may attend.

The numerous restrictions were viewed by other colonialists as an opportunity to study the effectiveness of these standards of social control. SANLC also was considered a social experiment that could be useful within South Africa after the war.

> Once the decision had been taken to send the S.A.N.L.C. to Europe a number of missionaries, Native Affairs Department officials and others concerned with "the native problem" realized fairly quickly that the scheme provided an ideal opportunity for testing—in what would, it was hoped, be carefully controlled conditions—the practicability and effects of the implementation of certain segregatory devices of social control; the lessons and results of this experiment could possibility be utilized in South Africa itself. It was perceived as a test . . . of the use to which the scheme could be put, and hence also the very frequent use of the terms "experiment" or "social experiment."[88]

Deployment and Work in France

Upon arrival in France, the men of SANLC loaded and unloaded trucks, trains, and ships; carried out road maintenance; built and repaired railways and roads; and cleared rail yards. They worked in petrol supply, Royal Engineer stores, and French forests, where they cut timber for construction. "Most, however, were employed in the French harbours of Le Havre, Rouen, and Dieppe where they unloaded ammunition, food supplies and timber, and transferred these to trains bound for the front." Some of the men with experience in South African mines did blasting in quarries. A small number also worked as clerks, interpreters, and hospital orderlies.[89]

When the first two battalions of the contingent arrived in December 1916, they were placed under the unified Directorate of Labour formed by the British Army, which made it difficult for South African officers to enforce "grand apartness." The directorate assigned some SANLC companies to forward areas, and German shelling resulted in some casualties. The Germans, aware of the SANLC camp near Dieppe, bombed it and dropped propaganda leaflets. One message declared that Germans hated black people and did not know what they were doing in a European war. Moreover, wherever the Africans were, they [Germans] would find them and destroy them.[90]

Some SANLC companies in areas of heavy shelling allegedly petitioned headquarters for relocation in compliance with their contract, which specified no employment in fighting zones. Others preferred to remain near the front, apparently because they did not want their loyalty and courage questioned. Eventually the companies were relocated after their segregated enclosures were built. It is not clear how much South African officers were involved in this effort, but they were quite supportive of the move, not out of concern for lives but because the new camps were under their control.[91]

Fighting on the Racial Front: The War within the War

The men of SANLC did not accept the constraints of segregation without a struggle. They were the only military laborers who lived in a barbed wire "prison" without free access to the world around them. Prisoners usually find ways to manipulate and resist the totalizing nature of institutionalized confinement. Members of SANLC learned to work the system, and their efforts to confront the inequality they faced on a daily basis were not without costs.[92] For example, on 23 July 1917, the "Charlie Incident" occurred.

In one of the camps dissatisfaction with the restrictions of the compound system exploded into violence that left thirteen Africans dead. An African (whose name is given only as "Charlie"), having finished working on a night shift, wanted to do his washing outside the compound. The officer in charge, however, ordered him to bring the water into the compound and do his washing there. Refusing to do this, Charlie was put under arrest, but the officer responsible, Captain Barrett, a chaplain, refused to give an explanation to Charlie's colleagues for his action. They then tried to release Charlie by force, and as a result were surrounded by white officers and N.C.O.s and fired upon, thirteen of their number being killed.[93]

In another instance, the men expressed a grievance over their food, which during the early months in France was acceptable and then deteriorated. Complaints through proper channels were ignored, so the men called a meeting and requested the attendance of officers. Many spoke out, but the compelling comments of Lance-Corporal Stimela Jason Jingoes drew the ire of the whites:

> My people, we must not be surprised: in South Africa, Bantu are often treated badly. I'm not surprised that this is starting here as well. We have brought that system with us.
>
> Look at the confusion that has been caused by the word *Native;* this word has been written on our lavatories so that White and Blacks need not use the same ones. But in doing this they have forgotten that here in France it is the French people who are *natives,* and they are white, and they are now using our lavatories, to the utter confusion of the South Africans here.
>
> We Bantu are often treated like dogs here by the white people from home, yet they forget that we are all here at war against a common enemy. Actually I made a mistake in saying that they treat us like dogs, because usually they treat their dogs very well indeed. They ignore the fact that we have left South Africa for the moment. We are in Europe, and we are at war, and we were promised decent treatment if we would fight the Germans.[94]

Jingoes was arrested and tried before a wounded captain recently reassigned from the front lines. Jingoes stated his case: "Sir, our meals have been changed from the usual rations to mealie-meal, which we are given from morning to night, sir, Monday to Monday, and the mealie-meal we get is bad. There are weevils in it. It is for you, sir, to judge where justice lies in this matter." The captain confirmed the truth of these assertions and then asked the white accusers—a chaplain, the sergeant-major, and the platoon sergeant—why they did not investigate. Their response: "As Natives we did not think they were telling the truth." The charges were dismissed, and the men of SANLC returned to having meals of meat, potatoes, rice, and bread.[95]

On a voyage back to South Africa on the SS *Militiades,* ten Africans were accused of mutiny on the high seas in November 1917. One man was killed, another was wounded, and eight were placed under armed guard. They were tried in Cape Town and sentenced to ten to twelve years in prison. Their case was reviewed, however, and they were released in May 1918.[96]

Persistent actions against SANLC segregation became a major concern for the senior officers, who realized they could not maintain the imprisonment policy indefinitely. In a confidential letter to the Union government, a high-ranking white officer described the men as resentful of their isolation and restrictions in comparison to other military laborers; they were characterized as "unruly" and as manifesting intemperate "nasty" attitudes. The South African government decided to end the "experiment" in January 1918.[97] The members of the contingent stayed in France until 1918, when most returned to South Africa.

At home, government officials praised the contingent for outstanding service, and British war medals were recommended for ninety-two men. Awards were given to white South African officers and NCOs as well as to Africans from Basutoland, Bechuanaland, and Swaziland. It is noteworthy that no black South Africans received medals, and war disablement pensions provided to white ex-servicemen were not given to Africans.[98]

Paying the Blood Price

A number of SANLC men who survived the war never returned home. A few went AWOL in France, and others went to England and West Africa when their ship put into ports in England, Nigeria (Lagos), and Sierra Leone (Freetown). As for those who died, estimates range around 1,100 among the 21,000 who served in SANLC; more than one-third of the deaths were due to tuberculosis and other pulmonary diseases.[99]

The greatest loss of lives occurred when the transport ship SS *Mendi*, en route to France in February 1917, sank within twenty-five minutes of colliding with another vessel in the English Channel, and 625 men perished. Of the 802 Africans on board, official reports stated 607 were "lost at sea." Some estimates put the number of casualties at 615.[100] On board were "Kroo boys" from West Africa, working as stewards, some of whom may have been among those lost.[101]

Among the black South Africans who died in World War I, some are buried in military cemeteries in France, others in England and Sierra Leone. Even the bodies recovered from the *Mendi* are widely dispersed. "Eight blacks were buried in the [U.K.] Milton cemetery at Portsmouth, one at Hastings, one at Littlehampton, one at Wimereux in France, south of Calais, and two in Holland (one at Wassenaar and one at Bergen-op-Zoom)."[102]

Transformation of Minds, Memories, and Activism

The SANLC had an effect on the politics and culture of South Africa. Many of the veterans and their families were participants or major cultural workers in the drive for liberation from the system of apartheid. For the men who went overseas, exposure to a world beyond their homeland opened their minds and imaginations to the prospects of personal and collective change. Before reaching France, transport ships stopped in Sierra Leone, which brought black South Africans into contact with the Krios and indigenous people of that British protectorate. "Marks Mokwena was particularly impressed by the fact that in Africa there were 'pure black negroes of very high educational attainments equal to that of the best Europeans.'" Once in France, the contingent was visited by French dignitaries, including Blaise Diagne of Senegal, who was a recruiting commissioner from 1917 to 1918. The SANLC men were impressed and wondered whether "such things [could] ever happen in our country."[103]

One experience with long-term consequences was the education provided in France by African chaplains and teachers who were part of the contingent. They offered instruction in reading, writing, mathematics, geography, and language translation. There is some evidence that the evening classes and the larger experience of passage made a difference for a number of the men. A. Masotho and Tsebo Macholela studied medicine in Edinburgh after their service ended. S. M. Bennett Ncwana, who benefited from the evening classes, became quite active in the trade union movement and initiated a publication titled *The Black Man*. Other activists in South African politics and trade unionism were Ben Nyombolo; Marks Mokwena, who was a *Mendi* survivor; and Doyle Modiakgotla, who witnessed the shooting of the thirteen men during the Charlie Incident. These examples do not mean that all SANLC veterans were in the forefront of the protracted struggle in South Africa, but some used their broadened knowledge and awareness to speak out against wrongs, participate in peasant and working class actions, and help end white domination.[104]

Jason Jingoes, in his autobiography, reflects on what it was like to travel abroad:

> We were aware, when we returned, that we were different from the other people at home. Our behavior, as we showed the South Africans, was something more than they expected from a Native, more like what was expected among them of a white man. We had copied the manners and customs of Europeans, and not only copied: we lived them, acted those customs right through.
>
> Well, we did not think of ourselves as white people, but we had learned many things since we left home and in some ways it was not easy to settle down.
>
> We tried to keep our memories alive, and our determination to return to France by

corresponding with our friends. . . . we corresponded for many years, but at last we lost touch.[105]

SANLC also served as an example. Speaking against the pass system at a meeting of the Bantu Women's League of Johannesburg in January 1918, one woman made the point that Africans had joined the forces in France but were still being killed and disrespected at home. Similar thoughts were expressed by the Transvaal Native National Congress at Vrededorp in April 1919 and by the deputation sent by the African Native National Congress (ANNC) to England in the same year.[106]

New traditions, folklore, sites, and memories were created as a result of SANLC. In the British military cemetery at Argue-la-Bataille near Dieppe, an engraved stone honors men of the contingent who died in France. The Holybrook Memorial in Southhampton, England, pays homage to those lost with the sinking of the *Mendi*.[107] "Smaller memorials appeared in South Africa—one in front of the Town Hall in Umtata has inscribed on it the names of those Africans from the Transkei who died in France."[108] Other memorials are located throughout South Africa and in other places from which SANLC men were recruited. In South Africa, these include Mendi Road in Port Elizabeth, a Mendi Memorial Creche for African babies in Queenstown, and tree plantings in Pietersburg with plaques naming the dead. Also, there is a war memorial in Maseru, Lesotho.[109]

The SANLC dead are not mentioned at the National War Memorial in South Africa. Sixty-eight years after the end of World War I, however, Africans were finally paid homage at the South African National War Memorial at the new museum in Delville Wood, France. In 1986, "a bronze plaque depicting the sinking of the *Mendi* was included among the mural decorations. . . . The Contingent's roll of honor was also placed there."[110]

Most important for black South Africans at the time was the loss of more than six hundred men in the *Mendi* sinking on 21 February 1917. This disaster became a focal point in the recollections of the veterans and other blacks throughout the Union of South Africa. A Mendi Memorial Club, started by a survivor, S. M. Bennet Ncwana, was at the forefront of annual countrywide observances, which included parades, religious observances, speeches, scholarships, music, and dance. In 1928 the Association of African Ministers passed the following resolution to maintain, in the forefront of African consciousness, the symbolic significance of those who made the ultimate sacrifice. The political nature of the resolution echoes the early expectations of the ANNC that if blacks served king and country at war, then they should expect postwar benefits of freedom and a more inclusive society.

To observe the *Mendi* Day of 21st February on which day all members assembled in solemn and reverent remembrance of the deeds of valour and sacrifice of the men of their race who went to serve their King and Country, hoping and believing that in the distribution of the spoils of war their compatriots and relatives may share in the blessings of peace and the opportunities guaranteed by the successful arms of the Allies.[111]

Into the 1950s annual *Mendi* observances provided a way for Africans to speak to the broader issues of racial oppression and the need to end apartheid. These yearly events were carefully monitored by the white minority government, which actively discouraged their continuation by harassing organizers and creating legal obstacles to the observance. As members of the contingent aged and died, memories began to fade, and the event is now almost forgotten. In his poem, "The Sinking of the *Mendi*," S. E. K. Mqhayi pays homage to the memory of "you who died for Africa."

> It was not for the King by any loyal tie,
> It was not for Britain you went out to die.
>
> . . .
>
> And when you left behind these hills, this earth,
> Your backs turned to the rivers of your birth,
> Black men of our blood, we said this thing—
> 'On that far off field you are our offering.'[112]

The British West Indies Regiment

For well over a year, the British Colonial Office and the War Office cogitated over whether to use black West Indians in the war. There were questions about the sources of funds to support these contingents, including pay, separation allowances, and pensions. But a considerable amount of discussion revolved around racist beliefs: this was a white man's war; blacks should not fight against white forces; blacks lack the intelligence and skills to become good soldiers; suitable only for work in hot climates, blacks would not be of much use in Europe. History belied these arguments.

At the outbreak of World War I, West Indians were serving in the armed forces in Africa. The British West India Regiment, formed in 1795, was used by the British in defense of colonial territories in the Caribbean and Africa, including the Ashanti War of 1823. Several battalions were deployed in the early stages of the Great War against the Germans in the Cameroons and in East Africa.[113] Due to the insatiable need for manpower, the British formed additional contingents of West Indians in April 1915.

The new entity was called the British West Indies Regiment (BWIR). "By the end of 1915 some 2,448 men and 48 officers had arrived in Britain and two battalions were ready for the field. . . . The 1st and 2nd battalions were representative of the entire West Indies; the 3rd, with a few exceptions, was composed mainly of the third Jamaican contingent."[114] The Bermuda Voluntary Artillery of Black Soldiers also served, as did recruits from Trinidad, British Guiana, Grenada, Barbados, the Bahamas, British Honduras, St. Lucia, St. Vincent, and the Leeward Islands. During the war eleven West Indian battalions were formed, comprised of 15,204 enlisted men and 397 officers. The largest number of volunteers were supplied by Jamaica— 9,977, or 66 percent; they were under the command of officers of "unmixed European blood" or at the very least not more than "one-sixteenth" of "one-thirty-second" Negro.[115]

The BWIR served in Egypt, Jordan, Palestine, France, England, Italy, and the East African theater near Mombasa, Kenya. With the exception of two battalions involved in fighting the Turks in the Middle East, neither the Bermudians nor the West Indians were actively engaged in combat against Europeans. Rather, they were employed as skilled and unskilled workers in "labor" battalions, to provide the infrastructure for "White fighting men"; they dug trenches, carried ammunition, loaded and unloaded ships, and the like. Some who were more skilled worked for the Royal Engineers as electricians, mechanics, and engineers.

> The battalions in France were attached to the British Expeditionary Force and were employed in all the main operations that had taken place, including the battles of the Somme, Arras, Messines and Ypres. Their work consisted chiefly of handling ammunition at the railheads and carrying it up to the batteries both day and night, digging cable trenches and emplacements for guns, often under heavy shell fire occasioning heavy casualties. Sometimes detachments were involved in loading and unloading at the docks at Boulogne, and in the construction of light railways. The 3rd battalion was in France from September 16 up to the armistice, working through both the winters of 1916–17 and 1917–18. Other battalions, like the 4th, spent one winter in France, and the other winter between France and Taranto Italy, where they worked on the quays in construction, unloading stores, and loading lighters for ships. The black contingent from Bermuda also served in the same capacity on the ammunition dumps for some time with the Canadian Corps subsequent to the capture of Vimy Ridge, May 1917.[116]

The BWIR performed gallantly and was often under heavy fire from the Germans; many men were decorated. According to Joseph, the BWIR had 1,953 casualties during World War I, 85 percent of whom died primarily from pulmonary illnesses. Another 185 were killed in action or by related wounds, and 697 were wounded.[117] Moreover, a number of black seamen lost their lives, including 1,000 who were shipped from Cardiff, England, and were killed at sea, plus another 400 who died from exposure after they were rescued.[118]

The presence of black soldiers in Europe led to a number of racial incidents during the war and after the armistice. For example, wounded soldiers, mainly of the BWIR, were attacked by South African whites convalescing at Belmont Road Military Auxiliary Hospital in Liverpool. Many BWIR survivors of the war remained in Britain and may have been attacked during the race riots of 1919, which erupted in Barry, Cardiff, Glasgow, Hull, Liverpool, London, Manchester, Newport, and Tyneside.[119]

Insurrection and Mobilization

A notable insurrection occurred at the BWIR's Cimino camp near Taranto, Italy, in December 1918. Immediately after the armistice, eight BWIR battalions were moved to the camp, where racial inequality continued, and abuse and humiliation remained part of their lives in the service of king and empire. The men were already upset by their lack of opportunity for advancement in rank, along with ineligibility for pay increases and other benefits. They received medical care in segregated "native facilities," and the white South African camp commander believed they should be treated as "niggers," not as British troops. The men also resented being assigned tasks normally given to civilian workers, such as washing dirty linen and cleaning latrines, not just their own but some belonging to members of the Italian corps.[120]

In early December, men of the 9th Battalion attacked officers and assaulted the unit commander. At the same time, 180 sergeants submitted petitions to the secretary of state for colonies regarding racist regulations that restricted their access to resources and benefits. "The outbreak continued for several days; men refused to work, a shooting and a bombing occurred, a 'generally insubordinate spirit prevailed.'"[121] The War Office sent a machine gun company and a battalion of white troops to suppress the revolt. Their orders were to disarm the BWIR, repatriate them to their homes in the Caribbean, and impose restrictions on the remaining three BWIR battalions, which had not yet arrived in Italy for demobilization. Leaders of the insurrection were arrested, charged with mutiny, and given prison sentences ranging from three to five years; one was given twenty years, and one who led a subsequent revolt was executed.[122]

An important development was the Caribbean League for the promotion of closer relations among West Indians.

The League was formed on 17 December 1918 by sergeants of the Regiment [BWIR] at a secret meeting in the sergeants' mess, at Cimino camp. At the three or four meetings held in December and early January, they discussed *inter alia* the general grievances experienced during the war, particularly the appointment of white non-commissioned officers in place of black non-commissioned officers. The demand was made that the black man should have freedom to govern himself and that force should be used if necessary to attain that object. Also a general strike by workers for higher wages was urged after demobilization.[123]

Although the league did not last long, it illustrates that a pan-nationalist sentiment was behind the "mutinous spirit" at Cimino, and it presaged a rise of black consciousness and anticolonialism in the diaspora. Moreover, the activism of the BWIR forced the British to review their policies, which resulted in some retroactive pay and benefits.

BLACK AMERICANS: "MAKING THE WORLD SAFE FOR DEMOCRACY"

When the United States declared war on Germany, at least a dozen African Americans were serving in the French Foreign Legion, assigned to the Marching Regiment with the Moroccans. Among them were Eugene Bullard and Bob Scanlon. In 1916 the two men were assigned to the 170th Infantry of the French Army and took part in a major assault against the Germans at Verdun. The legendary Bullard was promoted to corporal and received the French Order of the Day, equivalent to honorable mention for the croix de guerre, for helping other men when he was wounded. Bullard went on to flight school and joined the French Flying Corps. He is credited with destroying and inflicting heavy damage on German aircraft and flew for France until November 1917, when he was discharged for a disagreement with a senior officer. Bullard remained in France, where he entered the music business and fought again for France in World War II; he eventually returned to the United States after being wounded and smuggled out by the American consul. He died in New York City in 1961.[124]

When the United States entered the war on 6 April 1917 it used the slogan "Make the World Safe for Democracy." At the time, twenty thousand African Americans were on active duty in the U.S. Army and in the National Guard: "The Eighth Illinois, the Fifteenth New York, the separate battalions of the District of Columbia and of

Ohio, and the separate companies of Maryland, Connecticut, Massachusetts, and Tennessee."[125] The 24th and 25th Infantry Regiments and the 9th and 10th Cavalry Regiments did not see combat in Europe but were given assignments along the Mexican border or sent to the Philippines and Hawaii. The War Department dismissed, forced the retirement of, or reassigned high-ranking black officers of these units. The prevailing view of the U.S. military and politicians was that "colored" officers were unfit for major leadership positions and should be limited mostly to the ranks of first or second lieutenant. Colonel Charles Young, the highest ranking black in the U.S. Army, was forced to retire, and Captain Benjamin Oliver Davis was assigned to duty in the Philippines with the 9th Calvary, temporarily promoted to lieutenant colonel.[126]

Although the 24th and 25th Infantry Regiments were well trained, it is believed the War Department was fearful of them and how they might react to white officers. Moreover, a battalion of the 24th, after extended abuse by white civilians in Texas, armed themselves and on 23 August 1917 killed fifteen whites, including four policemen. Four men of the 24th were also killed, and twenty-one whites were wounded. There were several courts-martial. In one case, fifty-four men of the 24th were convicted of mutiny and murder: Forty-one were sentenced to life imprisonment, and thirteen were hanged on 22 December 1917. At subsequent trials, sixteen death sentences were handed down, six of which were carried out; the remainder were reduced to life in prison.[127]

Black Americans were eager to serve as enlisted men and as officers. "Before the end of the Selective Service enlistments, 2,290,55 blacks had registered, 367,000 of whom were called into the service."[128] The situation for officers was quite different, with strong resistance coming from white civil and government sectors. The NAACP made the case and received strong support from the black community through mass meetings and activism by college students, including a Central Committee of college men established at Howard University (Washington, D.C.) in May 1917. Eventually Congress approved the establishment of a segregated training camp for black Americans. This was not well received and was strongly denounced by sectors of the black community. In any case

On October 15, 1917, at Fort Des Moines, Iowa, 639 African Americans were commissioned—106 captains, 329 first lieutenants, and 204 second lieutenants. Later, at nonsegregated camps and in the field, other blacks received commissions in the army. At colleges and high schools throughout the country blacks prepared to become officer candidates and to serve the army in a variety of ways in the Students' Training Corps and the Reserve Officers Training Corps.

While African Americans were barred altogether from the marines and permitted to serve in the navy only in the most menial capacities, they served in almost every branch of the army except the pilot section of the aviation corps. After a long struggle they were permitted to join units of coast and field artillery. They were in the calvary, infantry, engineer corps, signal corps, medical corps, hospital and ambulance corps, veterinary corps, sanitary and ammunition trains, stevedore regiments, labor battalions, and depot brigades. Blacks also served as regimental adjutants, judge advocates, chaplains, intelligence officers, chemists, clerks, surveyors, drafters, auto repairers, motor truck operators, and mechanics.[129]

There were no black women in military service during World War I; they were not accepted by the Army Nurses Corps or the Red Cross. The Nurses Corps registered blacks after the armistice in December 1918 but then "logically" rejected them, on grounds that no black women were in the Army Medical Corps.[130] There were, however, four or five black women who worked in the European Theater. Three of them came under the auspices of the YMCA: Addie Waites Hunton, a former college dean; Kathryn Johnson; and Mrs. James Curtis, widow of a former ambassador to Liberia. During the last months of the war, pianist Helen Hagan was permitted to entertain the soldiers. Hunton, Curtis, and Johnson established a canteen for black American soldiers as they struggled to meet the needs of the men. "We had fitted out the first reading and reception room for the soldiers in our area . . . this room became known for its Chat Hour that came to fill it to overflow on Sundays at the twilight hour. Somehow it came to us that this was a lonely time for men."[131] Given the varied backgrounds of the men, a number of activities were initiated, including discussions of music, literature, the arts, politics and race relations; literacy courses; and assistance to help a few men to attend French universities after the war. During an influenza epidemic, they converted their living quarters into an infirmary for the men.[132] Hunton and Johnson coauthored a book about their experiences, *Two Colored Women with the American Expeditionary Forces*.[133]

War Service

The War Department formed two black divisions comprised of draftees, National Guardsmen, and volunteers. The 92nd Division—made up of the 365th, 366th, 367th, and 368th regiments—had artillery, signal, engineer, and machine gun components. Unlike other soldiers in the American Expeditionary Forces (AEF), the men of the 92nd were trained in different locations and not brought together until they arrived in France. White civilians protested the presence of too many black soldiers in their towns, so training sites were dispersed. More than fifty officers were demoted or reassigned because of their race and replaced by whites.[134] The 93rd, under black commanders with military experience, was composed of the 369th, 370th, 371st, and 372nd regiments. It was formed with "colored" National Guard units from Connecticut, the District of Columbia, Illinois, Maryland, Massachusetts, New York, and Ohio. These regiments arrived in France between late 1917 and mid-1918.

According to Astor, 404,308 African Americans served in the armed forces during World War I. Around 42,000 were combat soldiers, about 90 percent of whom were in the two infantry divisions, and the U.S. Navy enrolled 5,328 nonwhites in noncombat service and support jobs.[135] The rest, like the Africans and West Indians, were mainly laborers. They "built roads and bridges, loaded and unloaded tons of cargo, buried the dead, and assembled automobiles, trucks, ships, and airplanes. The work was very tedious and was completed under duress in less than desirable conditions. Most . . . were supervised, primarily and often brutally, by southern white officers."[136]

The 92nd and 93rd had different combat experiences and outcomes: The latter was under French command, and the former was under AEF command. Although serving under the French had its own problems, the 93rd had an honorable combat record; the men served alongside thousands of Africans who either were part of the Army of France or were incorporated into French divisions. The 369th was the first U.S. regiment placed into combat and spent a record number of days on the front. The 370th, which fought with French divisions at St. Mihiel and the Argonne Forest, captured Mt. Dessinges and other occupied territories, including places in Belgium, and held a sector of Canal L'Oise et Aisne without help.[137]

> The 371st and the 372nd Regiments [of the 93rd division] played vital roles in the defense of the Meuse-Argonne region. The 369th performed admirably in the fighting north of the Oise-Ardennes canal. It would be awarded more citations than any other regiment in the AEF. The first American unit to reach the Rhine River, the 369th fought for 191 consecutive days "without losing a trench, giving an inch or surrendering a prisoner." No other American unit served as long a span of nonstop combat. . . . The people of France awarded the 369th as a unit and 170 individual members its highest military honor, the Croix de Guerre. The 370th and 371st would receive the Croix as well.
>
> The 92nd Division's star did not shine so brilliantly. Remaining under AEF control, its men saw little action, although the 1st Battalion of the 367th Regiment was the recipient of a Croix de Guerre. The division did, however, fight capably in the war's final battle, the decisive American assault on the Hindenburg line. It is clear that the uninspiring

overall performance of the 92nd did not stem from any shortcomings inherent in the African-American fighting man. It was, rather, the result of a racist philosophy that pervaded the psyches of the military establishment. The 92nd had a high quotient of draftees in its ranks, unlike the 93rd, three-quarters of whose members were National Guardsmen. The 93rd had high-ranking black officers, the officers of the 92nd were mainly Southern whites. These commanders, furious over their assignment to a black unit, constantly and vehemently reviled their men as badly motivated cowards who were a detriment to overall morale.[138]

Jazz to Europe

There were two popular black military musical groups in France during the Great War. One was the 350th Field Artillery Band, directed by J. T. Baynum. The other, the 369th Regimental Band, led by Lt. James Reese Europe, is credited with being the first group of musicians to introduce jazz to Europe. Its drum major, Sgt. Noble Sissle, later became well known on Broadway as a singer, conductor, and composer. The band played for American and French troops in camps and hospitals and for civilians behind the lines and in Paris. Before entering the service, Lt. Europe conducted syncopated orchestras in New York, served as a musical director for Broadway shows, and gave concerts in Carnegie Hall. "Once the members of a French military band, unable to believe such strange jazz sounds could be produced by ordinary instruments, offered to exchange brasses and woodwinds with the Negro band. The Negroes played just as well on the French instruments, but the puzzled French soldiers could not produce jazz on the American ones."[139]

Anticipation and Reality

From beginning to end of the war, black men and women were not wanted in the armed forces. Only the insatiable need for manpower led the U.S. military to turn to the "reserve army" of black Americans. For them military service meant jobs, and they registered in large numbers—close to half a million. Blacks constituted a little less than 10 percent of the U.S. population but supplied 13 percent of inductees.[140] Also, there was the hope for a brighter future, for a trickle down effect from making the world safe for democracy. In other words, their service, loyalty, and sacrifices would bring benefits to them in the military and at home once the war ended. The reality was different. Even as they trained in various parts of the United States, blacks were rejected and attacked by white civilians and mistreated by white officers. They were rigidly segregated while fighting in Europe, and the Germans played upon this in a propaganda campaign. "In September 1918 Germans scattered circulars over the lines to demoralize . . . black troops, encouraging them not to be deluded into think- ing that they were fighting for humanity and democracy." The circulars asked whether they enjoyed the same rights as whites, were treated as second-class citizens, could eat in the same restaurants as whites. "Is lynching a lawful proceeding in a democratic country?"[141] There is no evidence of black desertions, but this propa- ganda reinforced what the men already knew.

The answers to the Germans' questions were vividly provided by the actions of white commanding officers. At the end of the war, as members of the 92nd Division waited at Brest for transport home, they were ordered to load coal for the boilers of the USS *Virginia*. The vessel's captain was pleased with their excellent work and wrote their company commander to express his thanks and praise for the exceptional dis- cipline and conduct of the men. Yet, he refused to provide passage for them, to main- tain the tradition of the no "colored troops" on his ship. In another case, the USS *Siboney* was carrying 399 whites and one black. The officers' mess could only seat 200, so meals were served in three shifts: "To maintain separation, the Navy served 200 whites, then the remaining 199, and finally the lone black officer, shunned throughout the trip by all but a single white man, ate at a third seating."[142]

The experience of the three black women YMCA workers, Hunton, Johnson, and Curtis, was not different. For their return trip:

They were placed on a deck below the white women. At meal time, they were given a secluded, poorly-ventilated part of the dining room. . . . When Kathryn Johnson protested, she was told that Southern workers on board the ship would feel insulted if the Negro workers ate in the same section as they, and that the Negroes "need not expect any such treatment as had been given them by the French."[143]

Racial Stigmatization and Representation

It is estimated that at the signing of the armistice, 750 black soldiers had been killed in action and more than 5,000 were wounded.[144] Although the valor of the African Americans was recognized by the French, the white and largely southern U.S. mili- tary remained strongly racist. During the downsizing and restructuring of the armed forces after the war, many typical opinions wound up in a study called the "Organization and Training of Negroes" at the General Staff College of Washington,

D.C. Some of the pseudo-scientific findings were that blacks make excellent soldiers but only under the command of whites; black soldiers have no confidence in their leaders, who lack moral integrity, so blacks should not be commissioned as officers; and because darkness terrifies blacks, especially during this time the capable and aggressive leadership of whites is required. A major conclusion of the study was: "The Negro is mentally inferior to the white in general. . . . In childhood the Negro is sharp, intelligent but on approaching adulthood change sets in as the brain fails to develop. Education cannot create mental powers, it can only develop that which is innate."[145]

Such racist thinking underlay the 1919 War Department decision to bar the enlistment of nonwhites except for those who were already soldiers in the regular army; moreover, those admitted could enter only the infantry, not the Air Force, Navy, or the Marine Corps. Blacks who re-enlisted drove trucks, worked security details, or groomed horses and tended stables at West Point for the cadets and staff.[146]

French Recognition at the End of the Twentieth Century

When African Americans returned to the United States, some—like the 369th—received a celebratory welcome in New York City. Black soldiers were excluded from the victory parade welcoming *all* returning American servicemen. In early 1999, the French consul-general to the United States, Richard Duque, presented his country's Legion of Honor medals to three thousand veterans of World War I to commemorate the 80th anniversary of the war's end. On 22 February 1999, two black Americans received their award at the French Consulate in New York: Herbert Young, age 112, and Robert Thomas, age 103, both residents of Manhattan. Young, born in Kingston, Jamaica, in 1886 and brought to the United States as a baby, died on 27 April 1999.[147] During a 28 June 1999, ceremony in Boston, Thomas Davis received the Cross of Knight in the Order of the French Legion of Honor; he served in France in World War I under General Pershing in the 809th Black Infantry.[148]

Black communities celebrated and memorialized black soldiers of the Great War. Harlem's Hell Fighters, for example, marched to James Reese Europe's band from lower Fifth Avenue to Harlem. The wealthy black entrepreneur Madam C. J. Walker hosted a two-day open house for the men and their families at her New York villa.[149] Large crowds in major cities such as Buffalo, St. Louis, and Chicago also gave festive welcomes to the African American troops.[150] The poem "The Colored Soldier," by Paul Laurence Dunbar, is a tribute to all the men who served, living and dead.

The Colored Soldiers

If the muse were mine to tempt it
And my feeble voice were strong,
If my tongue were trained to measures,
I would sing a stirring song.
I would sing a song heroic
Of those noble sons of Ham,
Of the gallant colored soldiers
Who fought for Uncle Sam!

In the early days you scorned them,
And with many a flip and flout
Said "These battles are the white man's
And the whites will fight them out."
Up the hills you fought and faltered,
In the vales you strove and bled,
While your ears still heard the thunder
Of the foes' advancing tread.

Then distress fell on the nation,
And the flag was drooping low;
Should the dust pollute your banner?
No! The nation shouted, No!
So when War, in savage triumph,
Spread abroad his funeral pall—
Then you called the colored soldiers,
And they answered to your call.

And like hounds unleashed and eager
For the life blood of the prey,
Sprung they forth and bore them bravely
In the thickest of the fray.
And where'er the fight was hottest,
Where the bullets fastest fell,
There they pressed unblanched and fearless
At the very mouth of hell. . . .

They have slept and marched and suffered
'Neath the same dark skies as you,
They have met as fierce a foeman
And have been as brave and true
And their deeds shall find a record
In the registry of Fame;
For their blood has cleansed completely
Every blot of Slavery's shame.
So all honor and all glory
To those noble sons of Ham—
The gallant colored soldiers
Who fought for uncle Sam!

—Paul Laurence Dunbar[151]

Changing as They Are Changed

World War I was a major period of transformation for the geosocially dispersed components of global Africa. The war had direct effects on those who left home and on those who remained behind. Life at home was (re)shaped by the economic ills resulting from imperialism and the changing world political economy, depressed farming and sharecropping conditions, higher "hut" and property taxes, and the loss of family members as soldiers or laborers, voluntary or forced. The latter especially disrupted family life and the organization of work in rural and urban areas. Depending on location, education, gender, and job skills, some were able to secure access to jobs vacated by white enlistees. A few openings occurred in clerical/technical fields and professional areas, such as teaching and missionary work.

Excluding professional soldiers in such military units as the WAFF, KAR, or the Tirailleurs Sènègalais, most men of African descent served in military labor regiments. In the Americas, voluntary enlistment was much more common than in Africa. In both places, changes occurred that would affect employment at war's end. In the Caribbean, the sugar industry became more mechanized and centralized due to large-scale capital investments from Europe and the United States. Machines replaced human labor, including the technology to convert cane juice into sugar, and corporate imperialism reduced the number of sugar plantation owners. In the United States, blacks in the North competed with European immigrants for jobs in the context of racial discrimination. In the South, the boll weevil and 1915 floods damaged cotton crops; this depressed agricultural production, which was further affected by increasing mechanization. These factors, along with racial discrimination and the exclusion of black farmers from government programs, made black labor redundant.

When World War I began Africa was fully integrated into the global economy under the control of European imperialists (Liberia and Ethiopia were the exceptions). Although the specific nature of the linkages depended upon land, natural resources, and location, one constant was the ability of colonialists to avail themselves of the labor power of Africans. Given the domination of Europeans politically, economically, and militarily, that labor could be mobilized through direct force or through the imposition of hut taxes. Workers in rural and urban areas were grossly underpaid, and the justification was rooted in racist ideologies. Even the persistent use of the term "Native" as a preface to various military units, jobs, residential areas, and the like was designed to keep blacks in their place. "Those properly of the nation are native to it, born and bred at its breast; Natives, by contrast, are those natural in racial kind to foreign, hostile, dominated lands. The latter are naive, simple, lack art, culture and capacity for rational self-determination."[152]

The role of the state, whether colonial or center, was critical to the entire process; it normalized racial and labor/class oppression. Racial oppression made labor easier to control. The state apparatus and agents articulated and legitimated the major principles of exclusion and domination and elaborated and controlled the various restrictions, directions, and prescriptions of behavior, including disrespect for the "Natives," "Coloreds," or "Negroes."[153] Although the forces of domination, especially the colonial power complex, pursued their interests, it was equally evident that global Africans pursued theirs. They repeatedly exerted their agency and acted in their own interests. Operating within cultures of control and domination, they were not always successful. Yet, whether in military or civilian life, they took advantage of opportunities and used the resources and degrees of freedom available to them. Their strategies included evasion, migration, millenarian movements, uprisings and revolts, strikes, and legal procedures. The examples of the Rehoboth Basters in German South-West Africa, the black soldiers in Texas, the BWIR in Taranto, or the SANLC in France call attention to the fact that, even in the military, victimization has its limits.

Active military service, in whatever capacity, resulted in the movement of African people across boundaries and empires. Global Africans came into contact with one another as they fought and labored, whether for the Axis or the Allies. For most, this was their first substantive exposure to others of African descent; most would have had little opportunity to acquire such knowledge from reading, travel, or other kinds of interactions. There were educated men in the various labor units, but the majority were poor people from rural backgrounds. These everyday people who survived the war acquired knowledge about other people and the larger world that affected their daily life, consciously or unconsciously. They transmitted their new level of awareness to those back home and to others with whom they shared pathways. They were to some degree agents of change and transformation.

This focus on World War I certainly does not mean that African people did not know they were oppressed or did not have a protracted history of struggle until 1914. The point is that the war was a particular period of historical transformation during which various forms and forces of conflict and struggle were experienced and crystallized. Beginning in the fifteenth century with the colonization of the Americas, Africans were uprooted and enslaved by Spain, Portugal, Britain, France, and other nations. During World War I, Africans were largely impressed laborers who fought within the domains ruled primarily by Britain, France, and Germany. This period has many similarities to the past and created many legacies for the future. Global Africa changes in relationship to the larger world ordering system of which it is an integral part, but social oppression, racism, and inequality are not immutable. Worldviews, beliefs, and ideologies are (re)shaped by larger forces and crystallize in specific situations at different times. The examples provided here point the way to more definitive analyses.

The vast majority of active participants in the Great War are deceased. Many of their experiences and legacies are lost forever. It is imperative that we rescue as much as possible from the historical "landscape of denial" and forgetfulness.[154] We stand to gain important understanding about the connectedness of global Africa, effecting change as it is being changed, at critical time-spaces in modern history.

It is not only the tumultuous world events such as major wars that demand our attention, but rather it is necessary to incorporate within our thinking the view of diaspora as a dynamic world or global phenomenon. The localized and geographically dispersed diaspora components originated as part of an expanding world political economy in the fifteenth century. It remains integral to ongoing world dynamics both contributing to and being impacted by the changing dialectics. World War I is, therefore, one time-space that calls attention to diaspora actors whose views and behaviors reflect imagined and real existence "between worlds," "in-betweenness," or "twoness, included and excluded, within extended and more encompassing geosocial spaces. Although the focus may be on a particular locality and cultural milieus, a global and comparative framework or context may be more heuristic. For example, phenomena thought to be qualitatively different and unique may indeed reflect differences in degree more than differences of kind. In the early twentieth century and at the beginning of the twenty-first century, a changing global Africa shares a larger history of interlinked and interdependent and world-changing social, political, and economic events and forces.

N O T E S

This chapter is dedicated to two of my brothers, Robert and Louis, who read drafts and provided extremely useful comments, and to the memory of my late husband, James. All three served honorably in the United States Armed Forces: Lieutenant Colonel Robert J. Simms, U.S. Army (retired); Louis M. Simms, Captain, U.S. Air Force (1969–1972); and Dr. James B. Hamilton, Sergeant (E-4), U.S. Marine Corps (1953–1956).

1. The Report of the Study Commission on U.S. Policy Toward Southern Africa, *South Africa: Time Running Out* (Berkeley: University of California Press, 1981), 103.
2. Roger Norman Buckley, *Slaves in Red Coats: The British West India Regiments, 1795–1815* (New Haven, Conn.: Yale University Press, 1979).
3. Myron J. Echenberg, "Paying the Blood Tax: Military Conscription in French West Africa, 1914–1929," *Canadian Journal of African Studies* 9, no. 2 (1975): 171–92, 173; and Shelby T. McCloy, *The Negro in France* (Lexington: University of Kentucky Press, 1961).
4. Echenberg, "Paying the Blood Tax," 174, 180; Nancy Ellen Lawler, *Soldiers of Misfortune: Ivoirien Tirailleurs of World War II* (Athens: Ohio University Press), 21.
5. For more details see Roger Perkins, *Regiments: Regiments and Corps of the British Empire and Commonwealth 1758–1993: A Critical Bibliography of Their Published Histories* (Chippenham, Wiltshire, U.K.: Antony Rowe, 1994); and F. W. Perry, *The Commonwealth Armies: Manpower and Organization in Two World Wars* (Manchester, U.K.: Manchester University Press, 1988).
6. A good source for details and discussion is Gerald Astor, *The Right to Fight: A History of African Americans in the Military* (Novato, Calif.: Presidio Press, 1998). Also see Morris J. MacGregor Jr. and Bernard C. Nalty, eds., *Blacks in the United States Armed Forces—Basic Documents*, 13 vols. (Wilmington, Del.: Scholarly Resources, 1977); Chuck Barth, *Buffalo Soldier History* (Tucson, Ariz.: Blue Horse Productions, 1997); Jack D. Foner, *Blacks and the Military in American History* (New York: Praeger, 1974); M. L. Lanning, *The African American Soldier from Crispus Attucks to Colin Powell* (New York: Birch Lane Press, 1997); Benjamin Quarles, *The Negro in the American Revolution* (Chapel Hill: University of North Carolina Press, 1961); and Gail Buckley, *American Patriots: The Story of Blacks in the Military from the Revolution to Desert Storm* (New York: Random House, 2001).
7. Research collected for forthcoming volumes in the African Diaspora Research Project.
8. Astor, *Right to Fight*, 15, 16–19.
9. Late in the war, when the Union was poised for victory, the Confederate Congress actually authorized the recruitment of black fighting units. The Confederate Congress, in February 1865 on the recommendation of General Robert E. Lee, passed a bill authorizing President Jefferson Davis to requisition a quota of black soldiers from each state. The bill did not mandate freedom for black soldiers. The bill passed the Confederate Congress on a vote of 40 to 37; the Confederate Senate defeated the measure on a single vote—with both senators from Lee's state of Virginia voting "no."

   Ironically, the Virginia legislature on 13 March 1865, enacted its own law for the enlistment of black soldiers—without mandating freedom. The two companies hastily organized in Richmond never saw action; the war came to an end in April 1865. No other Confederate state followed

Virginia's lead. James M. McPherson, *Battle Cry of Freedom*, (New York: Ballentine Books, 1989), 836–37.

10. W. E. B. DuBois, *Black Reconstruction in America, 1860–1880* (New York: Meridian Books/The World Publishing Co., 1964), 112; Astor, *Right to Fight*, 32; and James M. McPherson et al., *Blacks in America: Bibliographical Essays* (Garden City, N.Y.: Doubleday, 1971), 115.

11. McPherson et al., *Blacks in America*, 116.

12. Astor, *Right to Fight*, 46–47.

13. John Keegan, *The First World War* (New York: Vintage Books, 1998), 6, 135, 295, 298–99. Also see Martin Gilbert, *The First World War: A Complete History* (New York: Henry Holt and Co., 1994).

    For the French, June 1916 was the high point and crisis of the Verdun offensive; more than 200,000 men had been killed and wounded.

14. Echenberg, "Paying the Blood Tax," 175, 176: "Until the First World War the Senegalese Rifles were indeed a mercenary army, composed of volunteer soldiers attracted to the profession by premiums for enlistment, steady pay, promise of booty."

15. See the entire issue themed World War I and Africa of the *Journal of African History* 19, no. 1 (1978).

16. Melvin E. Page, "The War of *Thangata*: Nyasaland and the East African Campaign, 1914–1918," *Journal of African History* 19, no. 1 (1978): 87–100, 92.

17. C. M. Andrew and A. S. Kanya-Forstner, "France, Africa, and the First World War," *Journal of African History*, 19, no. 1 (1978): 16; Norman Clothier, *Black Valour: The South African Native Labour Contingent, 1916–1918, and the Sinking of the Mendi* (Pietermaritzburg, South Africa: University of Natal Press, 1987); Albert Grundlingh, *Fighting Their Own War: South African Blacks and the First World War* (Johannesburg, South Africa: Raven Press, 1987); B. P. Willan, "South African Native Labour Contingent, 1916–1918," *Journal of African History* 19, no. 1 (1978): 61–86; and David Killingray, "Repercussions of World War I in the Gold Coast," *Journal of African History*, 19, no. 1 (1978), 39–59.

18. For one of the most definitive and intelligent discussions of DuBois's shifting positions during the period, see David Levering Lewis, *W. E. B. DuBois: Biography of a Race, 1868–1919* (New York: Henry Holt and Co., 1993), 525–80.

19. Zygmunt Bauman, *Modernity and Ambivalence* (Ithaca, N.Y.: Cornell University Press, 1991), 121.

20. Grundlingh, *Fighting Their Own War*, 77.

21. Killingray, "Repercussions," 51–52.

22. Page, "*Thangata*," 88–89; Killingray, "Repercussions," 47–51; and Anne Summers and R. W. Johnson, "World War I Conscription and Social Change in Guinea," *Journal of African History* 19, no. 1 (1978): 28.

23. Killingray, "Repercussions," 42, 51, and 53 n. 66.

24. Page, "*Thangata*," 91.

25. Audrey Wipper, "The Gusii Rebels," in *Rebellion in Black Africa*, ed. Robert I. Rotberg (London: Oxford University Press, 1971), 175.

26. Ibid.

27. Page, "*Thangata*," 93.

28. Summers and Johnson, "World War I," 27.

29. Page, "*Thangata*," 87, 93.

30. Killingray, "Repercussions," 59, 41.

31. Ibid., 52.

32. Grundlingh, *Fighting Their Own War*, 69; Page, "*Thangata*," 89; and Killingray, "Repercussions," 47–48.

33. Summers and Johnson, "World War I," 27.

34. Grundlingh, *Fighting Their Own War*, 69; Summers and Johnson, "World War I," 27; Killingray, "Repercussions," 52–53; Page, "*Thangata*," 92.

35. Grundlingh, *Fighting Their Own War*, 49, 74; and Killingray, "Repercussions," 47.
36. Willan, "South African Native Labour," 63.
37. Ibid., 63–64.
38. Summers and Johnson, "World War I," 28.
39. Ibid., 28–29; Echenberg, "Paying the Blood Tax," 180–81; and Myron Echenberg, *Colonial Conscripts: The Tiraílleurs Senégalais in French West Africa, 1857–1960* (Portsmouth, N.H.: Heinemann, 1991), 44–45.
40. Grundlingh, *Fighting Their Own War*, 59; and Killingray, "Repercussions," 52.
41. World War I and Africa, *Journal of African History*, 19, no. 1 (1978).
42. Grundlingh, *Fighting Their Own War*, 19.
43. Elizabeth Isichei, *History of West Africa since 1800* (New York: Africana Publishing Company, 1977), 259.
44. George Shepperson and Thomas Price, *Independent African: John Chilembwe and the Origins, Setting and Significance of the Nyasaland Native Rising of 1915* (Edinburgh, U.K.: Edinburgh University Press, 1985), 113.
45. Ibid., 133–38.
46. Page, "*Thangata*," 90–91; Robert I. Rotberg, "Psychological Stress and the Question of Identity: Chilembwe's Revolt Reconsidered," in *Rebellion in Black Africa*, ed. Robert I. Rotberg (London: Oxford University Press, 1971), 133–63; Shepperson and Price, *Independent African*. On the diplomatic involvement of African Americans in Africa from the mid-nineteenth century through the early decades of the twentieth century, see Elliott P. Skinner, *African Americans and U.S. Policy toward Africa 1850–1924* (Washington, D.C.: Howard University Press, 1992). Other relevant works include Sylvia M. Jacobs, *Black American Perspectives on the European Partitioning of Africa, 1880–1920* (Westport, Conn.: Greenwood Press, 1981); and Walter L. Williams, *Black Americans and the Evangelization of Africa 1877–1900* (Madison: The University of Wisconsin Press, 1982).
47. Page, "*Thangata*," 94.
48. Grundlingh, *Fighting Their Own War*, 18.
49. Elizabeth Hopkins, "The Nyabingi Cult of Southwestern Uganda," in Rotberg, *Rebellion in Black Africa*, 60.
50. See Harold G. Marcus, *Haile Sellassie I, The Formative Years 1892–1936* (Lawrenceville, N.J.: The Red Sea Press, 1995), 17–18, and *The Life and Times of Menelik II, Ethiopia 1844–1913* (Lawrenceville, N.J.: The Red Sea Press, 1995), 249–81; Bahru Zewde, *A History of Modern Ethiopia 1855–1974* (Athens: Ohio University Press, 1991), 126–27; Bonnie Holcomb and Sisai Ibssa, *The Invention of Ethiopia: The Making of a Dependent Colonial State in Northeast Africa* (Trenton, N.J.: The Red Sea Press, 1990), 160–63; and Addis Hiwet, *Ethiopia: From Autocracy to Revolution* (London: Review of African Political Economy, Occasional Publication, no. 1, 1975). Many thanks to my research associate and friend, Getahun Benti, for bringing this movement to my attention.
51. Perry, *Commonwealth Armies*, 200.
52. Shelby Cullom Davis, *Reservoirs of Men: A History of Black Troops of French West Africa* (Geneva: Librairie Kundig, 1934), 142.
53. Andrew and Kanya-Forstner, "France, Africa, and the First World War," 14–16.
54. Echenberg, *Colonial Conscripts*, 46.
55. Isichei, *History of West Africa*, 259.
56. McCloy, *The Negro in France*, 192.
57. Ibid., 193.
58. Ibid., 194–95, 197.
59. Davis, *Reservoirs of Men*, 166.
60. Kenneth W. Grundy, *Soldiers without Politics: Blacks in the South African Armed Forces* (Berkeley: University of California Press, 1983), 52; Perkins, *Regiments*, 314; Clothier, *Black Valour*, 11; and

Willan, "South African Native Labour," 61–86.

61. Grundlingh, *Fighting Their Own War*, 86.

62. Ibid., 87, 90–91, 93.

63. Consult such works as David Theo Goldberg, *Racist Culture: Philosophy and the Politics of Meaning* (Oxford, U.K.: Blackwell, 1993); Stephen Jay Gould, *The Mismeasure of Man* (New York: W. W. Norton and Company, 1981); Ivan Hannaford, *Race: The History of an Idea in the West* (Washington, D.C.: Woodrow Wilson Center Press, 1996); James B. McKee, *Sociology and the Race Problem: The Failure of a Perspective* (Chicago: University of Illinois Press, 1993); and Steven Gregory and Roger Sanjek, *Race* (New Brunswick, N.J.: Rutgers University Press, 1994).

64. Personal correspondence from Werner Hillebrecht, National Library of Namibia, 25 June 1999.

65. See "Orchestrating Race, Nation, and Gender: African Peacekeepers in Germany, 1919–1920" in this volume.

66. Hillebrecht, personal correspondence, 25 June 1999.

67. Grundlingh, *Fighting Their Own War*, 88.

68. C. L. Joseph, "The British West Indies Regiment 1914–1918," *Journal of Caribbean History* 2 (May 1971): 105.

69. G. W. T. Hodges, "African Manpower Statistics for the British Forces in East Africa, 1914–1918," *Journal of African History* 19, no. 1 (1978): 101–16, 103.

70. Grundy, *Soldiers without Politics*, 53–54.

71. Perkins, *Regiments*, 257.

72. Perry, *Commonwealth Armies*, 200; and Perkins, *Regiments*, 233.

73. Hodges, "African Manpower Statistics," 104.

74. Ibid., 107.

75. Ibid., 115.

76. Page, "*Thangata*," 97–98.

77. Hodges, "African Manpower Statistics," 114–15.

78. Clothier, *Black Valour*, 8–9.

79. Joseph, "West Indies Regiment," 67.

80. Clothier, *Black Valour*, 20.

81. Ibid., 11; and Grundy, *Soldiers without Politics*, 52–55.

82. Clothier, *Black Valour*, 15, 26.

83. Grundlingh, *Fighting Their Own War*, 76.

84. Clothier, *Black Valour*, 13.

85. Grundlingh, *Fighting Their Own War*, 101.

86. Ibid., 74, 101, 104.

87. This listing is not exhaustive and is compiled from well-documented secondary sources. For details, see Clothier, *Black Valour*, 28–29, 124–27; Grundlingh, *Fighting Their Own War*, 106–7; and Willan, "South African Native Labor," 71–74.

88. Willan, "South African Native Labor," 71.

89. Ibid., 61; and Clothier, *Black Valour*, 109.

90. Willan, "South African Native Labor," 73. Willan's account is based on a diary kept by one of the Africans and later published. See J. and C. Perry, eds., *A Chief Is a Chief by the People: The Autobiography of Stimela Jason Jingoes* (Oxford, U.K.: Oxford University Press, 1975).

91. Clothier, *Black Valour*, 114; Willan, "South African Native Labor," 73–74; and Grundlingh, *Fighting Their Own War*, 97.

92. Clothier, *Black Valour*, 115, 160–63, and Grundlingh, *Fighting Their Own War*, 110–12.

93. Willan, "South African Native Labor," 79. Also see Grundlingh, *Fighting Their Own War*, 113; and Clothier, *Black Valour*, 161.

94. Perry and Perry, *A Chief Is a Chief*, quoted in Clothier, *Black Valour*, 129.

95. Ibid., 129–32; and Willan, "South African Native Labor," 79–80.

96. For details, see Clothier, *Black Valour,* 146–48; and Grundlingh, *Fighting Their Own War,* 110–11.

97. See Clothier, *Black Valour,* 114–15; Grundlingh, *Fighting Their Own War,* 106–14; and Willan, "South African Native Labor," 77–78.

98. Grundy, *Soldiers without Politics,* 56; and Clothier, *Black Valour,* 165, 172–73.

99. Clothier, *Black Valour,* 158; Grundlingh, *Fighting Their Own War,* 98.

100. Clothier, *Black Valour,* 1, 72–73, 96–100.

101. Ibid., 42.

102. Ibid., 99.

103. Willan, "South African Native Labor," 78; also see Clothier, *Black Valour,* 138; and Grundlingh, *Fighting Their Own War,* 126.

104. Clothier, *Black Valour,* 173; Grundlingh, *Fighting Their Own War,* 109, 130–33; Willan, "South African Native Labor," 83–84.

105. Clothier, *Black Valour,* p. 169.

106. Willan, "South African Native Labor," 84.

107. Clothier, *Black Valour,* 175.

108. Willan, "South African Native Labor," 85.

109. Clothier, *Black Valour,* 175–76.

110. Ibid., 177.

111. Ibid., 174–75.

112. Translated from Xhosa by Jack Cope and M. C. Mcanyangwa in Jack Cope and Ulys Krige, comps., *The Penguin Book of South African Verse* (Middlesex, U.K.: Penguin Books, 1968), 278–79.

113. See Buckley, *Slaves in Red Coats.*

114. Joseph, "West Indies Regiment," 103.

115. Ibid., 103–4, 111, 124.

116. Ibid., 112–13.

117. Ibid., 124.

118. Peter Fryer, *Staying Power: Black People in Britain since 1504* (Atlantic Highlands, N.J.: Humanities Press, 1984), 296; also see Joseph, "West Indies Regiment," 124.

119. For details, see Fryer, *Staying Power,* 294–311.

120. W. F. Elkins, "A Source of Black Nationalism in the Caribbean: The Revolt of the British West Indies Regiment at Taranto, Italy," *Science and Society* 34 (spring 1970): 99–103; and Joseph, "West Indies Regiment," 118–23.

121. Elkins, "A Source of Black Nationalism," 101.

122. Ibid., 102.

123. Joseph, "West Indies Regiment," 120.

124. Lawrence P. Scott and William M. Womack Sr., *Double V: The Civil Rights Struggle of the Tuskegee Airmen* (East Lansing: Michigan State University Press, 1994), 6–13, 20–21.

125. Ibid., 14; and John Hope Franklin and Alfred A. Moss Jr., *From Slavery to Freedom: A History of African Americans,* 8th ed. (New York: Alfred A. Knopf, 2000), 360.

126. Franklin and Moss, *From Slavery to Freedom,* 361–62; Astor, *Right to Fight,* 95–98; and Lou Potter with William Miles and Nina Rosenblum, *Liberators: Fighting on Two Fronts in World War II* (New York: Harcourt Brace Jovanovich, 1992), 23. Col. Young was forced to retire because of alleged high blood pressure. So he rode horseback from Ohio to Washington, D.C., to prove his fitness. The retirement board did not change its decision.

127. For an account of the events and the Houston riots see Potter, *Liberators,* 20–22; Astor, *Right to Fight,* 98–105; and Langston Hughes and Milton Meltzer, *A Pictorial History of the Negro in America,* 3rd ed. (New York: Crown, 1968), 263.

128. Franklin and Moss, *From Slavery to Freedom,* 360.

129. Ibid., 362–63.

130. Astor, *Right to Fight*, 110.

131. Quoted in Dorothy Schneider and Carl J. Schneider, *Into the Breach: American Women Overseas in World War I* (New York: Viking, 1919), 171.

132. Schneider, *Into the Breach*, 171.

133. Schneider, *Into the Breach*, 171. Chapter 6, "The Black Record," in Schneider is largely based on Hunton and Johnson.

134. Scott and Womack, *Double V*, 16–17.

135. Astor, *Right to Fight*, 110.

136. Scott and Womack, *Double V*, 19. This situation is also discussed in Arthur E. Barbeau and Florette Henri, *The Unknown Soldiers: Black American Troops in World War I* (New York: Da Capo, 1974).

137. Scott and Womack, *Double V*, 19.

138. Potter, *Liberators*, 26. Scott and Womack, *Double V*, also provide specific examples in support of this view.

139. Hughes and Meltzer, *Pictorial History*, 265.

140. Ibid., 262.

141. Paul Gordon Lauren, *Power and Prejudice: The Politics of Racial Discrimination* (Boulder, Colo.: Westview Press, 1988), 73.

142. Astor, *Right to Fight*, 124.

143. Sylvia G. L. Dannett, ed., *Profiles of Negro Womanhood: Twentieth Century II in Negro Heritage Library* (New York: M. W. Lads, 1964), 204.

144. Ibid. 123.

145. Ibid., 126–32.

146. Ibid., 133.

147. *JET*, 15 March 1999, 24–25; and *New York Times*, 28 April 1999, C-24.

148. *Christian Science Monitor*, 30 June 1999, 4.

149. A'Lelia Bundles, *On Her Own Ground: The Life and Times of Madam C. J. Walker* (New York: Scribner, 2001), 266–67.

150. Franklin and Moss, *From Slavery to Freedom*, 383.

151. The complete poem is found in Paul Laurence Dunbar, *The Complete Poems of Paul Laurence Dunbar* (New York: Dodd, Mead and Company, 1918), 50–52.

152. Goldberg, *Racist Culture*, 79.

153. Goldberg provides an excellent resource for understanding the role of the state and premises behind exclusion (ibid.).

154. James W. Loewen, *Lies Across America: What Our Historic Sites Get Wrong* (New York: New Press, 1999).

Brothers in Arms? African Soldiers in Interwar France

Dana S. Hale

IN 1954 RETIRED FRENCH GENERAL YVES DE BOISBOISSEL PUBLISHED A REVISED edition of his 1930 account of the contribution of sub-Saharan African soldiers to the defense of France during World War I. This new edition celebrated the centennial of the formal creation of sub-Saharan African units in the French Army. The title of his book, *Peaux noires, Coeurs blancs* (Black skins, white hearts), captured the view that a number of key French officers held of their subject troops from West Africa. The text, a collection of vignettes drawn from Boisboissel's years of command over black units, praised the commitment of African soldiers during the Great War and their heroism after the war. He argued that these Africans had wholeheartedly accepted the authority of the French state, which they saw as their liberator from oppressive African rulers. According to Boisboissel, African troops had the same heart as white soldiers defending their own native land.

General Boisboissel was part of a group of military figures who helped create the public image of a fiercely devoted corps of colonial troops, the Tirailleurs Sénégalais. These infantry riflemen came mainly from the French West African territories in Senegal, Ivory Coast, Guinea, Mauritania, Dahomey, Soudan, and Upper Volta. Boisboissel's book gave homage to General Louis Faidherbe of Senegal, the recognized founder of the Tirailleurs Sénégalais in the mid-nineteenth century, and to General Charles Mangin, the instigator of a recruitment campaign and the expanded use of black soldiers in the French Army beginning in 1912.[1] In fact, the purpose of the 1954 edition of *Peaux noires, Coeurs blancs* was to raise funds to reconstruct statues of

Mangin that the Germans destroyed during their occupation of France in the 1940s. The Germans removed the statues but were unable to erase public memories of Mangin and the African troops, praised by government officials for helping save France from defeat during World War I. Today, the myth of these ostensibly devoted and exceptionally courageous soldiers survives in nostalgic images of a grinning African soldier on Banania breakfast drink boxes and posters, war game figures, and collectibles invoking the age of French empire.

This essay focuses on the lives of African soldiers during the interwar years, when the myth of the Tirailleurs became more ingrained in the French popular imagination. Although scholars who study colonial soldiers serving France have not completed an in-depth examination of this period, several excellent works document the experiences of West African soldiers during World War I and World War II and provide context for this essay. Myron Echenberg's *Colonial Conscripts* describes the conscription and service of West African troops under French control until decolonization. Marc Michel's *L'Appel à l'Afrique* details the deployment of Africans on French soil during World War I and the reaction of Europeans to the use of black soldiers. Joe Lunn's *Memoirs of the Maelstrom* presents an oral history that describes how it felt for young men to leave their homes as conscripts in the French Army. These works demonstrate the fallacy of a uniformly recruited, submissive, and effective African force.[2]

A number of questions about the lives of African soldiers who remained in France after the Armistice surfaced while I was researching colonial propaganda during the Third French Republic. That investigation focused on one aspect of the lives of Tirailleurs Sénégalais in France—the ways that the government displayed them to its citizens at colonial expositions.[3] But beyond their participation in the expositions, what were the men's daily experiences as Africans displaced from their homeland? I wanted to learn more about the typical duties and activities of the soldiers and their living conditions at army bases. Using material gathered from military archives and other sources, I will present a general outline of the experiences and the public image of West African soldiers stationed in France from 1919 to 1939.

Many cite the fact that the French welcomed black American intellectuals and entertainers during this period as evidence of their racial tolerance.[4] A more valid assessment of French attitudes about race can be made from examining the treatment of the largest group of blacks residing in the country—the West African soldiers. I will argue that despite official propaganda, republican rhetoric, and public perceptions of the soldiers, West Africans conscripted into the French forces and serving in Europe between the wars experienced discriminatory treatment similar to that of other diaspora populations in the twentieth century. Military leaders increasingly saw the

African regiments as an integral part of national defense, yet they insisted on policies of segregation and unequal treatment.

AFRICAN SOLDIERS AFTER WORLD WAR I

In the months and years following World War I, due to the lack of French troops, French military officials came to rely on colonial forces to carry out the Armistice and Versailles Treaty. The War Ministry first decided to post West African and Malagasy soldiers in the Rhineland region of Germany to ensure the payment of reparations and disarmament. In response to this the German press mounted a massive anti-French campaign. They accused the troops of raping young German women, and they claimed the French knew that their colonial soldiers would commit such crimes. German newspapers and propagandists angrily referred to the African forces as the "black shame" on the Rhine. Although none of the alleged incidents was ever proved or prosecuted, the campaign persuaded the French to withdraw the Tirailleurs Sénégalais from the Rhineland in June 1920 and the Malagasy troops in November 1921.[5] Afterward, military and civilian officials continued to refute German accusations and lauded the Tirailleurs Sénégalais for their courage, submissiveness, and loyalty in books such as *Peaux noires* and at public celebrations.

The use of black soldiers in the Rhineland was the first in a series of colonial troop deployments that highlighted the importance of the African regiments in the military. In the first eight years after the Armistice, the French repatriated, recruited, and transferred large numbers of African troops. Thousands of combatants returned to their homeland, battalions of fresh recruits arrived from African ports, and seasoned and new soldiers found themselves sent to areas of colonial strife. Army officials garrisoned most of these forces in southern France in between assignments or while they awaited repatriation.

The history of the 12th Regiment of Tirailleurs Sénégalais illustrates this pattern. Created after the war in Turkey in 1920, the regiment served in Gallipoli for three years to collect remains. The regiment then experienced numerous troop transfers and postings in southeastern France between 1923 and 1925. In late 1925, the army command called the 12th Regiment to fight against Moroccan forces in the Rif War. After about a year of service in Morocco, the soldiers returned to Aix-en-Provence, France. Finally, in 1929 the regiment settled in La Rochelle, near Bordeaux, where it remained until 1939.[6]

African units were also sent to the Levant at the end of World War I to secure territory from the former Ottoman Empire that the French then administered by a League of Nations mandate. By 1922 there were more than 10,000 black troops in the region, compared to nearly 4,500 in France.[7] But two years later, the situation was nearly reversed. In an August 1923 directive, the minister of war announced plans to post 10,000 African troops in France permanently and cut back the number in the Levant to 2,000 by January 1924.[8] Another 1923 directive limited the soldiers' average stay outside his colony to 26 months.[9]

Arrivals of new conscripts and repatriations of soldiers in the interwar years took place primarily in Marseilles, with smaller sites in Bordeaux and, briefly, Le Havre. The majority of African units remained in an area that stretched about 150 kilometers east from Marseilles to Fréjus, just off the Riviera coast. A smaller number was garrisoned to the west in Perpignan, Montauban (north of Toulouse), and Mont-de-Marsan (south of Bordeaux). The information we have about the regiments stationed at Fréjus and Marseilles is perhaps the most useful. In addition to housing a number of regiments, Fréjus was the home of the Transitional Center of Indigenous Colonial Troops and the military school where African and Asian officers received their training.

The Transitional Center prepared new conscripts for military life with a one-month stay, prepared older ones for repatriation, and housed "convalescents" from units throughout France and others unable to handle the winter in their regular garrison (*hivernants*). Commanders from the center assigned tasks according to race, distinguishing among the Indochinese, Malagasy, and Senegalese (West African) soldiers. They gave the Senegalese the hardest manual tasks that required, in the words of one colonel, "an incorruptible fidelity." The Indochinese were given secretarial duties, and the Malagasy received jobs that required intelligence and some physical effort.[10]

Daily activities for soldiers in the center included morning exercise, regular training, and two half-hour sessions of French lessons. Shooting practice, field exercises, combat training, and training in the use of the gas mask took place on a weekly or monthly basis.[11] This program of activities was typical for the colonial regiments, which each numbered about 1,500 men. The commander of the Colonial Army in 1925, General Claudel, reported that using indigenous troops in France served not only military purposes but also cultural and political ones. Claudel claimed that training Africans and Asians in France was one of the best ways to produce "a successful evolution of our diverse races." Moreover, he believed that soldiers stationed in France would be less likely to join anticolonial movements when they returned home.[12]

LIFE IN THE GARRISONS

Military records and writings by French officials and observers permit us to reconstruct some of the conditions under which these men lived. Archived reports from periodic inspections of army bases provide the greatest number of details on their housing, food, and recreation. Most of these inspections took place in the fall, and the written reports that followed them informed superiors of inadequate conditions that could be corrected—at least in theory—before the arrival of winter.

Several reports noted substandard housing arrangements. A 1927 report on African troops in Aix-en-Provence noted that some men were sleeping in equipment storage areas and warehouses, which was a violation of military regulations.[13] In September 1928 Monsieur de la Pomelie, the controller for the caserne occupied by the 4th Regiment of Tirailleurs Sénégalais in Toulon-sur-Mer, remarked that the interior design of one barrack made it impossible to heat the bedrooms. Since the occupants were Africans who had a "great fear of the cold," the authorities decided to improve the building.[14] The commander of the Fréjus Transitional Center's three housing sites wrote his superior that the bathrooms were unheated except for the one attached to the convalescent ward. In fact, most of the bathrooms or washrooms were in the open air.[15] This might not have presented a problem most of the year, but the winter months in southeastern France brought periods of near-freezing weather. For many years army officials expressed concern over the effect of European weather on the health and performance of African troops.[16] The fact that Tirailleurs received minimally adequate clothing only exacerbated the situation.

Military inspectors identified other housing problems. The Toulon area inspector in 1928 noted that the barrack in nearby Camp Malbousquet leaked during the rainy season and was never meant for peacetime use. Other problems in regional casernes included fetid urinals, missing sink knobs, and broken staircases.[17] In November 1928, Monsieur Cunin, the controller for the 14th Regiment of Tirailleurs Sénégalais in Mont-de-Marsan, reported that the regiment saved money by using inexpensive straw beds for the colonial soldiers rather than the cloth mattresses on which the French soldiers slept. Cunin complained, however, that the straw beds were less than neat, and many were topped by torn or thin covers that needed to be replaced.[18] All these facts support one author's conclusion that barracks living in France for Africans could be particularly unhealthy.[19]

Colonial soldiers also received different treatment when it came to food and mess hall arrangements. The inspector of the 14th Regiment at Mont-de-Marsan cited the unit for not feeding the soldiers enough green vegetables when there was money in the budget to afford them.[20] At the Transitional Center in Fréjus in 1938, French commanders reaffirmed the status of soldiers from the colonies in relation to French soldiers in colonial units by the quality and quantity of dishware they could use. Africans had the use of soup plates for all their meals, whereas French soldiers were given regular plates as well. A team of West African and Malagasy cooks prepared the meals for all the soldiers at the center, but the French were to be served their entrées on earthenware serving platters; the African soldiers received their food in pots placed on the tables reserved for them. The French soldiers sat at their own tables equipped with an assortment of condiments, enjoyed wine with every meal, and were given dinner knives the colonial soldiers were not permitted to have.[21]

SOLDIERS AND THE CIVILIAN WORLD

Military commanders preferred to isolate colonial soldiers from populous areas or, when this was not possible, to control the ways African soldiers came into contact with the civilian population. The most common point of contact immediately after World War I was at hospitals and clinics where Africans recovered from battle injuries. African patients had close and sometimes lengthy contact with male and female hospital personnel. (A number of illustrations from the war period depict French nurses swooning over bedridden Tirailleurs or African soldiers pursuing nurses.) A second setting in which black soldiers interacted with French civilians was on work projects. After receiving a request from the prefect of the Var (southeast) in 1922, the War Ministry decided to allow colonial soldiers to volunteer as agricultural workers on an experimental, short-term basis. The only provisos were that their military instruction would not suffer and that they would receive no additional pay for the work.[22] Annual military reports and inspections indicate that these arrangements were rare for African soldiers.[23] Community officials, however, called on Tirailleurs in their regions to help in crisis situations when they needed additional manpower. In March 1930, soldiers from the 16th Regiment of Tirailleurs Sénégalais risked life and limb to rescue families during the massive floods of the Tarn River.[24] African units from the Marseilles garrison replaced striking dock workers in August 1938 during a period of great labor unrest.[25]

The soldiers based in Marseilles probably had the greatest opportunity to mingle with civilians because their barracks were located near busy areas of the city. Caserne Busserade, for example, stood close to the main train station, Gare Saint-

Charles. During the war, prostitutes received visits from African soldiers who obtained passes to leave their bases for short excursions into the surrounding neighborhoods. Visits to prostitutes, shops, and local cafés continued during the interwar years, when large numbers of soldiers resided in southern France. Some Africans established relationships with local women, stayed in France after their tour of duty, and married.[26]

West African soldiers also encountered the civilian world when they appeared before the French public in military and government-sponsored competitions, shows, and parades promoting the colonial empire. After the war, army officials at the Transitional Center created programs showcasing soldiers in cultural performances. Hundreds of Tirailleurs were dressed in African clothing, were instructed to sing, dance, and parade in costume to traditional drums and instruments, and were made to reenact cortèges of defeated West African rulers. They performed before the inhabitants of towns in the French Riviera during the 1920s. These Riviera festivals became the basis of colonial extravaganzas presented during the acclaimed 1931 International Colonial Exposition in Paris.[27]

In this period between the wars African regiments also performed in athletic events that showcased their physique and skills. One observer at a performance in Marseilles praised the black athletes as "suberb, strapping fellows . . . with sculptured musculature" visible under their white tank tops.[28] Local and national programs that featured black units reinforced images of African "primitive" strength and military usefulness before the public, and these additional activities helped keep the soldiers occupied.

At the colonial expositions of 1922 and 1931 organizers and military officials portrayed Africans as entertainers and willing fighters for the French. In an opening speech for the 1922 National Colonial Exposition in Marseilles, commerce minister Adrien Artaud called the soldiers "volunteers" who fought "next to their white brothers" to defend France.[29] On the exposition grounds sharply dressed Tirailleurs stood guard around the pavilions that held objects from their homelands and descriptions of how French commanders "pacified" backward African peoples. European visitors to such events knew nothing of the forced recruitment of these young men or of the crowded conditions, unequal treatment, and years spent away from home. The public accepted the official myth that many were volunteers, grateful for the "liberation" and "civilization" the French had brought them.

Conclusion

An examination of military records reveals the disjunction between government propaganda of the 1920s and 1930s and the real experiences of the Tirailleurs Sénégalais in France. Primarily, these colonial subjects provided an ongoing source of manpower for the decimated French forces. Army commanders deployed West African units to France, the Rhineland, the Levant, and Morocco to protect French interests. Few among the thousands of soldiers brought to France in these years came voluntarily. In fact, recruitment figures for 1921 reported only 1,926 volunteers among approximately 10,000 called into service.[30] The perceived success of the Tirailleurs and the need for soldiers to make up for French demographic weaknesses inspired military leaders to continue conscripting Africans in large numbers until World War II.[31]

French military leaders and government officials praised the contribution of Africans to the defense of the state but did not accord them equal treatment with white soldiers or other colonial groups when it came to duties and daily life in the garrisons. Army officers also required African soldiers to participate in athletic shows, musical performances, and colonial expositions for the benefit of Europeans eager for exotic entertainment. The speeches given by politicians and military figures at the 1922 and 1931 expositions painted images of fraternal ties between the métropole and its colonies and lauded black and white soldiers fighting together for France. Occasionally, white battalions and black battalions fought under the same leadership, but units maintained their racial divisions on and off the battlefield. Young African soldiers probably experienced few—if any—heartfelt bonds of brotherhood with French soldiers, from whom they were segregated in war and in peace.

NOTES

1. The conscription law of February 1912 instituted the increase in African forces. See Myron Echenberg, *Colonial Conscripts: The Tirailleurs Sénégalais in French West Africa, 1857–1960* (Portsmouth, N.H.: Heinemann, 1991), 25. Mangin's recommendations for expanding the colonial army are presented in *La Force Noire* (Paris: Hachette et Cie, 1910).
2. Echenberg, *Colonial Conscripts;* Marc Michel, *L'Appel à l'Afrique: Contributions et réactions à l'effort de guerre en A.O.F. (1914–1919)* (Paris: Publications de la Sorbonne, 1982); and Joe Lunn, *Memoirs of the Maelstrom: A Senegalese Oral History of the First World War* (Portsmouth, N.H.: Heinemann, 1999).
3. Dana Hale, "Races on Display: French Representation of the Colonial Native, 1886–1931" (Ph.D.

diss., Brandeis University, 1998).

4. African American writers, artists, and performers, such as Josephine Baker and Langston Hughes, claimed that they received better treatment in Paris than in the United States. My argument is that they represent a unique group, and their situation should be considered as one piece in the puzzle of racial attitudes and discrimination in France. In *Paris Noir: African Americans in the City of Light* (New York: Houghton Mifflin Company, 1996), Tyler Stovall maintains that the French were not always color-blind.

5. "Commissariat Général des Troupes Noires. La Campagne allemande contre des Troupes Noires," Archives Nationales, Fonds d'Outre-Mer (FOM), Affaires Politiques 534, Dossier 12.

6. "Historique du 12e Régiment de Tirailleur Sénégalais," 1 October 1920–1 November 1926; Cahier, 1 October 1920–10 November 1934; and "Journal des Marches d'operation," 23 September 1923–15 November 1926, Service Historique de l'Armée de Terre (hereafter, SHAT), 34 N 1090, Dossiers 1 and 2.

7. "Situation des Troupes Coloniales au 1er Janvier 1922," report of the Minister of War and Pensions to civil and military officials in Rabat, Mainz, Paris, Tunis, Beirut, and Algiers, SHAT 9 N 268, Dossier 1.

8. Ministre de la Guerre et des Pensions à MM, les Gouvernors Militaires de Paris et Lyon, le Général Commandant l'Armée Française du Rhin, les Généraux Commandant les 3e, 5e, 9e, 10e, 15e, 16e, 17e, 18e Corps d'Armée, et le Général Commandant le Corps d' Armée Coloniale, 4 August 1923, SHAT 9 N 268, Dossier 1. The figure does not include troops serving in the eastern border areas.

9. Effectifs 1922–1940, SHAT 9 N 269, Dossier 1. The regulation is mentioned in correspondence from the Ministre de la Guerre, Direction des troupes coloniales to the Etat-Major de l'Armée, 11 January 1924.

10. Colonel Marchand to Controller General Delande, 29 October 1931, Centre de Transition des Troupes Indigènes Coloniales, SHAT 8 N 208.

11. "Rapport d'inspection Générale en 1938," Colonel Ouvrard, commandant à Monsieur le Général de Division, Chef d'Etat major Général des Colonies, 30 September 1938, Centre de Transition des Troupes Indigènes Coloniales à Fréjus, 1938, SHAT 9 N 268, Dossier 1.

12. "Rapport du Général de Division Claudel, Commandant du Corps d'Armée Colonial et Inspecteur Général, au sujet des Troupes Coloniales stationées en France," 23 December 1925, SHAT 9 N 268, Dossier 1.

13. "Contrôle de Troupes, Tirailleurs Sénégalais en France, 1926–1935," report dated 11 August 1927, M. de la Pomelie 12th Regiment of Tirailleurs Sénégalais, Aix-en-Provence, SHAT 8 N 205.

14. "Contrôle de Troupes, Tirailleurs Sénégalais en France, 1926–1935," report dated 10 September 1928, M. de la Pomelie, Controller General, Toulon-sur-Mer, SHAT 8 N 205.

15. "Rapport d'inspection Générale en 1938," 30 September 1938, report from Colonel Ouvrard, Commandant le Centre, to the General of the Division of the Etat Major Général des Colonies, Centre de Transition des Troupes Indigènes Coloniales à Fréjus, SHAT 9 N 268, Dossier 1.

16. The annual report of the commander of the 4th Regiment of Tirailleurs Sénégalais noted that fourteen men had died during the year, primarily of pulmonary illnesses, including pneumonia and tuberculosis. See "Rapport Annuel, 1938," 15 September 1938, Colonel Blaizot, Commander of the 4th Regiment of Tirailleurs Sénégalais, 10, Régiment des Tirailleurs Sénégalais, Toulon, France, SHAT 34 N 1084. Africans performed poorly during winter campaigns, leading commanders to withdraw them from the front during the cold weather. The practice of *hivernage* continued in the interwar period. See Anthony Clayton, *France, Soldiers and Africa* (Washington, D.C.: Brassey's Defence, 1988), 344–45.

17. "Contrôle de Troupes, Tirailleurs Sénégalais en France, 1926–1935," reports dated 10 and 12 September 1928, M. de la Pomelie, Controller General, SHAT 8 N 205.

18. "Contrôle de Troupes, Tirailleurs Sénégalais en France, 1926–1935," report dated November 15,

1928, Cunin, Controller de Zème classe, Mont de Marsan, SHAT 8 N 205.

19. Clayton, *France*, 350.

20. "Contrôle de Troupes, Tirailleurs Sénégalais en France, 1926–1935," 14e Régiment, Mont-de-Marsan, 15 November 1928, Cunin, Controlleur de 2e classe, SHAT 8 N 205.

21. "Rapport d'inspection Générale en 1938," 30 September 1938, report from Colonel Ouvrard, commandant le Centre, to the General of the Division of the Etat Major Générale des Colonies, 5–12, Centre de Transition des Troupes Indigènes Coloniales à Fréjus, SHAT 9 N 268, Dossier 1.

22. "Service courant, 1921–1922, (Déplacement d'unités)," correspondence from Jung, Directeur des Troupes coloniales, to le Général Commandant la XVe Région, 12 May 1922, SHAT 7 N 2306, Dossier 12.

23. I have found only four other cases, all in the 1930s.

24. Yves de Boisboissel, *Peaux noires, Coeurs blancs* (Paris: Peyronnet, 1954), 108–9.

25. Reported in Clayton, *France*, 350.

26. Some of the former Tirailleurs interviewed by Lunn for *Memoires of the Maelstrom* tell of their comrades who married French women.

27. "Une babel coloniale aux Portes de Paris: Le Camp Saint Maur," *Le Monde illustré*, 10 October 1931, 230.

28. "Pour les Héroes de l'Armée Noire," *Journal Officiel de l'Exposition Coloniale, Marseille*, 31 August 1922, 8.

29. Adrien Artaud, *Exposition nationale coloniale de Marseille, Raport Général* (Marseille: Sémaphore, 1924), 413.

30. "Recrutement indigène de 1921," SHAT 9 N 269, Dossier 1, Effectifs 1922–1940. The recruitment chart for this year lists the number of volunteers and recruitment goals. Clayton gives 10,043 as the total conscripts for the year (*France*, 348).

31. The annual requests for new conscripts fluctuated but stayed near the 10,000 mark until the beginning of World War II, when they more than doubled. For 1908–54 statistics, see Echenberg, *Colonial Conscripts*, 27.

Increasing Resistance to Colonialism in Africa after the "Great War"

Ruth Simms Hamilton

AS EARLY AS 1916 MANY OF THE WORLD WAR I CONSCRIPTS FROM FRENCH West Africa began to return home, and within a few years Europeans were increasingly fearful of what they perceived as arrogant, subversive, and trouble-making behavior. In Guinea there were reports from military camps all over the country about disturbances due to dissatisfaction with back pay, long waits to be discharged, and inadequate food and clothing for the return to villages and towns. For example, soldiers were required to leave behind uniforms upon discharge, but since that was most likely their only clothing, the orders were simply ignored. In one camp the mutiny of more than 1,500 men went largely unpunished, partly because they outnumbered the authorities and had access to weapons.[1]

Many of the men who fought in France were influenced by socialism, and some joined the Ligue des Droits de l'Homme (League of the Rights of Man). Such exposure may have influenced many *anciens combattants* who engaged in union organizing and strikes among dock and railway workers in Conakry, Guinea. One veteran allegedly cleared all the construction workers off a new road when he compared their treatment to that of similar workers in France. He pointed out that black Africans, in their own land, were not well treated or paid adequately, and they still worked under the constraints of forced labor (*corvée*), which was outlawed in France in 1780. "And no African conscript who served in France can have failed to confront the stark contrast between the liberty, equality and fraternity which the Republic proclaimed for its citizens, and the disabilities which it imposed upon its [colonial] subjects."[2]

Many whites had objected to sending Africans to fight or even work in Europe; their exposure to European socialism could threaten continued white domination, and a little knowledge could be a dangerous thing. Many African conscripts were from rural areas and not very well educated, but their experiences abroad belied the racist ideology that blacks were childlike, subhuman, and incapable of learning on a par with Europeans. As in other parts of the diaspora, African veterans did not single-handedly destabilize colonialism, but their wartime service was life changing, with great implications for themselves and their communities. Their expanded level of consciousness would make it nearly impossible for them to be fully reintegrated into colonialist society.[3] Veterans, as cultural workers, were agents of change and transmitters of experiential knowledge, and they contributed in significant ways to the increasing tide of resistance.

New organizations were formed, such as the National Congress of British West Africa, established in Accra, Ghana, in 1920. Representatives from the Gold Coast, Gambia, Nigeria, and Sierra Leone saw the need to promote self-determination and eliminate racial discrimination. By 1921 cultural workers from the Francophone colonies had formed an organization with similar aims, Union Intercoloniale, which was soon followed by another group, Ligue Universelle pour la Défense de la Race Noire.[4]

Industrial workers also played an important part. In 1919 railway workers in Sierra Leone staged a strike for higher wages and were joined by two thousand striking police. During the same year the Industrial and Commercial Workers' Union of South Africa was formed; its first strike was launched in 1920 at Port Elizabeth, when laborers demanded and obtained a modest pay increase. There was a seamen's strike in Sierra Leone in 1929, and there were revolts in the French Congo in 1924, 1928, and 1930. A revolt against forced labor occurred in Ruanda-Urundi in 1929, with the daughter of the King of Ruanda as one of the leaders. In response, Belgian regiments and British detachments of the King's African Rifles (KAR) massacred more than a thousand Africans.[5]

After an earlier rebellion against Germany was suppressed and the leaders exiled to Cape Province in South Africa, the Bondelzwart people of South-West Africa (Namibia) revolted again. At the end of the war, the two leaders, Jacobus Christian and Abraham Morris, were denied permission to return to their homeland, which they eventually defied. Christian arrived in 1919 and Morris in 1921. When authorities attempted to arrest them, the Bondelzwarts and their headmen resisted. They seized arms from isolated white farms, and a major struggle erupted in May 1922. The Union of South Africa sent 455 men armed with the most advanced military equipment, including machine guns, and backed by airplanes. Even then it took them two weeks to bring the revolt to an end.[6]

Women and young girls were major participants in anti-colonial activism. Examples include the Ruanda princess noted above and Mandobe in the Kimbangu movement. One of the most significant revolts of the time involved Nigerian women. With the fall in prices for agrarian commodities, chiefs in Nigeria were instructed by the colonial state to impose higher taxes on market women. Thousands of them demonstrated against the government in 1929. In Aba, the capital of the Eastern Province at the time, women seized public buildings and held them for days. Soldiers of the West African Frontier Forces (WAFF) were ordered to shoot the women as they tried to escape, and the more than one hundred casualties included at least fifty deaths.

Several major social movements were quite notable in the 1920s, including the Kimbangu movement (1921) in the Belgian Congo (Zaire) and the Thuku movement (1921–22) in the East African Protectorate (Kenya). Simon Kimbangu, a carpenter, urged Africans to abandon the Christian missions and start their own independent churches. He had financial backing from elite Africans, and his following grew significantly, attracting students from British and French colonies. Plantation workers heeded his anti-European preachings and "left the plantations . . . in such large numbers that industry was disorganized," which was reinforced by the designation of Wednesday as the day of rest instead of Sunday. When the Belgian government ordered the arrest of Kimbangu, there were strikes and major acts of violence. Kimbangu was charged with using religion to overthrow the government and sentenced to death. His major assistants were tried and given prison terms that ranged from one year to life. Mandobe, "described as the most revolutionary woman in the Congo," received two years. The retaliatory violence and strikes by Kimbangu's followers prompted European traders to petition the king for a public hanging of Kimbangu, but when Africans let it be known that his death would result in a general massacre of whites, the home government commuted his sentence to life imprisonment and deported many of his assistants.[7]

In the East African Protectorate (Kenya), "land alienation, increase in settlers' political power, the Native Registration Ordinance, and the doubling of hut and poll taxes" contributed to the rise of Harry Thuku. On 7 June 1921, he became secretary of the Young Kikuyu Association, which was abandoned on 11 June for the more encompassing Africa Association, which cut across ethnic, racial, colonial state, and religious boundaries. On 1 July 1921, the title was changed to the East African Association (EAA), a "transnational" body within the region.[8] Thuku's advocacy of black solidarity had mass appeal, and some of his meetings attracted as many as twenty-five thousand people. He "embraced Christians, non-Christians, and Moslems in a much more deliberate way, and made the success of his non-sectarian policies a central theme in his publications."[9] Through correspondence and African envoys, Thuku built diaspora contacts that included such African Americans as Robert Moton, president of Tuskegee Institute, and Marcus Garvey of the Universal Negro Improvement Association (UNIA). Also, the NAACP's *Crisis* and UNIA's *Negro World* were in circulation in East Africa. Thuku issued his radical broadsheet, *Tangazo*, in December 1921. It often attacked missions and missionaries, had wide circulation, and was of considerable concern to colonial authorities.[10]

A mass protest meeting of the EAA in February 1922 was followed by the arrest of Thuku in March 1922. Thousands of his followers gathered to demand his release, and the KAR were ordered to fire on them, which resulted in many casualties and hundreds of arrests.[11] Marcus Garvey sent a letter of protest to the British Colonial Office, referring to

> the brutal manner in which your government has treated the Natives of Kenya East Africa. . . . [shooting] down a defenseless people in their own land for exercising their rights as men; such a policy will only tend to aggravate the many historic injustices heaped upon a race that will one day be placed in a position to truly defend itself not with mere sticks, clubs and stones but with the modern implements of science. . . . Again we ask you and your Government to be just to our race for surely we shall not forget you.[12]

Without a trial, Thuku was deported to "Kismay on the Somali border."[13]

Postwar resistance to colonial domination continued earlier struggles in the form of everyday defiance, evasion, flight, and various collective actions. After the Versailles Conference in 1919, liberation struggles in Africa seemed to expand in scale and scope of collective political and cultural actions that included global African collaboration and support. The powerful colonial state complex and its apparatus, including professional African military forces, remained brutally repressive, but the people as agents of change persisted as subjects of their own history.

NOTES

1. Anne Summers and R. W. Johnson, "World War I Conscription and Social Change in Guinea," *Journal of African History* 19, no. 1 (1978): 30.
2. Ibid., 29, 30–31.
3. Ibid., 37.
4. Paul Gordon Lauren, *Power and Prejudice: The Politics and Diplomacy of Racial Discrimination* (Boulder, Colo.: Westview Press, 1988), 105.

5. C. L. R. James, *A History of Pan-African Revolt* (Washington, D.C.: Drum and Spear Press, 1969), 48, 60–63.

6. Ibid., 63–66.

7. Ibid., 56–57.

8. Kenneth James King, *Pan-Africanism and Education: A Study of Race Philanthropy and Education in the Southern States of America and East Africa* (Oxford, Eng.: Clarendon Press, 1971), 65–66.

9. Ibid., 67.

10. Ibid., 67, 78.

11. The number injured and killed varies depending upon the sources. In *A History*, James states 150 people were murdered (58); In *Pan-Africanism*, King contends that twenty-five Africans were shot (79).

12. Garvey to David Lloyd George, 20 March 1922, quoted in Tony Martin, *Race First: The Ideological and Organizational Struggles of Marcus Garvey and the Universal Negro Improvement Association* (Westport, Conn.: Greenwood Press, 1976), 116.

13. James, *A History*, 58.

Orchestrating Race, Nation, and Gender: African Peacekeepers in Germany, 1919–1920

Ruth Simms Hamilton

AT THE CLOSE OF WORLD WAR I, THE TREATY OF VERSAILLES DEMANDED NOT only reparations but also occupation of Germany west of the Rhine River. From France's point of view, securing the southwestern part of Germany was necessary to prevent any subsequent aggression, and in this context French African forces entered the Ruhr Valley.[1] Between 1919 and 1921 Africans stationed in Germany included Algerians, Moroccans, Senegalese, and Tunisians.[2] Some of the larger cities in the occupied zone were Dusseldorf, Aachen, Köln, Coblenz, and Wiesbaden.[3]

During the peak of French occupation, in winter 1919, there were some 200,000 troops, but the number dropped to around 85,000 in January 1920. Troop strength varied by season, as many bivouacked in southern France during the winter, but in spring 1920 there were close to 42,000 Africans in the Ruhr Valley, and in spring 1921 around 45,000.[4] The commander of U.S. troops on the Rhine reported that "from January, 1919, to June, 1920, the average number of black troops in the French Army of the Rhine was 5,200, and of colored races, ranging from Moroccans to Malgaches [Madagascans], 20,000. In June, 1920, the black regiments were withdrawn; there remain the North Africans, the Malgaches, and a few black individuals in other regiments."[5] Although numbers vary depending on the source, there were far more "white" soldiers occupying the Rhine, but the focus of concern and discontent was directed toward the relatively small number of Senegalese soldiers. North Africans were targeted as well, but the main attention was directed toward the "coal-blacks."[6]

Germans were outraged that the French sent African occupation troops to the Rhineland. German colonization had been rationalized as a mission to raise an inferior race to a higher level of civilization; Africans were considered "childlike," "lazy," "born slaves," and subhuman.[7] The general population was conditioned to viewing Africans as exotic and primitive. In 1879, for example, Karl Hagenbeck exhibited them in his zoos at Stellingen because it was becoming more difficult to secure wild beasts from the African jungles, so he turned to *homo sapiens,* including Nubians, Somalis, and Hottentots.[8] In 1896 an exhibition of Ashantis in Budapest and at the Prater zoological gardens in Vienna was a focus of fascination for the "masses." According to Gilman, there was a predilection for Ashantis among the women of Vienna, who would "approach these Negroes under different pretexts for sexual encounters." The sexuality of the Ashantis was viewed by Europeans as inherently different from their own, and the Ashantis were representative of "blackness" as an abstraction, which "blackness" "signified the diseased but attractive Other for the Viennese."[9]

It was inconceivable that Africans should be posted on German soil, where "men were qualified by birth and blood connection to occupy the land."[10] Although the Germans used indigenous troops in their Africa campaign, they complained during the war about the use of African colonial troops against them, and they pleaded during armistice negotiations that "colored" troops not be part of the occupation forces. President Woodrow Wilson and the leaders of Britain and other European allies conveyed German concerns to the French but to no avail.[11] By the time the treaty took effect in January 1920, the Germans were already engaged in a major propaganda campaign against African troops, "The Black Horror on the Rhine."

The German Propaganda Assault

The German chancellor associated the presence of Africans with the denigration of sacred national symbols when he "imagined" Senegalese troops guarding the University of Frankfurt and Goethe House.[12] Political parties and organizations petitioned the National Assembly for their withdrawal, and some members of the assembly discussed the potential consequences of African occupation in relation to "moral and health dangers." A representative from the south-central province of Hessen expressed his concern for the female population of the Rhineland, impoverished by war and easily tempted: "Unfortunately, under these circumstances some part of the female population has not guarded their moral and national honor and have associated with the soldiers of occupation in offensive ways."[13] "German propaganda portrayed them as coal black savages from the African jungle."[14]

The German press played a major role in propagating vitriolic racialist discourse and stereotypes, and denigrating representations of Africans were presented in cartoon caricatures.[15] A newspaper account from Berlin provides a critical view of the propaganda campaign.

> The "black horror" is used to stir up the unenlightened chauvinist workers in white-guard Germany. Phantastic descriptions of excited old maids relating to the horror of the French occupation are being spread as actual facts. Even a German "Kultur Propaganda Film" ["The Black Horror on the Rhine"] is being shown, in which each white woman and each growing girl is forcibly seized by Negroes in French pay and violently enticed into a brothel. In Berlin and elsewhere extravagantly financed protest meetings of German people are held against "race destruction," and even official places such as the medical chambers are spreading inflammatory protests in the medical and daily press and give grossly exaggerated accounts of violent attacks of Negroes upon unprotected German women. Of course, outrages by young men in the French or English "garb of honor" may occur. Such things will happen as long as militarism sends young men into foreign lands against their will for the sake of conquest.[16]

Although most of the assertions were baseless, propaganda feeds negative images and calculated untruths to susceptible imaginations.

The establishment of brothels for occupying forces was one situation that fostered exaggerations. The French military ordered German city authorities to provide these for French troops. As shown in table 1, many were located in areas where North Africans and small units of Indo-Chinese and Senegalese were often posted. White artillery regiments and automobile corps also patronized the facilities. The brothel at Bad Ems was largely "used by Americans coming from Coblenz. The business is so lively, especially at night, that sometimes fourteen automobiles are parked in the street in front of the house."[17]

Sacred symbols of nation and whiteness were intertwined with such accusations as the abuse of white womanhood by uncontrollably oversexed African males; black rape and the degradation of white women; and the forced removal of citizens from their homes to make way for brothels costly to the German state and citizenry.[18] On the contrary, German entrepreneurs and the state expected to make a profit from the commerce of sex. Among sixteen descriptions of the circumstances and costs surrounding the establishment of brothels, in only one instance, Landau, was a large private home seized, which resulted in the displacement of four families. In most cases the businesses were subcontracted by the city authorities to private entrepreneurs.[19]

The mayor of one of the occupied cities stated:

Various cities have been formally compelled to establish brothels which, however, are also used by the white troops, men and officers. Sometimes the cities are compelled to acquire the houses needed. This was true in Speyer and Ludwigshafen, for instance. The business itself is carried on in those cities by entrepreneurs who are also responsible for recruiting the necessary personnel. In many cities, among them those named, there seem to have been no particular difficulties, although sometimes more or less gentle pressure may be exercised to induce women, even those already on the rolls of the morals police, to enter the public houses when the need arises.[20]

Women who had taken factory jobs when the men went off to war now faced hard times due to layoffs, and others had lost male breadwinners due to death or injuries. The economic and social fabric of Germany was in great disarray. Significant numbers of female factory workers "were turned out onto the streets as soon as their employment no longer brought profits to the war lords, and then they realized where they stood."[21] Were they concerned with guarding their "moral and national honor"? According to one newspaper account, three times more women than were needed sought work in the brothel at Ludwigshafen. "A war-widow, mother of four children, was among them."[22] It is likely that many women prostituted themselves for the first time in order to survive, in addition to those already on the radar of the "morals police."

Transnational Responses to Africans on the Rhine

One of the most pernicious propaganda campaigns against the African occupiers originated from Britain in the person of Edmund Dene Morel, who was a British radical, founder of the Union for Democratic Control (UDC), and member of the leftist Independent Labour Party (ILP). Born of a French father, he was originally named Georges Edmond Pierre Achille Morel-de-Ville.[23] A paternalistic protector of Africans, Morel was editor of *Africa Mail* and founder of the Congo Reform Association in 1904; he is credited for his efforts to terminate the regime of King Leopold in the Congo. Yet, in his 1919 work, *The Black Man's Burden,* he characterized Africans as "children" of the tropics, ill-equipped to survive capitalist exploitation, unlike European peasants, who possess an innate "force of character" unique to "white imperial people."[24]

Table 1. German Cities with Brothels for Occupation Troops, 1921

PLACE	BATTALIONS		REGIMENT	SOURCE OF REQUEST	DATE ESTABLISHED	# BROTHELS
	NUMBER	NATIONALITY				
Siegeburg	1	Tunisian	Riflemen No. 28	Occupation Authorities	Dec. 1918	1
Ludwigshafen	2	Moroccan	Colonial Infantry	French Local Commandant	Jan. 1919	1
Landau	1	Algerian	Riflemen #35	French Commandants	Jan. 1919	1
Speyer	1	Moroccan	Colonial Infantry	French Local Commandant	1920	1
Kastel	1	Moroccan	Riflemen No. 66	Occupation Authorities	1919	1
Weisenau (near Mainz)	1	Moroccan	Riflemen No. 66	French Chefferie du génie	1919	1
Bingen	1	Algerian	Riflemen No. 25	Delegates	April 1919	1
Griesheim	1	Algerian	Riflemen No. 33	Occupation Authorities	1919	1
Wiesbaden	2	Algerian	Riflemen No. 23	30th Army Corps	April 1919	2
Langen-schwalbach	1	Algerian	Riflemen No. 125	Occupation Authorities	Oct. 1919	1
Idstein	1	Algerian	Riflemen No. ?	Occupation Authorities	Dec. 1918	1
Hoechst am Main	1	Moroccan	Riflemen No. 66	Commandant	Dec. 1918, Oct. 1919, closed Nov. 1919	2
Bad Ems	1	Algerian	Riflemen No. 16	Occupation Authorities	Nov. 1921	1
Diez	1	Algerian	Riflemen No. 16	Commandant	Nov. 1919, June 1920	2
Kostheim	1	Algerian	Riflemen No. 53	French Chefferie du génie	1919	1
Total						18

Source: Papers of the Auswartiges Amt, 1922; and "The Black Troops on the Rhine," *The Nation* 112 (March 9, 1921): 365–66.

The Morel Factor

In an article published in London's *Daily Herald* on 10 April 1920, Morel launched a vicious racial propaganda assault against African soldiers. It followed a series of events four days earlier, when the French sent Moroccan units to occupy Frankfurt, Darmstadt, Hanau, and Hamburg in reprisal for the entry of German troops into the demilitarized zone. The Moroccans fired on a mob in Frankfurt and killed several civilians. Morel's front-page article appeared under the heading "Black Scourge in Europe/Sexual Horror Let Loose By France on Rhine/Disappearance of Young German Girls." The author vilified the "bestiality" of the black troops and labeled them "black savages," "primitive African barbarians," and "carriers of syphilis." The men were characterized as oversexed and said to have caused harm to white women for "well-known physiological reasons." Appealing to the fears of the working classes, Morel raised the specter that if men of the "backward races" can be used against an advanced civilization like the Germans, they can also be used against revolutionaries and workers in England and elsewhere.[25] (The economy of Great Britain was in turmoil, and working-class men and women expressed their rage against Africans, whom they saw as job competitors, in various riots.)

Morel continued to write about the "black menace" as passive instruments of capitalists and about the potential threat to European workers and revolutionary movements. All these ideas and more came together in his well-known pamphlet, *The Horror on the Rhine*,[26] in which the French are indicted for conscripting Africans, bringing tens of thousands into the heart of Europe, and quartering them upon European communities in time of peace. Moreover, Morel asks, will anyone who knows anything of tropical and subtropical Africa contend that sex is not central to the "sociology of that part of the world"? His response: "Nature opposes such obstacles to man in tropical Africa that strong *sex instinct* is essential to racial survival. If that strong sex instinct were non-existent, . . . the negro race would long ago have vanished from the face of the earth." Furthermore, "among the primitive—or the more natural . . . races inhabiting the tropical and sub-tropical areas of Africa, the *sex impulse* is a more *instinctive impulse* and precisely because it is so, a *more spontaneous, fiercer, less controllable impulse than among European peoples hedged in the complicated paraphernalia of convention and laws*" (emphasis added).[27]

Morel, whatever his political agenda, used primitivism as his major trope of racial expression. In his view, the childlike Africans are the racial Other in contrast to civilized Europeans, who are rational, logical, and scientific. In popular literature and discourse such as that found in *The Horror on the Rhine*, primitives are "conceived as childlike, intuitive, and spontaneous; they require the iron fist of 'European' governance and paternalistic guidance to control inherent physical violence and sexual drives."[28]

In most of the remainder of the pamphlet, Morel elaborates on the "outrages upon women," the establishment and operation of brothels, and purported evidence of "some eighty cases of rape and attempted rape" of German women and girls. Thousands of copies of the pamphlet were sold, and foreign-language editions were printed in Germany, France, the Netherlands, Spain, Portugal, and Italy.

Independent investigators found little truth to Morel's "horror." As during any occupation, there were abuses of civilians, such as the behavior of Germans in Africa and U.S. troops in Haiti (1915–34). The British government found the African troops were well behaved and the accusations exaggerated. Major General Henry T. Allen, commander of U.S. troops in the occupied Rhineland, issued a report assessing the situation.

> Germans have used the presence of these colored troops as the basis for a violent and exaggerated anti-French propaganda, . . . some German newspapers have honorably admitted such exaggeration. . . . Although, . . . *the discipline of the African troops is less perfect than that of their white comrades,* they are no such brute barbarians as they are pictured in the exaggerated propaganda here and abroad. And the presence of colored troops is no such special gall to Germans as it would be to Southerners in this country. . . . [There are] many cases of marriage freely contracted by German women with black soldiers. Gall and wormwood as any military occupation is to be occupied, and tyrannical as the occupiers are almost sure to be—as the Germans were in Belgium and as we are in Haiti—there are always cases of personal friendship and even love crossing the gulfs of hate and race.[29]

In Speyer, a reporter made the following observation:

> What I saw in the Imperial Theater under the title of The Black Horror . . . belong to the realm of imagination and are only produced in order to arouse popular feeling and to stir up passion and the spirit of revenge.
>
> What I saw with my own eyes in Speyer—white women around 9 o'clock in the evening in a side street in the vicinity of Altgurtel, joking with black soldiers, eating chocolate, and doing even more then that—certainly does not look like the acts of violence of the black troops.[30]

Claude McKay, a Harlem Renaissance writer from Jamaica, who was living in London in 1920, provides a concise and critical response to Morel's campaign.

Why all this obscene maniacal outburst about the sex vitality of black men . . . ? Rape is rape; the colour of the skin doesn't make it different. Negroes are no more over-sexed than caucasians; mulatto children in the West Indies and America were not the result of parthenogenesis. If Negro troops had syphilis, they contracted it from the white and yellow races. As for German women, in their economic plight they were selling themselves to anyone. I do not protest because I happen to be a negro . . . I write because I feel the ultimate result of your propaganda will be further strife and blood-spilling between whites and the many members of my race . . . who have been dumped down on the English docks since the ending of the European war.[31]

The United States

The Germans and Morel sought and received significant support in Europe and in the United States, Peru, and Argentina. The socialist connections of Morel also elicited support from well-known socialist activists and groups in Austria, Czechoslovakia, Denmark, France, Hungary, Ireland, Italy, The Netherlands, New Zealand, Norway, and Poland. Many were dissatisfied with the terms of the Treaty of Versailles, some were anti-war, and others were concerned about the spread of capitalism and imperialism.

In the United States, individuals and organized groups protested Germany's shame by lobbying Congress, writing letters to newspapers, and participating in demonstrations. Some journalists, "extreme leftists," politicians, and groups, including the Farm-Labor Party, were firmly behind Morel.[32] Efforts were led by the Steuben Society and the American Campaign Against the Horror on the Rhine (ACAHR). ACAHR was a group largely comprised of German and Irish Americans. It lobbied state and national legislators and the executive offices of government, raised money, and produced and distributed propaganda. German Americans were lobbied by Germany's Alliance Against the Black Terror "to unite and raise money to help carry on the campaign to impress upon Americans the awfulness and reality of the Black Terror in the Rhineland."[33]

On 28 February 1921, a protest rally of 12,000 at Madison Square Garden in New York City was characterized by one writer as a "love feast participated in by Sinn-Feiners and pro-Germans on equal terms." Another suggested that some Irish and German speakers were more anti-British than anti-French.

Many Americans of German descent came to Madison Square Garden believing that atrocities had really been visited upon their kinsmen by black soldiers in French uniform.

The American people should know, one New York speaker said, that these negroes "were dragged and coddled and inveigled out of the wilds of darkest Africa—Senegalese troops, thrown upon the white country of good virtuous, law-abiding citizens, such as German people know how to be, and there they are left to wreak their uncultured, untutored, uncivilized ways upon those innocent people." A resolution was passed declaring that these troops are victims of "an inhuman system of brutal conscription," and that something should be done to forestall the breach in the relations between this country and France to which their use is likely to lead. The resolution concludes with a petition to Congress "to instruct the President forthwith to inform the French Republic that the moral sense of the American people demands the immediate withdrawal of the uncivilized French colored troops from the occupied districts of Germany and the assurance that they will not be returned there, to the end that a speedy and permanent stop be put to the horror of the Rhine."[34]

There were those in the United States who were critical of the "horror stories," including the editors of and writers for *Crisis* and *The Nation*. There was a counter demonstration launched by the national commander of the American Legion, who saw ACAHR as driving a wedge between the United States and the people by whose side veterans had fought overseas; the rally on March 16 in Madison Square Garden drew approximately 25,000 participants, twice as many as the February pro-German protest. Carrie Chapman Catt, president of the National American Women's Suffrage Association, viewed the propaganda as a German American campaign based on a little truth and a great deal of falsehood. Moreover, the African troops had behaved no more shockingly than any others. "There is no Army of Occupation anywhere in the world about which such charges have not been made . . . one of the normal and inevitable results of the greatest of all atrocities, namely war itself."[35]

Lewis S. Gannett, an investigative reporter for *The Nation*, conducted interviews and studied police reports in Germany in 1920. He deemed five police reports to be authentic because of "cold, unemotional recitals of fact" and made the point that "women do not lightly report such experiences." Among the five reports,

> *not one of them refers to a crime committed by a Negro!* The five stories tell of twelve soldier brutes; seven of these were French Whites, five were Moroccans (largely Arab stock), and not one a Negro. There are Negroes, coal-black Negroes, on the Rhine, . . . they behave, on the whole better than the French Whites, and far better than the Moroccan Whites. The black race is enough maligned and abused without adding the dirty scores of the white race to its count.
>
> I talked in full, frank confidence with people of all stations in life who relieved their

hearts of accumulated complaints, but I found that Germans across the Rhine believed conditions to be worse than Germans in the Rhineland claimed them to be, just as German-Americans in this country believe them to be worse still. . . . The growth of venereal disease in the Rhineland, due largely to the white soldiers there, is appalling. I wish our German-American friends would make a frontal attack upon the very principle of military occupation and leave the Negro race apart. . . . There is a black horror on the Rhine, but it is not a Negro horror.[36]

Racial Solidarity of European Women

The appeal to European women and their responses make transparent the relationship between white female sexuality and larger geopolitics within a global system of racialized dominance. As shown in table 2, women in a vanquished Germany and in victorious nations were together in their opposition to Africans on the Rhine: primitive people must stay in their own country; they do not have sexual control; they are an outrage and an insult to white women worldwide. The Third International Congress of the Women's International League for Peace and Freedom met in Vienna on July 10–17, 1921, and passed a resolution opposing the military use of "native" populations.

Racism has no borders or frontiers. In fact, the positions of the women indicate that racism transcends nationalism and provides a larger relational space for European states to affirm their whiteness, their European peopleness. In the imperial competition for colonies, there was wide agreement on the mutual ideology of the White Man's Burden. Even the vanquished Germans and their allies could still feel they were part of the superior race. Even as losers, they were still winners as Europeans. Leading women and their organizations were unanimous in their defense of European civilization and in protecting the interests of their families and nations by making sure the Africans stayed in their place, colonized and respectful of their colonizers.

The solidarity of the women is a gendered expression of a European "we-ness," a "racist supranationalism." A common European identity reduces contrasts among European nations, and a self-confident and superior Western identity was reinforced by colonial and imperial successes.[37] Balibar's notion of a racist internationalism provides a frame of reference for analyzing European solidarity against the African soldiers in Germany.

A racial signifier has to transcend national differences and organize "transnational" solidarities so as to be able, in return, to ensure the effectivity of nationalism. Thus [anti-blackness] functioned on a European scale: each nationalism saw in the [black] . . .

its own specific enemy and the representative of all other "hereditary enemies"; this meant, then, that all nationalisms were defined against the *same* foil, the same [colonized, denationalized Other], and this has been a component of the very idea of Europe as the land of "modern" nation-states or, in other words, of civilization. At the same time, the European or Euro-American nations, locked in a bitter struggle to divide up the world into colonial empires, recognized that they formed a community and shared an "equality" through that very competition, a community and an equality to which they gave the name "White."[38]

By propagating and reinforcing racial stereotypes, European women, like the men, were active participants in dehumanizing Africans, keeping them in their "place" in Africa. At the same time, they perpetuated the mythical sacred white womanhood image, associated with whiteness and nationhood, as well as the polluted black male, associated with primitive and denationalized colonial subjects.

Articulating Race, Nation, and Gender

Defeated and occupied at the end of the war, Germany had to rescue and restore its state and its identity. Occupation by white soldiers was bad enough, but African soldiers on the Rhine—those "subhumans" the Germans had colonized and oppressed—added insult to injury. Knowing that many Europeans did not support the occupation in general, Germans used the presence of Africans to call attention to their plight and create antagonism toward the French. At a time when the European colonial and imperialistic system was being reordered, reinforced by ideologies of white racial superiority, the appeal to racism and racial imagery worked effectively for Germany. It not only reinforced German nationalism but also rallied support from other Europeans by invoking a sense of whiteness and common identity.

Racism helps produce the fictive ethnicity around which nationalism is organized. No community instituted by the nation-state possesses an inherent ethnic base. As social formations become nationalized, the populations within them are represented in the past or in the future as if they were a natural community, "possessing an identity of origins, culture and interests."[39] To reinforce this fictive or imaginary identity, race defines who is to be included or excluded. For example, one female member of the German National Assembly characterized the presence of African troops as "unnatural."[40] "All kinds of somatic or psychological features, both visible and invisible, may lend themselves to creating the fiction of a racial identity and

Table 2. Protests of European Women's Organizations against African Troops, 1920–21

BRITAIN[a]

- *Organization:* National Conference of Labour Women (London, April 1920); Women's International League for Peace and Freedom–British Division (London, April 1920)
- *Supporters*: London Daily Herald, Association of Women Clerks and Secretaries, Fabian Women's Group, Independent Women's Social and Political Union, National Federation of Women Teachers, Standing Committee of Industrial Women's Organizations, National Federation of Women Workers, Women's Co-operative Guild; 13 members of Parliament
- *Action*: Resolution; Protest Meeting; Resolution
- *Content*: Withdraw African troops (It's not race, it's development. Blacks do not have same powers of sexual control as developed races.); E. D. Morel main speaker; "That in the interest of good feeling between all the races of the world and the security of all women, this meeting calls upon the League of Nations to prohibit the importation into Europe for warlike purposes, of troops belonging to primitive peoples, and their use anywhere, except for purposes of police and defense in the country of their origin."[b]

FRANCE[c]

- *Organization*: Organization of French Socialist Women
- *Action*: Resolution
- *Content*: Withdraw African troops

GERMANY[d]

- *Organization*: Rhenish Women's League; 20 German women's organizations, in-

therefore to representing *natural* and hereditary differences between social groups either within the same nation or outside its frontiers."[41]

Germans' self-understanding of who they are as a nation has been long in the making. Germany did not become a nation-state until the late nineteenth century. Before that the pre-political nation was conceptualized in ethno-cultural terms, a *volksgemeinschaft* (organic) community linguistically and racially distinctive.[42] Themes of national virility, racial purity, and Aryanism were associated with German cluding women's society of German evangelical churches

- *Supporters*: Politicians and political organizations
- *Action*: Data collection publication; Work with governments of German states of Bavaria, Hesse, Prussia; Petition League of Nations
- *Content*: Focus on atrocities of "coloured soldiers"; Transmit depositions and police reports to E. D. Morel; Investigate the use of African troops on the Rhine

NETHERLANDS[e]

- *Organization*: Association of Dutch Women for Social Welfare
- *Action*: Petition League of Nations
- *Content*: Intervene on the Rhine

SWEDEN[f]

- *Organization*: 59 women's organizations
- *Action*: 50,000 women's signatures to a petition to League of Nations; Published pamphlet
- *Content*: Protest "atrocities of the French black troops in Germany"; "Coloured Frenchmen on the Rhine" expressed outrage upon womanhood throughout the world

a. See Reinders, "Racialism on the Left," 7–8.
b. Ibid., 8.
c. Ibid., 12.
d. Ibid., 14.
e. Ibid.
f. Nelson, "The Black Horror," 616; *The Literary Digest*, 22; Reinders, "Racialism on the Left," 14.

Robert C. Reinders, "Racialism on the Left: E. D. Morel and the 'Black Horror on the Rhine,'" *International Review of Social History* 13, part 1 (1968); Keith L. Nelson, "The Black Horror on the Rhine: Race as a Factor in Post–World War I Diplomacy," *Journal of Modern History* 42 (December 1970); *The Literary Digest* 66 (28 August 1920).

cultural, intellectual, and political traditions long before World War I. German citizenry was defined as a community of descent rooted in blood and racial purity; hence, Africans and other people of color were perceived as impure, negatively polluted, to be excluded from the national community. At the outbreak of the war, "the Reich had succeeded in integrating the differing, even antagonistic traditions of Prussian statehood and German nationhood. Yet the old dualism survived, the old tension between statist and ethnocultural components in the German tradition of nationhood."[43] The racialization of African soldiers was one way to express national-ism and nationhood.

Was the German state and its propaganda apparatus really concerned about brothels for occupying soldiers, the overwhelming majority of whom were Europeans? Or was the real concern about the dangers posed to the German state and its imperialist aims by working-class white women and the small number of African soldiers? Racist discourse in patriarchal societies presupposes sexism. Sexual control and restraint are perceived to be necessary to deal with the complexity of major social, political, and economic changes related to colonialism and the domination and con-trol of other people and societies.[44] Even before Germany became a state in 1871, its European identity was established in part by its appropriation of classical Greek her-itage, including the ideal "Greek male body as a subject position of cultural superior-ity." Along with purity and virility as central themes of nationhood, the beautiful body personified the beautiful nation. Maintaining the ideal of masculinity, as opposed to the uncontrolled instinctive or impulsive sexuality of tropical Africa, for example, was perceived to be essential to the order and health of the nation. Control and discipline of the body, as one indicator of national identity, helped to define the boundaries between normality and deviancy, masculinity and femininity, and racial superiority and inferiority. "Thus, nationalism used racist, sexist, [anti-African stereotypes] to redirect passion . . . to the body politic of the nation."[45]

Gendered imagery of the modern nation-state is associated with terms such as fatherland and motherland. As suggested by Delaney, the symbolic association of national identity with women's bodies is an especially powerful approach to natural-izing power. For example, Ataturk used his mother to draw an analogy to the moth-erland, "portraying injuries to one as if they were injuries to the other." Hence, if mother is injured, so is the nation.[46] Gender is placed within the context of repro-duction. "It is the coming together of sexualized bodies in a *natural* act of political procreation that gives rise to the *birth* of [the modern nation-state] as a body politic."[47] In many societies women often represent the symbolic figuration of cul-tural and ideological traditions; they are projected as the ideological reproducers or the "cultural carriers" of the state.[48]

Sacred white German womanhood was part of the mythology created to sym-bolize racial purity. In order to maintain the integrity of these beliefs so vital to national identity, German women were expected to stay in their place, ensuring chastity and purity. "The German woman had become the white desexualized mother-sister ideal, guardian of culture and morals and guarantee and basis of patri-archal identity."[49] Nothing would be more destabilizing to this myth than white working-class women and African soldiers who produced impure children (later derisively called the "Rhineland Bastards"). The propaganda machines continued to represent African soldiers as "black beast rapists," diseased and perverse sexualized figures. Newspaper editors, women and men who were active in politics—many from privileged social backgrounds—and others associated with religious groups that held views about the moral order of society questioned the morals of a "certain class of young German women."[50] These women were labeled the instigators of sex, and there was a defined need to control their sexuality. These women dared to display behavior that could potentially soil and corrupt the image of white female purity, which was on a par with God, nation, and empire. "Gender was 'an instrument of class,' a strategy that permitted the hegemony of middle-class norms which rendered working-class women . . . 'improperly gendered' by virtue of their distance from middle-class values."[51]

The dynamic between racial hierarchy and sexual anxiety was heightened by war, and there was major concern in the colonial centers about African and other colonial soldiers of color meeting and interacting with white women on equal terms, behavior that was hazardous to ideology and the practice of imperial colonial rule.

Race was a "crucial ruling strategy," and racial subordination was as critical to . . . imperialism at home as it was in the colonies. The war brought about an increasingly alarmist . . . vision of sexual disorder [between] "unruly" women and [nonwhite] colonials [who] were subject to far more rigorous controls than other groups. Sexual politics could not escape the tight bounds of race . . . nor could the politics of race exist except as marked by sexuality. These were "mutually determining" axes "necessarily implicated in one another."[52]

The case of African soldiers on the Rhine demonstrates the necessary relationship between racism and nationalism, both of which are articulated through sexism and gender. It also points out how gender can become an instrument of class within the framework of national sexual politics. All of this took place within the context of transcontinental colonialism and imperialism at the end of the Great War, when Germany was fighting for its national soul and political place in postwar geopolitical transitions. The competition for world economic and industrial supremacy involved the land, labor, and resources of colonized peoples and the struggle to make one's nation-state a dominant world player. The geosocial movement of African men as part of French occupation forces in Germany became a focal point to crystallize in the German mind the most deprecatory views of the black Other. Within this context, Germany exploited racial imagery, using African soldiers as scapegoats for broader world economic and political goals. No matter how small their numbers and how meager their circumstances, African diaspora peoples were indeed constitutive of, and mediated within and by, the larger world system.

NOTES

1. Donald S. Detwiler, *Germany: A Short History*, 2nd rev. ed. (Carbondale: Southern Illinois University Press, 1989), 172–78.
2. C. M. Andrew and A. S. Kanya-Forstner, "France, Africa and the First World War," *Journal of African History* 19, no. 1 (1978): 11–23.
3. Reiner Pommerin, *Sterilisierung der Rheinlandbastarde: Der Schicksal einer farbigen Minderheit, 1918–1937* (Dusseldorf: Droste Verlag, 1979), 8.
4. Keith L. Nelson, "The Black Horror on the Rhine: Race as a Factor in Post–World War I Diplomacy," *Journal of Modern History* 42 (December 1970): 610–11.
5. "The Black Troops on the Rhine," *The Nation* 112 (9 March 1921): 365.
6. Winston Churchill stated that "of 95,000 French troops stationed in the occupied zone, 7,500 were colonials, including one brigade of Senegalese." Nelson, "The Black Horror on the Rhine," 10. An account written in March 1921 claims "but one French regiment of troops of negroid origin in Germany" at that time (editorial, *Literary Digest*, 12 March 1921, 15). Davis reports that the French force totaled 85,000, of which "23,400 were native [African] troops, among them 7,490 Senegalese and Malagaches, the rest being Algerian and Moroccan." Shelby Cullom Davis, *Reservoirs of Men: A History of the Black Troops of French West Africa* (1934; Westport, Conn.: Negro Universities Press, 1970), 164.

    The issue of who was "truly" black added to the confusion. One source notes that the non-Senegalese troops were "Arab and Berber, who are of the Semitic branch of the white race, similar to the Jews, of whom there are so many now in Germany" (Pfalzzentrale Heidelberg, *Schwarze am Rhein: Ein Weltproblem* [Heidelberg: F. W. Schroeder Verlag, 1921], 14). This text is a German response to the French defense of the presence of African troops, and it is propaganda to the extent that it seeks to persuade public opinion that the occupation of Germany was an unjust act. Both the Germans and the French defined the Tunisians, Moroccans, and Algerians as Arabs and as racially distinct from the Senegalese, the Negroes.

    The German Foreign Office claimed that after March 1921 there were still fourteen or fifteen "brown regiments" (average strength 2,500) in addition to the seventeen colored regiments, which seemed to include at least two from Senegal (Auswartiges Amt. Nr. II/ab, R 995/Nr. 253, 28 February 1922). Berlin went so far as to send categorizations of the African troops to the German Embassy in Washington. The report makes the following distinctions: "Blacks = Negroes from Central Africa; Yellows = Malagasy, born in Madagascar, they are part Malaysian, part Negroid type; Browns = North Africans: Algerians, Tunisians and Moroccans. These 'Browns' from North Africa belong to the Caucasian race, are Semitic-Arab . . . ; Moors are mixtures of those two and Negroes" (Auswartiges Amt. Nr. I/ab, R 995/Nr. 253, Berlin, 27 March 1922). A supplement to the Foreign Office report cites a constant 65,000 white soldiers—summer and winter—but 23,000 "colored" troops during summer and 15,000 during the winter of 1920 (Ibid.).
7. See "Anti-Black Reigns of Terror in Great Britain and the Americas in 1919: Similarity and Simultaneity" in this book.
8. Karl Hagenbeck, *Von Tieren und Menschen. Erlebnisse und Erfahrung* (Berlin: Vita Deutsches

Verlagshaus, 1909). Also read the story of Ota Benga, a Congolese pygmy who was displaced by a missionary to be put on display at the 1904 World's Fair in St. Louis. See Phillips Verner Bradford and Harvey Blume, *Ota: The Pygmy in the Zoo* (New York: St. Martin's Press, 1992).

9. Sander L. Gilman, "Black Sexuality and Modern Consciousness," in *Blacks and German Culture*, ed. Reinhold Grimm and Jost Hermand (Madison: University of Wisconsin Press, 1986), 36–39.

10. Ivan Hannaford, *Race: The History of an Idea in the West* (Baltimore, Md.: Johns Hopkins University Press, 1966), 246.

11. Nelson, "Black Horror on the Rhine," 612–13.

12. Ibid., 615–16.

13. Pommerin, *Sterilisierung*, 23.

14. Sally Marks, "Black Watch on the Rhine: A Study in Propaganda, Prejudice, and Prurience," *European Studies Review* 13 (July 1983): 297–334.

15. See May Opitz, Katharina Oguntoye, and Dagmar Schultz, *Showing Our Colors: Afro-German Women Speak Out*, transl. Anne V. Adams et al. (Amherst: University of Massachusetts Press, 1992), 44–47; and *Literary Digest*, 28 August 1920, 22.

16. *The Nation* 113 (13 July 1921): 44.

17. "The Black Troops on the Rhine," 366.

18. Robert C. Reinders, "Racialism on the Left: E. D. Morel and the 'Black Horror on the Rhine,'" *International Review of Social History* 13, part 1 (1968): 4–6.

19. "The Black Troops on the Rhine," 366. "Ludwigshafen. . . . The city authorities bought two houses for 90,000 marks, and equipped one for 43,000 marks. The business was let out, and it is hoped to cover the costs by the rental. Bingen . . . The costs, 40,000 marks, are to be covered by interest at 5, and amortization at 2 per cent. Wiesbaden . . . two brothels were established upon demand by the French, at a cost of 58,542.32 marks, besides which the city provided equipment costing 100,000 marks, which the manager of the brothel is to pay for in monthly installments of 1,500 marks. Speyer . . . The city paid 50,000 marks to buy two houses; the business is rented out, the renter paying for the equipment, and it is hoped that the rent will pay for the purchase costs."

20. Ibid.

21. *The Nation* 113 (13 July 1921): 44.

22. Ibid.

23. Peter Fryer, *Staying Power: The History of Black People in Britain* (Atlantic Highlands, N.J.: Humanities Press, 1984), 317.

24. Reinders, "Racialism on the Left," 2–3; E. D. Morel, *The Black Man's Burden* (Manchester, England: National Labour Press, 1920).

25. Reinders, "Racialism on the Left," 1–2.

26. E. D. Morel, *The Horror on the Rhine*, 8th ed., Pamphlet No. 44, (Kingsway, London: St. Clements Press, April 1921).

27. Ibid., 8–10.

28. David Theo Goldberg, *Racist Culture: Philosophy and the Politics of Meaning* (Oxford, England: Blackwell, 1993), 156.

29. Emphasis added, "The Black Troops on the Rhine," 365. Also see *Literary Digest*, 12 March 1921, 15.

30. Reprinted from a newspaper in Speyer in *The Nation* 113 (13 July 1929): 44.

31. Reinders, "Racialism on the Left," 17, quoting a letter by Claude McKay, "A Black Man Replies," *Workers' Dreadnought*, 24 April 1920. Born in 1891 in Jamaica, McKay was well recognized and honored in his country before he left in 1912 to attend Tuskegee Institute in Alabama, where he stayed for a short time before attending Kansas State University. In 1919 he left the United States for Europe, and he lived in London until his return to the United States in 1921. In 1922 he visited the Soviet Union, Berlin, and Paris, and then he remained in Europe for about ten years. McKay, noted

for his poetry and fiction, died in 1948. His autobiography is entitled *A Long Way from Home* (New York: L. Furman, 1937).

32. Nelson, "The Black Horror on the Rhine," 620–23.

33. *Literary Digest,* 12 March , 1921, 14.

34. Ibid.

35. Ibid., 15.

36. Lewis S. Gannett, "The Horror on the Rhine Again," *The Nation* 113 (7 September 1921): 264.

37. Samir Amin, an economist, provides a historical perspective on this view of the world and the implications for its victims, the world's poor, in *Eurocentrism* (New York: Monthly Review Press, 1989). Goldberg also addresses the issue in *Racist Culture* (163–68).

38. Etienne Balibar, "The Nation Form: History and Ideology," in *Race, Nation, Class: Ambiguous Identities,* Etienne Balibar and Immanuel Wallerstein (London: Verso, 1991), 62.

39. Balibar, "The Nation Form," 96.

40. Reinders, "Racialism on the Left," 14.

41. Balibar, "The Nation Form," 99.

42. For details (in English) see Rogers Brubaker, *Citizenship and Nationhood in France and Germany* (Cambridge, Mass.: Harvard University Press, 1992); Alec G. Hargreaves and Jeremy Leaman, eds., *Racism, Ethnicity and Politics in Contemporary Europe* (Brookfield, Vt.: Edward Elgar Publishing, 1995); John Wrench and John Solomos, eds., *Racism and Migration in Western Europe* (Oxford, England: Berg Publishers, 1993); and Czarina Wilpert, "Ideological and Institutional Foundations of Racism in the Federal Republic of Germany," in Wrench and Solomos, *Racism,* 67–81.

43. Brubaker, *Citizenship and Nationhood,* 13.

44. Patricia Vertinsky, "Body Matters: Race, Gender and Perception of Physical Ability from Goethe to Weininger," in *Identity and Intolerance: Nationalism, Racism and Xenophobia in Germany and the United States,* ed. Norbert Finzsch and Dietmar Schirmer (Cambridge, England: Cambridge University Press, 1998), 331; and Balibar, "The Nation Form," 49.

45. Vertinsky, "Body Matters," 332–33.

46. C. Delaney, "Father State, Motherland, and the Birth of Modern Turkey," in *Naturalizing Power ,* ed. S. Yanagisako and C. Delaney (New York, N.Y.: Routledge, 1995), 186.

47. Hastings Donnan and Thomas M. Wilson, *Borders: Frontiers of Identity, Nation and State* (New York: Berg/Oxford International Publishers, 1999), 149.

48. See Floya Anthias and Nira Yuval-Davis, "Women and the Nation States," in *Nationalism,* ed. John Hutchinson and Anthony D. Smith (New York, N.Y.: Oxford University Press, 1994), 312–16.

49. Vertinsky, "Body Matters," 332.

50. *The Literary Digest,* 28 August 1920, 22.

51. Philippa Levine, "Battle Colors: Race, Sex, and Colonial Soldiers in World War I," in *Journal of Women's History* 9 (Winter 1998), 104–30, 116.

52. Ibid., 106.

Anti-Black Reigns of Terror in Great Britain and the Americas in 1919: Similarity and Simultaneity

Ruth Simms Hamilton

LTHOUGH IN 1919 THE PEACE CONFERENCE WAS HELD AT VERSAILLES AND THE Pan-African Conference took place in Paris, the year was not a peaceful one for large segments of global Africa. In Great Britain and the Americas, it was characterized by the most vitriolic expressions of racism and brutality directed at peoples of the African diaspora.

GREAT BRITAIN

The modern history of black people in Britain is linked to slavery in the West Indies and the slave trade in general. At least 20,000 enslaved Africans lived in England before 1772, and it is estimated that at least 40,000 blacks resided in Liverpool, Bristol, and other parts of the country by the turn of the century. In the late eighteenth century Pan-Africanism was foreshadowed by the publication in London of the writings of Ottobah Cugano *(Thoughts and Sentiments on the Evil and Wicked Traffic of the Slavery and Commerce of the Human Species, 1787)* and Olaudah Equiano *(The Interesting Narrative of the Life of Olaudah Equiano or Gustavus Vassa, the African, 1789).*[1]

Before World War I peoples of African descent who lived in Britain included students and those earning a living in various occupations that ranged from the professions to street begging. There were blacks in theology and religion, politics, medicine, law, business, the performing arts, sports, and journalism. They were writers, missionaries, nurses, civil servants, and personal servants of the wealthy. The vast majority belonged to the working class and lived very hard lives, and the largest number were seamen in places such as Barry, Cardiff, Glasgow, Hull, London, Liverpool, Newport, and Tyneside. At the outbreak of World War I many were recruited to work in munition and chemical factories for the navy and merchant marine, and for the numerous armies of the king.[2]

At the end of the war Britain was weakened militarily, politically, and economically. It had a major national debt as well as international debts, especially to the United States. A major social crisis affected the employment and livelihood of everyone. Many black seamen and laborers brought from the colonies remained after the war, but the need for their labor decreased as white servicemen returned. Shipping companies in major port cities would not hire or fired blacks and other foreign laborers. Demobilization substantially increased black unemployment in cities. "In one week alone, in the spring of 1919 about 120 black workers employed for years in the big Liverpool sugar refineries and oilcake mills were sacked [fired] because white workers now refused to work with them."[3] Such actions were repeated from Liverpool to London to South Wales, where white mobs attacked blacks, burned their homes, and inflicted physical and psychological violence. "White workers in bitter economic competition with black workers were mobilized into lynch mobs led by armed groups."[4]

The worst of these incidents took place in coastal cities such as Liverpool, where from between 2,000 to 5,000 blacks resided. In June 1919 roving gangs of whites that numbered up to 10,000 savagely beat and stabbed blacks on the street and looted and burned their homes. One site of some safety was the hall of the Ethiopian Association in Liverpool. Within the first ten days of June, as many as 700 men, women, and children took refuge there and were transferred in police vans to safer locations.[5] Between 6 and 11 June, crowds of whites in Newport also viciously attacked peoples of African, Chinese, and Greek descent. In Cardiff, where the black population rose from 700 before the war to more than 3,000 in early 1919, as many as 40 percent were unemployed. Demobilized, unskilled, and unemployed whites, with the aid of armed soldiers, attacked the homes and neighborhoods of Arabs, Egyptians, Portuguese, Malayans, Somalis, West Indians, and especially the heavily populated black settlement of Bute Town.

It was not unusual for foreign white soldiers and seamen to attack Africans and West Indians. Some of the soldiers who assisted white gangs were Australians. In one instance, two Scandinavian seamen stabbed a West Indian who refused to give them cigarettes. His friends retaliated at a pub frequented by Scandinavians, attacking them "with sticks, knives, razors, and pieces of iron taken from lamp-posts, knocking unconscious a policeman who tried to stop them." Police raided a boardinghouse to arrest the West Indians but were confronted with men armed with revolvers, knives, and other instruments. In another attack, a demobilized white soldier, joined by three other whites, accosted a French West Indian seaman, who fought back and stabbed to death the former soldier. The West Indian was then chased by a crowd and finally arrested. He was found guilty of manslaughter and sentenced to five years in prison.

There were riots and violent attacks against the African diaspora in London between April and June 1919. Black seamen were especially targeted; large crowds of whites gathered outside lodging houses used by them, cat-calling and insulting every black person who tried to enter. Coffee shops patronized by blacks were stormed and customers seized. In one instance, a Jamaican on leave from the Royal Navy was brutally attacked and fired into the crowd to defend himself; he was arrested but found not guilty. Many former members of the British West Indies Regiment, still in uniform, were also victims of violence. "For the entire black community in Britain, the final straw came a month after the riots, when it was decided not to allow any black troops to take part in London's victory celebrations: the much trumpeted Peace March on 19 July 1919."[6]

The white mobs outnumbered blacks, but they defended themselves as best they could. Some neighborhoods and communities decided to fight back rather than leave. In some areas of Cardiff, for example, they armed themselves, posted sentries, "and left no one in doubt of their mood."[7] Newspapers such as the *African Telegraph*, religious leaders, cultural workers, and organizations such as the Society of Peoples of African Origin and the Society of African Peoples, formed in 1919, acted in the interest of diaspora people under siege. They sent deputations to the British government and staged public protests, but the state and its institutions were not very responsive.

Other organizations were formed by diaspora students during the war years, including the African Student's Union of Great Britain and Ireland (1917). It is significant that the name was later changed, when a number of West Indian students joined, to the Union for Students of African Descent. Another example of transnational consciousness and action is the West African Students Union (1925), which in 1928 moved into a house put at its disposal for a year by Marcus Garvey. Paul Robeson became a financial patron of the union.[8]

The situation in Britain had major implications for black people in other parts of the empire, including the British West Indies.

[B]etween the time of their enlistment in the [British West Indies Regiment] and 1919 the soldiers had suffered massive blows to their dignity and their physical well-being. They had seen white and light-skinned West Indians accepted as fighting men while their own requests were met with procrastination; they had been confined for most of the war to fatigue duty, menial labour, carrying ammunition under heavy fire and garrison duty; they had seen comrades die from neglect in white-run hospitals; they had been subjected to every kind of petty racial abuse; their remuneration and benefits were usually inferior to those of white troops; and, with the war's end, even those benefits promised them were not forthcoming. And to further exacerbate matters, some of the returning soldiers had been involved in riots in Cardiff, Wales, during which British mobs had vented their racist fury against [them].[9]

Many of the riot victims, particularly demobilized soldiers, sailors, and merchant marines, were repatriated to the Caribbean. Resentful of their mistreatment during the war and afterward, they directed their violence toward the British in their Caribbean homelands. In July 1919, former members of the British West Indies Regiment (BWIR) staged an insurrection in British Honduras (Belize), while in Jamaica white seamen from HMS *Constance* were injured in hand-to-hand combat in Kingston. During the same month, "returnees" in Trinidad fought sailors from the HMS *Dartmouth*. Black seamen and military prisoners in the process of repatriation aboard the SS *Ocra* mutinied, and in St. Kitts the Universal Benevolent Association staged protests against the riots in Britain.[10] "Upon returning to Trinidad, the veterans imme-diately organized The Returned Soldier and Sailors Council and Organization which . . . may have been an offshoot of the Caribbean League . . . formed by West Indians in Taranto, Italy."[11] The 1919 revolutionary upheaval in Trinidad, including a dock strike, was a major jolt to British colonialism. At this critical juncture, structural inequalities and the cumulative experiences of returnees contributed to the growth of black consciousness and decolonization movements in the region.

THE UNITED STATES

Much has been written about what James Weldon Johnson labeled the "Red Summer" of 1919 in the United States.[12] Race riots, lynchings, the terror of the Ku Klux Klan, and racial oppression competed with stories about the "war to end all wars." One of the worst attacks had occurred two years earlier in East St. Louis, Illinois, where numerous blacks were killed, some of them burned alive in their houses, and at least 6,000 were driven from their homes. In 1919 there were eighty-three lynchings, including ten of black veterans still in uniform; more than two hundred rallies and public meetings were held by the KKK from New England to Indiana and Florida; and twenty-six race riots occurred across the United States in such locations as Elaine, Arkansas; Philadelphia and Chester, Pennsylvania; Omaha, Nebraska; Knoxville, Tennessee; Longview, Texas; Washington, D.C.; and Chicago, Illinois.[13] During the Chicago riot in July, blacks met mobs with mobs. The death toll was thirty-eight, and twenty-three of the dead were blacks.[14]

> The summer of 1919 . . . ushered in the greatest period of interracial strife the nation had ever witnessed. From June to the end of the year there were approximately twenty-five race riots. Some were large, others were small, and all were indicative of a thoroughly malodorous situation in race relations. Even after the war the migration of African Americans to urban centers continued and, in some areas, increased. Jobs were not so plentiful as during the war years, and competition strained the relations of whites and blacks. Meanwhile, the high rents in the segregated residential areas continued. Unrest and disappointment seized a considerable portion of the African-American population, and when it became clear that many whites were seeking to deprive them of some of the gains they had made during the war, blacks bristled into action and showed a willingness to defend themselves. . . . The riots were not confined to any section of the country. They were Northern and Southern, Eastern and Western—wherever whites and blacks undertook the task of living together. Egged on by native fascist organizations like the Ku Klux Klan, the lawless element of the population undertook to terrorize blacks into submission.[15]

In these post–World War I riots, white mobs entered the physical and social spaces of black communities and neighborhoods. This is a major contrast to the urban riots of the "burn baby burn" late twentieth century, when blacks in their spaces and places destroyed property of absentee landlords and others seen as interlopers. In fact, one can raise the question as to whether the early-twentieth-century racial disturbances should have been labeled riots. They were more like racial massacres. It appears that in both England and the United States the intention was to racially cleanse the cities of blacks.

In 1997, the state of Oklahoma, under the signature of Governor Frank Keating, established the Commission to Study the Tusla Race Riots of 1921, one of the most devastating conflicts during the period.[16] Based on rumor and newspaper vigilantism, armed white mobs killed, burned, and looted black Tulsa in less than twenty-four hours, between 31 May and 1 June 1921. Blacks were armed and fought back but were simply outnumbered and outgunned. The rumor that set off the riot was that a nineteen-year-old black man had accosted a white female elevator operator in a major downtown office building (during normal daytime business hours). The final report of the commission was issued 28 Februrary 2001.[17]

The report of the commission places the context of the riot within a "power" paradigm that provides a useful approach to understanding the similarity and simultaneity of the urban race riots of the time, at home and abroad. It was "one Oklahoma" distinguishable from another Oklahoma, the purpose of which was to keep "the other Oklahoma in its place, and that place was subordinate. That, after all was the object of suffrage requirement and segregation laws. No less was it the intent behind riots and lynching too. One Oklahoma was putting the other Oklahoma in its place." And it is this Oklahoma that had access to power, legal and extra-legal. While government may not have been the "essence" it was the "instrument" of the "one Oklahoma." For example, state officials deputized and armed as their agents white men who were already participating in the violence. Some of thee agents deliberately burned and destroyed homes and business in the black Greenwood district. Thus, in some instances government participated in or performed the deed. In no instances did government prevent or punish the deeds.[18] In Tulsa as well as in other cities of the United States and of England, men and women of the diaspora resisted, but authorities at local, state, and national levels were unwilling to provide protection to blacks or to curtail unruly whites intent on violent injurious behavior toward blacks. Often state authorities were in collusion with white mobs. This power complex of civil and state actors engaged in acts not only to subordinate blacks but to extirpate them socially and physically, as well.

Finally, the policy recommendations of the Oklahoma commission include "direct payments to riot survivors and descendants; a scholarship fund available to students affected by the riot; establishment of an economic development enterprise zone in the historic Greenwood district; a memorial for the riot victims."[19] Certainly the current movement and discussion concerning reparations for "global Africa" and the recommendations of the commission are not unrelated. The "one Oklahoma" symbolizes the violence and oppression directed toward "global Africa" and its enduring struggles lingering in the present. There is a compelling argument in favor of current governments making "monetary payment for past governments' unlawful acts," and thereby assuming those moral responsibilities that require moral responses today.[20]

The extensiveness and intensity of the violence during this time prompted a number of responses, such as the NAACP's Silent Protest Parade down Fifth Avenue in New York City on 28 July 1917. "More than 800 children, some as young as six dressed in white were followed by black men in dark suits, somewhere between 5,000 to

10,000 in all . . . marched speechlessly and solemnly to the beat of muffled drums." Banners carried such slogans as, "Treat Us So We May Love Our Country," "Mr. President [Woodrow Wilson] Why Not Make America Safe For Democracy?" "Your Hands Are Full of Blood," and "Give Me a Chance to Live."[21]

An Anti-Lynching Conference was held by the NAACP in May 1919 at Carnegie Hall in New York, during which its policy report, "Thirty Years of Lynchings in the United States, 1889–1918," was released. Findings included the following: there were more than 3,200 lynchings between 1889 and 1918, and most victims were black men; almost all occurred in the South, and Texas, Louisiana, Georgia, and Mississippi each had more than 300 victims; in 1918 alone, sixty-three blacks, five of whom were women, were lynched, as compared to five white men during the same year. The NAACP protest campaign included failed attempts to secure passage of anti-lynching legislation in Congress.

As attested by the following verse, one of the most poignant assaults against lynching was advanced by Abel Meeropol (Lewis Allan, pseudonym) in his song "Strange Fruit."

> Southern trees bear a strange fruit,
> Blood on the leaves and blood at the root,
> Black body swinging in the Southern breeze,
> Strange fruit hanging from the poplar trees.[22]

Written by Meeropol in 1939, the song was embedded in the popular memory and imagination by Billie Holiday, one of the most captivating and talented jazz artists of the twentieth century, who was only three years old during the Red Summer of 1919.[23]

Black migration from the rural South to northern and southern cities was directly tied to increased violence by whites. Paradoxically, the most vulnerable were maids and other workers employed in white homes and businesses, who had to enter white communities on a daily basis. In addition to the violence, economic conditions, such as job competition and the exploitation of whites and blacks by the owners of capital, contributed to the massive migration of blacks (and whites) from the South.

The Urban League, the National Baptist Convention, the Commission on Inter-racial Cooperation, the Universal Negro Improvement Association, Father Divine's social and religious movement, William Monroe Trotter's National Equal Rights League, and leftist groups such as the League of Struggle for Negro Rights and the National Negro Congress were quite active during the period.[24] The membership of the latter two groups was comparatively small and their influence was limited, but they "helped to dramatize the plight of the Negro and forced the NAACP to take more vigorous action in the pursuit of reform."[25] Claude McKay, noted literary figure of the Harlem Renaissance, in 1919 wrote one of his most famous poems in response to the carnage.[26]

> *If We Must Die*
> If we must die, let it not be like hogs
> Hunted and penned in an inglorious spot,
> While round us bark the mad and hungry dogs,
> Making their mock at our accursed lot.
> If we must die, O let us nobly die,
> So that our precious blood may not be shed
> In vain; then even the monsters we defy
> Shall be constrained to honor us though dead!
> O kinsmen! We must meet the common foe!
> Though far outnumbered let us show us brave,
> And for their thousand blows deal one death blow!
> What though before us lies the open grave?
> Like men we'll face the murderous, cowardly pack,
> Pressed to the wall, dying, but fighting back!

STRANGERS WITHIN

The diaspora experience in Britain and the Americas is a reminder of the phenomenon of strangerness, outsiderness, no matter how long blacks have resided "inside."

[The stranger is] the person who comes today and stays tomorrow. . . . Although he has not moved on, he has not quite overcome the freedom of coming and going. He is fixed within a particular spatial group, or with a group whose boundaries are similar to spatial boundaries. But his position in this group is determined, essentially by the fact that he has not belonged to it from the beginning, that he imports qualities into it, which do not and cannot stem from the group itself.[27]

The stranger is indeed someone who refuses to remain confined to the "far away" land or go away from our own and hence *a priori* defies the easy expedient of spatial or temporal segregation. The stranger comes into the life-world and settles here, and so—unlike the case of mere "unfamiliars"—it becomes relevant whether he is a friend or foe. . . . Yet, unlike other "straightforward" enemies, he is not kept at a secure distance, nor on the other side of the battleline. Worst still, he claims a right to be an object of *responsibility*—the well-known attribute of the *friend*. . . . He is a constant threat to the world's order.[28]

The violence directed against people of African descent after World War I was very much tied to factors of race, nation, and class. African people were already racialized. As colonial subjects they were "naturally inferior" and therefore of unequal merit, people who should be kept in their place. They were degenerates who would ultimately contaminate the white race through miscegenation. The fact that black men often worked alongside women in wartime industries and were married to or lived with white women may have threatened white males and reinforced their sense of powerlessness. The white working class, to which many of the men returning from the war belonged, was caught up in exploitation and the troubles of a turbulent economy. For them, however, the black strangers who came and stayed were the problem. Although many of the perceived strangers were fellow citizens and others were displaced workers who had helped meet wartime needs, they were redefined as the enemy. Racial violence was a form of labor control and reclamation of nation. All blacks were strangers, not nationals.

In the United States, blacks were the disenfranchised and racialized Other within. They were kept separate and had unequal access to jobs, education, housing, voting rights, and full participation in all aspects of society. Like many whites, they left the rural South and moved to urban areas in search of a better life, but once outside of their "proper" social spaces, they were perceived as a threat to white privilege and access. No longer confined to the southern plantations, they became strangers who were readily transformed into enemies, a threat to the white social order. In cities throughout the country, they were people who came today and stayed tomorrow.

One function of the nation-state is to eliminate strangers. "It is best not to meet strangers at all. If one cannot bypass the space they occupy or share, the next best solution is a meeting which is not really a meeting, . . . a *mismeeting*. . . . The art of mismeeting . . . is a denial of the stranger as a moral object and a moral subject. Or rather, exclusion of such situations as can accord the stranger moral significance."[29]

SIMILARITY AND SIMULTANEITY

The continued positioning of diaspora people on the lower tier within a world hierarchy of inequality is directly related to fifteenth-century Euro-American ideologies of conquest and oppression of "inferiors." World War I and its aftermath represented competition among the "superior" conquerors for world dominance and imperial power over the rest of the world. The United States and Great Britain were central to the restructuring, which had implications for social relations and economic opportunities for people everywhere but certainly within their respective nation-states. Given the significance of race in the construction of the modern world, the manifestations of racism and racist cultures in the early twentieth century, while culturally and spatially disparate, reflect an eerie similarity or "sameness." Moreover, the simultaneity of racial violence indicates that the localized and geographically dispersed peoples of the diaspora are fully integrated into the world or global system— politically, economically, and socially. Even as they act as subjects of their own history, they are also acted upon as objects in other people's history.

NOTES

1. Peter Fryer, *Staying Power: Black People in Britain since 1504* (Atlantic Highlands, N.J.: Humanities Press, 1984), chaps. 8 and 9; and Edward Scobie, *Black Britannia: A History of Blacks in Britain* (Chicago: Johnson Publishing, 1972), chaps. 6 and 7.
2. Fryer, *Staying Power,* 237, 294–97.
3. Ibid., 299. For details regarding the circumstances surrounding riots and violence during this period, see pages 298–316.
4. Ibid., 312, 315.
5. Ibid., 301–2. Unless otherwise noted most of this general overview is based on the work of Fryer, *Staying Power,* chap. 10.
6. Ibid., 315.
7. Fryer, *Staying Power,* 308.
8. Fryer, *Staying Power,* 325.
9. Tony Martin, "Revolutionary Upheaval in Trinidad, 1919: Views from British and American Sources," *Journal of Negro History* 58, no. 3 (July 1973): 314.
10. Fryer, *Staying Power,* 312–13.
11. Martin, "Revolutionary Upheaval," 314.
12. John Hope Franklin and Alfred A. Moss Jr., *From Slavery to Freedom: A History of African Americans,* 8th ed. (New York: Alfred A. Knopf, 2000), 384–92; James M. McPherson, *Blacks in America: Bibliographical Essays* (Garden City, N.Y.: Doubleday, 1971), 194–97; Langston Hughes and Milton Meltzer, *A Pictorial History of the Negro in America,* ed. C. Eric Lincoln and Milton Meltzer, 3rd rev. ed. (New York: Crown Publishers, 1968), 266–67; Deirdre Mullane, ed., *Crossing the Danger Water: Three Hundred Years of African-American Writing* (New York: Anchor Books/Doubleday, 1993), 460–67.
13. Hughes and Meltzer, *Pictorial History,* 267; Mullane, *Danger Water,* 460.
14. David Gordon Nielson, *Black Ethos: Northern Urban Negro Life and Thought, 1890–1930* (Westport, Conn.: Greenwood Press, 1977), 138–39.
15. Franklin and Moss, *From Slavery to Freedom,* 385–86.

16. For one of the more definitive accounts of the riot, see Scott Ellsworth, *Death in a Promised Land: The Tulsa Race Riot of 1921* (Baton Rouge: Louisiana State University Press, 1982).

17. "Tulsa Race Riot: A Report by the Oklahoma Commission to Study the Tulsa Race Riots of 1921" is available on the Web at *http://www.ok-history.mus.ok.us/trrc/freport.pdf* (last visited 9 January 2003).

18. Ibid., 11–19.

19. Ibid., ii.

20. Ibid., 19–21.

21. A. Lelia Bundles, *On Her Own Ground: The Life and Times of Madam C. J. Walker* (New York: Scribner, 2001), 207.

22. David Margolick, *Strange Fruit: The Biography of a Song* (New York: The Ecco Press, 2001), 1.

23. Ibid., 11–13.

24. For details see Franklin and Moss, *From Slavery to Freedom*, 392–99.

25. Albert P. Blaustein and Robert L. Zangrando, *Civil Rights and the American Negro: A Documentary History* (New York: Washington Square Press, 1968), 324. The recent biography of Madam C. J. Walker provides interesting personal perspectives on some of the participants in these organizations; see Bundles, *On Her Own Ground*.

26. Claude McKay, *Harlem Shadows* (New York: Harcourt Brace, 1922).

27. Kurt H. Wolff, trans. and ed., *The Sociology of Georg Simmel* (London: The Free Press of Glencoe and Collier-Macmillan, 1950), 402.

28. Zygmunt Bauman, *Modernity and Ambivalence* (Ithaca, N.Y.: Cornell University Press, 1991), 59.

29. Ibid., 62–63.

Contributors

Edward A. Alpers received his Ph.D. from the School of Oriental and African Studies, University of London, in 1966. He is a professor of history at the University of California at Los Angeles, where he served as dean of honors and undergraduate programs from 1985 to 1996. He has taught at the University of Dar es Salaam and has returned to Africa for research, including a Fulbright year at the Somali National University in Mogadishu. His research and writing focus on the political economy of international trade in eastern Africa through the nineteenth century, including the cultural dimensions of this exchange system and its impact on gender relations, with special attention to the wider world of the western Indian Ocean. He has served as president of the African Studies Association and chair of its National Program Committee, and has authored and edited a wide range of books, chapters, and scholarly articles.

Getahun Benti received his Ph.D. in African history from Michigan State University in 2000. He is an assistant professor in the department of history at Southern Illinois University in Carbondale. His research interests include urbanization-migration studies and the relationship between migration, language, and nationalism in Ethiopia.

Joy Gleason Carew is director of minority services at Illinois Wesleyan University.

Tim Carmichael, an assistant professor of history at College of Charleston, received his Ph.D. from Michigan State University in 2001. His research focuses on politics, culture, language, law, and Islam in Northeast/East Africa. He is currently writing articles about qat, Ethiopian literacy, and Somalis in Ethiopia.

Jorge Silva Castillo is the former director of the Centro de Estudios de Asia y Africa of El Colegio de Mexico and former secretary general of the Latin American Association for Asian and African Studies. He received his master's degree in Estudios Orientales from El Colegio de Mexico in 1965. He is currently researcher/professor at the Centro de Estudios de Asia y Africa in the field of ancient history of the ancient Near East.

Howard Dodson is a historian, lecturer, and Ph.D. candidate at the University of California, Berkeley. Dodson has worked for the Peace Corps as the director of credit union education programs for the National Credit Union Federation in Ecuador and as the director of minority recruitment and deputy director of campus recruiting. He has also served as the executive director of the Institute of the Black World in Atlanta, taught classes at Emory University, worked as a consultant to the National Endowment for the Humanities, and served as a project director for the Institute of the Black World. He is currently the director of the Schomburg Center for Research in Black Culture at the New York Public Library.

Raymond Familusi is a Ph.D. candidate in the department of sociology at Michigan State University. His dissertation examines relations of race, place and identity in late–twentieth century black political movements on the east coast of Canada (Nova Scotia). His research interests include expressions of place and identity among the descendants of nineteenth-century African "returnees" in Sierra Leone and Nigeria. He was a researcher-in-residence with the African Diaspora Research Project at Michigan State University.

Milfred C. Fierce is a former professor in the department of Africana studies at Brooklyn College–City University of New York. He received his PhD. in United States history from Columbia University. He is the author of several publications.

John T. Greene is a professor of religious studies and director of Michigan State University's Archaeology and History of Religion(s) Summer in Israel Program.

Dana S. Hale specializes in Modern European History. Her research interests concern French political, cultural and intellectual history, Francophone Africa, and the role of race in European expansion.

Ruth Simms Hamilton was a teacher and researcher at Michigan State University for thirty-five years, and she won many awards for her work. Ruth taught courses on international inequality and development, comparative race relations, international migration and diasporas, Third World urbanization and change, and sociological theory. She was professor of Sociology and Urban Affairs, director of the African Diaspora Research Project, and a core faculty member of the African Studies Center and Center for Latin American and Caribbean Studies at Michigan State University. TIAA-CREF, a national financial services leader, created the Hamilton Research Scholarship in 2004, in honor of Hamilton's work in minority and urban issues.

Michael Hanson is an assistant professor in the department of communication at the University of California at San Diego. He recently completed a Ph.D. at the University of California, Berkeley. His work examines black cultural politics, particularly music, diaspora, performance and identity. He was a researcher-in-residence with the African Diaspora Research Project at Michigan State University.

Joseph E. Harris, a distinguished professor of history emeritus at Howard University, lecturer, and author, has been recognized for his contributions in the fields of education and international studies. He is a renowned expert in the study of the African diaspora, and is currently helping to create a National Slavery Museum in Virginia along with L. Douglas Wilder, former governor of Virginia and current mayor of Richmond. In addition to Howard, Dr. Harris taught at the State University of New York–New Paltz. He received his Bachelor of Arts and Masters of Arts from Howard University and a Ph.D. in African History from Northwestern University.

Cassandra Pybus is one of Australia's best known and most admired nonfiction authors. Her book *The Devil and James McAuley* won the prestigious Adelaide Festival Award for Non-Fiction in 2000. She is the author of several other books, the editor of several books of essays, and the founding editor of the electronic journal *Australian Humanities Review*. Cassandra has a Ph.D. in history from Sydney University and is an ARC Senior Research Fellow at the University of Tasmania. She also has a Fulbright Senior Scholars Award for 2001–2.

Kimberly Eison Simmons earned her Ph.D. in anthropology at Michigan State University in 2002. She is an assistant professor in anthropology and African American studies at the University of South Carolina. Her areas of interest are identity formation, processes of racialization, cultural constructions of race and gender, women's organizations, African Diaspora, international migration, African American culture, Black ethnicities in the United States, and African diaspora communities in Latin America and the Hispanic Caribbean and the Dominican Republic in particular. She was a researcher-in-residence with the African Diaspora Research Project.

Michael C. Thornton is a professor of Afro-American Studies, Asian American Studies and Sociology at the University of Wisconsin in Madison. After receiving a B.S. from Michigan State University and a Ph.D. from the University of Michigan, he went on to teach at Eastern Michigan University and Cornell University. His work highlights issues related to ethnic/racial identity, relations among groups of color, aging and family. Areas of particular interest are ethnic identity among blacks and Asian Americans, Asian American and black mutual perceptions and attitudes towards other groups of color, ethnic differences in caring for the elderly, multiracial families and racial socialization.